THE LAW ON HOMELESSNESS

AUSTRALIA
LBC Information Services
Sydney

CANADA and USA
Carswell
Toronto

NEW ZEALAND
Brooker's
Auckland

SINGAPORE and MALAYSIA
Thomson Information (S.E. Asia)
Singapore

THE LAW ON HOMELESSNESS

by

ALASTAIR HUDSON

LONDON
SWEET & MAXWELL
1997

Published in 1997 by
Sweet & Maxwell Limited of
100 Avenue Road, London NW3 3PF
Computerset by LBJ Enterprises Ltd,
Aldermaston and Chilcompton
Printed and bound in Great Britain by
Clays Ltd, of St Ives plc

No natural forests were destroyed to make this product;
only farmed timber was used and replanted

**A CIP catalogue record for this book is
available from the British Library**

ISBN 0 421 580 704

"Poor naked wretches, wheresoe'er you are,
That bide the pelting of this pitiless storm,
How shall your houseless heads and unfed sides,
Your loop'd and window'd raggedness, defend you
From seasons such as these? O, I have ta'en
Too little care of this! Take physic pomp;
Expose thyself to feel what wretches feel . . . "

King Lear
Act III, Scene IV

The homeless: "the people you step on when you leave the opera."

Sir George Young, Minister for Housing,
Today, June 29, 1991

". . . popular dreads were assigned to open and shared space rather than the mythic sanctuary of the home. It was assumed that danger lived in the public places, not in the private domain . . . Home may be a frightening prison to a battered woman."

Beatrix Campbell
Goliath, Britain's Dangerous Places
Methuen (1993), p.168

PREFACE

This book is dedicated to a 16-year old girl I found huddled in a sleeping bag on Little Argyll Street in London's West End. She had been abused, dropped out of a school for the educationally-challenged, became addicted to heroin, then dependent on methadone and strong lager, and raped. For all the *Channel 4* documentaries, for all the magazine exposes, for all the copies of the *Big Issue* you buy on the street, nothing can bring home the misery of homelessness like opening yourself up to people who are living it. The Law on Homelessness is partly about people like her. However, it is more generally concerned with the 122,660 households accepted as homeless by local authorities in 1994. The tens of thousands of families living in uninhabitable accommodation. The book is written for lawyers and advisors — but the subject-matter concerns ordinary citizens and is, lamentably, all around us. So, the homeless people covered by this book are not simply those living in cardboard boxes on our main streets, eating scraps of other people's take-away dinners. It is about thousands of families living in appalling poverty in substandard housing in Britain in the 1990's.

While homelessness is about the contentious area of poverty, it is also one of the most frequently litigated areas of housing law. Importantly, for many legal advisors reading this book, it will deal with those clients who want to leave their current accommodation to be housed by local authorities; with those seeking to structure the break-up of a relationship; with those who are either elderly or teen-aged seeking shelter from their vulnerabilities; and for the care-in-the-community patients coping with a strange and frightening world. Understanding the statutory and common law rules on homelessness in this regard are vital to their life-choices at these critical times.

The structure of the book is as follows. The introduction considers the scale of homelessness in the English law jurisdiction and takes an historical view of the law dealing with homeless people since medieval times. The central thesis of this discussion is that attitudes to the indigent poor which were present in the Middle Ages, Victorian England and the Depression of the 1930s, are still identifiable in the common law of the 1990s.

The first substantive law section sets out to explain in outline the structure of Part VII of the Housing Act 1996 and the new Code of Guidance dealing with the law affecting homeless people. The next group of chapters considers procedural issues like making applications to local authorities, the right to notification of decisions and the means of challenging those decisions. The bulk of the text then considers in detail the statutory tests for deciding whether or not a person is homeless and then whether such a person is entitled to be accommodated permanently or temporarily by a local authority.

The last few chapters aim to complete the consideration of the law as it affects homeless people by considering the related issues of criminal sanctions against squatters and travellers; the civil law on adverse possession of land; and the means by which vacant possession of land is recovered from occupants. The central purpose, then, is to provide a survey of all of the law which affects people becoming homeless, people once they are homeless, and people seeking to be re-housed.

The approach I have taken with the new statutory provisions in the Housing Act 1996 is that much of the old case law will still be of some effect in interpreting the new statutory material. Therefore, the old case law is considered in detail, together with discussions of important new decisions like *Awua, Begum, Ben-al-Mabrouk* and *Mansoor*. However, the aim of this book is to go beyond the simple housing legislation and to deal with the full range of law dealing with homeless people. Therefore, there is some analysis of the relevant criminal law and an introduction to the law on adverse possession of land. All mistakes, omissions and infelicities of expression are entirely the fault of the author. The law is, to the best of my knowledge, correct as at January 1997.

In a civilised, mature democracy we can have little claim to success or communal self-worth while we allow hundreds of people to sleep on the pavements of our cities, thousands of families to live in uninhabitable conditions, and tens of thousands of children to grow up in excruciating poverty. It is often easy to reduce this blight to polemic or to economics, what is difficult is to accept it as an all-too-common human crisis lived out daily in our country. This is not a polemical text but its author does have a strongly-held belief that among our priorities as a society must be the restoration of some dignity and hope to those who suffer at the breaking-wheel of housing poverty.

There are many people who deserve my thanks in the preparation of this book. I am particularly grateful to those at my publishers who have supported me from the start with kind words and kind deeds. I also wish to express a debt of thanks to those working in the area who have allowed me a little closer to the work they do: in particular the people on the *Big Issue* who first blooded me in this field. My family have been, as ever, an inestimable support simply by being there and listening to me. But most of all, I would like to thank those homeless people who have shared a little of their lives with me on our mean streets. I thank them for connecting in me the prose in this subject with the passion in us all.

Alastair Hudson
January 1, 1997
Paper Buildings
Temple

CONTENTS

PART ONE
INTRODUCTORY

1. Introduction

2. Outline of Part VII of the Housing Act 1996

PART TWO
PROCEDURAL MATTERS

3. Applications

4. Inquiries

5. Decisions and Reviews

6. Notification and Reasons

7. Judicial Review

PART THREE
STATUTORY TESTS

PART FOUR
OTHER LAW AFFECTING HOMELESS PEOPLE

APPENDICES
MATERIALS

TABLE OF CASES

TABLE OF STATUTES

PART 1

INTRODUCTORY

CHAPTER 1

Introduction

There is a sense in which a writer feels a need to apologise in **1.01** starting a legal text with discussion of sociology and statistics. However, homelessness is not an ordinary legal subject and therefore an empirical introduction to the area is important. Its jurisprudential underpinnings and legal treatment cannot be separated from its social context. Understanding the human drama involved with homelessness is a necessity. In comprehending the law in this area, there is also a need to place it in its historical and political context before the reason for a number of the statutory provisions becomes clear.

The starting point is the human dilemma which presents itself **1.02** to every housing lawyer. The subject-matter of the law on homelessness is not visible to society at large; nor is the intensity of its suffering apparent to many who make legal decisions in this area. As Robert Wilson puts it in *"The Dispossessed"*:—

> "the true poverty opera takes place in the tiny rooms of council flats and houses. You have to get inside to see how bad it is. It is conducted in privacy".[1]

Street homelessness is clearly the obvious symptom of the disease of homelessness. In terms of statutory regulation and local authority responsibility, the bulk of the problem is hidden from public view. At the time of the census in 1991, there were in excess of 2,400 people sleeping rough in the United Kingdom, using pavements as a pillow. There is clearly a fundamental ethical issue for us all in allowing these lives to be thrown away, in allowing teenagers to risk everything huddled in doorways with small dogs.

---

[1] *The Dispossessed*, (Picador 1992), p.52.

The Scale of the Problem

1.03.   Street homelessness does not constitute the full extent of the problem. In the context of the law on homelessness, the street homeless are a numerically small part of the total problem. The term "homeless" also covers those living in accommodation which is not suitable for human habitation at all, or not suitable for the specific needs of the individual concerned. The full extent of the crisis is to be found in the cramped single rooms in bed-and-breakfast accommodation, infested with vermin and damp, that contain whole families.

1.04.   In 1994, local authorities accepted 122,660 households as being homeless on the terms of the legislation. The housing charity Shelter estimates that number to be closer to two million households. Therefore, there is a sizeable proportion of the population in housing which is considered to be uninhabitable or unsuitable for their occupation. Of these people, 30 per cent reported their accommodation was infested with vermin; 90 per cent did not know of any procedures for escape in event of fire; and 14 out of 15 mattresses did not satisfy British safety standards.

1.05.   As Robert Wilson puts it in *"The Dispossessed"*:—

"The homeless endure a harsh reality of social insecurity. The isolation of homelessness is hard to describe adequately . . . The indigent live in a dimension remote from the one in which we live. The world is different for the homeless. It is cold, wet, dangerous, lonely and marginal. It bears little resemblance to late twentieth-century life as lived by most people in western Europe . . . Perhaps homelessness is the single aspect of poverty that fiction tackles best. The revealed truth of fiction is sometimes a stronger truth than a fact too outrageous fully to comprehend. It is easy to see indigence as a phenomenon entirely removed from our own circumstances".[2]

1.06.   The necessary role of the lawyer in these circumstances is "to expose ourselves to feel what wretches feel" as Lear suggests. The legislation lays down restrictive categories of person who are entitled to accommodation or assistance. The approach of the courts in interpreting this legislation has been to make those categories even narrower than literal readings of the statute would suggest. The issue becomes difficult for over-stretched local

---

[2] *Ibid.*, p.52.

authorities who are working with limited resources. The attitude of
the legal system to the homeless appears to be founded in a long
tradition of considering the homeless to be an inherently trouble-
some and marginal class of people.

The History of the Law Dealing with the Homeless

It is a fact of our society's approach to the homeless that they are **1.07.**
a phenomenon removed from "real life" as lived by most of our
society. That mind-set is identifiable in much of the case law in
this area and in the Parliamentary Debates about the housing
legislation. There is a stream of thought which runs from the Poor
Law of 1530 through to the decisions of the Supreme Court in
1995: that is, that the indigent poor do not have a stake in our
society and are not deserving of any special favours from it.

Street Homelessness

Homeless people have been hounded since the days of the **1.08.**
medieval Poor Law. The ancient legislation, and even that of the
nineteenth century, referred to them as "rogues and vagabonds".
The Poor Law passed in 1530 aimed to licence begging and to
"outlaw vagabondage by the imposition of severe punishments".
The medieval Poor Laws were used in part to organise casual
labour in agricultural communities and provide occasional subsistence living for the poor. The responsibility for controlling such
people was placed on their local parishes. The penalties for
unlicensed begging and homelessness were criminal punishments.

The New Poor Law of the nineteenth century continued to deal **1.09.**
with the issue of homelessness as primarily a criminal matter. The
workhouses brought to life in Dickens' *Oliver Twist*, and his own
experiences of debtors' prisons, were the reality of the treatment of
the poor by the law. The spirit of Christian utilitarianism, and the
enforced links between the homeless and the parishes from which
they came originally, were key features of the treatment of the
indigent poor. Such organised, if harsh, benevolence has been
replaced by the hostels and pavements of today. There is still a
reliance on good works and charities running drop-in centres and
soup kitchens, to deal with the most obvious symptoms of a crisis
in the social provision of accommodation and subsistence levels of
income.

In his biography *"Dickens"*, Peter Ackroyd considers the novel- **1.10.**
ist's approach to the New Poor Law as presented in his serialised
novels and other writings at the time[3]:—

---

[3] *Dickens*, (Minerva) pp.232 *et seq.*

"What after all was the Poor Law doing? It was tearing families apart, by consigning sexes to different quarters within the same workhouse, and with the abolition of the "search for father" clause, it constituted the total disregard of the need of family life among the poor and the needy . . . it is possible to see why the New Poor Law provoked in Dickens angry memories of his own deprivation, of his own separation from his family, and his own obsessive comparison of the need for food with the need for love . . . Given the fact that the twin pre-occupations of the urban middle class were the fear of disease and the fear of theft, and that both of these were thought literally to spread in a miasma from the rookeries and the courts of the poor, it is important to note that Dickens was living alongside one of the most squalid areas in the whole metropolis".

1.11.   The Benthamite New Poor Law was seen as a punishment of the poor for being poor. As part of this social mood, the Vagrancy Act of 1824 was enacted "For the punishment of idle and disorderly Persons, and rogues and vagabonds, in that part of Great Britain called England". A disorderly person was defined in section 3 as including "every person . . . placing himself in any public place . . . to beg or gather alms". Section 4 empowered to the courts to sentence "incorrigible rogues" in this context to imprisonment or hard labour. Thus, the poorer you were, the greater the punishment you faced.

1.12.   This statute was re-enacted in the 1935 Vagrancy Act. The criminal offences were extended to cover those ". . . wandering abroad or lodging in any barn or outhouse" where they fail to give ". . . a good account of themselves . . ." and who are considered to be "rogues and vagabonds". The purpose of the statute was to criminalise those who were simply homeless, as well as those who begged.

1.13.   It is important to note that the 1824 Act had been introduced at the time of enormous social unrest with the reformist agitation of groups like the Chartists and the utilitarian zeal of the Benthamites. Street-level agitation caused by the new poor in the new industrial towns was the heart of the problem. Incarcerating people begging on the street therefore fitted the pattern of combating street-level activity with physical force. Similarly, the 1935 Vagrancy Act was enacted during the Great Depression at a time of agitation and profound economic hardship. Criminalising and marginalising those who are most poor has established itself as a feature of British history at times of social upheaval and economic difficulty.

Uninhabitable Accommodation

There is a long history of sub-standard accommodation in **1.14.** Britain. The Industrial Revolution brought agricultural workers into towns from poor accommodation in rural areas to poor, disease-ridden and cramped accommodation in towns. As E.P. Thompson explains in *"The Making of the English Working Class"*[4]:—

"... the houses themselves were better than those which many immigrants from the countryside had been accustomed. But as the new industrial towns grew old, so problems of water supply, sanitation, over-crowding, and use of homes for industrial occupations, multiplied, until we arrive at the appalling conditions revealed by the housing and sanitary inquiries of the 1840's".

The problem of people living in accommodation which was sub- **1.15.** standard was not dealt with by legal remedy until the creation of the Welfare State by the post-war Attlee administration. The "houseless heads" of the indigent poor were the object of early legislation. It was a later development when it was recognised that the poor live in-doors as well as out-of-doors.

The 1948 National Assistance Act was introduced to provide **1.16.** accommodation for those in urgent need where their need for housing was a result of unforeseen circumstances. The Act was the first piece of legislation to see homelessness as something other than a criminal issue rather than being a purely criminal matter, as with the Poor Laws and the Vagrancy Acts. However, as Moroney and Goodwin point out [5]:

"Whilst this offered improved options for homeless people and caused a shift in attitudes away from regarding homelessness as a criminal matter, it still failed to acknowledge homelessness as primarily a housing issue".

The Modern Legislation

It was the 1977 Housing (Homeless Persons) Act ("the 1977 **1.17.** Act") which confronted the deeper significance of the problem. The stated purpose of the legislation was to "change the outdated concept that homelessness was a social work problem and to place

---

[4] Penguin, as reprinted 1991, p.352.
[5] *"Homelessness — A Good Practice Guide"*; Shelter 1992, p.21.

it clearly in the sphere of housing".[6] However, the final form of the Act was considered by many Parliamentarians and others who applauded its aims as an inadequate piece of legislation for the problem which pandered too much to the local authority lobby. However, the legislation was enacted in the teeth of the general belief that those who would rely on the legislation were simply scroungers in any event.

1.18.   One of the underlying concerns of the law affecting homeless people is the need to discourage people from becoming homeless. This attitude was shown by the castigation of beggars in the earlier legislation. The Industrial Revolution marked the development of a trend towards considering the resources implications of providing an across-the-board poverty-relief system. The code dealing with "intentional homelessness" (Chapter 12, below) was introduced to the statute during its process through Parliament to ensure that people could not choose to leave accommodation which they did not like and insist upon being re-housed. Further, the categories of people eligible for aid has been restricted to those in "priority need" (as discussed in Chapter 10, below).

1.19.   The continued reactionary treatment of homeless people is demonstrated in the attitudes of Members of Parliament in the late twentieth century, for example, Ronald Bell, former M.P. for Beaconsfield, speaking in the House about the 1977 Act.[7] In his view the restricted purpose of that legislation should be to provide that:

> ". . . There must be two clearly defined categories of accommodation: healthy but uncomfortable accommodation for the bad cases, and other accommodation for people who are not so blameworthy . . ."

We are thrown back to notions of the "undeserving poor" once again. The disturbing fact of the law on homelessness is that such attitudes are not confined to blather of backwoodsmen in the House of Commons but also underpin judicial decisions in cases like *Puhlhofer*.

The Impact of the Puhlhofer Decision

1.20.   The speech of Lord Brightman in *Puhlhofer v. Hillingdon B.C.* [1986] A.C. 484 was central to the development of the law relating to homeless people. His Lordship took the view that it was not a

---

[6] Stephen Ross M.P., *Hansard* H.C. Vol. 926, cols. 898, 899, (18.2.77).
[7] *Hansard* Vol. 926, col. 944 (18.2.77).

priority expressed within the legislation that local authorities be required to find accommodation for homeless people which reached a standard of reasonableness. He conceded that there would be situations in which some shelter could not be termed "accommodation". The example given was Diogenes' tub. This might afford basic shelter but it did not rise to the level of something which could be described as "accommodation".

The law was altered after this decision to ensure that the 1.21. requirement of suitability was included in the legislation. However, *Puhlhofer* remains a seminal decision affecting the subsequent case law. It is seminal not because it represents current law but because the policy pronouncements which it makes still represent the underlying attitude of much of the case law concerning the homelessness legislation.

Broadly there are two schools of thought expressed in the cases: 1.22. the permissive and restrictive schools. The first school identifies the obligation imposed on a local authority by the legislation as being the duty to provide appropriate housing for the homeless. The second school considers the legislation as not requiring the homeless to be housed at all—rather, they are to be merely assisted in some way by the local authorities. Underlying the view of the second school is the stated conviction that local authorities are dealing with scarce resources and that the legislation should therefore be given restrictive interpretation.

Consequently, the circumstances in which the homeless are 1.23. entitled to be housed are greatly restricted by the literal interpretation given to the provisions in cases like *Puhlhofer*. The position for the legal advisor of applicants is that it is often difficult to manoeuvre through the complicated net of provisions. The effect of *Puhlhofer* continues even after legislation was introduced specifically to dilute its impact. For the restrictive school of thought, suitability was an issue for the local authority. The legislation was designed as a safety net for the needy and not as a counsel of perfection.

The issue of the suitability of accommodation has therefore 1.24. become the battleground between permissive and restrictive constructions of the homelessness legislation. The 1977 Act did not specify any quality of accommodation. Some of the early decisions, principally those of Lord Denning, sought to read in standards of appropriateness. Under these readings, local authorities would be required to live up to a spirit identified in the legislation that homeless people are to be housed wherever circumstances require it.

1.25.   The applicants in *Puhlhofer* were a married couple with two young children who were provided with accommodation in a bed-and-breakfast guest house by the respondent local authority. The authority had provided them with

> ". . . occupation of one room at the guest house containing a double and a single bed, a baby's cradle, dressing table, pram and steriliser unit. There were three bathrooms in the guest house, the total capacity of the guest house being 36 people or thereabouts. The applicants were in consequence compelled to eat out and to use a launderette for washing their own and the children's clothing. This expense absorbed most of their state benefit of £78 a week".

1.26.   Lord Brightman found, with the unanimous support of the House of Lords, that the concept of reasonableness was not to be read into the legislation in cases such as this to require the local authority to provide "suitable" accommodation.

1.27.   In Lord Brightman's view, the 1977 Act is an Act which saves the homeless from a lack of any help rather than imposing an obligation on local authorities to house them. While the Act has the word "housing" in its short title (as with the 1996 Act) "it is not an Act which imposes any duty on a local authority to house the homeless", in the words of Lord Brightman. Rather the Act was intended "to assist persons who are homeless, not an Act to provide them with homes". Lord Brightman was concerned, *inter alia*, that in the immediate wake of the introduction of the new legislation, the local authorities would not have had the time to increase the size of their housing stock to meet demand.

1.28.   Significantly the purpose of the legislation, in Lord Brightman's opinion, is that it "is intended to provide for the homeless a lifeline of last resort; not to enable them to make inroads into the local authority's waiting lists for applicants". The local authority are required to "balance the priority needs of the homeless on the one hand, and the legitimate aspirations of those of their housing waiting list on the other hand".

1.29.   The homeless are therefore categorised by Lord Brightman as the "undeserving poor". They are not identified as having "legitimate aspirations" of their own to be housed. The homeless do not have equal rights to other citizens for consideration in housing terms. On the one hand, there are those with legitimate aspirations, and on the other hand there are the homeless who impliedly lack such legitimacy.

The recent House of Lords decision in *Awua v. Brent L.B.C.*,[8] in **1.30.**
the speech of Lord Hoffmann, explicitly approves much of what is
said in *Puhlhofer*. Lord Hoffmann distinguished between the time
for which accommodation was offered and the quality of the
accommodation that was offered. With reference to the time for
which accommodation was offered, he held that it need be neither
permanent nor settled, provided that it was accommodation.
Further, he conceded that even though the legislation introduced
after *Puhlhofer* had reversed the issue whether the authority was
required to provide suitable accommodation the underlying
approach of *Puhlhofer* was nevertheless correct.

It would, of course, have been possible for Lord Hoffmann to **1.31.**
hold to the contrary: that accommodation could not be suitable
where it was only offered for a short period of time. Lord
Hoffmann's decision means that accommodation which is made
available for only a short time will be more likely to be considered
suitable because the applicant need only occupy it for a short
while. The opposite view is that the homeless applicant needs some
secure accommodation and therefore the authority should not be
allowed to avoid its obligations by offering only short term
accommodation. In this writer's opinion, *Awua* continues a judicial
tradition in the higher courts of seeking to limit the utility of the
accommodation which must be provided to the applicant.

The decision of the Court of Appeal in *Ben-el-Mabrouk*[9] does **1.32.**
suggest that the courts will take a broad view of what constitutes a
rational decision in this area by an authority. Where the authority
has great housing demands made of then, it appears that the courts
are accepting that these general circumstances will govern the
question whether or not accommodation is suitable. Therefore, the
court is entitled to consider the broader housing requirements of
the authority and its area in deciding whether or not accommodation is suitable.

This test appears to mirror the approach taken in *Puhlhofer* that **1.33.**
the court may be concerned about the impact on local authority
housing stocks of any decision that is made. The question of
whether or not the authority have been rational in their decision
making in this context might, therefore, be governed by the
broader exigencies of the housing management function. This is a
movement away from the erection of an objective standard of what
will and will not be suitable accommodation in the circumstances.

---

[8] [1995] 3 All ER 493.
[9] (1995) 27 H.L.R. 564.

Consequently, the ability of the applicant to assert that accommodation is unsuitable will be reduced in an area where there is great pressure for public-sector housing.

1.34.   Lord Hoffmann identified as "inconvenient"[10] the result that *Puhlhofer* required applicants to put themselves onto the street before they would be homeless because unsuitability of accommodation was not ground enough to make them homeless.

1.35.   Further Lord Brightman in *Puhlhofer* considered that those people who were contending that they were homeless should only be allowed to commence judicial proceedings in "exceptional cases". This was at a time when judicial review was the only remedy available to applicants — as set out in Chapter 7, below. This statement constituted the effective withdrawal of the ability of many people to access their rights under the homelessness legislation in many circumstances. It is hoped that the new appeals procedure introduced in the 1996 Act will enable applicants to question decisions without the complication of judicial review proceedings and without needing to cross the bridge erected in the way of access to those court remedies.

1.36.   The attitude presented in these leading judicial opinions does not, in this writer's opinion, represent an appropriate response to the homelessness problem either in the context of the homelessness legislation or at all. The "houseless heads and unfed sides" of the modern poor are a real concern for the legal system as well as the politicians. Restrictive interpretations of the legislation do not give effect to the underlying purpose of the legislation, nor do they constitute an answer to the greater social problems of homelessness.

Future Legislative Development

1.37.   The Government White Paper "Our Future Homes" proposes a reduction in the length of time for which accommodation need be made available to homeless people so that they are encouraged not to allow themselves to become homeless. The homeless would be entitled to only temporary accommodation for 12 months. This response to the housing problem appears to be a return to the medieval and Victorian notions of the undeserving poor needing a jolt out of the "giant idleness which destroys wealth and corrupts men".[11]

---

[10] [1995] 3 All E.R. 493 at 497.
[11] See this attitude discussed, *e.g.* in *The Five Giants* by Nicholas Timmins, (Fontana Press, 1996).

Writing at a time shortly before a General Election, there is the **1.38.** possibility of a new Labour Government which is committed to the phased release of capital receipts from the sale of council properties to reduce homelessness, and is also committed to the continuation of the Rough Sleepers Initiative and Foyer Schemes to provide housing and training for young people.

A new Code of Guidance to accompany Part VII of the Housing **1.39.** Act 1996 was issued in October 1996. The Code is similar in terms to the old codes issued under the 1985 legislation. Reference is made to the new code and its recommendations in the relevant discussions of the substantive law as set out below. However, there are sections of the Code of Guidance relating to "eligible persons" which had not been issued at the time of writing.

CHAPTER 2

Outline of Part VII of the Housing Act 1996

2.01. The aim of this chapter is to provide an introduction to the new provisions of the 1996 Act. The following chapters consider the case law and the statutory provisions in greater detail. It is hoped that an initial overview will enable the reader coming fresh to the subject or to the new statutory code to understand how the provisions knit together. Therefore, the chapter is divided between the definition provisions in Part VII which set out those people who will be homeless, the procedural provisions relating to the creation of the authority's liability, and other matters including the creation of criminal offences.

2.02. Under section 216(1) of the 1996 Act, the provisions of Part VII of the 1996 Act have effect in place of the provisions of Part III of the Housing Act 1985 and is to be construed as one with that Act. The provisions of Part VII do not apply in relation to an applicant whose application for accommodation, or assistance in obtaining accommodation, was made before the commencement of this Part.

Definitional Provisions

"Homeless"

2.03. The starting point for the legislation is defining those persons who are and are not homeless. The definition goes beyond those who are sleeping on the street. The statutory definition encompasses those who live in accommodation which is not suitable, such that they are considered not to have accommodation available for their occupation.

Section 175 of the 1996 Act sets out the central definition: **2.04.**

"(1) A person is homeless if he has no accommodation available for his occupation, in the United Kingdom or elsewhere, which he—

    (a) is entitled to occupy by virtue of an interest in it or by virtue of an order of a court,

    (b) has an express or implied licence to occupy, or

    (c) occupies as a residence by virtue of any enactment or rule of law giving him the right to remain in occupation or restricting the right of another person to recover possession."

Thus a person is homeless if she has no accommodation which is available for her occupation. That accommodation can be located either in the United Kingdom or outside it.

The individual must then satisfy one of three requirements as to **2.05.** rights in the property concerned. First, the individual must be entitled to occupy the accommodation either because she has an interest in it or because there is a court order granting the individual a right in the property.[1] Secondly, the individual must have an express or implied licence to occupy the accommodation. This does not require a legal or equitable interest in the property: rather a permission to occupy is adequate. Thirdly, the individual must occupy the property further to a statute or other rule of law which gives her the right either to occupy the accommodation or to be able to prevent others from occupying the property.

The definition is extended in section 175(2) to cover two **2.06.** situations in which the person has accommodation but either cannot gain access to it or in certain circumstances where the home is a moveable structure, such as a mobile home or barge. The first extension in section 175(2)(a) is where "he cannot secure entry to it". The second in section 175(2)(b) is where accommodation is a "moveable structure, vehicle or vessel designed or adapted for human habitation" and where "there is no place where he is entitled or permitted both to place it and to reside in it".

The qualification to this definition of "homeless" is to the **2.07.** definition of "accommodation". Under section 175(3) "a person shall not be treated as having accommodation unless it is accommodation which it would be reasonable for him to continue to occupy". The issue is therefore what type of accommodation is not

---

[1] Housing Act 1996, s. 175(1)(a).

reasonable for an individual to occupy . This issue is considered in detail in Chapter 9, below.

Homeless Person with Dependants

2.08.   The issue arises where the homeless person is not an individual applicant but a person who has dependants or co-habitees. Section 176 provides that:

> "Accommodation shall be regarded as available for a person's occupation only if it is available for occupation by him together with—
> (a) any other person who normally resides with him as a member of his family, or
> (b) any other person who might reasonably be expected to reside with him".

Therefore, section 176 provides that for all purposes in Part VII of the 1996 Act, any reference to an obligation to make accommodation available for a person's occupation is to be construed to include reference to member's of the individual's family or any person who might reasonably be expected to reside with her.

Reasonable Accommodation

2.09.   Under section 177(2) the reasonableness of a person continuing to occupy the accommodation regard may be had to the general circumstances surrounding housing in the district of the local housing authority to whom she has applied for accommodation or for assistance in obtaining accommodation. This reasonableness test applies on a retrospective basis to whether or not it would have been reasonable for the individual to occupy that accommodation.[2] There is provision[3] for the Secretary of State to create regulations for reasonableness in this circumstance.

2.10.   Section 210 sets out the test for whether or not accommodation is suitable for the applicant. The local housing authority is required to look specifically at Part IX (slum clearance), Part X (overcrowding) and Part XI (houses in multiple occupation).[4]

Persons from Abroad and Asylum Seekers

2.11.   One of the more complicated areas of the law on homelessness relates to the duties of local authorities to provide for people from outside the United Kingdom. Further in section 185 of the 1996

---

[2] s. 177(2).
[3] s. 177(3).
[4] s. 210(1).

Act "A person is not eligible for assistance under this Part if he is a person from abroad who is ineligible for housing assistance".

Under section 185(2) of the 1996 Act, a person who is subject to **2.12.** immigration control within the meaning of the Asylum and Immigration Act 1996 is not eligible for housing assistance.

There is a separate regime covering asylum seekers in the wake **2.13.** of the passage of the Asylum and Immigration Act 1996. An asylum seeker is not eligible for assistance under this Part if he has any accommodation in the United Kingdom, however temporary, available for his occupation.[5]

Local Connection

The applicant is required to satisfy the local connection pro- **2.14.** visions before being found statutorily homeless. This is done by the applicant showing that she has a local connection with the area of the local authority. There are echoes of the Poor Law in the requirement that the local authorities are required to take responsibility for people within their district. The definition of "local connection" is set out in section 199 of the 1996 Act.

A person has a local connection with the district of a local **2.15.** housing authority if he has a connection with it:

"(a) because he is, or in the past was, normally resident there, and that residence is or was of his own choice,
(b) because he is employed there,
(c) because of family associations, or
(d) because of special circumstances".

The applicant is therefore required to show that one of the **2.16.** following characteristics is satisfied. First, the applicant must show normal residence in the area. Secondly, the applicant may show that residence in the area is of her own choice. Thirdly, there may be some employment within the area. Fourthly, the applicant may show some family associations with the district covered by the local authority. Alternatively, the applicant may seek to show some special circumstances for the connection between the authority's area and herself.

Referrals to other Local Housing Authorities

It is an important part of the system of local connection that an **2.17.** authority is empowered to refer the applicant to another authority with which the recipient of the application believes the applicant to have a closer connection.

[5] s. 186(1).

Therefore, a local authority may discharge their functions under the Act where they pass their homeless people to another authority to be housed by that second authority. The rules governing the manner in which this is done are set out in sections 198 *et seq.* of Part VII to the 1996 Act.

2.18. The code under section 198 comes into operation where the applicant is in priority need and is not intentionally homeless.[6] The authority is able to consider a referral where they consider that all the conditions in the referral code are met. If they consider that the conditions are met for referral of the case to another local housing authority, the referring authority then notify that other authority of their opinion.

2.19. Importantly, the referring authority need not consider whether for the purposes of section 197 there is other suitable accommodation available for the applicant's use before proceeding under section 198.[7]

2.20. The conditions for referral to another authority are that the applicant has a local connection with the district of the second authority,[8] and the applicant will not run the risk of domestic violence in that other district.[9]

2.21. The notified authority are required to assist the notifying authority. It is therefore possible for obligations to reach the notified authority where the notifying authority are simply attempting to move the responsibility from themselves. The authority or body which is notified and requested to accommodate the applicant must co-operate in giving such assistance in effecting the request as is reasonable in the circumstances.[10]

2.22. When the notifying authority have decided whether the conditions for referral are met, that notifying authority shall notify the applicant of the decision and inform him of the reasons for it.[11] The notice must also inform the applicant of her right to request a review of the decision and of the time within which such a request must be made.

2.23. If it is decided that the conditions for referral are not met, the notifying authority must ensure that accommodation is available for occupation by the applicant until the authority have considered

[6] s. 198(1).
[7] *Ibid.*
[8] s. 198(2)(a).
[9] s. 198(2)(c).
[10] s. 213(1).
[11] s. 200(2).

whether other suitable accommodation is available for her occupation in their district.[12]

Any notice required to be given to an applicant under section 200 must be given in writing and, if not received by the applicant, must be treated as having been given to her if it is made available at the authority's office for a reasonable period for collection by her or on her behalf.[13]   **2.24.**

There is then a need for agreement between the two authorities as to the referral. Alternatively, the issue is referred to arbitration.   **2.25.**

Priority Need

It is a requirement of the 1996 Act, and also of its predecessor legislation, that the applicant establish she is in priority need before the obligations of the authority to provide accommodation for her use on ground of homelessness is satisfied. The precise obligations are considered below. The scope of the category "priority need" is set out in section 189 of the 1996 Act.   **2.26.**

The following have a priority need for accommodation: **2.27.**

"(a) a pregnant woman or a person with whom she resides or might reasonably be expected to reside;

(b) a person with whom dependent children reside or might reasonably be expected to reside;

(c) a person who is vulnerable as a result of old age, mental illness or handicap or physical disability or other special reason, or with whom such a person resides or might reasonably be expected to reside;

(d) a person who is homeless or threatened with homelessness as a result of an emergency such as flood, fire or other disaster."

Therefore, the Act retains the policy of seeking to provide people with accommodation not on the basis solely that they are homeless but rather where they satisfy some more stringent ground of eligibility for treatment. The statute is lenient in the sense that it recognises the need to house not only the person in priority need but also persons who could reasonably be expected to reside with such an individual. Thus, for example, while a pregnant woman would clearly fall within the definition of priority need of almost any measure, her co-habitee is similarly covered.   **2.28.**

[12] s. 200(3).
[13] s. 200(6).

2.29. It is open to the Secretary of State to create new categories of person who satisfy the test of "priority need" or may repeal, or amend, the categories of priority:[14] However, before making any such order, the Secretary of State must consult any associations which represent the relevant authorities, and indeed any other persons he considers appropriate.[15] Furthermore, no such order can be made unless a draft of it has been approved by resolution of each House of Parliament.[16]

Intentional Homelessness

2.30. As set out below in Chapter 12, the provisions relating to applicants who are adjudged to have become homeless intentionally were enacted to prevent people in accommodation from leaving their occupation deliberately so that they could be re-housed automatically, putting a huge strain on local authorities. Therefore, where an applicant has left accommodation intentionally, there is no duty to provide that applicant with permanent accommodation. Rather there are only limited duties to provide temporary accommodation and to provide advice and assistance, as discussed in Chapter 13, below.

2.31. The core of the definition of intentional homelessness is set out in section 191(1) of the 1996 Act:

"A person becomes homeless intentionally if he deliberately does or fails to do anything in consequence of which he ceases to occupy accommodation which is available for his occupation and which it would have been reasonable for him to continue to occupy".

Therefore, the test revolves around the applicant ceasing to occupy accommodation which was both available and reasonable for her to occupy, where that cessation of occupation is caused by some deliberate action or omission on her part. It is a central requirement that this act or omission is deliberate. An act or omission in good faith on the part of a person who was unaware of any relevant fact shall not be treated as deliberate.[17]

2.32. The test is extended by section 191(3) to include further situations in which a person is to be treated as becoming homeless intentionally. The two situations are where (1) the applicant enters into an arrangement under which she is required to cease to

---

[14] s. 189(2).
[15] s. 189(3).
[16] s. 189(4).
[17] s. 191(2).

occupy accommodation which it would have been reasonable for her to continue to occupy, and (2) the purpose of the arrangement is to enable her to become entitled to assistance under Part VII. It is a further requirement that there is no other good reason why she is homeless.

The issue arises where someone applies for housing and is given 2.33. assistance in finding other accommodation but fails to do so. The approach of the statute is that an applicant is to be considered intentionally homeless if she fails to find suitable accommodation after being given advice. Therefore, under section 191(4) an applicant who has been given advice or assistance to find accommodation (under section 197 (duty where other suitable alternative accommodation available)), but fails to secure suitable alternative accommodation will be considered to be homeless intentionally where it was reasonable to expect that she would find such accommodation.

"Threatened with Homelessness"

Within the core definition of "homeless", section 175(4) pro- 2.34. vides that "a person is threatened with homelessness if it is likely that she will become homeless within 28 days". Section 195(1) applies to the situation where the local housing authority are satisfied that an applicant is both threatened with homelessness and eligible for assistance. The local housing authority is obliged to take reasonable steps to secure that accommodation does not cease to be available for an applicant's occupation, if the authority are satisfied that the applicant has a priority need, and the authority are not satisfied that she became threatened with homelessness intentionally.[18]

The primary qualification to this provision is that it is always 2.35. subject to section 197 which sets out the authority's duty where there is other suitable accommodation available for the applicant's use, as considered below. Further, section 195(2) expressly does not affect any right the authority may have under the terms of a contract, an enactment or a rule of law to secure vacant possession of any accommodation.

Where the authority make available different accommodation 2.36. under section 195(2) from that occupied by the applicant at the time of her application, section 195(4) provides that the provisions of section 193(3) to (9) (period for which duty owed) and section

[18] s. 195(2).

194 (power exercisable after minimum period of duty) apply in relation to that duty under this section as they apply in relation to the duty under section 193.

Local Authority Obligations Towards the Homeless

2.37.   The core of Part VII is the catalogue of separate obligations which are placed upon the local authorities. The duties borne by a local authority with reference to any particular applicant depends upon the categorisation of the applicant within the foregoing classifications.

Obligation on Receiving an Application for Housing

2.38.   Section 183 deals with the situation where a local housing authority receives an application[19] for accommodation on the grounds of homelessness, or for assistance in obtaining accommodation.[20] The section applies where the local housing authority have reason to believe that the applicant is or may be homeless or threatened with homelessness. The provisions of section 183 and subsequent provisions do not affect a person's entitlement to advice and information under section 179 (duty to provide advisory services).[21]

Making Inquiries

2.39.   There is an obligation on the local housing authority to make inquiries where they have reason to believe that an applicant may be homeless or threatened with homelessness.[22] The inquiries that the local housing authority is required to make are those which are necessary to satisfy themselves of the following:[23]

"(a)   whether the applicant is eligible for assistance,[24] and
  (b)   if sowhether any duty, and if so what duty, is owed to him under the following provisions of this Part."[25]

The full extent of the local housing authority's obligation to make inquiries is considered below in Chapter 4.

2.40.   Chapter 5, below, considers the rules governing the making of decisions following requisite inquiries. The issue then arises as to the notifications which the authority must make, as considered in

---

[19] The term "applicant" is defined as meaning "a person making such an application" as referred to in s. 183.
[20] s. 183(1).
[21] s. 183(3).
[22] s. 184(1).
[23] s. 184(1).
[24] s. 184(1)(a).
[25] s. 184(1)(b).

Chapter 6, below. Any notice made under sections 184(3) or 184(4) must also inform the applicant of her right to request a review of the decision and of the time within which such a request must be made.[26] As to the time within which such requests must be made, see section 202 discussed at the end of this chapter and in detail in Chapter 5, below.

Obligation to Provide Advice and Assistance

Much of the scheme of duties set out in the 1985 legislation has **2.41.** been re-defined and slanted in favour of advice provision away from straightforward obligations to provide accommodation. The 1996 Act provides for a scheme of assistance by way of advice to all people in their authority's district relating to homelessness.[27] The advice and information that must be provided is "advice and information about homelessness and the prevention of homelessness".

The local housing authority is empowered to give any person by **2.42.** whom such advice and information is provided on behalf of the authority assistance by way of grant or loan.[28] The local housing authority may also assist any such person in a number of ways set out in the statute:[29]

"(a) by permitting him to use premises belonging to the authority,[30]
(b) by making available furniture or other goods, whether by way of gift, loan or otherwise,[31] and
(c) by making available the services of staff employed by the authority."[32]

The Secretary of State or a local housing authority may give **2.43.** assistance by way of grant or loan to voluntary organisations concerned with homelessness or matters relating to homelessness.[33] Powers are also given to local housing authorities to assist any such organisation.[34] The powers given are:—

"(a) permitting them to use premises belonging to the authority,[35]

---

[26] s. 184(5).
[27] s. 179(1).
[28] s. 179(2).
[29] At s. 179(3).
[30] s. 179(3)(a).
[31] s. 179(3)(b).
[32] s. 179(3)(c).
[33] s. 180(1).
[34] s. 180(2).
[35] s. 180(2)(a).

(b) making available furniture or other goods, whether by way
of gift, loan or otherwise,[36] and

(a) making available the services of staff employed by the
authority."[37]

For these purposes a "voluntary organisation" is a body whose
activities are not carried on for profit.[38] The voluntary organisation
cannot be a public or local authority.[39]

2.44.   The assistance which is required to be given, is not clearly set
out. Rather, the statute provides for an ad hoc system of giving
assistance. Section 181 sets out the terms and conditions on which
assistance is given under sections 179 or 180.[40] Under section
181(2), assistance is to be "on such terms, and subject to such
conditions, as the person giving the assistance may determine".
The section refers, in terms, to the giving of financial or similar
assistance. Such assistance to be given on the terms set out in the
section. Similarly, the statute reserves the power to recover the
assistance given where those conditions are not complied with.

2.45.   There are conditions placed on the pre-requisites for giving
assistance, under section 181(3). No assistance is to be given unless
the person to whom assistance is given undertakes the following
two things:

"(a) to use the money, furniture or other goods or premises for
a specified purpose,[41] and

(a) to provide such information as may reasonably be required
as to the manner in which the assistance is being used".[42]

There are further mandatory conditions to the giving of assistance under section 181 relating primarily to matters of record-
keeping.

*Local Authority Obligation to Provide Temporary
Accommodation*

2.46.   The obligation to provide temporary accommodation is to secure
that accommodation is available pending a decision as to the duty
(if any) owed to an applicant under Part VII of the 1996 Act.[43] A

---

[36] s. 180(2)(b).
[37] s. 180(2)(c).
[38] s. 180(3).
[39] *Ibid.*
[40] s. 181(1).
[41] s. 181(3)(a).
[42] s. 181(3)(b).
[43] s. 188(1).

local housing authority has an obligation to provide accommodation for the applicant if the local housing authority has reason to believe that the applicant may be homeless, is eligible for assistance and has a priority need.[44]

·Duties to Persons Found to be Homeless or Threatened with Homelessness

If the local housing authority are satisfied that the applicant is in **2.47.** priority need but that she became homeless intentionally[45], the authority is required to ensure that accommodation is available for the applicant's occupation for a period of time that will give the applicant a reasonable opportunity of finding accommodation.[46] The authority is also required to provide the applicant with advice and such assistance as they think necessary in respect of the applicant's search for accommodation.[47]

If the local housing authority are not satisfied that the applicant **2.48.** has a priority need and became homeless intentionally, they are required to provide her with the advice and assistance which they consider appropriate in relation to any attempts the applicant may make to secure that accommodation becomes available for her occupation.[48] This obligation applies where the local housing authority are satisfied that an applicant is homeless and eligible for assistance, are not satisfied that she has become homeless intentionally, and are satisfied that he does not have a priority need.

The Obligation where Priority Need but not Homeless Intentionally

Unless the local housing authority refers the application to **2.49.** another local housing authority, they are required to secure that accommodation is available for occupation by the applicant. Where the local housing authority are satisfied that an applicant is:

> homeless,
> eligible for assistance,
> has a priority need, and
> are not satisfied that he became homeless intentionally.[49]

section 193 takes effect where there is no other suitable accommodation available. The local housing authority are subject to the

---

[44] s. 188(1).
[45] The definition of becoming intentionally homeless is set out in s. 191.
[46] s. 190(2)(a).
[47] s. 190(2).
[48] s. 192(2).
[49] s. 193(1).

duty under section 193 for a period of two years ("the minimum
period"). After the end of that period, the authority is able to
continue to secure that accommodation is available for occupation
by the applicant, but are not obliged to do so.

Cessation of the Obligation

2.50.   The local housing authority ceases to be subject to the duty
under section 193 if the applicant refuses an offer of accommodation which the authority are satisfied is suitable for her and the
authority notify her that they regard themselves as having discharged their duty under this section.[50] This is in circumstances
where the applicant has been informed by the authority of the
possible consequence of refusal.[51]

2.51.   The local housing authority ceases to be subject to the duty
under section 193 if the applicant:—

> "(a) ceases to be eligible for assistance,
> (b) becomes homeless intentionally from the accommodation
>   made available for his occupation,
> (c) accepts an offer of accommodation under Part VI (alloca-
>   tion of housing), or,
> (d) otherwise voluntarily ceases to occupy as his only or
>   principal home the accommodation made available for his
>   occupation."[52]

2.52.   Further, the local housing authority ceases to be subject to the
duty under section 193 if:

> the applicant refuses an offer of accommodation under Part VI,
> after being informed of the possible consequence of refusal, and
> the authority are satisfied that the accommodation was suitable
> for the applicant and that it was reasonable for the applicant to
> accept it and notify the applicant accordingly within 21 days of
> the refusal.

2.53.   A person who ceases to be owed the duty set out in section 193
may make a fresh application to the authority for accommodation
or assistance in obtaining accommodation.

2.54.   In considering the question of young people's vulnerability, the
authority should have regard to section 20 and Part III of the
Children Act 1989. Section 20 requires local authorities to provide

---

[50] s. 193(5).
[51] *Ibid.*
[52] s. 193(6).

accommodation for children "in need" within their districts. Children in need are to be found accommodation (1) where there is no person having parental responsibility for them; (2) where they have been lost or abandoned; or (3) where the person who has been caring for them, can no longer care for them. Local authorities are required to provide accommodation where children have reached the age of sixteen and whose welfare the authority consider likely to be seriously prejudiced if they do not provide them with accommodation.

Power Exercisable After Minimum Period

It is open to a local housing authority to continue to secure that 2.55. accommodation is available for a person's occupation in circumstances where that authority was subject to the duty to provide accommodation under section 193 until the end of the minimum period.[53]

The local housing authority shall not continue to provide 2.56. accommodation in these circumstances unless they are satisfied on a review carried out under the terms of section 194 that a number of criteria are satisfied.[54] Those criteria are:

the applicant has a priority need,
there is no other suitable accommodation available for occupation by the applicant in the authority's district,
the applicant wishes the authority to continue securing that accommodation is available for his occupation, and
the authority shall not continue to provide accommodation in these circumstances for more than two years at a time, unless they are satisfied on a further review under section 194 in these circumstances.

The review under section 194 must be carried out, under section 2.57. 194(2), "towards the end of the minimum period, or subsequent two year period" with a view to enabling the authority to make an assessment of the likely situation at the end of that period. The authority must cease to provide accommodation in these circumstances if events occur such that, by virtue of sections 193(6) or 193(7), they would cease to be subject to any duty under that section.[55]

In circumstances where a local housing authority carry out a 2.58. review under section 194, the local housing authority is required to make such inquiries as the authority consider appropriate. The

[53] s. 194(1).
[54] s. 194(2).
[55] s. 194(3).

authority must then notify the applicant of their determination and of whether they propose to exercise, or continue to exercise, their power under section 194.

Threatened with Homelessness

2.59.   The authority are required to take reasonable steps to secure that accommodation does not cease to be available for the occupation of an applicant who is threatened with homelessness and is eligible for assistance.[56] If the authority are satisfied that she has a priority need, and are not satisfied that she became threatened with homelessness intentionally, they are required to take reasonable steps to secure that accommodation does not cease to be available for her occupation. Section 195(2) takes effect subject to section 197 (duty where other suitable accommodation available). Importantly, this provision does not affect any right of the authority to secure vacant possession of any accommodation. The authority is at liberty to commence proceedings to recover possession, in spite of the broader context of actions under section 195.

2.60.   In furthering the duty set out under section 195(2), the authority are required to secure that some accommodation is available for occupation by him.[57] This accommodation is required to be accommodation other than that occupied by the applicant when he made his application.[58]

2.61.   If the authority are not satisfied that the applicant has a priority need (or are satisfied that he has a priority need but is also satisfied that he became threatened with homelessness intentionally) they must provide her with appropriate advice and assistance to secure that accommodation does not cease to be available for her occupation.

Authority's Obligation where Applicant Threatened with Homelessness Intentionally

2.62.   The authority bears an obligation to furnish the applicant with advice and whatever assistance they consider appropriate in the circumstances in any attempts she may make to ensure that the accommodation which is available for her occupation does not cease to be so.[59] This obligation arises in circumstances where the authority are not satisfied that the applicant has a priority need, or

---

[56] s. 195(1).
[57] s. 195(4).
[58] *Ibid.*
[59] s. 195(5).

are satisfied that he has a priority need but are also satisfied that she became threatened with homelessness intentionally.

In deciding whether or not a person becomes threatened with 2.63. homelessness intentionally, regard must be had to section 196(1). A person becomes threatened with homelessness intentionally if she "deliberately does or fails to do anything the likely result of which is that he will be forced to leave accommodation which is available for his occupation and which it would have been reasonable for him to continue to occupy". There is a requirement therefore of failing to do some act which will result in being forced to quit accommodation with the joined caveats that the accommodation continued to be available and that it was reasonable for the applicant to continue to occupy that accommodation.

It is not clear whether accommodation can become available 2.64. after the application has been made and thus prevent the applicant from applying successfully or whether the availability is to be measured simply at the time of the application. The better view would appear to be that the accommodation must be unavailable at the time that the decision is made. Similarly, the reasonableness of the accommodation may alter with time (for example if refurbishing work is done on the property or the applicant becomes pregnant) — the best approach would appear to be to measure the situation at the time when the decision is made according to the inquiry results which the authority has available at that time. The crucial issue is whether or not the applicant can be housed or not at any particular time.

For the purposes of the discussion above, in deciding whether or 2.65. not a person became homeless intentionally, an act or omission in good faith on the part of a person who was unaware of any relevant fact is not to be treated as deliberate.

Further, a person is treated as becoming threatened with home- 2.66. lessness intentionally if she enters into an arrangement under which she is required to cease to occupy accommodation which it would have been reasonable for him to continue to occupy. The purpose of the arrangement must also have been to enable her to become entitled to assistance under Part VII. The final requirement is that there is no other good reason why she is threatened with homelessness.

The issue arises where someone applies for housing and is given 2.67. assistance in finding other accommodation but fails to do so. The approach of the statute is that an applicant is to be deemed threatened with homelessness intentionally if she fails to find suitable accommodation after being given advice and assistance, under section 197 (duty where other suitable alternative accommodation available). Therefore, an applicant who has been given advice or assistance to find accommodation, but fails to secure suitable alternative accommodation, will be considered to have become threatened homeless intentionally where it was reasonable to expect that she would find such accommodation.

Duty where Other Suitable Accommodation Available

2.68.   The duty on a local housing authority to provide accommodation where there is suitable accommodation available is set out in section 197. This section enables the local housing authority to avoid a duty to provide housing itself in circumstances where there is other accommodation which the applicant could occupy. There is a two-step introduction to this "get-out" for the authority and that is a requirement that the accommodation be:

> available to the applicant,
> suitable for the applicant, and
> is within the authority's district.

2.69.   Where the get-out is applicable, the local housing authority is required only to provide the applicant with such advice and assistance as the authority consider is reasonably required to enable him to secure such accommodation.

2.70.   The scope for the applicability of this get-out is set out in section 197(1). It applies where the local housing authority is under a duty under Part VII of the 1996 Act. In that case the local authority is required to secure that accommodation is available for occupation by an applicant,[60] or to secure that accommodation does not cease to be available for his occupation.[61] This applies where the authority is not satisfied that other suitable accommodation is available for occupation by her in its district.

2.71.   There are a number of areas in which this duty is expressly provided not to apply. Section 197(6) provides the complete list. The areas covered are: section 188 (interim duty to accommodate in case of apparent priority need), section 190(2)(a) (limited duty to person becoming homeless intentionally), or section 200(1), (3) or (4) (interim duties where case is considered for referral or referred).

---

[60] s. 197(1)(a).
[61] s. 197(1)(b).

The duty on the authority ceases in circumstances where the 2.72.
applicant fails to take reasonable steps to secure that accommodation for his occupation.[62]

Discharge of Housing Functions

The 1996 Act makes specific provision for the ways in which the 2.73.
local housing authority is deemed to satisfy, and thereby discharge,
their functions under Part VII. The only three ways in which they
can achieve this discharge are set out in section 206(1):

where the authority secures that suitable accommodation provided by; is available,
where the authority secures that he obtains suitable accommodation from some other person, or
where the authority secures that he is given such advice and
assistance as will secure that suitable accommodation is available from some other person.

There are requirements which can be imposed on the applicant 2.74.
or another person in relation to whom they are discharging such
functions.[63] A local housing authority may require such a person to
meet the cost of finding accommodation for him. In discharging
the functions under section 206, the local authority is required to
provide particular types of accommodation as set out in section
207(1). The accommodation must be one of the following types:

accommodation in a hostel within the meaning of section 622 of
the Housing Act 1985, or
accommodation leased to the authority.

Furthermore, that accommodation must be provided for more 2.75.
than two years in any period of three years. This time period of
two years need not be continuous—it is enough that the two years
are an aggregate two years out of the three.[64] This rule applies
irrespective of the number of applications for accommodation, or
assistance in obtaining accommodation, which the applicant
makes.

There is the question then of the authority's performance of its 2.76.
obligations when an applicant is placed for accommodation outside
the authority's own district. Section 208(1)provides that the local

[62] s. 197(3).
[63] s. 206(2).
[64] s. 207(1).

housing authority must secure that accommodation is available for
the occupation of the applicant in their district. This obligation is
circumscribed by the words "so far as reasonably practicable" in
discharging their housing functions.

2.77.   Much of local authority policy revolves around out-sourcing
housing to private sector landlords rather than maintaining a
public housing stock. The issue therefore arises, how the authority
discharges its obligations under the 1996 Act in this context.
Section 209(1) expressly deals with this situation. In this area, a
"private landlord" is defined as being a landlord who does not fall
within section 80(1) of the Housing Act 1985 (the landlord
condition for secure tenancies under that Act). The applicant in
this circumstance is defined as being "a person specified by the
authority".

2.78.   In any other circumstances where a tenancy is granted in
pursuance of arrangements under section 209 by a registered social
landlord to the applicant ("a person specified by the authority")
the tenancy cannot be an assured tenancy unless it is an assured
shorthold tenancy, and the landlord cannot convert the tenancy to
an assured tenancy[65]. The tenancy can be converted to an assured
tenancy where the accommodation is allocated to the tenant under
Part VI of the 1996 Act.

Damage to Personal Property

2.79.   There is then the issue of any personal property belonging to the
applicant and the respective duties of the parties to ensure that
such property is not damaged. Section 211 deals with this problem.
This section applies where a local housing authority have reason to
believe that there is danger of loss of, or damage to, any personal
property of an applicant by reason of his inability to protect or deal
with it, and that no other suitable arrangements have been or are
being made.

2.80.   The authority are required to take reasonable steps to prevent
loss of the applicant's property or to prevent or mitigate damage to
it in certain circumstances.[66] Those circumstances are where the
authority bear the interim duty to accommodate under section 188;
or the duties to persons found to be homeless or threatened with
homelessness under sections. 190, 193 or 195; or the duties to an

[65] s. 209(3).
[66] s. 211(2).

applicant whose case is considered for referral or referred under section 200. If the authority have not become subject to any of these duties, they may take any steps they consider reasonable for that purpose.[67]

The authority may decline to take action under this section **2.81.** except upon such conditions as they consider appropriate in the particular case. Those conditions may include making and recovery by the authority of reasonable charges for the action taken, or the disposal by the authority, in such circumstances as may be specified, of property in relation to which they have taken action.[68] The definition of "personal property" includes personal property of any person who might reasonably be expected to reside with her.[69]

In furtherance of this duty to protect an applicant's personal **2.82.** property, the authority can enter any premises which are the usual place of residence of the applicant at all reasonable times and deal with any personal property of hers in any way which is reasonably necessary.[70] This duty can be discharged by storing it or arranging for its storage. That place of residence can also be the applicant's usual last place of residence. Where the applicant asks the authority to move his personal property to a place he nominates, the authority is empowered to take the course of action set out in section 211(2). The authority may discharge their responsibilities under section 211 by doing as she asks, if it appears to them that the applicant's request is reasonable. If the authority does comply with the applicant's request in this way, the authority have no further duty or power to take action in relation to that property.[71] However, if such a request is made, the authority shall before complying with it inform the applicant of the consequence of their doing so.[72]

Section 212(3) sets out the position where the authority does not **2.83.** think there is any danger to the applicant's personal property. If the applicant does not make a request on the authority to deliver his personal property to a given place, the authority is not required to deliver that property to a given place if it believes that there is no danger to that property. Therefore, the authority cease to have

---

[67] s. 211(3).
[68] s. 211(4).
[69] s. 211(5).
[70] s. 212(1).
[71] s. 212(2).
[72] *Ibid.*

any duty or power to take action under section 211 when, in their opinion, there is no longer any reason to believe that there is a danger of loss of or damage to a person's personal property by reason of her inability to protect it or deal with it. This rule also applies where a request has been made by the applicant but it has not been acted upon. However, property stored as a result of action taken under section 211 may be kept in store and any conditions upon which it was taken into store continue to have effect.

2.84. Where the authority ceases to be subject to a duty to take action under section 211 in respect of an applicant's property, or ceases to have power to take such action, having previously taken such action, they must notify the applicant of that fact and of the reasons for it.[73] The notification must be given to the applicant by delivering it to her, or by leaving it, or sending it to her, at her last known address.[74] Again, the definition of personal property is provided to include personal property of any person who might reasonably be expected to reside with the applicant.

Statutory Review of Local Housing Authority Decisions

2.85. One of the developments in the 1996 legislation is the introduction of a means for the applicant to challenge the decision of the local authority without the need for judicial review proceedings. The possibility of bringing review proceedings under general principles of administrative law is considered in Chapter 7, below on "Judicial Review".

Right to Request Review of Decision

2.86. Under section 202 of the 1996 Act (reproduced below) the applicant has the right to request a review of the local housing authority's decision. The policy behind this procedure being in the statute is to restrict the number of cases which need to go to court.

2.87. The core part of the section provides that reviews can be sought in the prescribed cases as follows:—

　　(1) An applicant has the right to request a review of—

　　　(a) any decision of a local housing authority as to his eligibility for assistance,

　　　(b) any decision of a local housing authority as to what duty (if any) is owed to him under sections 190 to 193

[73] s. 212(4).
[74] s. 212(6).

and 195 to 197 (duties to persons found to be homeless or threatened with homelessness),

(c) any decision of a local housing authority to notify
another authority under section 198(1) (referral of
cases),

(d) any decision under section 198(5) whether the conditions are met for the referral of his case,

(e) any decision under section 200(3) or (4) (decision as to
duty owed to applicant whose case if considered for
referral or referred), or

(f) any decision of a local housing authority as to the
suitability of accommodation offered to him in discharge of their duty under any of the provisions
mentioned in paragraph (b) or (e)".

The Circumstances in which a Review can be Requested

The applicant is empowered by section 202(1) to request a **2.88.**
review. The applicant is in effect entitled to demand that a review
is held. Therefore, there is an automatic right of appeal. The
categories cover most of the main areas of local housing authority
discretion under Part VII of the 1996 Act.

The first category of review is with reference to any decision of a **2.89.**
local housing authority as to the applicant's eligibility for assistance. Assistance must be given by the local housing authority
regardless of whether or not the applicant is ultimately found to be
homeless.[75]

The second class is with reference to any decision of a local **2.90.**
housing authority as to what duty (if any) is owed to her under
sections 190 to 193 and 195 to 197. The local housing authority is
compelled to deal with people who have become homeless intentionally. Further local authorities have duties to persons who are
found to be homeless or who are threatened with homelessness.[76]

The third class[77]concerns any decision of a local housing author- **2.91.**
ity to refer homeless people within its district to another authority
under the terms of section 198(1). The fourth class concerns any
decision under section 198(5) whether the conditions are met for
the referral of his case.[78]

---

[75] s. 202(1)(a).
[76] s. 202(1)(b).
[77] s. 202(1)(c).
[78] s. 202(1)(d).

2.92.   The fifth class of case concerns any decision under section 200(3) or (4) being a decision under the duty which is owed to an applicant whose case is considered for referral or is actually referred.[79]

2.93.   The sixth class of case concerns any decision of a local housing authority as to the suitability of accommodation which is offered to the applicant in discharge of the authority's duty under any of the provisions mentioned in section 202(1)(b) or (e).[80]

Procedure Surrounding the Review

2.94.   To prevent persistent use of this system by those who are not content with the outcome of the review, section 202(2) provides that "There is no right to request a review of the decision reached on an earlier review". A request for a review must be made within 21 days of the time at which she is notified of the authority's decision. Alternatively, it is open to the authority to allow, in writing a longer period for the application.

2.95.   Where such a request is made, the authority is required to review its decision.[81] The 1996 Act does not create detailed procedures for the review to take place. Rather it restricts itself to creating the obligation to carrying out a review. The Secretary of State is given the capacity to develop a procedure for statutory reviews by regulation. Those regulations may also provide for the period within which the review must be carried out and notice given of the decision.

2.96.   There are some core, putative rules in section 203(4). These rules require the applicant to be notified of the reasons for the decision if the decision is:

> to confirm the original decision on any issue against the interests of the applicant, or
> to confirm a previous decision—
> to notify another authority under section 198 (referral of cases), or
> that the conditions are met for the referral of his case.

2.97.   Under section 203(5) the authority are required in any case to inform the applicant of his right to appeal to a county court on a point of law. Further the authority are required to notify the applicant of the period within which such an appeal must be made.

---

[79] s. 202(1)(e).
[80] s. 202(1)(f).
[81] s. 202(4).

Appeal from the Statutory Review

If an applicant is dissatisfied with the decision on the review, or 2.98. is not notified of the decision on the review within the time prescribed, she may appeal to the county court on any point of law arising from either or both of the reviewed decision and the original decision. On such an appeal the court may make such order confirming, quashing or varying the decision as it thinks fit.[82]

The appeal under section 204 must be brought within 21 days of 2.99. the applicant being notified of the decision; or it must be brought within 21 days of the date on which the applicant should have been notified of a decision on review.

Pending the outcome of the review, the authority may continue 2.100. to secure that accommodation is available for the applicant. The local authority are empowered to ensure that such accommodation is available during the period for appealing under this section against the authority's decision, and if an appeal is brought, until the appeal (and any further appeal) is finally determined.

Criminal Offences

There is one primary criminal offence created by the 1996 Act. 2.101.

False Statements or Omissions

The statute sets out a number of criminal offences committed in 2.102. connection with the provision of accommodation to homeless people. The first offence is set out in section 214, to deal with false statements made to the housing authority. The offence deals specifically with knowingly or recklessly making false statements or withholding information with the intention of making the authority believe that a person is entitled to accommodation under Part VII.

Therefore, under section 214(1):   2.103.

"(1) It is an offence for a person, with intent to induce a local housing authority to believe in connection with the exercise of their functions under this Part that he or another person is entitled to accommodation or assistance in accordance with the provisions of this Part, or is entitled to accommodation or assistance of a particular description—

---

[82] s. 204(3).

(a) knowingly or recklessly to make a statement which is false in a material particular, or

(a) knowingly to withhold information which the authority have reasonably required him to give in connection with the exercise of those functions".

Continuing Obligation

2.104.   There is a continuing obligation on the applicant under section 214(2) for the applicant not to omit to inform the authority of a change in circumstances. Thus, if before an applicant receives notification of the local housing authority's decision on her application, there is any change of facts material to his case, she must notify the authority as soon as possible.

2.105.   Any person who fails to comply with this obligation commits an offence under section 214(3). The authority shall explain to every applicant, in ordinary language, the duty imposed on her by subsection (2) and the effect of subsection (3). There are two statutory defences to section 214(2) set out in section 214(3). The first is that the applicant must show that she was not given the explanation required. The second is that the applicant had some other reasonable excuse for non-compliance. A person guilty of such an offence is liable on summary conviction to a fine not exceeding level 5 on the standard scale.[83]

---

[83] s. 214(4).

PART 2

PROCEDURAL MATTERS

CHAPTER 3

Applications

The duties of a housing authority under the 1996 Act arise only if **3.01.**
a person applies to a local housing authority to be housed. The
statute provides for categories of person to be deemed homeless but
there is no obligation for local authorities to seek out those people.
Rather, an application must be made in the first instance.

Who Can Make an Application?

Before discussing what constitutes an application and other **3.02.**
aspects of applications, the first question is: who can make an
application in the first place?

Applications from Persons Lacking Capacity

Part VII of the 1996 Act does not contain any express provisions **3.03.**
as to the capacity of a would-be applicant and indeed appears to
envisage applications by those who may have mental illness or
handicap, or at least by those with whom such a person resides or
might reasonably be expected to reside.

The question of whether the Act requires applicants to satisfy a **3.04.**
test of mental capacity before their applications are capable of
being accepted by a housing authority was the principal issue in
the joined appeals in *R. v. Tower Hamlets L.B.C., ex p. Rahman* and
R. v. Tower Hamlets L.B.C. ex p. Begum[1] which dealt with
applications by persons with mental and physical disabilities in
circumstances where a parent had previously made an application
which had been rejected on the ground of intentional homelessness. The Court of Appeal unanimously rejected the view that an

---

[1] [1993] 2 All E.R. 65, H.L.

applicant had to surmount a hurdle of demonstrating mental capacity before her application could be accepted by an authority. Furthermore, the Court of Appeal stated that the question whether a person was an applicant within the legislation was not a matter for the discretion of a housing authority.

3.05.   However, subsequently in *Begum*, the House of Lords overturned the Court of Appeal's decision, holding that it was implicitly a part of the Act that the duty to make an offer was only owed to those who had the capacity to understand and respond to such an offer and, if they accepted it, to undertake the responsibilities that would be involved. In the view of the majority in the House of Lords, a person lacking any such capacity would still be afforded protection by the appropriate provisions of the general social welfare legislation.

3.06.   Furthermore the majority of the House of Lords held that housing authorities had the discretion to decide whether or not a particular applicant lacked the capacity to make an application and that their decisions on this issue could only be reviewed by the courts on the grounds that it was *Wednesbury* unreasonable. The decision appears to return to the pre-1977 view that the housing requirement of homeless people in many cases can be considered to be classifiable as a social welfare rather than a housing issue.

3.07.   The decision of the House of Lords was not, however, unanimous with Lord Slynn's dissenting judgment arriving at a different interpretation of the Act. He identified a different purpose in what is now section 189 of the 1996 Act. This provision envisaged that persons who are vulnerable as a result of mental illness or handicap or physical disability would have a priority need for accommodation in their own right. Therefore, he argued that when such a person made an application to an authority, the applicant must establish whether she is homeless or threatened with homelessness, whether she has a priority need and finally whether she is intentionally homeless.

3.08.   In Lord Slynn's view, the insertion of a test of capacity before these steps was not warranted by the provisions of the Act. He considered that an applicant should not be excluded from the class of vulnerable persons who could establish a priority need because he or she was not capable of understanding the nature of details of a lease or contract. If the applicant had an existing carer or family who might reasonably be expected to reside with her, within terms of the Act, the accommodation must be available for their occupation also. Lord Slynn accepted that his interpretation might mean that a parent or carer who had personally become homeless might obtain accommodation as being a person who might reasonably be expected to reside with the person having a priority need.

Although it is the majority view of the House of Lords which **3.09.** represents the law as it presently stands, it is this writer's opinion that the view of the law adopted by the Court of Appeal and Lord Slynn is preferable to that of the majority of the House of Lords. There is no justification for implying a test of capacity into the Act, given that it is expressly the responsibility of local authorities to assess a person's capacity when they assess whether or not the applicant is in priority need.

While there is other social welfare legislation which might deal **3.10.** with this type of situation, as pointed out by the majority in the House of Lords, this is no reason to imply a supervening test of capacity into the homelessness legislation. Social welfare legislation essentially has a different purpose from housing legislation and may not be able to provide the accommodation needed for a vulnerable applicant. By reading in a test of capacity into the homelessness legislation, there is a risk that vulnerable applicants may be further disadvantaged by being deprived of the opportunity to rely on the homelessness legislation. They are therefore more likely to find themselves being passed back and forth between one local authority department and another. On a more positive note, it may be that Lord Slynn's dissenting speech might prove to be the basis for a future challenge on the same grounds, given that the House of Lords is not bound by its own decisions.

Applications by Dependent Children

Another category of persons who effectively lack capacity to **3.11.** make an application is that of dependent children in cases where their parents have already made an application and have been refused on the basis that they are intentionally homeless. See the discussion of *R. v. Oldham M.B.C., ex p. G*[2] below. In general, the position as dealt with by Lord Griffiths in *Garlick v. Oldham M.B.C.* was that dependent children were not included within the category of priority need in section 189 on the basis that it would be the responsibility of the child's parents to provide accommodation. Therefore, dependent children have no rights under the statute distinct from the rights of their parents.

[2] [1993] A.C. 509.

Applications by Asylum Seekers

3.12. The law governing asylum seekers in this context is considered in Chapter 8, below.

Applications by Illegal Entrants and Overstayers

3.13. The law governing illegal entrants and overstayers is considered in Chapter 8, below.

What is an Application?

3.14. For a housing authority's duties to arise under the homelessness legislation it is also necessary to establish that an application has actually been made. An application need not be in any particular form. An application need not necessarily be made in writing. Given the personal crisis that usually surrounds homelessness, it would often not be possible for the applicant to comply with such formalities in any event. Authorities should therefore allow applicants every opportunity to explain their circumstances fully and to have a friend, representative or interpreter present with them throughout the interview.

3.15. What is necessary, however, is that an applicant make it clear to the authority's officer that she is applying for assistance as a homeless person, or as a person threatened with homelessness. If a putative applicant merely inquires about housing availability, the authority are not obliged to provide advice or assistance. It should be noted that the Code of Guidance emphasises the importance of having well-trained staff to deal with applicants. Those persons who are not adept at local authority procedure or at seeking enforcement of their rights will require experienced staff to guide them through the process.

3.16. Although the distinction between an inquiry and an application in the urgent circumstances in which homeless people find themselves must be regarded as extremely tenuous, it is one that has continuing significance. In *R. v. Cherwell D.C., ex p. Howkins*,[3] for example, this distinction was crucial to the decision of the High Court to deny redress to a homeless person. The applicant's solicitor had merely inquired as to the council's intentions in respect of his client's housing needs. Therefore, it was held that there had been no application for accommodation. Consequently, there was nothing for the court to deal with.

[3] Unreported (May 14, 1984).

Forbes J. accepted that an application need not be made in writing but added that: "in order to be treated as an application an oral application has to be conducted in such a way that it is clear that it amounts to an application". This is an important decision for housing advisors, who should take note that in their dealings with housing authorities they should make it absolutely clear that their client is seeking assistance under Part VII of the 1996 Act.

By the same token, there can be no challenge by way of judicial **3.17.** review until the authority actually take a decision. In *R. v. Hillingdon L.B.C., ex p. Tinn*[4] a woman was advised by the Director of Housing that in the event of her having to sell her home because she was unable to meet mortgage repayments, she would need to make her own arrangements for rehousing. It was held that this did not amount to a decision because there had been no application. The authority were merely attempting to assist the individual by advising her what their attitude would be if she decided to sell her property. In these circumstances judicial review could not be granted because no application had been made and therefore no decision taken.

Local authorities should bear in mind, however, that provided **3.18.** an application for assistance has been made and there is prima facie evidence that the applicant is homeless or threatened with homelessness, the duty to make inquiries arises. This duty arises notwithstanding the fact that the applicants have not formally applied for assistance under the legislation. Furthermore, where an authority have received an application it cannot delay making inquiries as this amounts to a breach of the statutory duty. It should also be noted that failure of an authority to consider whether an applicant was homeless or threatened with homelessness, and failure to make appropriate inquiries, has been held to constitute maladministration by the Local Ombudsman.

Arrangements for Receiving Applications

A housing authority must make adequate arrangements for **3.19.** receiving applications from homeless persons. The Code's of Guidance's provisions on receiving applications are a considerable improvement over the previous provisions with new more detailed guidance on the issue and added emphasis on the quality of service provided to homeless people.

The interaction of these principles with judicial review is considered below in Chapter 7.

[4] (1988) 152 L.G.R. 750.

3.20.   The Code stresses that the duty to homeless people exists regardless of which department of the local authority the applicant approaches and that authorities should be aware of the need to recognise people who should be treated as homeless, even if no formal application is made. Arrangements should be in place to monitor all applications and to ensure that all applicants are referred speedily to the department which deals with homelessness.

3.21.   Furthermore, the Code recommends that authorities should aim to provide access at reasonable opening hours to suit the times when applicants are most likely to attend and provide 24-hour emergency cover. The office should be accessible. The service provided should be well publicised.

3.22.   In *R. v. London Borough Camden, ex p. Gillan*[5] the housing authority only opened their homeless persons unit for three hours on weekdays and provided no cover at weekends. Applications could only be made by telephone and applicants were unable to meet officials unless they presented themselves at the unit by 9.30 a.m. The Divisional Court found that these arrangements were unlawful. May L.J. held that there was a duty on housing authorities to take reasonable steps to hear and adjudicate on applications by homeless persons and that in heavily populated areas reasonable provision might require 24-hour cover.

3.23.   Staff training clearly plays a very important role in ensuring that the arrangements for receiving applications work effectively and that applicants are dealt with speedily, sensitively and appropriately. The key word here must be "appropriately" in this writer's opinion. Further, the Code also emphasises the importance of having well-trained staff.

Interpreters and Intermediaries

3.24.   The importance of having an interpreter present when interviewing applicants whose native language is not English can be seen from *R. v. Surrey Heath Borough Council, ex p. Li.*[6] Mr Li was occupying property with his family. The property was owned by the relative of a former employer. Mr Li and his family were licensees of the property. When Mr Li found new work he was told to leave the accommodation. He applied to the local housing authority for accommodation. The interviewing housing officer

---

[5] (1988) 21 H.L.R. 114.
[6] (1986) 18 H.L.R. 79.

told him that it was necessary for the owner to obtain a court order before he could be required to leave the accommodation. Hodgson J. held that the advice that the applicant could remain in occupation until a possession order is made was wrong. Consequently he quashed the decision that Mr Li was homeless. The housing official stated further that he was not convinced that Mr Li was telling the truth in response to questions and in explaining the factors which had led to his homelessness. Hodgson held that: "one frequently finds there to be inconsistencies caused by a lack of communication or for some other reason". Therefore it was ill-advised to find such facts in these circumstances.

In *R. v. Tower Hamlets L.B.C., ex p. Jalika Begum*[7] Poppelwell J. 3.25. recognised that it was impossible to have an official interpreter present on all occasions and that authorities must therefore satisfy themselves, as part of the interviewing process, that the interpreter was saying what the applicant wanted to say. He went on to hold that where there was doubt about the competence of an interpreter the test which should be applied was whether it had been shown that, to the knowledge of the housing authority, the interpreter was not competent to conduct the interview.

In *Jalika Begum* inconsistencies had emerged in the applicant's 3.26. version of events over the course of two interviews resulting in a decision that the applicant was intentionally homeless. The decision was challenged on the basis that the authority had failed to take sufficient account of alleged difficulties with the interpretation of what the applicant had wanted to say. However, in the light of the evidence from the experienced housing officer who had conducted the interview and who regarded the interpreter as sufficiently competent, Poppelwell J. held that there was not a sufficient case for interfering with the authority's decision on the basis of incompetent interpretation. Further, there was sufficient conflict between the two versions to enable the authority to conclude that there had been a lack of truth.

There will also be, in the case of people with hearing difficulties, 3.27. a need for an intermediary to ensure that the applicant is able to understand the procedure for making an application.

Separate Applications

An application is at the instance of a person not a family. It is 3.28. open to each member of a family unit to apply for assistance, However, the joined appeals *R. v. Oldham M.B.C., ex p. G*[8] and *R.*

[7] (1990) 24 H.L.R. 230.
[8] [1993] A.C. 509.

v. Bexley L.B.C., ex p. B[9] established that it is not open to dependent children to make a separate application in cases where their parents have already made an application and have been refused on the basis that they are intentionally homeless. In these appeals the applicants were four-year old dependent children of the applicant parents. Lord Griffiths held that:

". . . if a family has lost its rights to priority treatment through intentional homelessness the parent cannot achieve the same result through the back door by an application in the name of a dependent child; if he could it would mean that the disqualification of intentional homelessness had no application to families with dependent children; if this had been the intention of Parliament it would surely have said so".

However, as Lord Griffiths pointed out, there is other social welfare legislation that provides for the accommodation and welfare of children which might be applicable in this situation.

3.29.   Likewise, a person who otherwise lacks capacity to make an application cannot make a separate application in circumstances where her parent has previously made an application which has been refused on the ground that she is intentionally homeless.

3.30.   The reason it is important that each family member should be able to apply for assistance separately, and have their applications considered separately, is because one member of the family should not necessarily be held responsible for the actions of another member of the family who is found to be homeless intentionally.

3.31.   In certain circumstances the courts will permit a housing authority to consider separate applications jointly provided the authority take into account any additional material which relates only to one of the applicants. For example, in *R. v. Swansea C.C., ex p. Thomas*[10] where cohabitees each applied for assistance, Woolf J. indicated that had the authority not considered the special circumstances of the male cohabitee, who was in prison at the time when the conduct took place on which the authority's finding of intentional homelessness was based, he would almost certainly have overturned their decision.

3.32.   Similarly, in *R. v. Eastleigh B.C., ex p. Beattie (No. 2)*[11] where a husband and wife each applied for assistance it was held that the wife had not become homeless intentionally and therefore the

[9] [1993] A.C. 509.
[10] (1983) 9 H.L.R. 64.
[11] [1984] Fam. Law 115.

authority had a duty to provide accommodation for her and for her family, notwithstanding the fact that the husband was found to be intentionally homeless on the basis of his application.

Where members of a family unit each apply to an authority for **3.33.** assistance under the legislation it may be necessary for the authority to interview them separately. For example, in *R. v. West Dorset D.C., ex p. Phillips*[12] Webster J. held that where as a result of conduct of the applicant it was evident that the authority had a duty to make further inquiries as to whether the applicant had acquiesced in her husband's drinking, it was necessary for them to "make further inquiries as to her own situation and that not in the presence of her husband".

It would appear from these cases, therefore, that if there are **3.34.** factors which justify the conclusions that the members of the same family should not be treated as having been homeless for the same reasons (for example where a wife was unable to prevent her husband from spending the rent money on drink or was unable to control the anti-social behaviour of other members of the family) then separate applications should be made. The authority may also be required to conduct such inquiries and consider such applications in a way that enables all parties to put their case openly and without fear of any reprisals, as in *Phillips*.

Joint Applications

The legislation is concerned with homeless persons and not **3.35.** homeless families. Therefore, as has been stated, an application for housing must be treated as an application made by an individual. Nevertheless, where a joint application is made to an authority then, in the absence of a request from one or both of the joint applicants for their cases to be treated separately, an authority may consider the application as a joint application. Alternatively, where material comes to light when considering a joint application which points to the need to consider the circumstances of each of the joint applicants separately, an authority may consider the application as a separate application.

Subsequent Applications

One of the great problems facing applicants who have been **3.36.** rejected once when applying for housing on grounds of homelessness, is the point at which the "stigma" of failure wears off and

[12] (1984) 17 H.L.R. 336.

subsequent applications are permitted. If an applicant makes a fresh application without putting forward new grounds or additional information, the authority may reject that application on the basis of their previous inquiries because there has been no material change in the applicant's circumstances. In *Delhaye v. Oswestry B.C.*[13] an applicant who had been provided with temporary accommodation because he was judged to have become homeless intentionally reapplied to the authority for assistance. As there had been no material change in the appellant's circumstances which would justify further assistance from the council, it was held that the applicant was not entitled to a second bite at the cherry.

3.37.   However, if in a fresh application an applicant puts forward fresh grounds or additional information, the housing authority must make further inquiries. For example, in *R. v. Ealing L.B.C., ex p. McBain*[14], the Court of Appeal held that when an applicant, who had previously refused an offer of accommodation, had a second child, this constituted a material change in her circumstances. The reason for this deemed change in circumstances was that the birth of the second child made the accommodation previously offered to her unsuitable.

3.38.   If an authority reopen their inquiries it is possible for it to set right an unlawful decision made on the basis of previous inquiries. For example, in *R. v. Hambledon D.C., ex p. Geoghan*,[15] Forbes J. indicated that if the authority's decision that a couple had become homeless intentionally had been based on their original inquiries, he would have quashed it on the grounds that the authority had failed to inquire into the couple's reasons for leaving their previous accommodation. However, the authority had dealt with this matter in the subsequent inquiries and therefore its later decision could not be quashed because it would be futile to do so.

3.39.   In addition Forbes J. held that it was open to a housing authority to reopen inquiries without a fresh application being submitted to them. He held:

> "the council were also entitled to re-open the matter of their own accord if they took the view that they were no longer satisfied upon the matters which they had to be satisfied and in relation to which appropriate enquiries had to be made".

It should be noted that a request for a decision to be reconsidered or reviewed in the light of new material is not to be

[13] *The Times,* July 29, 1980.
[14] [1986] 1 All E.R. 13.
[15] [1985] J.P.L. 394.

regarded as a fresh application and imposes no duties upon a housing authority. However, in the interests of fairness, it is a matter for the housing authority to make clear to the applicant whether they are merely reviewing their earlier decision in the light of new material or whether, as was the case in Geoghan, they are re-opening their inquiries with a view to reaching a decision.

Applications to Different Authorities

There is no prohibition on an applicant to apply to any number **3.40.** of authorities for assistance. For example, in *R. v. Slough B.C., ex p. Ealing L.B.C.*[16] two families had been found to have become intentionally homeless by the first authority. They later applied to the second authority, which concluded that they had not become homeless intentionally. The decision of the second authority was held to displace the earlier decision of the first authority. Consequently, the first authority were compelled to provide the families with accommodation under the statute.

Local Councillors and Housing Policy

The involvement of local councillors in the allocation of council **3.41.** housing has been widely criticised. The basis for much of this criticism is that the allocation of council housing should be administered by professional housing staff, rather than by local politicians, if it is to be seen to be fair. This criticism of the involvement of local councillors in housing decision making would appear to apply with equal force to the processing of applications under the homeless persons legislation. In *R. v. Preseli D.C., ex p. Fisher*[17] the council passed a motion to protect the district from squatters and from "any nomad who wants to live in the area". McCullough J. held that while he could understand and sympathise with the councillors' sentiments, the local councillors should be required to allow council officers to apply the law and have cognisance of the Code of Guidance — they should not be bound by the outcome of a debate such as this.

The Availability of Damages

In *R. v. Northavon D.C., ex p. Palmer*[18] P sought damages against **3.42.** the authority for failure to process her housing application time-ously. P first applied when her and her family were squatters on

[16] *op cit.*
[17] (1984) 17 H.L.R. 147.
[18] (1995) 27 H.L.R. 576.

the point of eviction. She applied a second time when she and her family were required to move to a caravan. The authority held that she was neither homeless nor threatened with homelessness. Prior to the hearing for judicial review, the authority conceded that P was homeless. Sir Thomas Bingham M.R. held that P could not recover damages except for breach of a private law duty to provide housing. It was held that she could not establish such a private law duty until the authority's public law decision-making function has been concluded. That was a function which only the authority could perform.

CHAPTER 4

Inquiries

Making Inquiries

There is an obligation on the local housing authority to make **4.01.**
inquiries where they have reason to believe that an applicant may
be homeless or threatened with homelessness.[1] The inquiries that
the local housing authority is required to make are those which are
necessary to satisfy themselves of the following:[2]

"(a) whether the applicant is eligible for assistance,[3] and
(b) if so whether any duty, and if so what duty, is owed to him
under the following provisions of this Part,[4]

The local housing authority may also make inquiries as to
whether the applicant has a local connection with the district of
another local housing authority in England, Wales or Scotland.[5]
On completing their inquiries, the authority is required to notify
the applicant of their decision.[6]

The local housing authority is then required to inform the **4.02.**
applicant of the reasons for its decision, where any issue making
up that decision is decided against the interests of the applicant.[7] If
the authority have notified, or intend to notify, another local

[1] Housing Act 1996, s. 184(1).
[2] *Ibid.*
[3] s. 184(1)(a).
[4] s. 184(1)(b).
[5] s. 184(2).
[6] s. 184(3).
[7] *Ibid.*

housing authority under section 198 (referral of cases), they are required to notify the applicant of that decision and inform him of the reasons for it at the same time.[8]

4.03. Any notice made under subsection (3) or (4) must also inform the applicant of her right to request a review of the decision and of the time within which such a request must be made.[9] As to the time within which such requests must be made, see the discussion of section 202 below.

4.04. A notice which is required to be given to a person under section 184 shall be given in writing.[10] If the notice is not received by her, it shall be treated as having been given to her if it is made available at the authority's office for a reasonable period for collection by her or on her behalf.[11]

4.05. Section 183 deals with the situation where a local housing authority receives an application for accommodation on the grounds of homelessness, or for assistance in obtaining accommodation.[12] (The term "applicant" is defined as meaning "a person making such an application" as referred to in section 183.) The section applies where the local housing authority have reason to believe that the applicant is or may be homeless or threatened with homelessness. The definition of whether a person is "homeless" or not is contained in section 175 and discussed below in Chapter 8.

4.06. The provisions of section 183 and subsequent provisions do not affect a person's entitlement to advice and information under section 179 (duty to provide advisory services)[13] as discussed in Chapter 13, below.

The Form of Inquiries

4.07. As set out above, there is an obligation on the local housing authority to make inquiries where they have reason to believe that an applicant may be homeless or threatened with homelessness.[14] As discussed the purpose of the inquiries is to ascertain the applicant's eligibility for assistance, what duties are owed to her,

---

[8] s. 184(4).
[9] s. 184(5).
[10] s. 184(6).
[11] *Ibid.*
[12] s. 183(1).
[13] s. 183(3).
[14] s. 184(1).

and also a power to make inquiries as to whether the applicant has a local connection with the district of another local housing authority.[15]

In *R. v. Lambeth L.B.C., ex p. Miah*,[16] Latham J. considered a **4.08.** case in which allegations had been made that the applicant, who had been provided with temporary accommodation, was letting that accommodation out to other people. Having decided that the applicant was homeless in 1992, the authority made further inquiries in the wake of the allegations in 1993 and came to the conclusion that the applicant was not in fact homeless. Latham J. held that the process of inquiries was a stage by stage process which resulted in the original determination in 1992. The authority was bound by this decision. There was no scope for any further inquiry nor was there any further application from this applicant which required a further inquiry.

In *R. v. Tower Hamlets L.B.C., ex p. Khatun*,[17] the Court of **4.09.** Appeal considered a case of intentional homelessness where the applicant had come from Bangladesh to England to marry. She lived with her parents-in-law for five years before the family went to Bangladesh on holiday and stayed for two years. She returned to England to live with her parents-in-law again. She was told to leave by her mother-in-law because the house was overcrowded. The applicant wife therefore applied to the authority to be housed on grounds of homelessness. The applicant was interviewed twice and 11 reasons were given by the authority why she was considered to have become intentionally homeless. Neill L.J. held that she had only a reasonable expectation that she would be housed when she returned to the United Kingdom. Furthermore, the judge at first instance had held that the interviews were inherently flawed on the basis that they were conducted by an employee of the authority. Neill L.J. found that it was for the authority to decide on the method for appropriate inquiries.

Assistance under Section 183 *et seq.*

References to "assistance under this Part" in the statute mean **4.10.** the benefit of any function under section 183 and the following provisions of Part VII of the 1996 Act relating to accommodation, or assistance in obtaining accommodation. References to being "eligible for assistance" refers to an applicant not excluded from

[15] *Ibid.*
[16] (1995) 27 H.L.R. 21.
[17] (1995) 27 H.L.R. 465.

such assistance by section 185 (persons from abroad not eligible for housing assistance) or section 186 (asylum seekers and their dependants).

Judicial Review Cases under Homelessness Legislation

Duty to Make Inquiries

4.11.   Local authorities bear duties to make inquiries with reference to those applying for housing on the basis of homelessness. The issue arises as to the type and scope of inquiries which the authority is required to make. The scope of this duty is discussed in greater detail at Chapter 13, below. There is a line to be drawn between the obligation of local authorities to conduct original research and to rely on information gleaned from other sources or from information already known to the authority.

4.12.   There has been judicial criticism of local authorities which have found applicants to be homeless where they have completed application forms giving permanent addresses. In those cases Lord Denning in *Tickner v. Mole Valley D.C.*[18] criticised the local authority for relying solely on the fact that the applicants had completed those boxes without making any further inquiries as to whether or not the applicants did have permanent homes. Inquiries ought to have been made at those addresses to see whether they were capable of being occupied as a home or not.

    The law on judicial review in this area is considered in detail below in Chapter 7.

The Code of Guidance

4.13.   Clearly the Code of Guidance has a part to play in making decisions as to what will and will not be required to be investigated. The role of the Code in judicial review proceedings is potentially important. The Code sets out best practice in some areas and guidance in others. Therefore, deviance from the suggested course in the Code would appear to be prima facie evidence of irrational or unreasonable procedures or decision-making on the part of the local authority.

4.14.   Given that the Code does not have the effect of law itself, it would be difficult to argue that ignorance of the Code was necessarily a misdirection in law. However, it would be a contributory factor alongside an analysis of what the law in fact requires

[18] Legal Action, August 1980.

the local authority to do. Training staff in the operation of the Code is also considered by the new code itself, to be an important part of best practice in this area.

CHAPTER 5

Decisions and Reviews

Decisions

5.01. The case law relating to decisions in themselves is thin: rather, it concentrates on the effect of decisions and the rationality of decisions. Under the law generally, there is an obligation to make decisions. Where the authority fails to come to a decision it would appear to be in prima facie breach of its duties to decide as specified under Part VII. Applying the principle in *Cocks v. Thanet D.C.*[1], the authority is only liable under this head where it refuses to make any offer of accommodation at all. Where some decision is made, it is not possible to argue that that decision is a breach of statutory duty: as considered below in Chapter 7. An authority will also be susceptible to judicial review where the manner in which the decision is made is irrational. These principles are considered in outline here. Those relating to judicial review proceedings are considered below in Chapter 7 on "Judicial Review".

5.02.   On completing their inquiries, the authority is required to notify the applicant of their decision.[2] The local housing authority is required to inform the applicant of the reasons for their decision if any issue making up that decision is decided against the interests of the applicant.[3] If the authority have notified, or intend to notify, another local housing authority under section 198 (referral of cases), they are required to notify the applicant of that decision and inform her of the reasons for it at the same time.[4]

---

[1] [1983] 2 A.C. 286.
[2] Housing Act 1996, s. 184(3).
[3] *Ibid.*
[4] s. 184(4).

Any notice made under subsection (3) or (4) must also inform 5.03.
the applicant of her right to request a review of the decision and of
the time within which such a request for a review must be made.[5]
As to the time within which such requests must be made, see the
discussion of section 202 below.

A notice which is required to be given to a person under section 5.04.
184 must be given in writing.[6] If the notice is not received by the
applicant, it is nevertheless treated as having been given to her if it
is made available at the authority's office for a reasonable period
for collection by her or on her behalf.[7]

The authority is therefore required to reach a decision as set out 5.05.
in *R. v. Ealing L.B.C., ex p. Sidhu,*[8] although there is no explicit
statutory obligation to reach a decision generally under Part VII,
only to notify the applicant of such a decision once made.

Obligation not to Fetter own Decision-Making Power

A decision reached without making the proper inquiries will be 5.06.
an invalid decision. The most obvious examples of this principle
occur where an authority seeks to give effect to a blanket policy
without considering the precise circumstances of the case before it.
For example, where an entire family is treated as intentionally
homeless where they fall into arrears of rent this would constitute
an invalid decision in relation to such family if no inquiries are
made as to the reason for the rent arrears.

Where the inquiries suggest that the applicant has become 5.07.
homeless intentionally but there is doubt or uncertainty in the
matter, it should be resolved in favour of the applicant: (*R. v. North
Devon D.C., ex p. Lewis*[9], *R. v. Gravesham B.C., ex p. Winchester; R.
v. Thurrock D.C., ex p. Williams*).[10] An authority is entitled to take
the particular circumstances of an applicant into account in
reaching a decision whether or not to believe the evidence the
applicant produces. In the same way, the authority is entitled to
take into account previous inconsistent statements of an applicant.
However, in judicial review proceedings, the court is entitled to
take into account the factual basis for this decision. That there are
inconsistencies in an applicant's statement will not necessarily be

[5] s. 184(5).
[6] s. 184(6).
[7] *Ibid.*
[8] (1982) 2 H.L.R. 45.
[9] [1981] 1 W.L.R. 328.
[10] (1981) 1 H.L.R. 128.

the basis for finding dishonesty. There may be a number of different reasons for inconsistencies or errors in an applicant's statements in this circumstance — such as inability to communicate, mental illness and so forth. The criminal consequences of false statements are considered in detail in Chapter 15, below.

5.08.   In *R. v. Gateshead M.B.C., ex p. Lauder*[11] L sought judicial review of two decisions of the authority to the effect that L's points for being overcrowded under the authority's letting policy would be suspended for a year. L further contended that G's letting policy in relation to the suspension of points advantage was unlawful. L and her three sons had moved into accommodation occupied by her parents and disabled brother. L left previous accommodation following violent treatment by her husband. The accommodation was considered to be overcrowded within the terms of the authority's letting policy. L was found to be unintentionally homeless. Points were suspended when L turned down accommodation offered to her because it was outside her chosen area. The authority decided that it had discharged its duty and L was placed on the housing waiting list. Potts J. held that the 1985 Act provided for a discretion exercisable by local authorities dealing with a provision of accommodation to those suffering overcrowding. The inclusion of the word "will" in its policy meant that it would not be flexible in the operation of that policy — therefore its discretion was being unlawfully fettered in relation to any decision made as a result of that policy.

5.09.   When an authority takes a decision in connection with its powers and responsibilities under Part VII, the decision is made on the basis of information which is known to the authority at the time of the application. As set out below in Chapter 7, where an authority fails to take into account a relevant piece of information, or takes into account a piece of irrelevant information, there will be prima facie grounds for an application for judicial review of that decision.

5.10.   However, it would appear that it would not be open to an applicant to seek judicial review of a decision which failed to take into account a matter which came to the knowledge of the authority only after it had taken its decision. The only liability attaching to the authority in those circumstances would be an allegation that it had failed to make proper inquiries — this issue is considered in Chapter 4 above. The question then would be whether or not the authority had been irrational in failing to make

[11] Unreported (May 16, 1996).

proper inquiries or whether the new information could be put before the authority so that it could re-open its inquiries as part of the decision-making process. A decision not to re-open inquiries would similarly be subject to judicial review.

Where there are changes of fact, the applicant is under a 5.11. continuing duty to inform the authority of material changes in respect of the application. The authority's decision must, reasonably, be made on the basis of information known or available to it at the date of the decision (rather than at the date of the application). The applicant's duty to inform the authority of changes would seem to continue until the notification of the decision because that is the time that the decision becomes actionable by the applicant. The issues will arise in connection with the time lag between the termination of inquiries and the communication of the decision to the applicant. This will clearly be a matter of fact in the circumstances of any case and subject to the *Wednesbury* standards of reasonableness as considered in Chapter 7 below.

The Applicant's Credibility as a Reason for a Decision

Frequently, authorities will reach decisions in respect of an 5.12. applicant based on some view of the applicant's credibility or on the basis of some professional opinion which has not been communicated to the applicant. Thus, in *R. v. Kensington and Chelsea R.L.B.C., ex p. Campbell*[12] C, the applicant, and her three children left accommodation in Birmingham to escape domestic violence. C applied to Westminster C.C. as homeless and was accepted as unintentionally homeless and in priority need. In February 1994 she was interviewed to assess whether or not she was entitled to accommodation under the homelessness legislation. In June 1994, she was offered a flat on the 27th floor of a high-rise block. C refused the offer because she suffered from vertigo. She was examined by a consultant psychiatrist who concluded that she was suffering from post-traumatic stress disorder and exhibiting symptoms of depression and vertigo. It was the consultant's opinion that it would be intolerable for her to live in a high-rise block. The council's medical officer concluded that the offer was suitable in spite of the report. C was informed of this decision although no reasons were given for it and no explanation was given as to the rejection of the psychiatrist's report.

At the proceedings for judicial review the council produced an 5.13. affidavit which contended that C's evidence was uncorroborated. Sir Louis Blom-Cooper Q.C. held that if the council was casting

[12] (1996) 28 H.L.R. 160.

doubt on the applicant's credibility, the interests of natural justice demanded that these matters be put to her so that inquiries could be made. The council was found to have been gratuitously dismissive in rejecting the psychiatrist's report and in refusing to give reasons for their decision.

Issues to be Taken into Account

5.14.   The authority are required to have regard to all relevant factors. The issue then often arises at what point the authority can stop taking into account new factors. In *Barry v. Newham L.B.*[13] a decision to evict a tenant for arrears was accompanied by notification that they were considered to have become homeless intentionally. The court did not uphold the validity of either the decision or the notification on the basis that it preceded the application itself. It was held that where an authority must take into account information and material which had come to their attention between the time of a decision to evict the applicant and a decision made under the 1977 Act.[14] All circumstances up until the time of the decision must be taken into account.[15] Therefore, while a possession order is relevant no finding of intention can automatically follow.[16]

5.15.   While the obligation to reach a decision generally is not spelled out, it is implied in the legislation. An authority may not defer the obligation in the hope or expectation of a change where that change might reduce its duties (such as loss of priority need status). However, it may be that in an appropriate case a short-term deferral may be permissible where there is a valid reason for the authority to believe that there will be a material change in the applicant's circumstances.

5.16.   Generally, when the authority have ended their inquiries, they must make their decision. At first sight this might seem to impose a strict obligation on authorities. As mentioned above, there are situations under Part VII where the legislation admits of changes in the applicant's circumstances. However, it is this writer's view that the authority should not seek to delay a decision solely in a haphazard hope that there might be some change. This structure of

[13] (1980) LAG Bulletin 142. See however, the decision in *Zold v. Bristol C.C.* (1981) December LAG Bulletin 287.
[14] *Barry v. Newham L.B.* (1980) LAG Bulletin 142; *Zold v. Bristol C.C.* (1981) December LAG Bulletin 287; see also *Devenport, (n. 15, below).*
[15] *Devenport v. Salford C.C.* (1983) 8 H.L.R. 54, C.A., and *R. v. Swansea C.C., ex p. John* (1982) 9 H.L.R. 56.
[16] *Ibid.*

the legislation follows that in the 1977 Act when the position of security of tenure for tenants of local authorities was very different.

Reviews of Decisions

This section deals with the ability of the applicant to bring 5.17. proceedings to enforce the obligations of the local authority or to challenge a decision of that authority. There are therefore two separate questions. The first is how the local housing authority can be forced to carry out an obligation which they otherwise have not performed. The second is the means by which an applicant can contest the decision of a local housing authority that they have no obligation to perform.

Part VII of the 1996 Act does not create its own scheme for 5.18. enforcing the rights and obligations which it creates. What is available under section 202 of the 1996 Act is the ability to have a review of a decision made by a local housing authority.

Statutory Review under the 1996 Act

The statutory review procedure is a new provision, not found in 5.19. the 1985 Act. The aim is to provide a quicker and structured mechanism than court procedures for applicants to object to the decision made by the authority. Section 202 sets out the circumstances in which the right to such a review arises. Sections 203 and 204 of the 1996 Act create procedures for the review of a local authority decision and for appeal to a county court on a point of law from such a review.

Right to Request Review of Decision

Under section 202 of the 1996 Act (reproduced below) the 5.20. applicant has the right to request a review of the local housing authority's decision in the circumstances set out in the section. The policy behind this procedure being in the statute is to restrict the number of cases which need to go to court. Rather, a system of appeal is built into the procedure for making applications for housing on grounds of homelessness.

The core part of the section provides that reviews can be sought 5.21. in the prescribed cases as follows. An applicant has the right to request a review of:

"(a) any decision of a local housing authority as to his eligibility for assistance,
(b) any decision of a local housing authority as to what duty (if any) is owed to him under sections 190 to 193 and 195

to 197 (duties to persons found to be homeless or threatened with homelessness),

(c) any decision of a local housing authority to notify another
authority under section 198(1) (referral of cases),

(d) any decision under section 198(5) whether the conditions
are met for the referral of his case,

(e) any decision under section 200(3) or (4) (decision as to
duty owed to applicant whose case is considered for
referral or referred), or

(f) any decision of a local housing authority as to the
suitability of accommodation offered to him in discharge
of their duty under any of the provisions mentioned in
paragraph (b) or (e)".

The Circumstances in which a Review can be Requested

5.22.   The applicant is empowered by section 202(1) to request a
review. From the precise wording of the provision, it would appear
that the applicant is in effect entitled to demand that a review is
held. There is no restriction on the circumstances in which a
review is held, subject to what is said below about timing and the
number of applications. Therefore, there is no prima facie restriction or embargo against purely vexatious or misguided requests for
review. Therefore, there appears to be an automatic right of appeal.
The categories cover most of the main areas of local housing
authority discretion under Part VII of the 1996 Act.

5.23.   The first class of review is set out in section 202(1)(a) with
reference to any decision of a local housing authority as to the
applicant's eligibility for assistance. Assistance, as discussed generally in Chapter 13, below, is required to be given by the local
housing authority regardless of whether or not the applicant is
ultimately found to be homeless.

5.24.   The second class of review is set out in section 202(1)(b) with
reference to any decision of a local housing authority as to what
duty (if any) is owed to him under sections 190 to 193 and 195 to
197. The local housing authority is compelled, as discussed in
Chapter 13, below, to deal with people who have become homeless
intentionally. Further local authorities have duties to persons who
are found to be homeless or who are threatened with homelessness.

5.25.   The third class under section 202(1)(c) concerns any decision of
a local housing authority to refer homeless people within its
district to another authority under the terms of section 198(1). The
fourth class under section 202(1)(d) concerns any decision under
section 198(5) whether the conditions are met for the referral of his
case.

The fifth class of case under section 202(1)(e) concerns any **5.26.** decision under section 200(3) or (4) being a decision under the duty which is owed to an applicant whose case is considered for referral or is actually referred.

The sixth class of case under section 202(1)(f) concerns any **5.27.** decision of a local housing authority as to the suitability of accommodation which is offered to the applicant in discharge of the authority's duty under any of the provisions mentioned in section 202(1)(b) or (e).

Procedure for Commencing the Review

To prevent persistent use of this system by those who are not **5.28.** content with the outcome of the review, section 202(2) provides that "There is no right to request a review of the decision reached on an earlier review". This effectively draws a line under the statutory review procedure after the applicant has had "one bite of the cherry". Instead, the applicant is thrown back on the general legal remedies discussed in Chapter 7, below.

The applicant is required by section 202(3) to make the request **5.29.** for a review within 21 days of the time at which she is notified of the authority's decision. Alternatively, under the same provision, it is open to the authority, in writing, to allow a longer period for the application.

Where such a request is made, the authority is required to **5.30.** review its decision.[17] The 1996 Act does not create detailed procedures for the form in which the review is to take place. Rather it restricts itself to creating the obligation to carrying out a review. Under section 203(1), the Secretary of State is empowered to create a procedure to be followed in connection with the statutory review under section 202. Under section 203(7), provision may be made by regulations as to the period within which the review must be carried out and notice given of the decision.

The remainder of section 203 restricts itself to an outline for the **5.31.** possible procedure which expressly does not restrict the freedom of the Secretary of State to create a procedure *de novo*. Section 203(2) provides that the regulations may require the decision on review to be made by a person of appropriate seniority not involved in the original decision, andset out the circumstances in which the applicant is entitled to an oral hearing. Further the regulations

---

[17] s. 202(4).

may provide whether the applicant may be represented, and by whom the applicant may be represented, at such a hearing. In any event the authority is required to notify the applicant of the decision on the review.[18]

5.32.   The putative rules in section 203(4) require the applicant to be notified of the reasons for the decision if the decision is:

to confirm the original decision on any issue against the interests of the applicant, or

to confirm a previous decision—
  to notify another authority under section 198 (referral of cases), or
  that the conditions are met for the referral of his case.

Under section 203(5) the authority is required in any case to inform the applicant of her right to appeal to a county court on a point of law. Further the authority is required to notify the applicant of the period within which such an appeal must be made.

5.33.   Further to section 203(6), notice of the decision is not treated as given unless and until the applicant has been informed of her right to an appeal to the court, and where applicable of the reasons for the decision. Section 203(8) provides that any notice under section 203 must be given in writing. Where the notice is not received by the applicant it must be treated as having been given if it is made available at the authority's office for a reasonable period for collection by him or on his behalf.

Appeal from the Statutory Review

5.34.   Section 204 deals with situations in which the applicant is dissatisfied with the result of the review. Section 204(1) provides that if an applicant is dissatisfied with the decision on the review, or is not notified of the decision on the review within the time prescribed, she may appeal to the county court on any point of law arising from either or both of the reviewed decision and the original decision. On such an appeal the court may make such order confirming, quashing or varying the decision as it thinks fit.[19]

5.35   The appeal under section 204 must be brought within 21 days of the applicant being notified of the decision.[20] Alternatively, the appeal under section 204 must be brought within 21 days of the

---

[18] s. 203(3).
[19] s. 204(3).
[20] s. 204(2).

date on which the applicant should have been notified of a decision on review.[21] This latter situation obtains where the applicant is not notified of the decision but notice is made sufficiently available to her as set out in section 203(8).

The issue arises: what of the applicant's need for accommo- **5.36.** dation while the review is being held? Further to section 204(4), where the authority was under a duty under any of section 188, 190 or 200 of the 1996 Act to secure that accommodation is available for the applicant's occupation, they may continue to secure that accommodation is so available. The local authority is empowered to ensure that such accommodation is available:

"(a) during the period for appealing under this section against the authority's decision, and
(b) if an appeal is brought, until the appeal (and any further appeal) is finally determined."

[21] *Ibid.*

CHAPTER 6

Notification and Reasons

Notification

6.01. The authority are required to notify the applicant of their decision whether or not favourable to the applicant. The authority are also required to provide reasons for their decision. The decision must be notified, as discussed in Chapter 5 above, at the completion of inquiries at the point in time when the decision is taken. The issue for the applicant is then to demonstrate the point in time at which notification ought to have taken place.

6.02. The authority are also required to notify the applicant of any reasons behind a decision which goes against her. The duty of notification and to give reasons has been held to be independent of any substantive duties to make inquiries or to provide accommodation: *(R. v. Beverley B.C., ex p. McPhee.)*[1]

Reasons

6.03. The purpose of giving reasons is to enable the applicant to consider them and decide whether or not to appeal. Therefore, it is possible to see whether or not a decision is defective in some way.[2] As held by Sir Thomas Bingham M.R. in *R. v. Croydon L.B., ex p. Graham*[3], after acknowledging that the making of decisions under Part VII is the business solely of the authorities:

---

[1] *The Times*, October 27, 1978.
[2] *Thornton v. Kirklees M.B.C.* [1979] Q.B. 626; *R. v. Tynedale D.C., ex p. Shield* (1987) 22 H.L.R. 144; *R. v. Northampton B.C., ex p. Carpenter* (1991) 25 H.L.R. 349.
[3] (1993) 26 H.L.R. 286.

"There is, nonetheless, an obligation under the Act to give reasons and that must impose on the council a duty to give reasons which are intelligible and which convey to the applicant the reasons why the application has been rejected in such a way that if they disclose an error of reasoning the applicant may take such steps as may be indicated".

There is, therefore, an obligation on authorities to make decision **6.04.** notices clear, such that the applicant can be certain of all of the reasons for the decision. There will not be a sufficient notification where that notification is not clear.[4] The courts will frequently find a decision invalid where there has been insufficient notification.[5] The decisions of Housing Benefit Review Boards will be subject to the same principles.[6] The authority will also be prevented generally from relying on extraneous material to justify the decision made.[7]

There will be circumstances where the courts will not rely on **6.05.** the precise words of the reasons given. The measure here will be whether or not the authority can be said to have discharged their obligations properly in the notification given to the applicant. The cases in this area have tended to concern findings of intentional homelessness where the court has been of the view that the decision that the applicant was intentionally homeless was reasonable in the circumstances.[8]

The applicant in *R. v. Kensington and Chelsea R.L.B.C., ex p.* **6.06.** *Grillo*[9] was offered seventh floor accommodation although she contended that this was unsuitable because of her partner's asthma.

---

[4] *R. v. Islington L.B.C., ex p. Hinds* (1995) 28 H.L.R. 302.

[5] *R. v. Tower Hamlets L.B., ex p. Monaf* (1988) 20 H.L.R. 529; *R. v. Slough B.C., ex p. Khan* (1995) 27 H.L.R. 492; *R. v. Sedgemoor D.C., ex p. McCarthy* (1996) 28 H.L.R. 608.

[6] *R. v. Housing Benefit Review Board, ex p. Thomas* (1991) 25 H.L.R. 1; *R. v. Housing Benefit Review Board for East Devon D.C., ex p. Gibson* (1993) 25 H.L.R. 487; *R. v. Sefton M.B.C., ex p. Cunningham* (1991) 23 H.L.R. 534; *R. v. Solihull M.B.C. Housing Benefit Review Board, ex p. Simpson* (1994) 27 H.L.R. 41; *R. v. Sutton L.B., ex p. Partridge* (1994) 28 H.L.R. 315.

[7] In *R. v. Croydon L.B., ex p. Graham* (1993) 26 H.L.R. 286; *R. v. City of Westminster, ex p. Ermakov* [1995] 8 Admin L.R. 389; *R. v. Southwark L.B., ex p. Dagou* (1995) 28 H.L.R. 72; *R. v. Cardiff C.C., ex p. John* (1982) 9 H.L.R. 56. Except perhaps where the evidence is simply explanatory of things said in the notification: *Hobbs v. Sutton L.B.C.* (1993) 26 H.L.R. 286.

[8] *R. v. Hillingdon L.B.C., ex p. Islam* [1983] 1 A.C. 688; *R. v. City of Westminster, ex p. Chambers* (1982) 6 H.L.R. 15; *R. v. Hillingdon L.B.C., ex p. H* (1988) 20 H.L.R. 559. See the probanda in *City of Gloucester v. Miles* (1985) 17 H.L.R. 292 as discussed in Chapter 12, below.

[9] [1995] N.P.C. 85.

The applicant also produced evidence as to her own problems with arthritis. The authority rejected the medical evidence adduced on behalf of the applicant and her partner. Neill L.J. found that the authority was under no duty to give reasons so long as the decision was within policy guidelines in this context. While there might be an implied duty to give reasons in some circumstances, this was found to be a case where the authority had activated a voluntary appeals procedure and therefore was not one in which giving reasons could be required. Perhaps this is an unfortunate judgment. The authority appear to have fettered their discretion by giving a decision in accordance solely with policy guidelines.

CHAPTER 7

Judicial Review

Court-Based Remedies

When will the Courts Intervene?

This section deals primarily with the ability of the applicant to **7.01.** bring proceedings to enforce the obligations of the local authority. Below is the statutory procedure by which an applicant can challenge a decision of that authority.

The difficulty with enforcing the obligations of the local housing **7.02.** authority on behalf of the applicant is the discretionary ambit which the decision-making obligations contain. The 1996 Act, as with its predecessor legislation, is worded in terms of the local authority being "satisfied", or "having reason to believe" or "being of the opinion that" such and such is the case. Therefore, the applicant is forced to challenge the opinion or belief of the authority and not simply challenge the existence of a legal rule. The practical implications of this phraseology should not be under-estimated. Not only is the applicant required to demonstrate to a tribunal that, beyond the local authority's own procedures, she has a given right, but also that the local authority has mis-directed itself or made an error, and so on. The nature of the burden of proving eligibility is therefore increased.

An example is the burden that an applicant bears of demonstrat- **7.03.** ing that she is in priority need before being classified as being statutorily homeless. A person is in priority need where the local authority are "satisfied" that that is the case. The local authority bear the burden of making accommodation available to a person which they "have reason to believe" is homeless and in priority need. Similarly, the local connection requirements are satisfied when the local housing authority are "of the opinion" that the applicant fulfils the criteria as set out in Chapter 2, above, in outline.

7.04.   There is great difficulty in the situation where an applicant is contending that she is the victim of domestic violence. Section 177(1) provides that an applicant is not to be considered as having available accommodation where it is probable that continued occupation will lead to domestic violence against her. This is on grounds that it is not reasonable for that person to continue to occupy the accommodation.[1] There is no provision as to who bears the burden of proof that domestic violence is probable. In situations where domestic violence has occurred, it will clearly be easier to demonstrate the probability of its recurrence in the future. Particularly where the violence has occurred on a systematic basis in the past, its probability of repetition will be easier to judge.

7.05.   This test will be a difficult one for local housing authorities to apply in practice. The definition of "domestic violence" includes threats which are likely to be carried out. Therefore, it would appear that an applicant can produce evidence or testimony of threats coupled with a real expectation that they will be put into practice. For the legal adviser there is a difficult line to draw here between becoming homeless intentionally and leaving accommodation because it is unreasonable to continue to occupy it on grounds of anticipated domestic violence.

7.06.   The policy behind the legislation is clear: co-habitees should not be required to suffer violence to themselves or their dependants and be trapped in that accommodation. Rather, domestic violence should be combated and the individual should be eligible to be re-housed away from the abusive relationship. The difficulty of discharging the burden of proof here, however, carries enormous risks for applicants in some circumstances.

7.07.   There is, therefore, a general difficulty for the local housing authority to reach decisions on the basis of mixed fact and opinion. The local authority bears the burden of carrying out inquiries in certain circumstances (as discussed in Chapter 4, above). Those obligations therefore bring knowledge of facts to the local authority's decision. However, in deciding whether or not a person is occupying accommodation which is reasonable, or whether it is probable that threats of violence will lead to violence, the authority is necessarily thrown into speculation on the back of its researches.

[1] Housing Act 1996, s. 177(1).

Not only does this pose problems for the local authority but it **7.08.** creates difficulties for homeless people and people in unacceptable situations to assert their civil rights. Therefore, the problems become problems of enforcement and ability to challenge decisions of public bodies.

For the applicant, the situation is complicated by demonstrating **7.09.** that the authority has a particular policy in relation to particular sets of circumstances. For example, it may be that the applicant is able to demonstrate that the authority has fettered its discretion in relation to the personal circumstances of the applicant. The frame of mind of the authority therefore becomes a factor in the applicant's assertion of her civil rights in this circumstance.

The Judicial Approach to Judicial Review

The applicant is therefore thrown onto the principles of judicial **7.10.** review to seek an answer to problems caused by the decisions of the local authority. Therefore, it is a matter for the local authority's decision and the court will not replace that decision with one of its own. The local authority must therefore be demonstrated to have acted unreasonably in accordance with the *Wednesbury*[2] principles.

The attitude of the courts to the widespread use of judicial **7.11.** review proceedings in this area was set out most clearly in the following extended extract from the speech of Lord Brightman in *Puhlhofer*[3]:

"I am troubled at the prolific use of judicial review for the purpose of challenging the performance by local authorities of their functions under the Act of 1977. Parliament intended the local authority to be the judge of fact. The Act abounds with the formula when, or if, the housing authority are satisfied as to this, or that, or have reasons to believe this, or that. Although the action or inaction of a local authority is clearly susceptible to judicial review where they have misconstrued the Act, or abused their powers or otherwise acted perversely, I think that great restraint should be exercised in giving leave to proceed by judicial review. The plight of the homeless is a desperate one, and the plight of the applicants in the present case commands the deepest sympathy. But it is not, in my opinion, appropriate that the remedy of judicial review, which is a discretionary remedy, should be made use of to monitor the actions of local authorities under the Act save in the exceptional case. The

[2] *Associated Provincial Picture Houses v. Wednesbury Corp.* [1948] 1 K.B. 223.
[3] *Puhlhofer v. Hillingdon L.B.C.* [1986] A.C. 484.

ground upon which the courts will review the exercise of an administrative discretion is abuse of power — *e.g.*: bad faith, a mistake in construing the limits of the power, a procedural irregularity, or unreasonableness in the *Wednesbury* sense — unreasonableness verging on an absurdity: see the speech of Lord Scarman in *R. v. Secretary of State for the Environment, ex p. Nottinghamshire C.C.*[4]. Where the existence or non-existence of a fact is left to the judgment and discretion of a public body and that fact involves a broad spectrum ranging from the obvious to the debatable to the just conceivable, it is the duty of the court to leave the decision of that fact to the public body to whom Parliament has entrusted the decision-making power save in a case where it is obvious that the public body, consciously or unconsciously, are acting perversely . . . I express the hope that there will be a lessening in the number of challenges which are mounted against public authorities who are endeavouring, in extremely difficult circumstances, to perform their duties under the Homeless Persons Act with due regard for all their other housing problems".

Judicial Review and the 1996 Act

7.12. The comments of Lord Brightman, quoted above, in *Puhlhofer* set out the attitude of the courts to this day in considering judicial review applications in the area of homelessness. While *Puhlhofer* does indicate a judicial reluctance to allow too many reviews by the courts of local authority decisions, those decisions are still open to review in the right circumstances.

7.13. What Lord Brightman's words do achieve is a raising of the barrier at the initial stage of seeking leave to bring judicial review. The impact of *Puhlhofer*, as followed in a number of more recent decisions, is to provide that it is in the "exceptional case" only that the applicant should be permitted to proceed by way of judicial review.

7.14. The *Wednesbury* principles are as set out below. There are a number of classical statements relating to this area of law. Particularly that of Lord Scarman in *Council of Civil Service Unions v. Minister for the Civil Service*[5]:

"One can conveniently classify under three heads the grounds upon which administrative action is subject to control by judicial review. The first ground I would call "illegality", the

[4] [1986] A.C. 240.
[5] [1985] A.C. 374.

second "irrationality" and the third "procedural impropriety" . . ."

Or in the speech of Lord Scarman in *R. v. Secretary of State for* **7.15.** *the Environment, ex p. Nottinghamshire C.C.*[6]:

"The ground upon which the court will review the exercise of an administrative decision by a public officer is abuse of power. Power can be abused in a number of ways: by a mistake of law in misconstruing the limits imposed by statute (or by common law in the case of a common law power) upon the scope of the power; by procedural irregularity; by unreasonableness in the *Wednesbury* sense; or by bad faith or an improper motive in its exercise . . ."

The main substantive principles on which the law on judicial **7.16.** review are based in the context of applications by homeless people are:

The authority must take into account all the relevant factors before making their decision.
An authority must similarly ignore all irrelevant factors.
The authority must not make a decision which has no factual basis. The decision must be based on the facts before the authority.
The authority must act neither in bad faith nor dishonestly.
The authority must direct themselves properly in law. A decision which is reached as a result of a misunderstanding or a misapplication of the law will not have been reached properly.
The authority must act in a way which promotes and does not conflict with the objects or policy of the statute.
The authority must not fetter their discretion by approaching decisions solely on the basis of the application of a pre-determined policy.
The authority cannot delegate decisions which are properly to be made solely by them to some other person or body of persons.
The authority must act in accordance with natural justice.

The burden of proof in such cases is borne by the applicant. The **7.17.** applicant is required to demonstrate that the decision should be quashed for one of the reasons set out above. Therefore, the applicant is required to demonstrate that she is entitled to be considered homeless in the given circumstance and that the decision of the authority that she is not homeless offended one of

---

[6] [1986] A.C. 240 at 249.

the principles set out above. There is therefore both a factual and a substantive legal basis for the application for judicial review.

7.18.   The common thread in the principles of administrative law is that there has been some lack of probity in decision-making or some error in procedure by the authority. On the one hand, the decision which is sought to be made void by the applicant must have been arrived at by some perversion of the rules of natural justice, or as a result of some policy of the authority which works to the detriment of the applicant. Alternatively, there must have been some break-down in the decision-making procedure of the authority.

Specific Judicial Review Cases Dealing with Homelessness

7.19.   It must be remembered that the legislation places the obligation and the power to make decisions in this area on the local authorities. The courts will therefore be careful to review decisions only on the basis of the *Wednesbury* principles but not to re-make the decision in any way.[7]

Duty to Make Inquiries

7.20.   Local authorities bear duties to make inquiries with reference to those applying for housing on the basis of homelessness. The issue arises as to the type and scope of inquiries which the authority are required to make. (The scope of this duty is discussed in greater detail at chapter 4, above.) There is a line to be drawn between the obligation of local authorities to conduct original research, and the ability to rely on information gleaned from other sources or from information already known to the authority.

7.21.   There has been judicial criticism of local authorities which have found applicants to be homeless where they have completed application forms giving permanent addresses. In those cases Lord Denning in *Tickner v. Mole Valley D.C.*[8] criticised the local authority for relying solely on the fact that the applicants had completed those boxes without making any further inquiries as to whether or not the applicants did in fact have permanent homes. In his Lordship's opinion, inquiries ought to have been made at those addresses to see whether they were capable of being occupied as a home or not.

---

[7] *R. v. Wycombe D.C., ex p. Mahsood* (1988) 20 H.L.R. 683; *R. v. Hertsmere B.C., ex p. Sedaghat* Unreported (March 7, 1984).
[8] Legal Action, August 1980.

The question arises: what constitutes reasonable inquiry- 7.22.
making? In *Rose*[9] the local authority assumed that a woman who
stayed temporarily with her father after her arrival in the United
Kingdom, had become homeless intentionally when she ceased to
live with him. The court held that the authority should have made
further inquiries as to whether she had ceased to live there
voluntarily and what the reasons for her leaving had been.
Similarly in *Paris*,[10] the authority found that the applicant was
intentionally homeless in the wake of a couple coming to the
United Kingdom without a prior accommodation arrangement.
The authority did not make inquiries about the accommodation
which the couple had been forced to leave in Italy to see whether it
had either been available for them to occupy or had been reasonable for them to continue to occupy it.

There is a similar stream of case law related to findings of 7.23.
priority need. In *Ryedale*, it was held that the obligation to make
inquiries covered all questions relevant to priority need under
what is now section 189 of the 1996 Act. In *Carroll*[11], the court
quashed a decision of a local authority that the applicant was not
in priority need on the basis that it had relied exclusively on its
own medical officer's opinion as to the applicant's vulnerability,
despite the fact that the applicant had raised a number of issues
other than purely medical arguments. This case can be contrasted
with *Banbury*[12] where the local authority was able to adduce
evidence that it had considered the issue of vulnerability for itself
and had not simply approved the opinion of its own medical
officer. However, on the facts of *Di Domenico*[13] it was held that a
medical opinion by itself was sufficient to enable the local authority to reach its decision.

In *R. v. Camden L.B.C., ex p. Adair*[14] A sought judicial review of 7.24.
Camden's decision not to transfer his tenancy under their discretionary "relationship and breakdown policy" and Camden's finding that he was homeless but not in priority need. A argued that
Camden had failed to take into account relevant considerations,
considered irrelevant matters and failed to give reasons for their
decision. A also argued that, in relation to their finding on priority
need, Camden had failed to make proper inquiries as required by

---

[9] *R. v. Wandsworth L.B., ex p. Rose* (1983) 11 H.L.R. 105.
[10] *R. v. Reigate and Banstead B.C., ex p. Paris* (1984) 17 H.L.R. 103.
[11] *R. v. Lambeth L.B., ex p. Carroll* (1987) 20 H.L.R. 142; also *R. v. Brent L.B., ex p. Omar* (1991) 23 H.L.R. 446.
[12] *R. v. Wandsworth B.C., ex p. Banbury* (1986) 19 H.L.R. 76.
[13] *R. v. Reigate and Banstead B.C., ex p. Di Domenico* (1987) 20 H.L.R. 153.
[14] Unreported (April 2, 1996).

the then section 62(2)(a) of the 1985 Act. The assessment form made no reference to the threats of violence received by A which were relevant to A's vulnerability under section 59(1)(c) and which were known by the District Housing Office.

Stephen Richards Q.C., sitting as a judge in the High Court, held that the application should be allowed in part. Camden's "relationship and breakdown policy" was discretionary. Camden had considered all the relevant matters and were entitled to take into account factors such as A's previous housing history. The decision letter adequately dealt with the reasons for the decision considered and that there was no special feature of the decision which required particular explanation. The application in relation to this decision was therefore dismissed. However, a local authority, in making inquiries to decide whether an applicant was in priority need, were obliged to make adequate inquiries of other local authorities where the applicant had indicated that his dealings with such other authorities were relevant to his application. The authority were required to inform the applicant of the reasons for its decision when informing him that he was not in priority need. However, the letter sent by Camden merely contained a general formula rather than clear reasoning. The decision was therefore unlawful and quashed.

7.25.   The issue of the authority's conduct of inquiries has been considered in a number of cases. Authorities are generally required to chase all leads relating to non-payment of rent of mortgage payments until they are satisfied as to the applicant's culpability for such non-payment. A female applicant in *Phillips*[15] became very distressed in front of a local authority official when asked about her husband's drinking habits. The court held that her outburst should have alerted the authority to make further and better inquiries into the background of her application. In particular they should have considered the applicant and her husband's individual shares of responsibility for their mortgage arrears in the context of the drinking. Similarly, the applicant in *Joyce*[16] had suffered difficulties as a result of mortgage arrears accruing over property. The authority had not made any inquiries as to why those arrears had arisen nor had it taken into account, therefore, any relevant factors which would have arisen if such inquiries had been made.

7.26.   In some cases, information will be provided via legal advisers. The authority may well decide that it will rely on the oral representations of the applicant at interview instead. In *Walters*[17],

---

[15] *R. v. West Dorset D.C., ex p. Phillips* (1984) 17 H.L.R. 336.
[16] *R. v. Wyre B.C., ex p. Joyce* (1983) 11 H.L.R. 73.
[17] *R. v. Woodspring D.C., ex p. Walters* (1984) 16 H.L.R. 66.

the applicant's solicitor put information before the authority which might have led the authority to find the applicant homeless if the authority had pursued that information. That the authority did not pursue that information, led the court to hold that the authority had not made sufficient inquiries. Further, it was held that the authority had failed to understand that it was their own duty to make inquiries in response to that information, rather than leaving the burden of proving homelessness entirely on the applicant.

In *Fisher*[18], it was held that if the accommodation which the applicant last occupied before making the application was no longer available or not suitable for occupation by the applicant, the authority must make inquiries going back to the last accommodation which the applicant occupied — even where that means making inquiries going back some number of years. The case of *Henderson*[19] did set out the obligation of applicants as being to put the local authority in possession of such facts as would require it to make investigation. For example, the condition of previously occupied accommodation. **7.27.**

Founding an Application for Review by Entering the Property

There are a stream of seemingly harsh cases which suggest that an applicant cannot found a claim for judicial review on the basis that accommodation is not reasonable unless and until the applicant has actually gone into occupation of those premises. The response of many authorities where the applicant has failed to accept an offer of accommodation is to treat their duties to the applicant as having terminated and then to let the offered accommodation to another person. **7.28.**

In *R. v. Newham L.B.C., ex p, Begum*[20] B entered the United Kingdom from Bangladesh in 1990. She sought to appeal against her offer of accommodation under the 1985 Act. The offer was made to her following the authority's decision that she had not become homeless intentionally and that she was in priority need. She refused to move into the accommodation on the basis that she had suffered racial abuse on visiting the premises for the first time. The authority decided that there were no exceptional circumstances and considered that they had therefore carried out their duty to B. B sought judicial review of this decision on the basis that there were exceptional circumstances justifying B refusing the accommodation on this occasion. Richards J. held that although **7.29.**

---

[18] *R. v. Preseli D.C., ex p. Fisher* (1984) 17 H.L.R. 147.
[19] *R. v. Wandsworth B.C., ex p. Henderson and Hayes* (1986) 18 H.L.R. 522.
[20] Unreported (February 5, 1996).

earlier letters had failed to consider whether there was an exceptional circumstance in the light of the racial abuse, the letter from
the Director of Housing demonstrated that the matter had been reconsidered with full knowledge of the facts and that he was
entitled to decide that it was nevertheless reasonable for B to move
into the property.

7.30.   Further, Richards J. held that under the true construction of the
authority's procedure, once it had been decided that exceptional
circumstances did not apply, then the applicant should be given
the opportunity to move into the property in order to exercise her
right of appeal. In this, Richards J. was following *R. v. Wycombe
D.C., ex p. Hazeltine*[21]. In this case the judge exercised his
discretion against B as she had not shown any intention of moving
into the property in order to found an appeal. In that case, the
property had by then already been let to someone else.

7.31.   The issue is then what the authority must do to demonstrate
that it has acted reasonably, at the time at which the applicant
becomes homeless. In *R. v. Croydon L.B.C., ex p. Jarvis*[22] the
authority decided that the time at which the applicant-tenant
became homeless, was the time at which the landlord took
possession proceedings and obtained an order for possession.
Where the tenant had only received notice to quit, she was not
homeless at that time. Andrew Collins Q.C. held that the decision
was not unreasonable because the authority had considered the
reasonableness of the applicant remaining in occupation, the
general housing situation in the authority's district and the
provisions of the Code of Guidance.

7.32.   In cases where the applicant has a very real anticipation of being
the victim of violence or intimidation, or that some other harm
will be caused to her, if she takes up occupation, the above cases
would seem to offer little sensitivity to the danger that the
applicant might therefore be forced to run.

Misplaced Burden

7.33.   The burden is on the authority to make inquiries and is not on
the applicant to prove that she is homeless. In *R. v. Woodspring
D.C., ex p. Walters*[23] the authority required that the applicant
demonstrate positively that her husband, who was a serving
member of the RAF in Cyprus, had lost married persons' quarters

---

[21] (1993) 25 H.L.R. 313.
[22] (1994) 26 H.L.R. 194.
[23] (1984) 16 H.L.R. 73.

after she returned to England. Taylor J. held that the burden was on the authority to make inquiries and not on the applicant to prove that accommodation was no longer available.

However, it may not be clear whether or not an application has **7.34.** been made. It is a matter for the authority to decide whether or not it is seised of an application under Part VII: (*R. v. Lambeth L.B.C. ex p. Pattinson*)[24]. Therefore, the authority will not be under a duty to make any inquiries until it is seised of an application. However, in *R. v. Sefton M.B.C., ex p. Healis*[25], Harrison J. held that where an applicant had applied for a transfer to other council accommodation, on the basis that it was no longer reasonable for her to continue to occupy her accommodation, clearly constituted both a request for a transfer and an application for housing on grounds of homelessness.

The Code of Guidance

Given that the Code of Guidance does not have the effect of law **7.35.** itself, it would be difficult to argue that ignorance of the Code was necessarily a misdirection in law. However, it would be a contributory factor alongside an analysis of what the law in fact requires the local authority to do. The Code of Guidance will have a part to play in making decisions as to what will and will not be required to be investigated and whether or not the authority has reasonably discharged its duties under Part VII. The role of the Code in judicial review proceedings is potentially important. The Code sets out best practice in some areas and guidance in others. Therefore, deviance from the suggested course in the Code would be prima facie evidence of irrational or unreasonable procedures or decision-making on the part of the local authority.

Misdirection in Law Generally

There are a number of examples of potential misapplications of **7.36.** the legal rules, including misplacing the burden of proof in relation to intentional homelessness cases onto the applicant and away from the local authority itself, as considered above. There is also the semantic question of the various standards of proof required by the different formulations: "is satisfied that", "is of the opinion that", and "has reason to believe".

There are a number of cases in which the local authority have **7.37.** misdirected themselves in situations where the applicant was formerly living with another person who has been found to have

---

[24] (1996) 28 H.L.R. 214
[25] *The Times*, May 2, 1994.

made herself homeless intentionally. In the case of *Lewis*[27] it was held that such applicants are not to be treated as though they are a single family unit. Rather, each is entitled to separate consideration.[27]

7.38.　　One of the clearest examples of the wrongful application of a policy was in the case of *Tilley*[28]. The London Borough of Wandsworth decided that no assistance would be given under the provisions of the Children and Young Persons Act 1963 to people who had been found to have become homeless intentionally under the terms of the 1977 Act. The policy as set down did not permit of any exceptions. In the opinion of the Court of Appeal, the policy was wholly invalid. Templeman L.J. considered that the policy would have been invalid even where it had been "hedged about with exceptions". Its concrete nature did not permit of any exceptions nor of any consideration of the merits of any individual case. However, the remainder of the Court of Appeal was less didactic in their views, considering that a policy which is intended to operate as a guideline, and which does not prevent the consideration of the merits of individual cases, will be valid.

7.39.　　It would appear that the law is, therefore, that a blanket policy which is applied regardless of the merits of individual cases, will be unlawful. The difficulty for the applicant is always to prove that a decision has been made in such a way. It is usual for the applicant to have to prove by cross-examination of a witness for the local authority that the policy was applied rigidly. However, in circumstances where the same conditions are applied to different types of applicant (for example those with or without families of similar sizes), it would be for the local authority to rebut a presumption that a blanket policy is in fact being enforced.

7.40.　　For example, in *R. v. Canterbury C.C. ex p Gillespie*,[29] there was a policy restricting certain categories of applicant from registering on the authority's waiting list. It was found that the policy operated as a rule rather than as a general approach subject to exceptions. Therefore, it was held to be unlawful. Similarly, a blanket policy which considered all applicants who were in rent arrears as having become homeless intentionally would be held to be an unlawful fetter on the discretion to make decisions.

---

[26] *R. v. North Devon D.C., ex p. Lewis* [1981] 1 W.L.R. 328; see also *R. v. Thurrock B.C., ex p. Williams* (1981) 1 H.L.R. 128.
[27] This rule was restated in the case of *R. v. Swansea C.C., ex p. John* (1982) 9 H.L.R. 56. In neither case did the court find for the applicant on the facts.
[28] *A.-G. ex rel Tilley v. Wandsworth L.B.* [1981] 1 W.L.R. 854.
[29] (1986) H.L.R. 7.

It is for the local authority to demonstrate, for example, that **7.41.**
obligations to provide accommodation where it is reasonable to do
so for so long as it is reasonable to do so, are not operating a
blanket policy where all of their applicants are provided with such
accommodation for identical periods of time. (See, for example,
Chapter 12, below, on "Intentional Homelessness".)

In *Lally*,[30] the Kensington and Chelsea local authority admitted **7.42.**
to a policy of providing accommodation for only 14 days for those
who were in priority need but had become homeless intentionally.
The court held that they had not discharged their duty under
section 65(3) of the 1985 Act.

The county court case of *Stubbs* demonstrates that a local **7.43.**
authority cannot simply follow the decision of another body. In
that case, the authority held that an applicant had become
homeless intentionally merely because he had been the subject of a
possession order on the grounds of nuisance and annoyance to
neighbours. The court which heard the applicant's challenge to the
authority had also heard the possession action:

"In the ordinary course of events I might have suspended an
order based on the nuisance . . . I took the view however, that
because of the friction in this case such an order would not be
satisfactory".

Therefore, the issue was whether or not it was reasonable to
make the order—this did not depend solely on the behaviour of
the evicted tenant, but also on other factors. Equating this
situation with intentional homelessness would be to misunder-
stand the operation of the discretionary grounds for possession and
to fail to ask the specific questions which are raised by the 1996
Act. The duty of the authority is to reach their own decision, to
which a court order will be one of the relevant factors. Nor can one
authority merely rubber stamp the decision of another authority or
of an expert such as a medical officer (whether or not that person is
employed by it).

Frequently, the issue of intentional homelessness also poses **7.44.**
questions about natural justice in practice. For example, in the
county court case of *Afan*, inquiries were made of the family with
whom the applicants has been living, until they became homeless.
The applicants were given no opportunity to comment upon what
had been said, even though what had been said reflected badly
upon them, and would have been strongly disputed.

[30] *Lally v. Kensington and Chelsea R.L.B.C.*, *The Times*, March 26, 1980.

7.45. Thus in *Stubbs* there was an unfair failure to put to the applicants the basis for the authority's decision even though it was emphasised that there is no duty to go so far as to conduct an hearing. In general it would appear to be safer to pose the challenge on the ground of want of procedural propriety. Although there may be no duty to conduct a hearing, if the authority customarily grants a hearing to those who may be found to be intentionally homeless, there would seem to be a want of procedural propriety in an individual case if it fails to do so.

7.46. In any challenge to an authority's decision, the reasons for a decision given by an authority will often form the starting point of the proceedings. There has been a tendency to approach the matter on a broadly-based basis. The court will identify whether or not the decision of the local authority can be sustained on any ground rather than simply on the ground suggested by the authority.

Judicial Review Procedure in Outline

7.47. Challenging the decision of a local authority is usually done in the Divisional Court of the High Court on an application for judicial review under Order 53 of the Rules of the Supreme Court. It is common that such applications are heard by a single judge of the High Court. The Divisional Court may quash a decision of the local authority (certiorari), or it may compel the authority to make a decision or a particular decision (mandamus), or may prohibit an authority from taking some action (prohibition). It may also make a declaration under R.S.C. Order 53, rule 1(2) to declare such decision *ultra vires* or void. There can, however, be no challenge before a decision has been made under the terms of Part VII (except in circumstances where the local authority is recalcitrantly refusing to make a decision at all). Therefore, where an applicant has been warned that if accommodation were quit, she would be considered intentionally homeless, relief was refused on the basis that she had not yet been threatened with homelessness (as discussed in Chapter 8, below).[31] The court would not make a declaration on the basis that this would pre-empt the authority's statutory responsibility under the 1996 Act.

7.48. In an appropriate case, the court may also award damages as compensation for wrongful action, or a wrongful refusal to act.[32] Leave must be sought to bring an application for judicial review,

[31] *R. v. Hillingdon L.B., ex p. Tinn* (1988) 20 H.L.R. 305.
[32] R.S.C. Ord. 53, r.7.

and this is done generally by ex parte application, in writing or by application for an oral hearing.[33] A refusal of leave on an application for an oral hearing may be renewed by oral application. Leave is to be granted only in obvious or exceptional cases.[34]

Application for leave must be made: 7.49.

"promptly and in any event within three months from the date when the grounds for the application first arose unless the Court considers that there is good reason for extending the period".[35]

The court will be reluctant to grant leave where an application is outwith this time period. When certiorari is sought, time runs from the date of the decision.[36] When leave is granted out of time, this is not a final ruling that relief will be granted. The fact that the application was out of time may still be raised by the authority at the full hearing of the application for judicial review itself. However, delay in obtaining legal aid may constitute an acceptable reason for granting leave belatedly.

The application for leave is by way of notice, giving a descrip- 7.50. tion of the applicant, the relief sought, the grounds on which relief is sought, the name and address of solicitors acting for the applicant, the applicant's address for service, and an affidavit verifying the facts relied on. Where there is any delay the reasons for such delay are to be set out in the notice. Therefore, their truth is to be attested to by affidavit.

If leave is granted, copies of the notice, the statement and the 7.51. supporting affidavit or affidavits must be served on the respondent: without the leave of the court, no further grounds may be relied upon, or relief sought, or affidavits used at the hearing. Where the respondent files an affidavit in reply, the court generally grants leave to introduce a further affidavit in reply dealing with new matters raised in the respondent's affidavit.

Application can be made during the course of proceedings for 7.52. discovery, which can be important in proceedings to enable the applicant to have sight of more documents than are in her possession. It is usual that all the applicant has is the notification of the decision and correspondence. There should not usually be a problem in accessing all documents relating to the reasons for

---

[33] *Ibid.* r.3.
[34] See, *e.g.* the dicta of Lord Brightman in *Puhlhofer* (see para. 7.11, above).
[35] R.S.C. Ord. 53, r.4.
[36] *Ibid.*, r.4.

making the decision. It will only be documents prepared in readiness for legal action which will attract privilege. This discovery process may throw up correspondence with others, potentially even prejudicial remarks made by officers of the local authority or others.

Breach of Statutory Duty

7.53.   As an alternative to bringing proceedings for judicial review, the applicant may seek to bring proceedings for breach of statutory duty. It may be that the applicant contends that the authority has failed to carry out its duty to such an extent that it could properly be said not to have carried out its duty at all. However, the decision of the High Court in *R. v. Westminster C.C. ex p. Tansey*[37] has limited the potential for any action in this context. Applying the principle in *Cocks v. Thanet D.C.*[38], the authority is only liable under this head where it refuses to make any offer of accommodation at all. Where some decision is made, it is not possible to argue that that decision is a breach of statutory duty. Rather, an action must be brought for judicial review of the decision that is made. The Court of Appeal found that this aspect of the High Court's judgment was obiter. The point therefore remains at issue.

7.54.   Comparatively few cases are brought by this method. The route of judicial review being used instead. There is clearly some overlap. For a local authority to have failed to exercise its decision-making power or to have done so in such a way that it appears to be breach of its duty altogether, would generally found an action for judicial review.

7.55.   The appropriate remedy in cases of torts such as that for breach of statutory duty is damages for loss of out-of-pocket expense. Therefore, the tortious route offers little more remedy than that under judicial review in any event.

Relief

7.56.   Homeless people require housing. Homeless people require housing immediately. The problem with the methods of seeking relief outlined above is that they take some time to come into effect. Therefore, it will often be important for an applicant to obtain interlocutory, intermediate relief.

---

[37] (1988) 20 H.L.R. 520.
[38] [1983] 2 A.C. 286.

Interim Relief

Interlocutory relief is available in judicial review proceedings 7.57. and under breach of statutory duty proceedings. It is usual in the case of judicial review proceedings for the interlocutory relief sought to be obtained should be stated in the notice. The most common form of interlocutory relief sought is that the applicant be housed pending a trial of the action. On this basis, where the interlocutory application is successful, there will be no need to pursue the action to trial.

In cases alleging breach of duty by the authority, Lord Denning 7.58. held in *De Falco*[39] that there is a need to show a strong prima facie case of breach. Part of the justification for this different approach is that the applicant will generally not be in a position to give an undertaking for damages in the event that the case is lost. Some commentators have raised the question as to what loss would be suffered by the authority on the basis that the accommodated applicant would be required to pay rent or would receive rent from housing benefit claims in any event.

It has been the subject of some academic comment that Lord 7.59. Denning gave an apparently conflicting judgment in *Allen v. Jumbo Holdings*[40] where the owners of an aircraft were the subject of a Mareva injunction which prevented the aircraft from being removed from the jurisdiction. Lord Denning held in that case that "I do not see why a poor plaintiff should be denied a *Mareva Injunction* just because he is poor, whereas a rich plaintiff would get it". The principle in this latter case would appear to be infringed by the rule in the former.

In the case of *Hammell*[41] it was argued that the effect of the 7.60. *Puhlhofer* judgment in the House of Lords was a necessity to show "exceptional circumstances" before an interlocutory injunction would be granted. It was held that it was sufficient to show that there were grounds for leave to be granted to proceed with judicial review for the application for interlocutory relief to be made. *De Falco*[42] was followed in these circumstances. In *Barry*, it was held that there was a presumption that a local authority should be subject to an injunction against excluding the applicant from accommodation which she is currently occupying until the decision in the trial of the action. The Court of Appeal in *Thornton v.*

[39] [1980] Q.B. 460, C.A.
[40] [1980] 1 W.L.R. 1252.
[41] *Hammel v. Kensington and Chelsea R.L.B.C.* (1988) 20 H.L.R. 666.
[42] [1980] Q.B. 460, C.A.

Kirklees M.B.C.[43] has underlined that *ex parte* orders should not normally be granted. The exceptions to this rule would appear to be in circumstances where there has been some wilful disregard of statutory duty.

Final Relief

7.61.   In the case of judicial review proceedings, the court will quash the decision or compel that action is taken. The court will not make the decision itself. In *Tickner*[44] for example, the court refused to make a declaration that the applicant was not homeless intentionally because that would have been to interfere with the decision of the authority. However, it is often the case that in fact the authority are left with no alternative but to reach a particular decision on the basis of the court's judgment.

7.62.   In the wake of quashing a decision, the parties are at least back at the position of the interim position before the authority made the original decision. For example, where an authority irrationally believed, in the court's opinion, that an applicant was not in priority need, the authority are left in the position effectively of being required to believe that the applicant is in priority need unless other pressing factors exist.

7.63.   In *R. v. Northavon D.C., ex p. Palmer*[45], P sought damages against the authority for failure to process her housing application timeously. P first applied when her and her family were squatters on the point of eviction. She applied a second time when she and her family were required to move to a caravan. The authority held that she was neither homeless nor threatened with homelessness. Prior to the hearing for judicial review, the authority conceded that P was homeless. Sir Thomas Bingham M.R. held that P could not recover damages except for breach of a private law duty to provide housing. It was held that she could not establish such a private law duty until the authority's public law decision-making function has been concluded. That was a function which only the authority could perform.

[43] [1979] Q.B. 626.
[44] *Tickner v. Mole Valley D.C.* (1980) August LAG Bulletin. 187, C.A.
[45] (1995) 27 H.L.R. 576.

PART 3

STATUTORY TESTS

CHAPTER 8

Homelessness

This chapter deals with the definition of homelessness under the **8.01.** Housing Act 1996. Section 175 of the 1996 Act sets out the core definition of the situation in which an applicant will be considered homeless. It is a pre-requisite of fixing a local housing authority with an obligation for having responsibility for housing an applicant that the individual is homeless. The definition is expressed in terms of those situations in which an applicant will not be considered to be homeless. Therefore an applicant will seek to remain outside the definition in section 175(1) to be eligible for housing on grounds of homelessness.

The starting point for the 1996 legislation is therefore defining **8.02.** those persons who are not homeless. Section 175 is one component of the whole of the definition. The full range of requirements, as set out in Chapter 2, above, are that the applicant is homeless, in priority need, has a local connection with the authority's district and has not become homeless intentionally. The core of the definition goes beyond those who are sleeping on the street. The statutory definition encompasses those who are living in unsuitable accommodation, as discussed below, and those living in temporary accommodation which is tantamount to having no accommodation at all.

The Statutory Definition of "Homeless"

Introductory

Section 175 of the 1996 Act sets out the central definition. **8.03.**

> "(1) A person is homeless if he has no accommodation available for his occupation, in the United Kingdom or elsewhere, which he—

(a) is entitled to occupy by virtue of an interest in it or by virtue of an order of a court,

(b) has an express or implied licence to occupy, or

(c) occupies as a residence by virtue of any enactment or rule of law giving him the right to remain in occupation or restricting the right of another person to recover possession."

A person is homeless if she has no accommodation which is available for her occupation. That accommodation can be located either in the United Kingdom or outside it.

8.04. The individual must then satisfy one of three requirements as to rights in the property concerned. First, the individual must be entitled to occupy the accommodation either because she has an interest in it or because there is a court order granting the individual a right in the property.[1] The question arises: what kind of interest is it that the individual must have in the property or what kind of right must be granted by the court order?

8.05. Secondly, the individual must have an express or implied licence to occupy the accommodation. This does not require a legal or equitable interest in the property. Rather a permission to occupy is adequate.

8.06. Thirdly, the individual must occupy the property further to a statute or other rule of law which gives her the right either to occupy the accommodation or to be able to prevent others from occupying the property.

8.07. The definition is extended in section 175(2) to cover two situations in which the person has accommodation but either cannot gain access to it or in certain circumstances where the home is a moveable structure, such as a mobile home or barge. The first extension in section 175(2)(a) is where "he cannot secure entry to it". The second in section 175(2)(b) is where accommodation is a "moveable structure, vehicle or vessel designed or adapted for human habitation" and where "there is no place where he is entitled or permitted both to place it and to reside in it".

8.08. The qualification to this definition of "homeless" is to the definition of "accommodation". Under section 175(3) "a person shall not be treated as having accommodation unless it is accommodation which it would be reasonable for him to continue to

---

[1] Housing Act 1996, s. 175(1)(a).

occupy". The issue is therefore what type of accommodation is not reasonable for an individual to occupy. This issue is considered in detail in Chapter 9, below.

The issue is then the time at which the applicant becomes **8.09.** homeless. *R. v. Croydon L.B.C., ex p. Jarvis*[2] held that the point in time at which the applicant becomes homeless in the circumstances of an assured shorthold tenancy, is the time at which the landlord takes possession proceedings and obtains an order for possession. Where the tenant has received notice to quit, she is not homeless at that time. Andrew Collins Q.C. held that the decision was not unreasonable because the authority had considered the reasonableness of the applicant remaining in occupation, the general housing situation in the authority's district and the provisions of the Code of Guidance.

The question of the time at which a person becomes homeless **8.10.** was considered in *R. v. Hillingdon L.B.C., ex p. Bax*[3] where the applicant lived in a houseboat. The authority considered that he had always been homeless because he had never had a permanent place of mooring for the boat. It was held that the applicant had a licence to travel the waterways and therefore was not homeless until the houseboat was lost.

Under section 175(4) "a person is threatened with homelessness **8.11.** if it is likely that he will become homeless within 28 days".

No accommodation

Meaning of "accommodation". In the joined appeals of *R. v.* **8.12.** *Wandsworth L.B.C., ex p. Mansoor* and *R. v. Wandsworth L.B.C., ex p. Wingrove*[4] the applicants applied separately to their local authority for accommodation on the ground that they were homeless. The authority found with reference to both that they were intentionally homeless but also in priority need. It was the authority's policy to make only one offer of suitable accommodation. The authority offered assured shorthold tenancies in the private sector in discharge of this duty. The offer was for a period of months with a reasonable chance of renewal thereafter. Both applicants sought judicial review on the basis that the offers lacked the appropriate degree of permanence or the quality of indefinite duration required by the Act. The Court of Appeal held that this

[2] (1994) 26 H.L.R. 194.
[3] December 1992 *Legal Action* 21.
[4] [1996] 3 All E.R. 913.

offer of accommodation was suitable for someone who was intentionally homeless and in priority need. *Awua* was applied on the basis that these offers were reasonable.

8.13.   In *R. v. Hillingdon L.B.C., ex p. Puhlhofer*,[5] Mr and Mrs *Puhlhofer* were living with their two young children temporarily in bed-and-breakfast accommodation in a guest house. The couple had one single bedroom with no means of washing clothes or of cooking. They applied to the local authority for accommodation as homeless people because the room was inadequate for their needs. The council decided that they were not homeless or threatened with homelessness within the meaning of section 1(1) of the 1977 Act. The applicants sought judicial review of the council's decision that they were not homeless and claimed that the term "accommodation" meant "appropriate accommodation".

8.14.   **The statutory test.**Under Part III of the 1985 Housing Act, it was only accommodation in England, Wales or Scotland which counted in deciding whether or not a person was homeless. Section 175(1) of the 1996 Act provides that a person is homeless if he has no accommodation available for his occupation in the United Kingdom or elsewhere. It is important to note that the accommodation can be in the United Kingdom or elsewhere. It is no longer the case that, as happened under the Housing Act 1985, an individual can own property outside the United Kingdom and still be considered homeless in the United Kingdom for the purposes of the 1996 Act.

8.15.   There remains the obligation on a local authority (as set out below) to consider the application for housing on grounds of homelessness until such time as they are satisfied that the applicant does have accommodation available outside the United Kingdom.

8.16.   The development of the law in this context appears to be in step with the Asylum and Immigration Act 1996 which introduced a new code for dealing with those seeking entry to the United Kingdom or asylum or citizenship within it. There are a number of provisions in the 1996 legislation which do not mirror the 1985 Act, which deal with the position of asylum seekers or putative immigrants.

8.17.   The 1977 Act did not specify want of accommodation in England, Wales or Scotland. It had been accepted in the case law, however, that only accommodation in England, Wales or Scotland

---

[5] [1986] A.C. 484.

should be taken into account and that the courts will consider the legislation only on that limited basis.

The early case law in this area dealt with claims by local **8.18.** authorities that they bore no further responsibility to house persons living in temporary accommodation as persons who were homeless. The courts held that there was no necessary inconsistency between being homeless and having some temporary accommodation available. In the first case the applicants were women living in refuges (as in cases such as *Cynon Valley* and *Sidhu,* discussed below). In *Cynon Valley*[6] the judge held that:

"It was important that refuges be seen as temporary crisis accommodation, and that women living in refuges were still homeless under the terms of the Act. If it was suggested that they were not homeless it would be necessary for voluntary organisations to issue immediate 28 days' notice when women came in so that they would be under threat of homelessness. This would be totally undesirable and would simply add stress to stress. If living in crisis accommodation took women out of the "homeless" category then the Act was being watered down and its protection would be removed from a whole class of persons that it was set up to help and for whom it was extremely important".

In *R. v. Ealing L.B.C. ex p. Sidhu*[7] the applicant had been **8.19.** subjected to violence by her husband. She left and went to stay at a women's refuge with her children. She was granted interim care and control of the children by court order. She then applied to Ealing Borough Council for accommodation under the terms of the 1977 Act. The authority decided that she was not homeless. The authority decided further that they would not consider the applicant to be in priority need until she obtained a final court order granting her care and control of the children. Hodgson J. quashed the decision of the authority. He held that the fact that the applicant was accommodated in a refuge did not justify the authority's decision that she was not homeless. The applicant ought to have been considered as being in priority need because she had dependent children living with her — despite the fact that she did not have a final court order granting her care and control over the children.

Hodgson J. in Sidhu said the following:

". . . what I think is plain beyond peradventure the correct construction of this Act, I find it in the speech of Lord Lowry in

---

[6] *Williams v. Cynon Valley Council* (1980) January LAG Bulletin 16.
[7] (1982) 2 H.L.R. 45.

Din v. Wandsworth L.B.C. I think that all I need read are two short sentences from Lord Lowry's speech: 'I consider that to be homeless and to have found some temporary accommodation are not mutually inconsistent concepts. Nor does a person cease to be homeless merely by having a roof over his head or a lodging, however precarious' ".

8.20.   In the second case[8] the applicant was a man staying in a night shelter on a night-by-night basis. He ran the risk of being turned away on any particular evening if the shelter was full. Short-term accommodation of this type would not constitute settled accommodation of the kind which would be a break in a period of intentional homelessness. It would appear that their authority has been reinforced.

8.21.   In each of these cases, the occupants were mere licensees. Such rights to occupy, were not rights in property—the applicants therefore were capable of falling within the definition under section 58(2) of the 1985 Act.

The Person for Whom the Accommodation is Provided

Homeless Person with Dependants

8.22.   The issue arises where the homeless person is not an individual but has dependants or co-habitees. Therefore, section 176 provides:

"176[9] Accommodation shall be regarded as available for a person's occupation only if it is available for occupation by him together with—
(a) any other person who normally resides with him as a member of his family, or
(b) any other person who might reasonably be expected to reside with him".

---

[8] *Bowers.*
[9] Cut from section 176:
(X) Accommodation shall not be regarded as available for a person's occupation if—
(a) he cannot secure entry to it, or
(b) it consists of a moveable structure, vehicle or vessel designed or adapted for human habitation and there is no place where he is entitled or permitted both to place it and to reside in it.
(Y) Accommodation shall not be regarded as available for a person's occupation unless it is accommodation which it would be reasonable for him to continue to occupy.

Section 176 provides that throughout Part VII of the 1996 Act, any reference to an obligation to made accommodation available for a person's occupation are to be construed to include reference to member's of the individual's family or any person who might reasonably be expected to reside with him.

The difficulty of deciding whether or not a person is homeless is **8.23.** confused where that person is not a single applicant. Where there are dependants or persons with whom the applicant usually resides, or can be expected to reside, the issue arises whether the homeless test is satisfied. Where persons other than the applicant are to be taken into account, the relevant right to occupy must be such that both applicant and other person can reside in the accommodation in question. Those other persons will be taken into account only where they normally reside with the applicant and those other persons do so as a member of the applicant's family or in circumstances where it would be reasonable for them to live together.

The issue arises where the homeless person is not an individual **8.24.** but has dependants or co-habitees. Section 176 provides that throughout Part VII of the 1996 Act, any reference to an obligation to made accommodation available for a person's occupation are to be construed to include references to members of the applicant's family or any person who might reasonably be expected to reside with him.

Therefore, someone who would reasonably be expected to reside **8.25.** with the applicant, is not to be taken into account unless she does normally live with the applicant. However, someone who is a member of the applicant's family is not to be taken into account unless she does normally live with the applicant: but need not be shown to do so reasonably.

The Code of Guidance under the 1985 legislation suggested that **8.26.** "member of the family" would cover family relationships where there is a blood or marriage nexus between two people.

In the context of persons who might reasonably be expected to **8.27.** reside with the applicant, the Code of Guidance considered that the following categories would fall within the class: co-habiting couples, adults with foster children, and elderly or disabled people who live with carers. It appears to be sufficient that, in this context, those persons do not form a family with the applicant. The personal nexus between them will be adequate to satisfy section 176. This categorisation is mirrored in the new Code of Guidance.

8.28.   There may be situations in which the categories of person, discussed in the previous paragraph, do not live with the applicant because they have separated as a result of having no accommodation. Homelessness itself might be the reason why the test under section 176 might not be satisfied at the date the application is made.

8.29.   Alternatively, the situation may arise where a family has never lived together, either at all or not in the United Kingdom. In *R. v. Hillingdon L.B. ex p. Islam*[10] Mr Islam was a Bangladeshi who settled in the United Kingdom, having been granted indefinite leave to remain. From time to time he visited Bangladesh. He was married in Bangladesh and had children with his wife. She lived in Bangladesh until she obtained entry clearance to the United Kingdom. Mr Islam had not lived with his wife before this time. His wife came to England and was housed temporarily by Mr Islam's landlord. The landlord later evicted Mr Islam, the wife and their children. Mr Islam sought to be housed by the authority as a homeless person. The authority decided that Mr Islam was not in priority need because his dependents were not homeless on the basis that his wife and children were not, in these circumstances, persons who might reasonably be expected to reside with him. The authority's reason for this finding was Mr Islam had organised that his wife and family leave Bangladesh deliberately to come and live with him.

8.30.   At first instance, Glidewell J. held that Mr Islam was in priority need but was intentionally homeless. The matter reached the House of Lords on the issue whether or not Mr Islam was intentionally homeless. In allowing his appeal, the House of Lords held that the room from which Mr Islam was evicted was not accommodation available for him and his family because of its inadequacy for their communal occupation. It was found that it would not have been reasonable for them to have occupied it as a family. The House of Lords held further that Mr Islam could not be said to have been occupying accommodation with his wife and children in Bangladesh given that his family was ordinarily resident in Bangladesh while he had been ordinarily resident in England. Therefore, he had not ceased to occupy any accommodation in Bangladesh — there was no accommodation which Mr Islam could be said to have given up.

8.31.   The issue might arise where a married couple has always lived with one set of their parents. The question would be whether or not they were homeless at a time when they left their parents'

[10] [1983] 1 A.C. 688; See also *R. v. Eastleigh B.C. ex p. Beattie (No. 1)* (1983) 10 H.L.R. 134.

home. The first issue would be whether they become voluntarily homeless when they left their parents. The answer would then be in the precise reason for their leaving. Therefore, where such a couple leaves their parents' accommodation when their parents' tenancy comes to an end, the couple would have quit the property involuntarily. The authorities would indicate that the couple would not be intentionally homeless in these circumstances.

The Decision as to Homelessness

The burden is on the authority to make inquiries and is not on **8.32.** the applicant to prove that she is homeless. In *R. v. Woodspring D.C., ex p. Walters*[11] the authority required that the applicant demonstrate positively that her husband, who was a serving member of the R.A.F. in Cyprus, had lost married persons' quarters after she returned to England. Taylor J. held that the burden was on the authority to make inquiries and not on the applicant to prove that accommodation was no longer available.

In *R. v. Islington L.B.C., ex p. Hassan,*[12] an order for possession **8.33.** was obtained against the applicant. The applicant was found to be homeless by the authority. The landlord informed him that the order would not have been enforced if he agreed to have housing benefit paid directly to the landlord. The authority found him intentionally homeless because he knew of his landlord's offer after the accommodation was lost. It was held that the authority could not rely on events which happened after the authority had found that the applicant was homeless.

The authority's officer must be scrupulous to keep personal **8.34.** value judgments separate from the issue of homelessness. In *R. v. Tower Hamlets L.B.C., ex p. Hoque*[13] it was held that where a local authority officer decided that overcrowding in a property was due to the applicant's own decision to increase the size of his family, the decision would be quashed.

It may not be clear whether or not an application has been **8.35.** made. It is a matter for the authority to decide whether or not it is seised of an application under Part VII: (*R. v. Lambeth L.B.C. ex p. Pattinson*[14]). However, in *R. v. Sefton M.B.C., ex p. Healis*[15] Harrison J. held that where an applicant had applied for a transfer to other

[11] (1984) 16 H.L.R. 73.
[12] (1995) 27 H.L.R. 485.
[13] *The Times*, July 20, 1993.
[14] (1996) 28 H.L.R. 214.
[15] *The Times*, May 2, 1994.

council accommodation on the basis that it was no longer reasonable for her to continue to occupy her accommodation, clearly
constituted both a request for a transfer and an application for
housing on grounds of homelessness.

8.36. The question is therefore: will a material change in the applicant's circumstances require the authority to provide housing for
the applicant. The issue arises whether pregnancy constitutes a
material change in circumstances such that there is a new application. In *R. v. Ealing L.B.C., ex p. McBain*[16] the applicant became
pregnant and applied for housing. The authority offered her
accommodation which she refused. She became pregnant a second
time and applied for housing on ground of homelessness and
priority need. The authority refused on the basis that they had
already discharged their obligation to her. The Court of Appeal
held that the authority's obligations to her were revived by a
material change in her circumstances.

Rights of Occupation

8.37. Under the terms of section 175 of the 1996 Act, the applicant is
required to have certain types of right in property before being
found to have accommodation available. There are three requirements as to rights in the property concerned, and a individual will
be found to have accommodation available if any of the three
requirements are satisfied.

Occupation under Interest or Court Order

8.38. First, the applicant must be entitled to occupy the accommodation either because he has an interest in it or because there is a
court order granting the applicant a right to the accommodation.[17]
The two issues to be considered are therefore: the type of interest
the applicant must have in the property and alternatively the type
of right which must be granted by the court order.

8.39. The first point to be made is that that right must be sufficient to
grant the applicant the ability to occupy the accommodation.
Where there are dependents, or other people who normally reside
with the applicant, that right must be a right which also covers
their accommodation at the property.[18]

8.40. It would appear that the interest referred to in section 175(1)(a)
must be some kind of legal or equitable interest in the property.
Those with a legal interest would clearly include a freeholder or

---

[16] (1986) 18 H.L.R. 59.
[17] Housing Act 1996, s. 175(1)(a).
[18] See, *e.g. R. v. Hillingdon L.B. ex p. Islam* (see n.10, above).

long leaseholder. Similarly, short periodic leases would be captured by the section. Those with interests under a trust of land[19] would similarly appear to be caught on the basis that they have some equitable interest in the property.[20] Therefore, where an equitable interest comes to an end or is converted into a right in the proceeds of the sale of the property, the applicant would cease to have an interest in the property and therefore be potentially within the definition of "homeless" under section 175.

The further issue is, therefore, with reference to an order of the **8.41.** court giving a person a right in property. This is a matter of construing any court order made. The types of order which would seem to be caught most clearly are the following. Orders made with reference to family disputes under matrimonial legislation generally. For example, orders giving rights of occupation made under the Matrimonial Homes Act 1983 or the Family Law Act 1996. Orders made on the grounds of proprietary estoppel or constructive trust which give the applicant rights to occupy the property for life[21] or to occupy for some period of time[22] or which recognise that the plaintiff has some right in the property[23].

A person who occupies under the terms of a licence may be **8.42.** prevented from being defined as homeless where he still has a right in the property but has ceased to live there. Section 175(1) provides that the applicant be entitled to occupy the premises. There is no let out for such an applicant who no longer wishes to occupy that property — it would appear that the applicant would not even get to the stage of contending whether or not she was intentionally homeless because she would not satisfy the test under section 175 in any event. Where that person voluntarily gives up the right in the accommodation, she is at risk of being intentionally homeless.

Occupation under Licence

The second means by which an applicant has accommodation **8.43.** available is where she has a licence to occupy that accommodation. Under English law this may be an express or an implied licence.

---

[19] Or formerly "trust for sale", see Trusts and Appointments of Land Act 1996.
[20] See, *e.g. Williams & Glyn's Bank v. Boland,* [1981] A.C. 487, and *Lloyds Bank v. Rosset,* [1988] 132 S.J. 1698.
[21] *Pascoe v. Turner,* [1979] 1 W.L.R. 431.
[22] *Coombes v. Smith,* [1986] 1 W.L.R. 808.
[23] See, *e.g. Williams & Glyn's Bank v. Boland,* [1981] A.C. 487, and *Lloyds Bank v. Rosset,* [1988] 132 S.J. 1698.

Under Scots law the equivalent is a right or permission, or an implied right or permission to occupy. Neither of these sets or rights requires a legal or equitable interest in the property. Therefore, those occupying property as lodgers or flatsharers, rather than as tenants, will occupy under a licence.[24] Where the applicant occupies under the terms of a service licence which is connected to the terms of a contract of employment, the licence to occupy will terminate at the date of the termination of that contract.

8.44. In *R. v. Tower Hamlets L.B.C., ex p. Miah*,[25] the Court of Appeal held that for the purposes of section 79 of the 1985 Act, where a person occupies accommodation on the terms of a licence (being a lesser interest granted from a leased interest), that person is not a secure tenant for the purposes of the 1985 Act.

8.45. In *R. v. Portsmouth C.C., ex p. Knight*[26] the applicant had occupied accommodation as part of his employment with a wine merchant. He was dismissed and left the accommodation before his employer obtained a possession order. The authority argued that he was intentionally homeless. Woolf J. held that the applicant had become a trespasser from the time he lost his employment and therefore it was not reasonable for the authority to decide that he was intentionally homeless.

8.46. In *R. v. Kensington and Chelsea R.L.B.C., ex p. Minton*[27] a housekeeper resigned her occupation and thereby lost her accommodation. Her former employer offered to let her live in the property again. The local authority contended that this offer meant that she was not homeless. Macpherson J. held that she did not have accommodation within the meaning of section 175 of the 1996 Act because she had lost her previous licence to occupy the property and the new offer did not constitute accommodation in itself.

Occupation by Enactment or Restriction

8.47. Thirdly, the applicant will not be homeless where she has accommodation available further to a statute or other rule of law which gives her the right either to occupy the accommodation or to be able to prevent others from occupying the property. This accommodation must be occupied in conjunction with dependents and persons with whom the applicant is usually expected to reside.

---

[24] *A.-G. Securities v. Vaughan*, [1990] 1 A.C. 417.
[25] [1992] 2 All E.R. 667.
[26] (1983) 10 H.L.R. 115.
[27] (1988) 20 H.L.R. 648.

The significant difference between section 175(1)(a) (right to **8.48.** occupy accommodation) and section 175(1)(c) (occupation under an enactment or by restriction) is that the former (discussed above) does not require that the applicant is in occupation to fall outside the homeless test. However, the test for occupation by enactment or restriction under section 175(1)(c) requires that the applicant be in occupation to fall outside the homeless test.

There are a number of statutes to which this provision could **8.49.** relate. The clearest is the Protection from Eviction Act 1977. The rights granted by that Act ensure that a tenant occupying a tenancy not under the Rent Acts cannot be evicted without a court order. Therefore, the tenant acquires a right to occupy the property even after the termination of a fixed term tenancy. The 1977 Act protects persons occupying under the benefit of a restricted contract further to section 19 of the Rent Act 1997.

A person occupying property under the terms of the Housing **8.50.** Act 1988 or Part IV of the Housing Act 1985, occupies under the terms of the tenancy and then by the terms of the statutory security of tenure provisions. Therefore, the tenant occupies under the terms of either Act until the date of a court order requiring him to give up possession of the property to the landlord. Tenants under long leaseholds will frequently occupy property after the termination of the fixed-term tenancy on the basis of a statutorily extended tenancy. Therefore, the tenant will similarly acquire a right to occupy under that statute.

Matrimonial homes legislation, and the domestic violence and **8.51.** other provisions of the Family Law Act 1996, provide that spouses and other co-habitants have rights of occupation or grant rights restricting the ability of others to recover possession.

The rights of those occupying under adverse possession have **8.52.** only restricted rights which will generally not entitle them to remain in occupation or to restrict others from going into occupation of the accommodation. The position of squatters and others in adverse possession is considered below in Chapter 14. In short, squatters will generally not satisfy the first two categories under section 175. In this writer's opinion, it is unlikely that they will fall within section 175(1)(c) in any event. The legislation does not give squatters rights to exclude others. The accommodation which squatters provide for themselves is nothing more than temporary accommodation in which they have no rights. As such, they cannot be said to fall within the mischief of Part VII of the 1996 Act.

Unsuitable Accommodation

Reasonableness of Accommodation

8.53.   The above discussion of the core definition in Part VII of the 1996 Act of the "homeless", has proceeded on the basis that an individual must either not have accommodation, or have only restricted rights to occupy temporary accommodation. The other aspect which might make an applicant homeless for the purposes of the 1996 Act, is where she is living in accommodation which is unsuitable.

8.54.   Section 175(3) provides that "A person shall not be treated as having accommodation unless it is accommodation which it would be reasonable for him to continue to occupy". Therefore, there is a qualification to the core test in section 175(1) and (2) where the accommodation is not reasonable for the applicant to continue to occupy. Subsection (3) is drafted in terms that the applicant must be in occupation and that it is continued occupation which is unreasonable. Consequently, if the factor which makes the occupation not reasonable is removed, the applicant will not be able to rely upon section 175(3) because it may then be reasonable to continue to occupy the accommodation.

8.55.   There are two situations set out in the legislation at section 177 as to the reasonableness of continuing to occupy the legislation:

cases where the applicant has suffered domestic violence or the risk of domestic violence
cases where it is unreasonable to occupy accommodation in the general circumstances of housing in an area.

8.56.   There is no express provision within section 177 that the provision in section 175(3) is restricted to the categories of reasonableness set out in section 177. Therefore, it is possible for there to be factors which make accommodation unreasonable to occupy beyond those categories set out in section 177. While the opening words in section 177(1) do bear the interpretation that the Subsection is intended to be restrictive, it cannot be the case because there are further express statutory categories of reasonableness set out in section 177(2) and (3). Therefore, it is this writer's opinion that the legislation is capable of allowing a number of causes which make accommodation not reasonable to occupy.

General Circumstances

8.57.   Under section 177(2), in considering the reasonableness of a person continuing to occupy the accommodation regard may be had to the general circumstances surrounding housing in the district of the local housing authority to whom she has applied for accommodation or for assistance in obtaining accommodation. This reasonableness test applies on a retrospective basis to whether or not it would have been reasonable for the individual to occupy that accommodation.[28] Therefore, the applicant can seek to justify having left accommodation retrospectively by arguing that the circumstances at the time of leaving the accommodation rendered the decision to leave reasonable.

This wording appeared in the amended housing legislation in response to the *Puhlhofer* decision. The intention was to restore people living in unacceptable accommodation to the category of those who are homeless. *Puhlhofer*, in effect, removed such people from the definition. Therefore, this wording was added to mimic part of the test for intentional homelessness and reinforce that construction of the legislation. Case law before *Puhlhofer* held that accommodation which it was unreasonable to continue to occupy should be disregarded in decided whether or not an applicant was homeless. **8.58.**

In *Gloucester v. Miles*,[29] Mrs Miles and her husband were joint tenants of their property. Mrs Miles went to stay with friends after her husband left her. Her husband ransacked the house after she had moved out, thus making it uninhabitable. The council changed the locks when they learned of this. Mrs Miles applied to the council for housing on the grounds that she was homeless. The Court of Appeal accepted her argument that she was not homeless when she left to stay with friends. It was the vandalism which caused her homelessness. Therefore, she was not intentionally homeless. **8.59.**

The Code of Guidance, lists a number of criteria to which the local authority should refer when deciding whether or not an applicant is homeless: **8.60.**

physical conditions,
overcrowding (not necessarily statutory overcrowding),
the type of accommodation,
violence or threats of violence from outside the home,
the cost of remaining in property compared to the applicant's means and security of tenure.

Where the applicant contends that permanent accommodation is unsuitable, it is possible for the court to order that the applicant be

---

[28] Housing Act 1996, s.177(2).
[29] (1985) 17 H.L.R. 292.

placed in alternative temporary accommodation pending trial: (*R. v. Haringey L.B.C., ex p. Flynn;*[30] *R. v. Haringey L.B.C., ex p. Ulger*[31]).

8.61.   In deciding whether or not accommodation is overcrowded, the authority must consider whether the number of people occupying the property is reasonable — the authority cannot simply rely on the statutory definitions of what will and will not constitute overcrowding: (*R. v. Westminster C.C., ex p. Alouat*[32]).

8.62.   In *R. v. Medina B.C., ex p. Dee*[33] the applicant occupied a beach chalet when she became pregnant. She received medical advice that there was risk to the unborn baby if she continued to occupy the damp and mould-infested chalet. The local authority decided that the chalet was fit for human habitation. Henry J. held that it was not reasonable for the authority to expect the applicant to ignore medical opinion in this context.

8.63.   In *R. v. Kensington and Chelsea R.L.B.C., ex p. Kassam*[34] the applicant occupied a small, one-bedroomed flat with her son and daughter. The conditions caused her daughter to develop a depressive illness. The applicant sought housing on the basis that the accommodation was unsuitable for her daughter to move back in after receiving medical care. The authority decided that she was not homeless. The authority's decision was quashed on the basis that they had not considered whether there was a requirement for full-time live-in care for her daughter. The authority did not give sufficient reasons in the context of the live-in care arrangements.

8.64.   The reasonableness of occupying or continuing to occupy accommodation is considered below in Chapter 9.

Domestic Violence

8.65.   Section 177(1) provides that it is not reasonable for a person to continue to occupy accommodation if it is probable that this will lead to domestic violence against that person or categories of prescribed persons. Therefore, where an individual is the victim of domestic violence it is considered not reasonable for a person to continue to occupy accommodation, with the result that such a person can be considered to be homeless where having accommodation where the domestic violence will probably occur is the only reason for refusing to categorise that person as being homeless.

---

[30] June 1995 *Legal Action* 21.
[31] December 1992 *Legal Action* 21.
[32] (1989) 21 H.L.R. 47.
[33] (1992) 24 H.L.R. 562.
[34] (1994) 26 H.L.R. 455.

For this purpose "domestic violence", in relation to a person, **8.66.** means violence from a person with whom she is associated, or threats of violence from such a person which are likely to be carried out.[35]

The test of reasonableness is extended beyond the individual **8.67.** homeless person.[36] It is not reasonable for that person to continue to occupy the accommodation if it is probable that a person who normally lives with him as a member of his family[37], or any other person who might reasonably be expected to reside with her, bears the same risk of domestic violence.[38]

Section 177(1) provides that an applicant is not to be considered **8.68.** as having available accommodation where it is probable that continued occupation will lead to domestic violence against her. This is on grounds that it is not reasonable for that person to continue to occupy the accommodation.[39] There is no provision as to who bears the burden of proof that domestic violence is probable. In situations where domestic violence has occurred, it will clearly be easier to demonstrate its probability; particularly where the violence has occurred on a systematic basis in the past, its probability will be easier to judge.

This test will be a difficult one for local housing authorities to **8.69.** apply in practice. The definition of "domestic violence" includes threats which are likely to be carried out. Therefore, it would appear that an applicant can produce evidence or testimony of threats coupled with a real expectation that they will be put into practice. For the legal adviser there is a difficult line here between becoming intentionally homeless and leaving accommodation

---

[35] Housing Act 1996, s.177(1).

[36] "(1) ... from some other person residing in it or to threats of violence from some other person residing in it and likely to carry out the threats.

(2) In determining whether it would be, or would have been, reasonable for a person to continue to occupy accommodation, regard may be had to the general circumstances prevailing in relation to housing in the district of the local housing authority to whom he has applied for accommodation or for assistance in obtaining accommodation.

(3) The Secretary of State may by order specify—

(a) other circumstances in which it is to be regarded as reasonable or not reasonable for a person to continue to occupy accommodation, and

(b) other matters to be taken into account or disregarded in determining whether it would be, or would have been, reasonable for a person to continue to occupy accommodation".

[37] Housing Act 1996, s.177(1)(a).

[38] s. 177(1)(b).

[39] s. 177(1).

because it is unreasonable to continue to occupy it on grounds of expected domestic violence.

8.70.   In *R. v. Broxbourne B.C. ex p. Willmoth*[40] the applicant was a woman who had been forced to leave accommodation as a result of the actions of her violent former partner. That partner did not live with her, but the applicant contended that she should be housed outside the borough of Hackney where the violence took place. The respondent authority decided she was not homeless because it was reasonable that she continue to live in Hackney. The authority contended that it was the rights to the property which decided whether or not the applicant was homeless. On these facts, she continued to have a right to occupy the property under her tenancy. Sir John Megaw, giving the judgment of the Court of Appeal held that the correct application of the statute (now section 175) was that the authority look at all of the circumstances related to continued occupation. In his words:

> "It may be the duty of the housing authority to consider also circumstances, matters and factors which may fall outside the limited consideration of the actual quality of physical accommodation itself . . . Just as the difficulties created by a staircase or other approach to accommodation, to an applicant with physical infirmities, is relevant to reasonableness, so also are threats of violence, even though those threats come from one who is not resident in the accommodation".[41]

8.71.   The policy behind the legislation is clear: co-habitees should not be required to suffer violence to themselves or their dependents and be trapped in that accommodation. Rather, domestic violence should be combated and the individual should be eligible to be re-housed away from the abusive relationship. The difficulty of discharging the burden of proof here carries enormous risks for applicants in some circumstances.

8.72.   In *R. v. Purbeck D.C. ex p. Cadney*[42] the applicant left her husband due to his violence and went to live with another man. She left her new partner after three months. Nolan J. held that the applicant had not attempted to gain access to the matrimonial home and therefore there was no direct evidence that she would suffer violence if she did attempt to gain access to the property. Consequently, the local housing authority could not be said to have erred in failing to find that she was homeless.

---

[40] (1990) 22 H.L.R. 118.
[41] (1990) 22 H.L.R. 118 at 127.
[42] [1986] 2 F.L.R. 158.

Statutory Reasonableness

Section 177(3) provides that the Secretary of State may create **8.73.** orders to set out tests for reasonableness in this circumstance. Such orders may specify other circumstances in which it is to be regarded as reasonable or not reasonable for a person to continue to occupy accommodation.[43] The orders may also specify other matters which are to be taken into account (or alternatively disregarded) in determining whether it would be, or would have been, reasonable for a person to continue to occupy the accommodation.[44]

Deemed Homelessness

There are categories of homelessness which are deemed to exist **8.74.** in circumstances where the applicant would otherwise fall outside the core test in section 175 as discussed above.

Eviction

The 1985 legislation contained provisions as to eviction of the **8.75.** applicant or a situation in which it was impossible for the applicant to gain access to the accommodation being tantamount to eviction. This would lead under section 58(3) of the 1985 Act to a person being deemed to be homeless in these circumstances. This provision is reproduced in section 175(2)(a) of the 1996 Act.

The issue has therefore become, in relation to the 1985 legisla- **8.76.** tion, whether the applicant is intentionally homeless for failing to pursue the legal remedies open to him. However, that there is a theoretical legal remedy does not take account of the fact that the statute is aimed at what is "reasonable". There are many circumstances in which it would not be reasonable to pursue a legal or other remedy: for example, where that will not prevent a landlord securing vacant possession by court order in the future.

In *R. v. Portsmouth C.C., ex p. Knight*[45] the applicant had **8.77.** occupied accommodation as part of his employment with a wine merchant. He was dismissed and left the accommodation before his employer obtained a possession order. The authority argued that he was intentionally homeless. Woolf J. held that the applicant had become a trespasser from the time he lost his employment and therefore it was not reasonable for the authority to decide that he was intentionally homeless.

[43] Housing Act 1996, s.177(3)(a).
[44] s. 177(3)(b).
[45] (1983) 10 H.L.R. 115.

Movable Structures

8.78. The definition of "homelessness" is extended in section 175(2) to cover two situations in which the person has accommodation but either cannot gain access to it or in certain circumstances where the home is a moveable structure, such as a mobile home or barge, that is a "moveable structure, vehicle or vessel designed or adapted for human habitation" and where "there is no place where he is entitled or permitted both to place it and to reside in it".

8.79. *Smith v. Wokingham*[46] was a case in which a family had been housed after being held to be homeless by a local authority. The interim housing consisted of a caravan which was parked on land owned by the local authority. The family lived in the caravan for two and half years on the land although they had no express permission to live in the caravan on that land. The county court held that the local authority had acquiesced in the family's presence on the land. Therefore the occupants had permission to be on the land and therefore were not homeless within the terms of section 175(2)(b).

8.80. In *R. v. Chiltern D.C. ex p. Roberts*[47] the applicants were travelling showmen who made their way around the country in mobile homes. The applicants were required to quit a permanent site at a time when they were about the embark on a tour where there would be available site for their mobile homes. The applicants argued that they were either homeless or threatened with homelessness on grounds that they did not have a place where they were entitled to live with a degree of permanence and continuity. Pill J. held that at the start of their tour they were not homeless, nor were they threatened with homelessness. The term "reside" (as reproduced in section 175(2)(b)) means "live or occupy". Until the end of the tour, the applicants were not homeless because they would have places to reside on their way around the country.

8.81. It is important to note that where persons give addresses as their current address, that is not to be confused with that applicant having a "home" or "permanent residence". In *Tickner*[48] it was held that people living in mobile homes who had given addresses which belonged variously to mother-in-laws and divorced husbands could not be considered as permanent addresses. This was so because the mother-in-law and the divorced husband would not

---

[46] [1980] LAG Bulletin 9.
[47] (1991) 23 H.L.R. 387.
[48] *R. v. Mole Valley, ex p. Tickner* (1980) August LAG Bulletin 187, C.A.

consent to having the applicant back to live at that address. Therefore, the applicants had been correctly found to be homeless in this circumstance.

Persons Eligible for Assistance

Persons from Abroad

There are categories of person who are expressly denied **8.82.** qualification as homeless persons subject to the provisions of Part VII of the 1996 Act. The first category of person excluded is set out in section 185 of the 1996 Act:

"(1) A person is not eligible for assistance under this Part if he is a person from abroad who is ineligible for housing assistance".

Under section 185(2) of the 1996 Act, a person who is subject to immigration control within the meaning of the Asylum and Immigration Act 1996 is not eligible for housing assistance. This is unless he is of a particular class of persons prescribed by regulations made by the Secretary of State.[49]

Beyond those persons specified under the Asylum and Immigra- **8.83.** tion Act 1996 or other immigration legislation, the Secretary of State is empowered to create regulations specifying other categories of person who are to be treated for the purposes of this Part as persons from abroad who are ineligible for housing assistance.[50]

There is a disregard for people from abroad who are not eligible **8.84.** for housing assistance, under section 185(4). The effect of the subsection is that such a person is disregarded in determining whether another person either is homeless (or threatened with homelessness),[51] or has a priority need[52] for accommodation[53].

An immigrant who obtained entry to the United Kingdom by **8.85.** deceit was held to be outside any obligation on the local housing authority to whom they had applied for housing to be furnished with permanent accommodation: (*R. v. Secretary of State for the Environment, ex p. Tower Hamlets L.B.C.*[54]).

[49] Housing Act 1996, s.185(2).
[50] s. 185(3).
[51] s. 185(4)(a).
[52] As defined by section 189.
[53] s. 185(4)(b).
[54] [1993] 3 All E.R. 439.

8.86.   In *R. v. Westminster C.C., ex p. Castelli*,[55] the Court of Appeal considered a case where an Italian national, who had come to the United Kingdom legally to look for work, brought judicial review proceedings against the authority for refusing to provide him with temporary accommodation. Since arriving in the United Kingdom, the applicant had suffered bouts of illness making him unable to work. The authority argued that he was no longer a "qualified person" within article 6 of the Immigration (European Economic Area) Order 1994, and therefore had no right of abode in the United Kingdom. Evans L.J. held that the authority was wrong to find that they had no duty to the applicant under the homelessness legislation. Although he was no longer a qualified person, he had not been asked to leave the United Kingdom and was under no obligation to seek leave to remain. Therefore, the authority should have found that he was entitled to remain and to be housed under what is now Part VII of the 1996 Act.

Asylum Seekers

8.87.   There is a separate regime covering asylum seekers in the wake of the passage of the Asylum and Immigration Act 1996. An asylum seeker is not eligible for assistance under this Part if he has any accommodation in the United Kingdom, however temporary, available for his occupation.[56] The issue arises when a person becomes an asylum seeker for the purposes of section 186. Under section 186(2), a person who makes a claim for asylum[57] becomes an asylum seeker at the time when his claim is recorded by the Secretary of State as having been made.[58] A person ceases to be an asylum seeker at the time when his claim is recorded by the Secretary of State as having been finally determined or abandoned.[59]

8.88.   The decision in *R. v. Hillingdon L.B.C., ex p. Streeting*[60] has been reversed by the 1996 Act and the Asylum and Immigration Act 1996. In that case the Court of Appeal held that an applicant who came from overseas and who satisfied all the other criteria of what is now Part VII, must be housed by the local authority to which she applies regardless of local connection.

---

[55] *The Times*, February 27, 1996.
[56] Housing Act 1996, s.186(1).
[57] A claim for asylum is defined as a claim made by a person that it would be contrary to the United Kingdom's obligations under the Convention relating to the Status of Refugees for him to be removed from, or required to leave, the United Kingdom: section 186(5).
[58] s. 186(2)(a).
[59] s. 186(2)(b).
[60] [1980] 1 W.L.R. 1430.

Section 186 covers the dependent's of asylum seekers in the **8.89.**
same way, where that dependent is not by virtue of section 185 a
person from abroad who is ineligible for housing assistance.[61] The
following categories of person are defined as dependents of an
asylum seeker: (1) a person who is his spouse or a child of his
under the age of eighteen, and (2) who has neither a right of abode
in the United Kingdom nor indefinite leave under the Immigration Act 1971 to enter or remain in the United Kingdom.[62]

A person becomes a dependent of an asylum seeker at the time
when she is recorded by the Secretary of State as being a
dependent of the asylum seeker.[63] That person ceases to be a
dependent of an asylum seeker at the time when the person whose
dependent she is ceases to be an asylumseeker.[64] Alternatively that
person ceases to be such a dependent at the time when she is
recorded by the Secretary of State as ceasing to be a dependent of
the asylum seeker, if that is earlier.[65]

An immigrant who obtained entry to the United Kingdom by **8.90.**
deceit was held to be outside any obligation on the local housing
authority to whom they had applied for housing to be furnished
with permanent accommodation: (*R. v. Secretary of State for the
Environment, ex p. Tower Hamlets L.B.C.*[66]).

In *R. v. Kensington and Chelsea R.L.B.C., ex p Kihara*[67] K and **8.91.**
other asylum seekers who had no right to housing benefit and were
debarred from employment, sought judicial review of decisions by
several local authorities that they were not in priority need for
housing. It was submitted that their situation fell within the "other
special reason" for vulnerability in determining priority need
under the 1985 Act. Popplewell J. held the position of the
applicants differed greatly from that of ordinary homeless people as
they were considerably more vulnerable. They were less able to
secure accommodation than the ordinary homeless person and
would suffer more than the ordinary person without such accommodation: (*R. v. Waveney D.C., ex p Bowers*[68] and *Ortiz v. City of
Westminster*[69]). However, the provisions of priority need under
section 189 should be construed narrowly. The words "other

---

[61] Housing Act 1996, s. 186(1).
[62] s. 186(4).
[63] s. 186(3)(a).
[64] s. 186(3)(b).
[65] *Ibid.*
[66] [1993] 3 All E.R. 439.
[67] Unreported (April 18, 1996).
[68] (1983) 15 H.L.R. 118.
[69] (1995) 27 H.L.R. 364.

special reason" should be considered in the light of the preceding words "old age, mental illness or handicap or physical disability" in line with the *ejusdem generis* rule. The reasons related to problems of a physical or mental nature did not extend to impecuniosity, in line with *Noble v. South Herefordshire D.C.*[70] and *Wilson v. Nithsdale D.C.*[71]

8.92.   On appeal to the Court of Appeal, in *R. v. Kensington and Chelsea R.L.B.C., ex p. Kihara,*[72] K and other asylum seekers who had no right to housing benefit or to obtain employment to provide an income, appealed against the refusal of their applications for judicial review of local authority decisions that they were not in priority need for housing. In this case, the lack of access to income or capital, the absence of friends or family in the United Kingdom and an inability to speak English stood the applicants apart from most homeless persons.

Threatened with Homelessness

8.93.   Under section 175(4) "a person is threatened with homelessness if it is likely that he will become homeless within 28 days". While this is the given period of time, prudent policy on behalf of local authorities would appear to be to take action as early as possible in relation to persons becoming homeless.

---

[70] (1983) 17 H.L.R. 80.
[71] 1992 S.L.T. 1131.
[72] *The Independent,* July 3, 1996.

CHAPTER 9

Suitable Accommodation

The question of accommodation is central to Part VII of the 1996 **9.01.**
Act. What is also key to this area is the question whether or not
the accommodation in question is suitable for occupation by the
applicant. The case law since *Puhlhofer* has also considered whether
or not the law places any additional requirement on the local
authority to provide accommodation of a particular quality.

There are a number of issues which arise from the concept of **9.02.**
"suitability" of accommodation. There is a distinction to be made
whether accommodation is suitable because it is not offered to the
applicant for a long enough period of time. Alternatively, it may be
that the accommodation is not in a suitable condition. In either
regard, it may be said by the applicant to be inappropriate. The
issue of suitability may arise where other provisions of the 1985
Housing Act, such as overcrowding and slum clearance, would
suggest that the accommodation is not appropriate.

It is an important part of the provision of social accommodation, **9.03.**
whether by a local authority or procured from a private landlord or
voluntary body on their behalf, that those persons who are without
homes fit for the purpose are not suitably housed. The social cost
of the housing crisis is caused as much by unsuitable accommodation as by the lack of any accommodation. For example, the
problems caused to families by people being housed in bed-and-
breakfast accommodation is critical in the United Kingdom at the
time of writing. As discussed in Chapter 1, above, the most recent
(1994) figure of 122,660 households living in accommodation
which is so inadequate that they are officially recognised as being
homeless, is the extent of the current problem in this area.

It is therefore a vital part of giving effect to the statutory **9.04.**
provisions that housing is both of the necessary quality and that it
is suitable both for the individual applicant and those with whom
she resides.

The Impact of the *Puhlhofer* Decision: "Suitability"

9.05.   The seminal decision in the House of Lords in the area of homelessness was the speech of Lord Brightman in *Puhlhofer v. Hillingdon B.C.*[1] It is seminal not because it represents the law in its entirety today, but because the policy pronouncements which it makes still represent the underlying drift of much of the case law dealing with the homelessness legislation. There are two streams of thought: the first is that the duty to assist the homeless should be read so as to be of broad application; the second is that local authorities are dealing with scarce resources and that the legislation should therefore be given restrictive interpretation. Consequently, the circumstances in which the homeless are entitled to be housed are greatly restricted by the literal interpretation given to the provisions. The position for the legal advisor of applicants is that it is often difficult to manoeuvre through the complicated net of provisions. The effect of *Puhlhofer* continues even after legislation was introduced specifically to dilute its impact.

9.06.   The issue of the suitability of accommodation has therefore become the battleground between permissive and restrictive constructions of the legislation. The 1977 Act did not specify any quality of accommodation and some of the early decisions, principally those of Lord Denning, sought to read in standards of appropriateness. Thus local authorities would be required to live up to a spirit identified in the legislation and not just its plain words. For the restrictive school of thought, suitability was an issue for the local authority. The legislation was designed as a safety net for the needy and not as a counsel of perfection.

9.07.   The applicants in *Puhlhofer* were a married couple with two young children who were provided with accommodation in a bed-and-breakfast guest house by the respondent local authority. They contended that the authority had not discharged its duty to them on the basis that the accommodation was not appropriate accommodation for them. Lord Brightman described the accommodation as:

> ". . . occupation of one room at the guest house containing a double and a single bed, a baby's cradle, dressing table, pram and steriliser unit. There were three bathrooms in the guest house, the total capacity of the guest house being 36 people or thereabouts. The applicants were in consequence compelled to eat out and to use a launderette for washing their own and the

[1] [1986] A.C. 484.

children's clothing. This expense absorbed most of their state benefit of £78 a week".

The applicants relied on the decision of the Court of Appeal in *Parr v. Wye*[2] that accommodation was required to be "appropriate", as set out in the decisions of Lord Denning and Eveleigh L.JJ. In that case the applicants had been living in a motor home and were offered accommodation in Birmingham, 200 miles away from the authority's district. The Court of Appeal in *Puhlhofer* expressed a number of different opinions as to this issue. Ackner L.J. considered that accommodation must be "appropriate" or "reasonable". Whereas Glidewell and Slade L.JJ. could see no requirement to impute the concept of reasonableness into the definition of accommodation.

Lord Brightman found, with the unanimous support of the **9.08.** House of Lords, that the concept of reasonableness was not to be read into the legislation. The policy reasons behind this decision appear to be as much the motivating factors as a literal reading of the statute. The 1977 Act was considered to be an Act which saves the homeless from a lack of any help rather than imposing an obligation to house them. Further, local authorities were found to have restricted resources which must be distributed between the homeless and others on the waiting lists.

Lord Brightman did consider, with greater sympathy than the **9.09.** argument as to an absolute standard of suitability, the arguments that accommodation might not be appropriate where it is beyond the applicant's means rather than because it is not in a suitable condition.

Looking more broadly, the decision of the Court of Appeal in **9.10.** *Ben-el-Mabrouk* does suggest that the courts will take a broad view of what constitutes a rational decision in this area by an authority. Where the authority has great housing demands made of it, it appears that the courts are accepting that these general circumstances will govern the question whether or not accommodation is suitable. This is a movement away from the erection of an objective standard of what will and will not be suitable accommodation in the circumstances. Consequently, the ability of the applicant to assert that accommodation is unsuitable will be reduced in an area where there is great pressure for public sector housing.

[2] (1982) 2 H.L.R. 71.

Common Law Suitability after *Puhlhofer:* the Time Element

9.11.   The House of Lords decision in *Awua v. Brent L.B.C.*[3] in the speech of Lord Hoffmann approves much of what is said in *Puhlhofer* at the policy level. Clearly, the ratio of *Puhlhofer*, concerning suitability, has been overtaken by the legislative amendments discussed below. The issue in *Awua* was whether or not the original local authority, Tower Hamlets, was required to provide settled accommodation in pursuance of its duty to house the applicant. The second authority, Brent, contended that the applicant had become intentionally homeless on the basis that she refused temporary accommodation offered to her by Tower Hamlets and was consequently evicted from her other accommodation in Tower Hamlets. The applicant argued that Tower Hamlets was required to provide her with "settled" accommodation. Given that the authority had only offered her non-permanent accommodation she contended that she was still homeless. In the words of Lord Hoffmann, she had been offered a "short life" house. Lord Hoffmann held that there was no requirement in section 60 of the 1985 legislation that the accommodation be "settled".

9.12.   Lord Hoffmann distinguished between the time for which accommodation was offered and the quality of the accommodation that was offered. With reference to the time for which accommodation was offered, he held that it need be neither permanent nor settled, provided that it was accommodation. Further, he conceded that the legislation introduced after *Puhlhofer* had reversed the issue whether the authority was required to provide a suitable quality of accommodation.

9.13.   However, the issue of suitability of accommodation would be linked to the amount of time which the applicant would be required to remain in it. Thus, a family required to occupy cramped accommodation for only a short period of time might not succeed in an argument that that accommodation was unsuitable. Therefore, the test for suitability is circumscribed by the element of time during which occupation will take place. Where the applicant contends that the purportedly long-term accommodation is unsuitable, it is possible for the court to order that the applicant be placed in alternative temporary accommodation pending trial: (*R. v. Haringey L.B.C., ex p. Flynn,*[4] *R. v. Haringey L.B.C., ex p. Ulger*[5]).

---

[3] [1995] 3 All E.R. 493.
[4] June 1995 *Legal Action* 21.
[5] December 1992 *Legal Action* 21.

It would, of course, have been possible for Lord Hoffmann to **9.14.**
hold to the contrary: that accommodation could not be suitable
where it was only offered for a short period of time. Instead, the
brevity of the accommodation's availability is used to make
suitable accommodation which would otherwise be unsuitable. In
this writer's opinion, *Awua* continues a judicial tradition in the
higher courts of seeking to limit the utility of the accommodation
which must be provided to the applicant.

Suitable Accommodation

Following the preceding discussion of the notion of suitability, **9.15.**
the 1996 Act does provide some system for defining the term in
different circumstances. Section 210 sets out the core test for
whether or not accommodation is suitable for the applicant. This
legislative change was added to the Housing Act 1985 to reverse
the impact of the decision in *Puhlhofer*. By section 210, the local
housing authority is required to have regard to specified provisions
of the Housing Act 1985. The authority are required to look in
particular at Part IX (slum clearance), Part X (overcrowding) and
Part XI (houses in multiple occupation).[6]

The statute makes provision for the Secretary of State to create **9.16.**
regulations by order to specify circumstances in which accommodation is or is not to be regarded as suitable for a person,[7] and also
those matters which are to be taken into account or disregarded in
determining whether accommodation is suitable for a person.[8] At
the date of writing, no such regulations have been created.

Statutory Reasonableness

Section 177(3) provides, in the context of deciding whether or **9.17.**
not an applicant is homeless, that the Secretary of State may create
orders to set out tests for reasonableness in this circumstance. Such
orders may specify other circumstances in which it is to be
regarded as reasonable or not reasonable for a person to continue
to occupy accommodation.[9] The orders may also specify other
matters which are to be taken into account (or alternatively
disregarded) in determining whether it would be, or would have
been, reasonable for a person to continue to occupy the
accommodation.[10]

[6] Housing Act 1996, s. 210(1).
[7] s. 210(2)(a).
[8] s. 210(2)(b).
[9] s. 177(3)(a).
[10] s. 177(3)(b).

9.18.   In *Ali v. Tower Hamlets L.B.C.*,[11] the Court of Appeal held that
the statutory duties to provide suitable accommodation for homeless people required an authority to make a subjective judgment as
to what constituted suitable accommodation before carrying out
the executive function of securing accommodation for the applicant. The Court envisages a two-stage process in the authority's
decision-making procedure. It was held that the public law duties
of the authority were not discharged until they had reached their
decision as to what type of accommodation was to be provided for
the applicant. The only means of challenging this decision was by
judicial review. Therefore, there was no ground on which to base a
claim for a private law injunction.[12] The dicta of Lord Bridge in
Cocks v. Thanet[13] were applied here in preventing tortious
principles from being used to enforce the authority's obligations.

9.19.   The case of *R. v. Kensington and Chelsea R.L.B.C., ex p. Ben-el-
Mabrouk*[14] saw the Court of Appeal take a very straightforward view
of the way in which local authorities are required to ensure that
accommodation is suitable within the terms of the statutory
requirement. The Court of Appeal approved attempts by the
authority to organise some means by which the accommodation
could be made suitable, rather than simply reaching a decision
which would effectively require the authority to re-house the
applicant.

9.20.   The applicant in *Ben-el-Mabrouk* lived with his wife and child on
the fifth floor of a building which was occupied by a number of
families. The lift did not operate, there was only one internal
staircase and there was no fire escape. Consequently, the applicant
contended that the accommodation was not suitable because it was
not safe. The applicant argued, *inter alia*, that the lack of fire
escapes meant that the property was not safe. The further issue is
whether or not the accommodation can be held to be unsuitable
because the applicant simply does not like it. The authority's
director of environmental health decided that the options for
improvement be put to the owner of the property. Sir Thomas
Bingham M.R. held that it was not irrational for the authority to
seek to solve the problem by approaching the owner of the
property in this way. In his view, the court must look to the
problems faced by the authority with 4,500 properties under their

---

[11] [1992] 3 All E.R. 512.
[12] See however, *Roy v. Kensington and Chelsea and Westminster Family Practitioner
Committee* [1992] 1 All E.R. 705.
[13] [1982] 3 All E.R. 1135, at 1137-1139.
[14] (1995) 27 H.L.R. 564.

control. In the circumstances of those problems, seeking a structured solution with the owner of the property was neither irrational nor perverse.

The decision of the Court of Appeal to consider the broader **9.21.** housing requirements of the authority and its area, mirrors the approach taken in *Puhlhofer* that the court may be concerned about the broader ramifications were the case before it to set a precedent in dealings with the authority's housing stock. The question of whether or not the authority has been rational in its decision-making in this context, might therefore be governed by the broader exigencies of the housing management function.

"Homeless" and the Reasonableness of Accommodation

The definition in Part VII of "homeless", includes a provision **9.22.** that an applicant is homeless for the purposes of the 1996 Act, in circumstances where she is living in accommodation which is unsuitable for her occupation. Subsection 175(3) provides that:

> "(3) A person shall not be treated as having accommodation unless it is accommodation which it would be reasonable for him to continue to occupy".

Therefore there is a qualification to the core test in section 175(1) and (2) in the situation where the accommodation is not reasonable for the applicant to continue to occupy it. The provision is drafted in terms that the applicant must be in occupation of some accommodation and that continued occupation of that accommodation is unreasonable. The status of accommodation as reasonable or not reasonable may alter over time depending on the applicant's circumstances. Therefore, if the factor which makes the occupation unreasonable is removed, the applicant will not be able to rely upon section 175(3) if it has then become reasonable to occupy the accommodation. Similarly, where the applicant becomes pregnant, accommodation may cease to be suitable for a pregnant woman.

There are two situations set out in the legislation at section 177 **9.23.** as to the reasonableness of continuing to occupy:

cases where the applicant has suffered domestic violence or the risk of domestic violence;
cases where it is unreasonable to occupy accommodation in the general circumstances of housing in an area.

There is no express provision within section 177 that the provision in section 175(3) is restricted to the categories of reasonableness set out in section 177. Therefore, it is possible for there to be factors which make accommodation unreasonable to occupy outside the terms of those categories set out in section 177. While the opening words in section 177(1) do bear the interpretation that the subsection is intended to be restrictive, it is submitted that this cannot be the case because there are further express statutory categories of reasonableness set out in section 177(2) and (3). Therefore, it is this writer's opinion that the legislation is capable of allowing a number of causes which make accommodation not reasonable to occupy, not restricted to those in section 177(1).

9.24. In *R. v. Kensington and Chelsea R.L.B.C., ex p. Kassam*[15] the applicant occupied a small, one-bedroomed flat with her son and daughter. The conditions caused her daughter to develop a depressive illness. She left the property to receive treatment for this condition. The applicant sought housing on the basis that the accommodation was unsuitable for her daughter to move back in after receiving medical care. The authority decided that she was not homeless because the accommodation was suitable. The authority's decision was quashed on the basis that they had not considered whether there was a requirement for full-time live-in care for her daughter. Consequently, it could be said that the accommodation was not suitable in this context. The authority did not give sufficient reasons in the context of the live-in care arrangements.

Domestic Violence[16]

9.25. Section 177(1) provides that it is not reasonable for a person to continue to occupy accommodation if it is probable that this will lead to domestic violence against that person or categories of prescribed persons.

9.26. Section 177(1) provides:

"(1) It is not reasonable for a person to continue to occupy accommodation if it is probable that this will lead to domestic violence against him, or against—
 (a) a person who normally resides with him as a member of his family, or
 (b) any other person who might reasonably be expected to reside with him".

[15] (1994) 26 H.L.R. 455.
[16] This issue is considered in detail in Chapter 8, above and also in the context of intentional homelessness in Chapter 12, below.

Therefore, where an individual is the victim of domestic violence it is considered not reasonable for her to continue to occupy the accommodation where that domestic violence took place. The upshot of this provision is that such a person can be considered to be homeless despite having accommodation available for her occupation, where domestic violence will probably be inflicted on her. Clearly this categorisation applies if leaving the accommodation due to the domestic violence would be the only reason for refusing to categorise that person as being homeless.

For this purpose "domestic violence", in relation to a person, 9.27. means violence from a person with whom he is associated, or threats of violence from such a person which are likely to be carried out.[17]

The test of reasonableness is extended beyond the individual 9.28. homeless person.[18] It is not reasonable for that person to continue to occupy the accommodation if it is probable that a person who normally lives with her as a member of her family[19], or any other person who might reasonably be expected to reside with her, bears the same risk of domestic violence.[20]

Section 177(1) provides that an applicant is not to be considered 9.29. as having accommodation available where it is probable that continued occupation will lead to domestic violence against her. This is on grounds that it is not reasonable for that person to continue to occupy the accommodation.[21] That is, there is some likelihood of domestic violence rather than simply a fear that it may happen. There is no provision in the statute as to who bears the burden of proof that domestic violence is probable. It is

---

[17] Housing Act 1996, s. 177(1).
[18] "(1) . . . from some other person residing in it or to threats of violence from some other person residing in it and likely to carry out the threats.
(2) In determining whether it would be, or would have been, reasonable for a person to continue to occupy accommodation, regard may be had to the general circumstances prevailing in relation to housing in the district of the local housing authority to whom he has applied for accommodation or for assistance in obtaining accommodation.
(3) The Secretary of State may by order specify—
(a) other circumstances in which it is to be regarded as reasonable or not reasonable for a person to continue to occupy accommodation, and
(b) other matters to be taken into account or disregarded in determining whether it would be, or would have been, reasonable for a person to continue to occupy accommodation".
[19] Housing Act 1996, s. 177(1)(a).
[20] s. 177(1)(b).
[21] s. 177(1).

possible that the applicant be required to bear the burden as the person alleging the likelihood of domestic violence. However, the better view would appear to be that the authority be required to bear that burden as part of its duty to make inquiries, as discussed in Chapter 4, above. In this regard, it would be incumbent on the applicant to provide the authority with the necessary information. In situations where domestic violence has occurred in the past, it will clearly be easier to demonstrate its probability in the future. Particularly where the violence has occurred on a systematic basis in the past, its probability will be easier to judge.

9.30. This test will be a difficult one for local housing authorities to apply in practice. The definition of "domestic violence" includes threats which are likely to be carried out. Therefore, it would appear that an applicant may produce evidence or testimony of threats coupled with a real expectation that they will be put into practice. For the legal adviser there is a difficult line here between the applicant becoming intentionally homeless and leaving accommodation because it is unreasonable to continue to occupy it on grounds of expected domestic violence, and remaining in occupation and continuing to suffer abuse. In the interests of the abused client, obtaining a restraining order against the abusive co-habitee removes the risk of the client being found to be intentionally homeless.

9.31. The policy behind the legislation is clear: co-habitees should not be required to suffer violence to themselves or their dependants and be trapped in that accommodation. Rather, domestic violence should be combated and the individual should be eligible to be re-housed away from the abusive relationship. The difficulty of discharging the burden of proof here carries enormous risks for applicants in some circumstances.

9.32. In *R. v. Purbeck D.C. ex p. Cadney*[22] the applicant was the joint owner of the matrimonial home. She left her husband due to his violence and went to live with another man, D. D asked her to leave after three months. The applicant did not seek to return to the matrimonial home because she was frightened that her husband would resume his violence towards her. The applicant sought judicial review of the authority's decision that she was not required to be re-housed. Nolan J. held that the applicant had not attempted, on the evidence before him, to gain access to the matrimonial home and therefore there was no direct evidence that she would suffer violence if she did attempt to gain access to the

[22] [1986] 2 F.L.R. 158.

property. Therefore, the local housing authority could not be said to have made an error in failing to find that she was homeless.

Clearly, this imposes a difficult obligation on the applicant. On **9.33.** the basis of Nolan J.'s judgment, it would appear that the applicant is required to attempt to re-enter the property and thus demonstrate that the resumption of domestic violence occurred. In many cases, it is likely that applicants will choose not to run this risk. Therefore, many potentially applications will be spoiled by insisting that the individual put herself at risk in any event. The decision in *Cadney* appears to run contrary to the policy behind the statute by exposing applicants to the risk of domestic violence.

It is common for women not only to leave accommodation due **9.34.** to domestic violence but also to leave the area in which they live entirely. The fear is that, if they continue to live locally, their abusive co-habitee will find them and continue the abuse. There is, therefore, some cross-relation with the issue of local connection, set out in Chapter 11, below. The result might well be that a local authority will seek to refer the applicant back to the area where she was living originally. Alternatively, it may be that the authority would take the view that while domestic violence caused her to leave the accommodation and the area, the domestic violence was no longer a threat at the time of the application. A referral back to the area where the abuse took place runs the risk of the resumption of the abuse.

This risk is perhaps shown up in *R. v. Kensington and Chelsea* **9.35.** *R.L.B.C., ex p. Moncada*[23] M sought judicial review of a decision of the authority which found that M and his two sons were not homeless. M was the joint tenant of a four bedroom house with his ex-wife. M no longer lived at the premises which were occupied by his ex-wife and their daughter. There was a dispute over whether the ex-wife's new partner, W, was living at the house or was merely a frequent visitor. M had been in prison for a drugs offence and was currently on licence. There had been an incident in which W had assaulted one of the sons. The decision letter from K stated that, although not an ideal arrangement, it was possible for M and his sons to live at the former matrimonial home. M argued that the decision was unreasonable, especially considering the incident between W and M's son. In addition, due to the history of trouble with W, there was a danger that M's licence would be at risk. Popplewell J. held that it was possible for the court to interfere only where the authority had made a perverse decision. On the

---

[23] Unreported (April 24, 1996).

facts it was a reasonable decision which the authority was at liberty to make — even though the decision was perhaps not an ideal one.

9.36. The issue also arises whether the applicant is intentionally homeless, as set out in Chapter 12, below. For the victim of domestic violence, there are a number of potential difficulties not only connected to producing evidence but also to demonstrating a number of different parts of the legal requirements are present.

Violence, Other than Domestic Violence

9.37. The issue arises: what of an applicant who is not suffering domestic violence but is the victim, or potential victim, of other forms of violence directed against her. In *R. v. Northavon D.C., ex p. Smith*[24] the issue arose between the duty to provide housing under what is now Part VII of the 1996 Act and that under section 27 of the Children Act 1989 to provide for the welfare of children in the local authority's district. The applicant and his wife had five children under the age of ten. They left accommodation as a result of violence and harassment. The local authority accepted that they were homeless and in priority need but that they were homeless intentionally. Therefore, the local authority provided them with temporary bed and breakfast accommodation. The applicant and his wife approached the county council to seek accommodation from them in line with its obligations under section 27 of the 1989 Act. Further to that provision the county council requested the local authority to provide accommodation on the basis that the applicants were held not to be entitled under the 1985 Act. It was held by the Court of Appeal that in accordance with section 27(2), the county council was required to protect the welfare of the children and was empowered to make a request of another authority. This obligation obtained even in circumstances where the local authority had lawfully decided that it was not obliged to house the applicant and his family permanently under the 1985 Act. These duties were held not to be inconsistent because the requirements of section 27 of the 1989 Act referred to the needs of the children and not the accommodation and priority need of the applicant. The local authority had not responded lawfully to the request made by the county council because it had not given reasons for its decision in this context. As Sir Thomas Bingham M.R. held[25]:

> "Reading these two statutory codes side by side, I find a clear parliamentary intention that children in need should not fall between them".

[24] [1993] 4 All E.R. 731.
[25] [1993] 4 All E.R. 731 at 740.

Person for Whom the Accommodation must be Suitable

There are a stream of cases where the question arises for whom **9.38.** the accommodation must be unsuitable. It is common that it is not the applicant living alone for whom the accommodation is unsuitable. In such circumstances a change in the applicant's own medical condition would raise the issue. More usually it is the dependents of the applicant or an impending pregnancy which raise the issue of the property being unsuitable for the accommodation of the applicant.

In *R. v. Newham L.B.C., ex p. Dada*[26] the Court of Appeal **9.39.** considered the plight of the applicants, Mr and Mrs Dada, who had been accepted as being unintentionally homeless and in priority need because Mrs Dada was pregnant. The couple were offered one bedroom accommodation on the seventh floor of a building in multiple occupation. It was held by Glidewell L.J. that the legislation referred to a "person" or a "living person" with whom the applicant could reasonably be expected to reside. Therefore, the prospective child with which Mrs Dada was pregnant did not constitute a "living person". Consequently, the applicant was not able to rely on the condition of a child as yet unborn in contending that the accommodation was not suitable.

Further, in *Dada,* the applicants contended that the authority's **9.40.** appeals procedure required that the applicant go into occupation of the accommodation before arguing that it was unsuitable. It was held that the procedure was not unreasonable because the appeals officer reviewed all those offers which had been made and which had been unreasonably refused. Therefore, there was held to be satisfactory consideration of the issues involved in the application.

In *R. v. Brent L.B.C., ex p. Yusuf*[27] The applicant was a Somalian **9.41.** who had been granted exceptional leave to remain in the United Kingdom on her application for asylum. She began living with a man, who had already been resident at the address where they cohabited, and she became pregnant. The relationship ended. In the applicant's opinion, conditions at the house were not suitable for bringing up a child. The house was dirty and frequently full of her former partner's drunken friends. Consequently, the applicant left the house and went to stay with a friend. She applied to the

[26] [1995] 2 All E.R. 522.
[27] Unreported (November 8, 1995).

authority for housing. The authority considered that the applicant
had become homeless intentionally. The applicant contended that
the authority should have considered that the applicant was
pregnant when they made their decision.

9.42.   Turner J. applied the rule in *Din v. Wandsworth L.B.C.*[28] He held
that the decision whether or not an applicant was homelessness
must be based on the conditions at the time of the application and
not on what might happen in the future. The applicant's contention that she would not be able to live in the accommodation when
her child was born was not relevant at the time when the
application was made. There was four months of the pregnancy left
to run at the time when the applicant left the accommodation and
therefore it was not a current event at that time. What is not clear
is whether the applicant could have argued that the conditions
might have affected the pregnancy. Therefore, there would have
been an impact on the applicant at the time of the application, thus
making it a current issue at the time of the application.

9.43.   The authority is able however, to seek to solve the unsuitability
in the accommodation without needing to take action immediately
to re-locate the applicant. For example, the case of *R. v. Kensington
and Chelsea R.L.B.C., ex p. Ben-el-Mabrouk*[29] saw the Court of
Appeal take a very realpolitik approach to the means by which
local authorities ensure that accommodation is suitable. The
applicant contended that the accommodation is not suitable
because it is not safe or, alternatively, because the applicant simply
does not like it. Sir Thomas Bingham M.R. held that it was not
irrational for the authority to seek to solve the problem by
approaching the owner of the property to install fire escapes and
other amenities. In his view, the court must look to the problems
faced by a local authority with 4,500 properties under their control.
In the circumstances of those problems, seeking a structured
solution with the owner of the property was neither irrational nor
perverse.

9.44.   Furthermore, the obligations on the authority are not absolute.
Some unsuitability in the property is permissible provided that the
authority acts reasonably to deal with that defect. The applicant in
R. v. Kensington and Chelsea R.L.B.C., ex p. Grillo[30] was offered
seventh floor accommodation. The applicant contended that this
was unsuitable because of her partner's asthma. The applicant also

[28] [1983] 1 A.C. 657.
[29] (1995) 27 H.L.R. 564.
[30] [1995] N.P.C. 85.

produced evidence as to her own problems with arthritis. The authority made its offer again having rejected the medical evidence adduced on behalf of the applicant and her partner. The applicant brought judicial review proceedings on the joint basis that the decision was not one which a reasonable authority would have come to and, further, that no reasons had been given for the decision.

Neill L.J. held that the offer of accommodation was reasonable **9.45.** and within the *Wednesbury* guidelines. The authority was required to consider all the housing needs in its district. The lift was found to be out of order only occasionally. Further, the authority were under no duty to give reasons so long as the decision was within policy guidelines. While there might be an implied duty to give reasons in some circumstances, this was found to be a case where the authority had activated a voluntary appeals procedure and therefore was not one in which giving reasons could be required.

General Circumstances

Under section 177(2), in considering the reasonableness of a **9.46.** person continuing to occupy the accommodation, regard may be had to the general circumstances surrounding housing in the authority's district. The statute requires consideration of housing conditions in the district of the local housing authority to whom the applicant has applied for accommodation or for assistance in obtaining accommodation. This reasonableness test applies on a retrospective basis to whether or not it would have been reasonable for the individual to occupy that accommodation at the time the application was made.[31] Therefore, the applicant can seek to justify having left accommodation retrospectively by arguing that the general circumstances at the time of leaving the accommodation rendered the decision to leave reasonable.

This wording appeared in the amended housing legislation in **9.47.** response to the *Puhlhofer* decision. The intention was to restore people living in unacceptable accommodation to the category of those who are homeless. *Puhlhofer*, as discussed above, removed the notion of suitability from the definition of "accommodation". Therefore, this wording was added to mimic part of the test for intentional homelessness and re-inforce that construction of the legislation. The case law before *Puhlhofer* held that accommodation which it was unreasonable to continue to occupy should be disregarded in deciding whether or not an applicant was homeless.

[31] Housing Act 1996, s. 177(2).

9.48.   The Code of Guidance lists a number of criteria for deciding
whether or not an applicant is homeless:

affordability;
physical conditions;
overcrowding (not necessarily statutory overcrowding);
the type of accommodation;
violence or threats of violence from outside the home;
security of tenure.

The reasonableness of occupying or continuing to occupy
accommodation is considered below in the Chapter 12 on Intentional Homelessness. The issue usually resolves itself into the
question: was the applicant homeless when she left the accommodation because of its unsuitability, or did she become homeless
intentionally?

Duty where Other Suitable Accommodation Available

9.49.   The qualification to this definition of "homeless" is to the
definition of "accommodation". Under section 175(3) "a person
shall not be treated as having accommodation unless it is accommodation which it would be reasonable for him to continue to
occupy". The issue is therefore what type of accommodation is not
reasonable for an individual to continue to occupy. Further to the
decision in *Awua*, applying *Puhlhofer*, there is also the anterior
question whether the shelter constitutes accommodation in any
event.

The Terms of the Duty

9.50.   The extent of the duty on a local housing authority to provide
accommodation for the applicant where there is suitable accommodation available is set out in section 197. The scope for the
applicability of this duty is set out in section 197(1). It applies
where the local housing authority are under a duty under Part VII
of the 1996 Act. In that case the local authority is required to
secure that accommodation is available for occupation by an
applicant,[32] or to secure that accommodation does not cease to be
available for his occupation.[33] This applies where the authority are
not satisfied that other suitable accommodation is available for
occupation by her in their district.

9.51.   There are a number of areas in which this duty is expressly
provided not to apply. Section 197(6) provides the complete list,
that is: section 188 (interim duty to accommodate in case of

[32] s. 197(1)(a)
[33] s. 197(1)(b).

apparent priority need), section 190(2)(a) (limited duty to person becoming homeless intentionally), or section 200(1), (3) or (4) (interim duties where case is considered for referral or referred).

The duty on the authority ceases in circumstances where the **9.52.** applicant fails to take reasonable steps to secure that accommodation is available for her occupation.[34]

Section 197 does enable the local housing authority to avoid the **9.53.** duty to provide housing themselves in circumstances where there is other accommodation which the applicant could occupy. There is a two-step introduction to this exclusion of the authority's obligation and that is a requirement that the accommodation be:

available to the applicant,
suitable for the applicant, and
is within the authority's district.

Where this exclusion is applicable, the local housing authority is required to provide the applicant with such advice and assistance as the authority consider is reasonably required to enable her to secure such accommodation.[35]

The Scope of the Duty

The issue arises as to the sort of advice and assistance that the **9.54.** local authority are required to provide. The authority must have regard to all the circumstances.[36] Some of the factors which the authority is required to look to as part of its duty include the characteristics and personal circumstances of the applicant,[37] and the state of the local housing market and the type of accommodation available.[38]

In the circumstances of this particular duty, accommodation is **9.55.** not regarded as available for occupation by the applicant if it is available only with assistance beyond what the authority consider is reasonable in the circumstances.[39] The ambit of this subsection is therefore to discount accommodation which would require, in effect, unreasonable levels of assistance to procure such accommodation for the applicant's benefit.

[34] s. 197(3).
[35] s. 197(2).
[36] s. 197(4).
[37] s. 197(4)(a).
[38] s. 197(4)(b).
[39] s. 197(5).

Intentional Homelessness and Suitability for Occupation

9.56.   Section 191 provides that: "A person becomes homeless intentionally if he deliberately does or fails to do anything in consequence of which he ceases to occupy accommodation which is available for his occupation and which it would have been reasonable for him to continue to occupy".

9.57.   At the time of the cessation, the statute requires that accommodation must actually be available for her occupation. However, there is a different standard with reference to the issue of reasonableness. The test of reasonableness is phrased in the conditional: "would have been reasonable". This phrasing suggests that continued occupation need not have been reasonable at the time of cessation of occupation on a literal reading of the words. Rather, the authority is required to assess whether it would have been reasonable to continue to occupy, not whether it was.

9.58.   As discussed above, *R. v. Kensington and Chelsea R.L.B.C., ex p. Ben-el-Mabrouk*[40] saw the Court of Appeal take a straightforward approach to the means by which local authorities ensure that accommodation is suitable. Sir Thomas Bingham M.R. held that it was not irrational for the authority to seek to solve the problem by approaching the owner of the property in this way. In his view, the court must look to the general pressures of housing demand faced by the authority. Therefore, a solution reached with the owner of the property to deal with the problems complained of was neither irrational nor perverse.

Condition of Housing

9.59.   There is no specific guidance given in Part VII as to what will constitute "reasonable" in these circumstances. For example, none of the categories from the 1985 Act are incorporated into Part VII, such as unfitness for human habitation, to constitute situations in which it would be reasonable to give up accommodation. The old Code only suggests that the local authority is required to carry out a balancing exercise between the applicant's reasons for quitting the accommodation and "whether there is a housing shortage or whether there are many people living in the area in worse conditions than the applicant" (*R. v. Westminster C.C., ex p Ali*[41]; *R. v. Reigate and Banstead B.C., ex p. Paris*[42]). It should be borne in

---

[40] (1995) 27 H.L.R. 564.
[41] (1984) 11 H.L.R. 72.
[42] (1984) 17 H.L.R. 103.

mind that this type of information is unlikely to be available to the applicants.

The Scottish Code does not contain a definition of reasonable- **9.60.** ness on the basis that it is better to consider the issue in the light of each person's circumstances and not attempt to erect an artificial standard. What the Scottish Code does do is identify those things which will point to unsuitability if they do not exist: "the absence of important facilities such as provision for heating, ready access to piped water supply, a sink, or a water closet should normally be regarded as making it unreasonable for the applicant to occupy the accommodation . . ." or where conditions in the property have "degenerated to such a point where they could not in all the circumstances be expected to live either because of overcrowding, lack of basic amenities or severe emotional stress," as in the Scottish Code. It would appear that being without certain facilities on a short-term basis is less likely to lead to such a finding.

Overcrowded Accommodation

The authority is required to consider the condition of the **9.61.** housing which is available to the applicant currently, as well as any accommodation which the applicant has left. For example, the failure of a housing authority to consider whether it was reasonable for a family of six to continue to live in a two-bedroomed house led to their decision being quashed in *R. v. Eastleigh B.C., ex p. Beattie*.[43] Conditions which are grossly overcrowded will not be accepted as reasonable were held to include the situation where an applicant lived with this wife and five young children in one room measuring 12ft by 10ft. Simply because there had been two rooms 12ft by 12ft available for sole occupation by the applicant and his family in Bangladesh did not necessarily mean such accommodation continued to be so available. The court held that there must be proper investigation of claims of overcrowding — where an applicant left accommodation which was stated to be overcrowded but where the dimensions of the accommodation and which members of the family were occupying it were not clarified at interview, it could not be said that it would have been reasonable to continue to occupy such accommodation.

The authority's officer must be scrupulous to keep personal **9.62.** value judgments separate from the issue of homelessness. In *R. v. Tower Hamlets L.B.C., ex p. Hoque*[44] it was held that where a local authority officer decided that overcrowding in a property was due

---

[43] (1983) 10 H.L.R. 134.
[44] *The Times*, July 20, 1993.

to the applicant's own decision to increase the size of his family, the decision would be quashed.

9.63. In deciding whether or not accommodation is overcrowded, the authority must consider whether the number of people occupying the property is reasonable — the authority cannot simply rely on the statutory definitions of what will and will not constitute overcrowding: (*R. v. Westminster C.C., ex p. Alouat*[45]).

9.64. In *R. v. Gateshead M.B.C., ex p. Lauder*,[46] Potts J. held that the 1985 Act provided for a discretion exercisable by local authorities dealing with the provision of accommodation to those suffering overcrowding. The authority had included the word "will" in its policy, which had the result that that policy would not be flexible in its operation. Consequently, the authority's discretion was being unlawfully fettered in relation to any decision made as a result of that policy.

Accommodation Unfit for Human Occupation

9.65. The authority will generally have regard to the statutory definitions of unfitness for human habitation in considering this ground. Where this ground is satisfied, it will enable the applicant to remain outside the definition of intentional homelessness. In the case of *Lester*, set out above, the court did suggest that the authority should reconsider the position of an applicant whose infant son had been hospitalised due to the alleged damp housing conditions.

9.66. In accordance with what is said above in *R. v. Westminster C.C., ex p. Alouat*,[47] it would appear that in deciding whether or not accommodation is overcrowded, the authority must consider whether the number of people occupying the property is reasonable. The authority cannot simply rely on the statutory definitions of what will and will not constitute overcrowding.

9.67. The property will be unsuitable where it is unsafe, as in *R. v. Kensington and Chelsea R.L.B.C., ex p. Ben-el-Mabrouk*.[48] However, in that case the Court of Appeal considered that it was neither irrational nor perverse to seek a structured solution with the owner of the property to the applicant's allegations that the building was unsafe due to the lift being inoperable, there being only one

---

[45] (1989) 21 H.L.R. 47.
[46] Unreported (May 16, 1996).
[47] (1989) 21 H.L.R. 47.
[48] (1995) 27 H.L.R. 564.

internal staircase and there being no fire escape. The Court of Appeal were particularly concerned about the problems faced by the authority with 4,500 properties under their control, as considered above.

Inappropriate Accommodation

As considered in Chapter 12 "Intentional Homelessness", it may **9.68.** be that it is not appropriate to occupy accommodation because of any one of a number of environmental factors. The applicant may find it difficult to establish that a decision is in contravention of the *Wednesbury* principles where an authority considers accommodation was satisfactory and where the applicant has sought to base her contentions on purely minor and personal matters.

Claims about unsuitability such as it being unreasonable to **9.69.** occupy accommodation because the accommodation was located on a "bad", drug-infested estate must be addressed and investigated: (*R. v. Westminster C.C., ex p Bishop*[49]).

Cost

It is not reasonable to continue to occupy accommodation where **9.70.** the cost is excessive. The court took the view in *Tinn*[50] that:

"it cannot be reasonable for a person to continue to occupy accommodation when they can no longer discharge their fiscal obligations in relation to that accommodation, that is to say, pay the rent and make the mortgage repayments, without so straining their resources as to deprive themselves of the ordinary necessities of life, such as food, clothing, heat, transport and so forth".

So, in *R. v. Westminster C.C., ex p. Obeid*[51] O applied for judicial review of the authority's decision that she was intentionally homeless. She and her family were housed by the authority in temporary accommodation and were then offered permanent accommodation, which they accepted. They had reservations about the offered accommodation on health grounds. Therefore, worried about the property's suitability, they found private rented accommodation before moving into the property offered to them by the council. They considered the private accommodation more suitable and moved in after ascertaining that housing benefit would be payable. They subsequently discovered, however, that their housing benefit was subject to a reduction because the rent on that

---

[49] (1993) 25 H.L.R. 459.
[50] *R. v. Hillingdon L.B.C., ex p. Tinn* (1988) 20 H.L.R. 305.
[51] *The Times*, July 16, 1996.

property was deemed by the rent officer to be unreasonably high in comparison with rent payable for suitable alternative accommodation. The family were unable to pay the shortfall. An application was made to the authority for housing, which the local authority refused; finding instead that O was intentionally homeless. The issue to determined was whether O's assumption that the rent would be covered by housing benefit meant that she was "unaware" of a "relevant fact". Carnwath J. held that the authority ought to have found that O did not become homeless intentionally. There was no question but that O had acted in good faith and her genuine misapprehension concerning her housing benefit entitlement amounted to being unaware of a relevant fact.

9.71. This decision follows the rules set down in *R. v. Exeter C.C., ex p. Tranckle*[52] and also *R. v. Ealing L.B.C., ex p. Sukhija*.[53]

Employment Prospects

9.72. In *R. v. Hammersmith and Fulham L.B.C., ex p. Duro-Rama*,[54] the applicants had lived in the United Kingdom from 1964 until 1979 when they returned to Spain to care for a relative. The family returned to the United Kingdom when the husband's entitlement to Spanish social security benefits expired. The husband obtained work and a flat to rent. Later the family were evicted from their accommodation and applied for housing. The council, however, held that they were intentionally homeless because they had voluntarily left accommodation in Spain which it would have been reasonable to continue to occupy.

9.73. The applicants contended that the council should have considered the unavailability of social security benefits in Spain. The authority argued that it was only matters directly related to the housing which were relevant. Woolf J. rejected the authority's contention and observed that section 17(4) of the 1977 Act was couched in permissive language and was not to be regarded as exhaustive. Consequently, the local housing authority must have regard to the applicant's employment prospects and the lack of social security benefits available in the country he left.

9.74. This leaves the applicant with the difficulty of verifying her claims about her employment position. Thus, while the principle, laid down in *Duro-Rama*, that employment prospects are a relevant matter to be considered by a housing authority has been accepted

---

[52] (1994) 26 H.L.R. 244.
[53] (1994) 26 H.L.R. 726.
[54] (1983) 81 L.G.R. 702.

as valid, later cases show that in practice the result is variable. For example, in *Mazzaccherini v. Argyll and Bute D.C.*[55] Lord Jauncey rejected the submission that it was incumbent on the authority to make exhaustive inquiries into the labour market in Glasgow as compared to Dunoon for a person with the applicant's qualification.

In *R. v. Kensington and Chelsea R.L.B.C., ex p. Cunha*,[56] Otton J. **9.75.** stated that to require the housing authority to inquire into employment conditions in Brazil would be to place an unwarranted burden on them. More recently in *R. v. Winchester C.C. ex p. Ashton*[57] a middle-aged woman was offered a one-year contract in Winchester which she hoped would lead to more permanent employment. She had been unemployed for six years prior to this living in private rented accommodation in Tunbridge Wells. She obtained a non-secure tenancy in a council flat in Winchester which she lost when she was made redundant after 11 months. The council deemed her intentionally homeless because she had given up private rented accommodation to move to take up the job. It was held by the Court of Appeal that the applicant was entitled to "grasp the opportunity for employment that had come her way after six years" without being considered to be intentionally homeless.

Medical Facilities

The principle of looking beyond purely housing-related consid- **9.76.** erations established in *Duro-Rama*, has not had overwhelming indorsement in all courts. For example, the courts have not overturned intentionality decisions, where, among the stated reasons for giving up accommodation, was to seek better facilities in Britain.

In *R. v. Medina B.C., ex p. Dee*[58] the applicant occupied a beach **9.77.** chalet when she became pregnant. She received medical advice that there was risk to the unborn baby if she continued to occupy the damp and mould-infested chalet. The local authority decided that the chalet was fit for human habitation. Henry J. held that it was not reasonable for the authority to expect the applicant to ignore medical opinion in this context. Therefore she should be accepted as having been homeless at the time of her application.

In *R. v. Kensington and Chelsea R.L.B.C., ex p Assister*[59] Sedley J. **9.78.** held that on an application for judicial review of a local authority's decision that accommodation offered to a homeless applicant was

---

[55] 1987 S.C.L.R. 475.
[56] (1988) 21 H.L.R. 16.
[57] (1992) 24 H.L.R. 520.
[58] (1992) 24 H.L.R. 562.
[59] *The Times*, 20 August 1996.

suitable, the authority should assist the court by adducing an explanation from the medical officer of how he reached his conclusion, where that medical practitioner had presented his conclusion on suitability without giving reasons, despite her claim to have special medical needs, where the authority made their decision.

Conditions in the Authority's Area

9.79.   The question of the availability of required medical services is one which appears regularly in the context of suitability of housing. While it would appear reasonable to deal with this issue as falling within the judgment in *Duro-Rama* (set out above) that the court should look beyond factors which are related solely and directly to housing. In determining the reasonableness of accommodation authorities may have regard to the general circumstances prevailing in relation to housing in their areas.

9.80.   This issue has been considered by the House of Lords. The question of whether or not a person has to wait until a possession order is granted before leaving accommodation depended, in the view of Lord Fraser, in *Din v. Wandsworth L.B.C.*[60] on overall housing conditions and prevailing demand for accommodation in the areas of the housing authority. In this case the Din family quit accommodation linked to Mr Din's employment and began to live with relatives to avoid incurring further rent and rate arrears. Observing that accommodation in the area of Inner London is scarce, the House of Lords suggested that it was not reasonable for the Dins to quit their accommodation. However, if the same issue had arisen in another part of the country where accommodation was under less pressure the position might have been different, according to Lord Fraser. It is noteworthy that in their affidavits in judicial review cases authorities are wont to give detailed information of the extent, turnover and demand on the housing stock. The issue is one that is measured on the facts in any case and in any local authority's area.

9.81.   In *Ali*[61] McCullough J. expressed the view that it was astonishing that anyone should regard it as reasonable that a family of seven should continue to live in one room measuring 12ft by 10 ft. He added that in the absence of the evidence that the general housing circumstances in the area were so desperate that it would be reasonable to accept such gross overcrowding, he was driven to the conclusion that the question of reasonableness had not been properly determined by the authority.

[60] [1983] 1 A.C. 657 at 671.
[61] (1983) 11 H.L.R. 83.

Exceptional Circumstances

The issue then arises whether there is a residuary category of 9.82. circumstances in which applicants will be able to contend that their accommodation is not suitable.

In *R. v. Newham L.B.C., ex p. Begum*[62] B entered the United 9.83. Kingdom from Bangladesh in 1990. She sought to appeal against her offer of accommodation under the 1985 Act following the authority's decision that she was not intentionally homeless and in priority need. She refused to move into the premises on the basis that she had suffered racial abuse on visiting the premises for the first time. The authority decided that there were not exceptional circumstances and therefore they had carried out their duty to B. B sought judicial review of this decision on the basis that there were exceptional circumstances justifying B refusing the accommodation on this occasion.

Richards J. held that although earlier letters had failed to consider whether there was an exceptional circumstance in the light of the correct facts, the letter from the Director of Housing demonstrated that the matter had been reconsidered with full knowledge of the facts and that he was entitled to decide that it was nevertheless reasonable for B to move into the property. Further, Richards J. held that under the true construction of the authority's procedure once it had been decided that exceptional circumstances did not apply, then the applicant should be given the opportunity to move into the property in order to exercise her right of appeal. His Lordship followed *R. v. Wycombe D.C., ex p. Hazeltine*[63] in this regard. The judge exercised his discretion against B as she had not shown any intention of moving into the property in order to appeal and the property had already been let to someone else.

Guidelines for the Authority's Decision

In *Ali v. Tower Hamlets L.B.C.,*[64] the Court of Appeal held that 9.84. the statutory duties to provide suitable accommodation for homeless people required an authority to make a subjective judgment as to what constituted suitable accommodation, before carrying out the executive function of securing accommodation for the applicant. Therefore, there is a two-stage process envisaged. The public law duties of the authority were not discharged until it had

[62] Unreported (February 5, 1996).
[63] (1993) 25 H.L.R. 313.
[64] [1992] 3 All E.R. 512.

completed deciding what type of accommodation was to be provided for the applicant. The only means of challenging this power was by judicial review. Therefore, there was no ground on which to base a claim for a private law injunction. The case of *Roy v. Kensington and Chelsea and Westminster Family Practitioner Committee*[65] was distinguished: the dicta of Lord Bridge in *Cocks v. Thanet*[66] were applied.

9.85.   The authority's officer must be scrupulous to keep personal value judgments separate from the issue of homelessness. In *R. v. Tower Hamlets L.B.C., ex p. Hoque*[67] it was held that where a local authority officer decided that overcrowding in a property was due to the applicant's own decision to increase the size of his family, the decision would be quashed.

9.86.   Where the applicant contends that the purportedly long-term accommodation is unsuitable, it is possible for the court to order that the applicant be placed in alternative temporary accommodation pending trial: (*R. v. Haringey L.B.C., ex p. Flynn*[68]; *R. v. Haringey L.B.C., ex p. Ulger*[69]).

---

[65] [1992] 1 All E.R. 705.
[66] [1982] 3 All E.R. 1135 at 1137-1139.
[67] *The Times*, July 20, 1993.
[68] June 1995 *Legal Action* 21.
[69] December 1992 *Legal Action* 21.

CHAPTER 10

Priority Need

As considered in earlier chapters, the legislation does not impose **10.01.** an obligation on local authorities to house all persons who are without suitable accommodation. It is required that the applicant come within one of the categories of priority need. The policy underlying this legislation demonstrates the policies in favour of keeping families intact. Thus, where there are dependent children involved, it is usual that the parent (or potential guardian) applicant will fall within the category of priority need. Similarly, those who are vulnerable (for some reason other than simply being without permanent accommodation) may fall within the requirements.

There are differing obligations on local authorities depending on **10.02.** whether the applicants are found to be in priority need and also where the applicants are not in priority need at all.

"Priority Need"

It is a requirement of the 1996 Act, and also of its predecessor **10.03.** legislation, that the applicant establish she is in "priority need for accommodation" before the statute will impose obligations on the authority to provide accommodation for the applicant's use on the ground of homelessness. The scope of the category "priority need" is set out in section 189 of the 1996 Act.

The following have a priority need for accommodation: **10.04.**

"(a) a pregnant woman or a person with whom she resides or might reasonably be expected to reside;
(b) a person with whom dependent children reside or might reasonably be expected to reside;

    (c) a person who is vulnerable as a result of old age, mental illness or handicap or physical disability or other special reason, or with whom such a person resides or might reasonably be expected to reside;

    (d) a person who is homeless or threatened with homelessness as a result of an emergency such as flood, fire or other disaster".

10.05. The 1996 Act retains the policy of seeking to provide people with accommodation not on the basis solely that they are homeless but rather where they satisfy some more stringent ground of eligibility for treatment. The four main categories considered below therefore are:—

pregnant women
those with dependent children
those who are vulnerable
victims of emergencies

10.06. The statute recognises the need to house not only the person in priority need but also persons who could reasonably be expected to reside with such an individual. Thus, for example, while a pregnant woman would clearly fall within the definition of priority need on almost any measure, her co-habitee is similarly covered.

10.07. While priority need is the important category for deciding whether or not a person is entitled to be provided with accommodation on grounds of homelessness, a local authority is still required not to fetter its discretion when deciding whether or not a person is vulnerable as a result of some "special reason". As discussed above with reference to judicial review proceedings in this area, it is incumbent on all housing authorities to consider each case on its merits. While the authorities frequently develop policies relating to the types of person they consider to be homeless as a result of some "special reason", the applicant is entitled to individual consideration.

10.08. It should also be remembered that local authorities are required to provide advice and assistance to those applicants who are not found to be in priority need. There is an obligation on every local housing authority to secure that free advice and information is available to any person in their district.[1] The advice and information that must be provided is "advice and information about homelessness and the prevention of homelessness".[2] These provisions are discussed in greater detail in Chapter 13, below.

[1] Housing Act 1996, s. 179(1).
[2] *Ibid.*

Pregnant Women

The applicant is entitled to be considered in priority need from **10.09.**
the moment of conception. It was the practice of a number of
authorities under the 1977 legislation to consider women entitled
only when they reached a given stage in the pregnancy. Therefore,
those who had only recently conceived were not entitled to be
housed on the basis of pregnancy. Clearly, it is an arbitrary
decision to reach a policy which discriminates between women
who are in different stages of the process. Similarly, it does not
take account of the needs of any pregnant woman to a suitable
living environment. The modern view must be somewhat clearer.
A woman is in priority need because she is pregnant and not
because she is in a particular stage of pregnancy.

What may be at issue is whether present accommodation is **10.10.**
unsuitable because of pregnancy or because it would be unsuitable
for a young child once born. In *R. v. Newham L.B.C., ex p. Dada*[3]
the Court of Appeal considered the plight of the applicants, Mr
and Mrs Dada, who had been accepted as being unintentionally
homeless and in priority need because Mrs Dada was pregnant.
They were offered one bedroom accommodation on the seventh
floor of a building. It was held by Glidewell L.J. that the
legislation referred to a "person" or a "living person" with whom
the applicant could reasonably be expected to reside and therefore
the prospective child with which Mrs Dada was pregnant did not
constitute a "living person".
Therefore, the applicant was not able to rely on the condition of
a child as yet unborn in contending that the accommodation was
not suitable. Further the applicants contended that the authority's
appeals procedure required that the applicant go into occupation of
the accommodation before arguing that it was unsuitable. It was
held that the procedure was not unreasonable because the appeals
officer reviewed all offers made which had been unreasonably
refused.

It should also be noted that "a person with whom [the pregnant **10.11.**
woman] resides or might reasonably be expected to reside" also
falls within the definition of priority need for these purposes.
Therefore, a partner or co-habitee, whether or not the father of the
child, is entitled to be considered as falling within the entitlement
to housing under Part VII.

[3] [1995] 2 All E.R. 522.

Dependent Children

10.12.   The issue arose under the predecessor to section 189(1)(b) (section 59(1) of the 1985 Act) whether section 189(1) required that the applicant both live and reside with the dependent children where the applicant contended that dependent children were living with her: particularly the words "reside or might reasonably be expected to reside". In the case of *Islam*[4] it was held that the tests were alternative. Therefore, it was not necessary for the applicant to show that the child was both resident and reasonably expected to be resident with the applicant.

10.13.   Given these arguments, the wording of section 189(1)(b) (which is identical to that of the 1985 Act) appears to be clear. The definition of priority need encompasses "a person with whom dependent children reside or might reasonably be expected to reside". The applicant can be residing with the applicant or it may be reasonable to expect that the child will reside with the applicant. The two halves of the test are considered separately.

"Resides with"

10.14.   First, the residence test. The requirement on the words of the statute is that there be residence with the applicant. The issue arises as to the nature of such residence. For example, there may be a question with reference to parents who have separated where the child does not live with either parent permanently. It may be that the child lives with other family members or is temporarily in foster care. In homelessness cases it will often be the case that the parent places the child with adults who are in more permanent accommodation.

10.15.   The use of the word "residence" indicates that the correct standard appears to fall somewhere between the permanence of "living with" and the temporary nature of "staying with". There is a need to show some continuity of residence without, seemingly, permanence.

10.16.   The authorities are occasionally guilty of being overly technical in applying the test for priority need where the children are not living with the parents at the time of the application. For example, in *R. v. Lewisham L.B.C., ex p. Creppy*[5] the married applicant couple went abroad temporarily and placed the children with a

---

[4] *R. v. Hillingdon L.B. ex p. Islam* [1983] 1 A.C. 688
[5] (1992) 24 H.L.R. 121.

carer. On their return they were homeless and applied to the authority to be housed. The authority argued that they were not in priority need because the children were not living with them at the time of the application. The Court of Appeal took a very straight-forward approach that this decision was "plainly inaccurate" (in the words of Russell L.J.). Furthermore the decision was found to be without justification on these facts.

"Reasonably be expected to reside"

The expression "might reasonably be expected to reside" would **10.17.** appear to cover the situation in which dependent children are required to live with other relatives or adults while the parents go through a period of homelessness. Therefore, where the parental relationship breaks down and the children reside in the short term with a parent who is not entitled to keep the children, or where the children reside temporarily with other relatives during the period of homelessness, this should not count against their parent being found to be in priority need for accommodation.

The underlying aim of the legislation is that families should not **10.18.** be broken up by reason of homelessness. This is clearly an important social objective. Therefore, it is similarly important that the legislation is not interpreted in such a way that parents are forced either to keep children in sub-standard accommodation to maintain their claim for housing, nor to break up the family unit rather than place the children with relatives in the short term.

There is the further problem of children who are living outside **10.19.** the United Kingdom at the time of the application. It might be that those children are to be considered reasonably expected to reside with the applicant, even though the applicant is inside the United Kingdom and the children outside the United Kingdom at the time of the application. It would appear the best practice is to consider that such children are dependents of the applicant where they are dependent upon her despite the issue of location. The issue then becomes one relating to the rights of asylum seekers and non-British nationals to accommodation under Part VII. On this issue see Chapter 8, above, and the section on asylum seekers.

In *R. v. Westminster C.C., ex p. Catelli (No. 2); R. v. Westminster* **10.20.** *C.C., ex p. Garcia*[6] the applicants sought judicial review of the authority's decision not to house them under the 1985 legislation. The applicants were both HIV positive and therefore categorised as

[6] (1995) 92 L.S.Gaz. 28.

being in priority need due to their vulnerability. The authority contended that the first applicant was not lawfully in the United Kingdom and that the second applicant had failed the habitual residence test for income support. Therefore, the authority contended that they owed no duties to house either applicant. Roger Henderson Q.C. sitting in the High Court held that it was for the local authority to decide, after making inquiries, whether or not the applicants fell within the category for homelessness. Therefore, no duty was owed to the applicants as people who were not entitled to a right of admission to reside in the United Kingdom.

10.21. As discussed above, in *R. v. Lewisham L.B.C., ex p. Creppy*[7] the Court of Appeal held that applicants were in priority need where the children were not actually living with them at the time of the application.

10.22. In *R. v. Kingswood B.C., ex p. Smith-Morse*,[8] S was homeless and applied to the local authority to be housed. The local authority decided that he was not in priority need as having a dependent child because his son's main residence was with S's ex-wife. S sought judicial review of the decision. Sir Louis Blom-Cooper held that the qualification "main" given to the term "residence" by the authority was a misdirection in law. The issue the authority should have considered, following *Vagliviello*, was whether the child resided with his father or not. The question should not have been a comparison of time spent between father and mother. The issue for the applicant was whether the applicant had a dependent child in these circumstances. The authority's duty was to consider the future care of the child and not just past arrangements.

10.23. In *R. v. Lambeth L.B.C., ex p. Bodunrin*[9] an overseas student was staying in a single person's hostel when he was unexpectedly visited by his children. He applied for housing on grounds of homelessness. He was found to be homeless because the accommodation was not available for his children's occupation. The issue arose whether he was in priority need. The court held that it was not reasonable for the authority to find that he was homeless in these circumstances and yet find that he was not in priority need where the children were people who were normally expected to reside with him.

---

[7] (1992) 24 H.L.R. 121.
[8] [1995] 2 F.L.R. 137.
[9] (1992) 24 H.L.R. 647.

"*Residence*"

In *R. v. Ealing L.B.C. ex p. Sidhu*[10], the applicant was living in a **10.24.** women's refuge. She had an interim custody order granted in her favour by a county court. The local authority contended that they were not required to consider her application until a full custody order was obtained. It was held unnecessary to wait for a final custody order in deciding the issue of priority need. Furthermore, the authority would not be at liberty to delay any decision to satisfy itself whether or not there would be any change in the applicant's circumstances with regard to the custody order. Therefore, the authority could not take into account the chance of the applicant losing the custody application at a final hearing of the matter.

In *Sidhu*, it was a significant point in considering the applicant's **10.25.** status as being in priority need that the dependent children were residing with her at the time of the application. The issue may be different where the children are not so residing. Had the custody order not been a full order and had the children not been residing with the applicant, this point in *Sidhu* might have been decided differently.

"*Dependent*"

The further issue is whether the child must be wholly depend- **10.26.** ent upon the applicant or whether it is sufficient that the child is partly dependent upon the applicant and upon other persons. In *R. v. Lambeth L.B.C., ex p. Vagliviello*[11] it was held that the authority had directed themselves incorrectly when they decided that the applicant was not in priority need where the children were not dependent entirely upon her. Rather it is possible for a child to be resident with and dependent upon more than one person, when only one of those persons is applying for housing under Part VII.

In a similar situation to *Vaglivello*, the male applicant in *R. v.* **10.27.** *Port Talbot B.C., ex p. MacCarthy*[12] obtained access to his child for part of the week. The authority contended, on receiving his application for housing, that the child did not "normally reside with him" and therefore he was not in priority need. The Court of Appeal held that the authority had impliedly considered the issue of normal residence with the father and it was for them to decide whether or not there would be normal residence.

---

[10] (1982) 2 H.L.R. 45.
[11] (1990) 22 H.L.R. 392, C.A.
[12] (1991) 23 H.L.R. 207.

10.28. There is clearly some difference here with *Vaglivello* where the Court of Appeal held that the test simply requires that one child live with the applicant. The reconciliation of these cases seems to be that it is a matter of fact for the authority whether or not the child normally resides with the parent applicant. However, if a child does normally reside with the parent, then that should be enough to constitute priority need without needing the child to live wholly and exclusively with the applicant.

10.29. The term "dependent" is not itself defined in Part VII. The Code of Guidance prepared under the 1985 legislation suggested that all children under the age of 16 should be considered to be dependent. Generally, older children should also be considered to be dependent where they are not able to or do not in fact support themselves. This would appear to cover children not of the age of majority. The Code of Guidance has some slight commentary relating specifically to the plight of young people suggesting some allowance for their added susceptibility. Lack of parental care, educational disadvantages and histories of abuse or disadvantage are highlighted as concerns for the local authority in this context.[12a]

10.30. In *R. v. Kensington and Chelsea R.L.B.C., ex p. Amarfio*[13] the Court of Appeal considered the issue of the meaning of "dependent" within the context of "priority need". The applicant had applied for housing from the authority for himself and his 18-year old son. His son had begun a two-year youth training scheme in connection with which he received a weekly allowance. Nourse L.J. held that once a child had gone into full-time occupation he could not be a dependent within the meaning of the statute. A young person on such a scheme was held to be in full-time employment.

10.31. Where a father occupies accommodation which it is unreasonable for him to occupy with dependent children, he is entitled to have the presence of the dependent children residing with him for the first time taken into account in deciding whether or not he is in priority need. Thus, in *R. v. Lambeth L.B.C. ex p. Bodunrin*[14] a local authority were held to have misdirected themselves where they had, on these facts, taken the approach that the applicant was not homeless and that the issue of priority need was not therefore one that needed to be considered. Rather, the authority should

---

[12a] See para. 14.10.
[13] (1995) 27 H.L.R. 543.
[14] (1992) 24 H.L.R. 647.

have considered whether or not the applicant was in priority need as a result of having dependent children residing with him in unsuitable accommodation as part of their decision whether or not he was homeless. It was held that there was priority need in these circumstances.

Vulnerable Persons

"Vulnerable"

The term "vulnerable" is not defined in the legislation. The 10.32. clues as to interpretation are contained in the categories of vulnerability which are set out in the statute. In *R. v. Waveney D.C. ex p. Bowers*,[15] vulnerability was considered to cover persons "less able to fend for [themselves] so that injury or detriment will result where a less vulnerable man would be able to cope without harmful effects". The test is therefore a comparison by the court of the applicant with an objectively ascertained reasonable applicant of reasonable ability to cope with her own housing difficulties.

Therefore, it would appear that there must be some infirmity or 10.33. characteristic of the applicant which marks out her vulnerability from that of other applicants. For example, cases of alcoholism will not demonstrate vulnerability by themselves on the grounds set out in the Act. It would be necessary for the applicant to demonstrate that this condition fell within one of the other grounds of vulnerability. Of itself, it will not qualify.

Some Scottish decisions have followed this approach (in particu- 10.34. lar Lord Prosser in *Wilson*) on the basis that one applicant cannot be considered vulnerable just because there might be a different applicant who is less vulnerable. Therefore, an alcoholic is not vulnerable purely because there is another applicant elsewhere who is not an alcoholic or whose alcoholism is less acute. Establishing an objective standard of vulnerability would be the only means of reaching a rational solution to this issue.

Connexity and Burden of Proof

Alternatively, it might be that the vulnerability arises solely with 10.35. reference to obtaining or maintaining housing. The extent of the vulnerability is something which must be susceptible of proof by the applicant. For example, the case of *R. v. Reigate and Banstead B.C., ex p. Di Domenico*[16] considered an epileptic applicant who

---

[15] [1983] Q.B. 238.
[16] (1980) 20 H.L.R. 153.

contended that he was vulnerable within the terms of the Act on the basis that he had difficulty in finding or maintaining housing. It was held that the applicant could not be considered to be vulnerable purely on account of his condition because he had not adduced factual evidence that he was vulnerable in this regard. The applicant is therefore required to bear a burden of proof in this regard.

10.36.   Further, in *R. v. Wandsworth B.C., ex p. Banbury*,[17] for example, it was held that the issue of whether or not epilepsy would amount to vulnerability was a matter of fact and degree in any case. For example, where it could be shown that the attacks occurred with severity and frequency, the claim would be successful. It would be the duty of the authority in any case to seek suitable evidence but also to come to an independent decision: therefore the authority could not simply indorse the view of its own medical officer without considering that opinion in the context of the housing application.

Voluntary Vulnerability

10.37.   There has been a distinction made in some of the cases between "voluntary" and "involuntary" vulnerability. In the case of *R. v. Waveney D.C., ex p. Bowers*,[18] Waller J. considered that where a man became vulnerable through his drinking, this was voluntary vulnerability and therefore the applicant would not fall within the category of priority need. However, in circumstances where the applicant had been injured in a car accident, and became vulnerable as a result, this was involuntary vulnerability which would mean that he would fall within the category of priority need.

10.38.   The issue of vulnerability necessarily resolves itself to a question of fact in any case. Where an Italian woman was found to be of sub-normal intelligence and had difficulty communicating at all due to her intellectual difficulties, it was held that the authority was wrong in failing to take into account her condition when deciding that there was no evidence of vulnerability (*R. v. Bath C.C., ex p. Sangermano*[19]).

10.39.   Therefore, there would appear to be reasons for creating further sub-divisions in the test of vulnerability. There is precedent for distinguishing between those applicants who become vulnerable "through choice" and those who are vulnerable "through no fault

[17] (1987) 19 H.L.R. 76.
[18] [1983] Q.B. 238.
[19] (1984) 17 H.L.R. 94.

of their own". An applicant wishing to show vulnerability in a case where it is not clear whether or not dependency or illness resulted from some consensual act might be required to adduce some factual evidence of a pre-disposition to such vulnerability. In the case of those addicted to drugs, evidence of dependency or some other reason would be required to demonstrate a lack of choice.

In *R. v. Westminster C.C., ex p. Ortiz*[20] the applicant was **10.40.** considered not "vulnerable" by the authority on discharge from a detoxification unit where she had been treated for drink and drugs addiction. The Court of Appeal took the view that she was not at a disadvantage in obtaining housing and therefore not vulnerable within the statutory meaning. Simon Brown L.J. was satisfied that she was at no disadvantage because of the number of hostel places, including places for those with addiction problems. Therefore, even after treatment for a medically recognised condition, there is no presumption of proof of vulnerability.

Old Age

The category of "old age", as considered in the Code of **10.41.** Guidance, is a term designed to catch those experiencing difficulty in finding accommodation due to their age. Again the issue arises whether the vulnerability must be connected to the difficulty in finding accommodation or whether the applicant can be experiencing such difficulty and incidentally be in old age. Under the Code of Guidance, the status of those over 60 should be considered with care in each instance.

Mental Illness or Handicap

It is suggested that in seeking to assess mental illness or **10.42.** handicap, the authority should have regard to the medical advice and assistance being provided to the applicant and also to that which has been provided to the applicant in the past. The authority should also consult with social services personnel who are involved with the applicant or who are responsible for her welfare. In general it is considered that the main issues to be taken into account should be the relationship between the mental impairment and the applicant's housing difficulties. The extent and duration of the mental illness or handicap will therefore be significant factors in this consideration.

Clearly, particular attention needs to be paid to the requirements **10.43.** of former psychiatric patients; those in secure units; and those in local authority care for psychological illness or handicap. The Code

[20] (1995) 27 H.L.R. 364.

suggests that the authority appoint a particular homelessness officer to deal with this category of patient. In many cases it will be possible to manage the discharge of such persons from formal care into accommodation. However, it will also be necessary to cope with direct approaches from those who seek accommodation entirely independently of any structure: for example, where they have been care-in-the-community patients.

10.44.　　There is a distinction made between mental illness and mental handicap. The former is simply to do with diagnosable illness; the latter is concerned with subnormality or psychosis. Not all subnormality will constitute vulnerability, rather it will be for the authority to consider the medical evidence put before them and make any necessary inquiries.

10.45.　　Under *Garlick v. Oldham M.B.C.*[21] it was held by the House of Lords that it was not the intention of the priority-need provisions to grant a right of application to dependent children to claim rights to accommodation. In this case, the applicant sought to apply on behalf of a child suffering from mental illness. It was held that there was no specific capacity to a person who was unfit through mental illness to make an application or even to instruct another to make such an application on her behalf. The Act required that an applicant be able to understand and respond to such an offer. If a person was caring for another who was suffering from mental illness, then that person would have a right to be housed thus enabling her to look after the disabled person. The result of this decision is the regrettable effect that there are no independent rights for the disabled. The local housing authority will bear no obligation to them specifically.

Physical Disability

10.46.　　The issue of physical disability will be a matter of medical fact and degree, as it is with mental illness and disability (considered above). Where an applicant is in receipt of a benefit related to physical disability, such as incapacity benefit, this would appear to raise a presumption of vulnerability. The much-criticised policy of care-in-the-community introduced by the Conservative Government, does make the issue of assessing physical disability in this way more problematical.

10.47.　　In assessing physical handicap, the authority should have regard to the medical advice and assistance being provided to the applicant. The authority should also consult with social services

---

[21] [1993] 2 All E.R. 65.

personnel who are involved with the applicant or who are responsible for her welfare. In general it is considered that the main
issues to be taken into account should be the relationship between
the disability and the applicant's housing difficulties. The extent
and duration of the handicap will therefore be significant factors in
this consideration.

In this context it is important to note that being in priority need **10.48.**
as a result of physical disability, will not necessarily lead to an offer
of a particular type of accommodation. The applicant in *R. v.*
Kensington and Chelsea R.L.B.C., ex p. Grillo[22] was offered seventh
floor accommodation although she contended that this was unsuitable because of her partner's asthma. The applicant also produced
evidence as to her own problems with arthritis. The authority
rejected the medical evidence adduced on behalf of the applicant
and her partner. Neill L.J. held that the offer of accommodation
was reasonable and within the *Wednesbury* guidelines because the
authority was required to consider all the housing needs in its
district. The defects complained of by the applicant were found to
be either only slight or only present occasionally. The result is that
the authority need not tailor their decision to the specific requirements of the applicant. Rather, the broader context of the authority's obligations can intervene.

Equally controversially, Neill L.J. found that the authority were **10.49.**
under no duty to give reasons so long as the decision was within
policy guidelines in this context. While there might be an implied
duty to give reasons in some circumstances, this was found to be a
case where the authority had activated a voluntary appeals procedure and therefore was not one in which giving reasons could be
required. Perhaps this is an unfortunate judgment. The authority
appears to have fettered its discretion by giving a decision in
accordance solely with policy guidelines.

Other Special Reason

The difficulty with this final category is the extent to which it is **10.50.**
to be interpreted *ejusdem generis* with the preceding statutory
examples of vulnerability. The approach of the courts has demonstrated that no court will be astute to find an "other special
reason". The situations in which such reasons have been found
have tended to be in relation to very serious personal circumstances, as discussed below. It is clear, for example, that language
difficulties alone will not constitute an "other special reason".

---

[22] [1995] N.P.C. 85.

10.51. Categories of special reason for young persons might include risk of physical or sexual abuse in the home. Similarly, risks associated with drug abuse or being induced into prostitution would constitute special reasons. In the case of *Kelly*,[23] Lord Ross held that two 16-year-old girls who were without assets or accommodation, and who allegedly had been the victims of violence, had the requisite degree of vulnerability to fall within the definition of priority need. Exceptionally, on those facts it was held that it need not be conclusively proved that the young women had been the victims of violence, in spite of the lack of evidence of such violence in the area.

10.52. With certain categories of young person, there will be a greater degree of vulnerability than with others. For example, those who have been in local authority care or those who are young offenders. Similarly, those young people with educational difficulties may be in priority need where those difficulties impair their ability to find or keep accommodation.

10.53. Domestic violence will constitute a special reason. Therefore, persons who are at risk from domestic violence at their accommodation will be in priority need. The violence need not necessarily be caused by a co-habitee of the young person. It is sufficient that there be some violence or harassment surrounding the accommodation. As part of this consideration of domestic violence, questions of harassment on grounds of race, gender or sexual orientation should similarly be taken into account as a risk impacting on the applicant's vulnerability.

10.54. In *Garlick v. Oldham M.B.C.*[24] it was held by the House of Lords that it was not the intention of the priority-need provisions to grant a right of application to dependent children to claim rights to accommodation themselves. It was expected that that right would be granted to their parents, thus securing accommodation for their occupation. This is in spite of section 20 of the Children Act 1989 as discussed below. Therefore, a dependent child could not claim to be in priority need as a vulnerable person within the definition of "special reason".

10.55. Where the child was unfit to make an application and an adult applied on behalf of the child, the House of Lords in *Garlick* held that the Act required that an applicant be able to understand and respond to such an offer. Therefore, if a person was caring for

[23] 1986 S.L.T. 169.
[24] [1993] 2 All E.R. 65.

another who was suffering from mental illness, then that person would have a right to be housed thus enabling her to look after the disabled person.

Children Act 1989, Part III. In considering the question of **10.56.** young people's vulnerability, the authority should have regard to section 20 and Part III of the Children Act 1989. Section 17 of the 1989 Act requires local authorities to safeguard and promote the welfare of children within their area. Section 20 requires local authorities to provide accommodation for children "in need" within their district. Children in need are to be found accommodation where there is no person having parental responsibility for them; where they have been lost or abandoned; or where the person who has been caring for them can no longer care for them. Local authorities are required to provide accommodation for young people where those people have reached the age of sixteen and whose welfare the authority consider likely to be seriously prejudiced if they do not provide them with accommodation.

Violence. While domestic violence will constitute a special **10.57.** reason, there is a more difficult category of violence not caused by a co-habitee. The issue of harassment on grounds of race, gender or sexual orientation should similarly be taken into account as a risk impacting on the applicant's vulnerability.

In *R. v. Camden L.B.C., ex p. Adair*[25] A sought judicial review of **10.58.** Camden's decision not to transfer his tenancy under their discretionary "relationship and breakdown policy" and Camden's finding that he was homeless but not in priority need. A argued that Camden had failed to take into account relevant considerations, considered irrelevant matters and failed to give reasons for their decision. A also argued that, in relation to their finding on priority need, Camden had failed to make proper inquiries as required by the legislation. The assessment form made no reference to the threats of violence received by A which were relevant to the issue of A's vulnerability and which were known by the District Housing Office. Stephen Richards Q.C., sitting as a judge in the High Court, held that the application should be allowed in part. Camden's "relationship and breakdown policy" was discretionary. Camden considered all the relevant matters and were entitled to take into account factors such as A's previous housing history.

The decision letter dealt adequately with the reasons for the **10.59.** decision and considered that there was no special feature of the decision which required particular explanation. The application in

[25] Unreported (April 2, 1996).

relation to this decision was therefore dismissed. However, a local authority, in making inquiries to decide whether an applicant was in priority need, was obliged to make adequate inquiries of other local authorities where the applicant had indicated that his dealings with such authorities were relevant to his application. The authority was required to inform the applicant of the reasons for its decision when informing him that he was not in priority need. The letter sent by Camden merely contained a general formula rather than clear reasoning. The decision was therefore unlawful and quashed.

Emergency Homelessness

10.60.   The emergency category is derived from section 21(1)(b) of the National Assistance Act 1948. The applicant is required to be "homeless or threatened with homelessness as a result of an emergency such as flood, fire or other disaster". The definitions of "homeless" and "threatened with homelessness" are set out in section 175 of the 1996 Act.

10.61.   What is required of the legislation is that the incident giving rise to the homelessness is both an emergency and a form of disaster. The definition of "disaster" for these purposes is something similar to a flood or a fire: (Noble v. South Herefordshire D.C.[26]). In *Noble* there was a demolition order effected over the applicant's accommodation before the applicant had taken up occupation. The applicant contended that the demolition constituted an emergency. However, the authority succeeded on the basis that the proposed action did not constitute an emergency. It was held that this did not constitute an emergency — partly because the applicant was entitled to compensation in any event under the Land Compensation Act 1973.

10.62.   Where an applicant is unlawfully evicted, she may be in priority need. In *R. v. Bristol C.C. ex p. Bradic*[27] it was accepted by Sir Louis Blom-Cooper that a single unlawful eviction may constitute an emergency situation. This would be an extension of the logic that sudden, unlawful evictions could constitute such an emergency.

10.63.   The issue of what constitutes a disaster was then considered by the Court of Appeal in *R. v. Bristol C.C., ex p. Bradic.*[28] The term was given a restrictive meaning. The applicant returned from a trip

---

[26] (1983) 17 H.L.R. 80, C.A.
[27] (1995) 27 H.L.R. 584.
[28] *Ibid.*

to find that the locks had been changed on his accommodation and his personal property removed. He contended that he was home-less and in priority need because the unlawful eviction constituted a "disaster" within the legislation. Roch L.J. held that it was not Parliament's intention that every emergency which resulted in a person becoming homeless was intended to create priority need. The types of emergencies which were to be considered to fall within the definition were emergencies which caused physical damage to the property thus making the accommodation inhabitable.

However, being imprisoned does not itself constitute a "disas- **10.64.** ter" within Part VII. The point was considered in a preliminary appeal where the applicant appeared in person before securing housing in any event (*R. v. Secretary of State for the Home Office ex p. Toft*[29]).

There is some academic commentary which suggests that the **10.65.** collapse of a property in circumstances where the occupier is uninsured, should lead the authority to find that the occupier is homeless within the meaning of Part VII. In principle this would appear to be correct on the basis that the collapse of the property is a disaster tantamount to fire or flood on the condition of the property for occupation by the applicant. The difficulty may be in comparison with *Noble* where the demolition order required destruction of the property. *Noble* may be capable of distinction on the basis that the applicant knew of the demolition order in advance. Therefore, there was not the quality of sudden emergency as in *Bradic*.

In *R. v. Walsall M.B.C., ex p. Price*[30] P was served with an order **10.66.** for possession on grounds of non-payment of rent and non-compliance with tenancy conditions. The council wished to demol-ish the houses in P's street and therefore demolished the properties either side of P's accommodation. P's accommodation was there-fore exposed to damp, rodent infestation and an accumulation of sewerage. P was evicted and applied to be housed on grounds of homelessness. P was found not to be homeless. Judicial review was sought on the basis that insufficient inquiries were made and that the council should have considered what caused P to become homeless in the first place. P contended that his situation should have been considered to be an emergency. Harrison J. held that the officer had failed to inquire into the demolition and therefore had

[29] Unreported, QBD (May 25, 1993).
[30] Unreported (September 7, 19960.

failed to make adequate inquiries.[31] The term "emergency" must refer to something urgent and not an accumulation of events over time. Therefore, the gradual accretion of events in this case could not constitute an emergency.

Future Regulation

10.67.   It is open to the Secretary of State to create new categories of person who satisfy the test of "priority need" or may repeal, or amend, the categories of priority.[32] However, before making any such order, the Secretary of State must consult any associations which represent the relevant authorities, and indeed any other persons he considers appropriate.[33] Furthermore, no such order can be made unless a draft of it has been approved by resolution of each House of Parliament.[34] No such regulations had been made as at the date of going to print.

Obligation where Priority Need but not Homeless Intentionally

10.68.   The detail of the obligations borne by the authority where the applicant is in priority need for accommodation are discussed in greater detail below in Chapter 13. However, it may be useful to rehearse some of that discussion in this chapter to pursue some of the contextual discussion about the impact of being in priority need. Where the applicant is in priority need but not homeless intentionally, the local housing authority are required to ensure that accommodation is available for occupation by the applicant under section 192(2).This duty arises specifically where the local housing authority are satisfied that an applicant is homeless, eligible for assistance, has a priority need, and is not satisfied that he became homeless intentionally.[35]

10.69.   The local housing authority are subject to the duty under section 193 for a period of two years ("the minimum period"). This is subject to the remaining provisions of section 193. After the end of that period, the authority is empowered to continue to secure that accommodation is available for occupation by the applicant, but are not obliged to do so.[36]

---

[31] See also Bayani [1991] C.L.Y. 1987.
[32] Housing Act 1996, s.189(2).
[33] s. 189(3).
[34] s. 189(4).
[35] s. 193(1).
[36] s. 193(3) and further s. 194.

Cessation of the Obligation

The local housing authority ceases to be subject to the duty **10.70.** under section 193 if the applicant refuses an offer of accommodation which the authority are satisfied is suitable for her and the authority notify her that they regard themselves as having discharged their duty under this section.[37] This is in circumstances where the applicant has been informed by the authority of the possible consequence of refusal.[38]

The local housing authority ceases to be subject to the duty **10.71.** under section 193 if the applicant ceases to be eligible for assistance; becomes homeless intentionally from the accommodation made available for his occupation; accepts an offer of accommodation under Part VI of the 1996 Act; or otherwise voluntarily ceases to occupy the accommodation made available for his occupation as his only or principal home.

Further, the local housing authority ceases to be subject to the **10.72.** duty under section 193 if the applicant refuses an offer of accommodation under Part VI (in the given circumstances) and can therefore notify the applicant accordingly within 21 days of the refusal. A person who ceases to be owed the duty set out in section 193 may make a fresh application to the authority for accommodation or assistance in obtaining accommodation.[39]

Where a local housing authority carry out a review under section **10.73.** 194, the local housing authority is required to make such inquiries as are considered appropriate to decide whether to use their power to provide such accommodation. On completing the review, the authority must notify the applicant of their determination and of whether they propose to exercise, or continue to exercise, their power under section 194.[40]

Alternatively, the authority may give notice to the applicant that **10.74.** they are to withdraw the accommodation provided under section 194 in the applicant's case[41] either as a result the review or otherwise.[42]

---

[37] s. 193(5).
[38] *Ibid.*
[39] s. 193(9).
[40] s. 194(4).
[41] s. 194(5).
[42] *Ibid.*

10.75.   Where the local housing authority are satisfied that an applicant is threatened with homelessness and is eligible for assistance,[43] they are required to take reasonable steps to secure that accommodation remains available for her occupation.[44] If the authority are satisfied that she has a priority need,[45] and do not believe that she became threatened with homelessness intentionally,[46] they are required to take reasonable steps to secure that accommodation remains available for her occupation. The only circumscription on this power is where there is other suitable accommodation available.

10.76.   Importantly, this does not affect any right of the authority to secure vacant possession of any accommodation provided to the authority.[47] The authority are at liberty to commence proceedings to recover possession, in spite of the broader context of actions under section 195.

10.77.   Where the authority are not satisfied that the applicant has a priority need,[48] or are satisfied that she has a priority need but are also satisfied that she became threatened with homelessness intentionally,[49] they must provide her with the advice and assistance which they consider appropriate in the circumstances in any attempts the applicant may make to secure that accommodation does not cease to be available for her occupation.[50]

---

[43] s. 195(1).
[44] s. 195(2).
[45] s. 195(2)(a).
[46] s. 195(2)(b).
[47] s. 195(3).
[48] s. 195(5)(a).
[49] s. 195(5)(b).
[50] s. 195(5).

CHAPTER 11

Local Connection

In *R. v. Slough B.C. ex p. Ealing L.B.C.*,[1] Lord Denning M.R. said **11.01.** that he considered the local connection provisions of the homelessness legislation to be curiously reminiscent of the Poor Law of 1601. He said[2]:

> "To us old folk this is a repeat performance of the disputes under the Poor Law 200 years ago. In those days each parish was responsible for the relief of those who were poor and unable to work. When a poor man moved from one parish to another, the question arose: which parish was responsible? The disputes, Blackstone tells us, "created an infinity of expensive law-suits between contending neighbourhoods, concerning those settlements and removals". Under that system, paupers could be returned to the parishes "where they had a settlement"."

Similarly, it is a requirement in the 1996 Act that any person **11.02.** seeking housing on the grounds of homelessness be able to demonstrate that she has a local connection with the district of the authority to which she is making her application. An authority is not bound to provide accommodation for any person who does not have a local connection with that area.

It is one of the weaknesses of the system that homeless people **11.03.** are liable to be moved from place to place. The process is described by Lord Denning in *R. v. Slough B.C. ex p. Ealing L.B.C.*[3] as being a "game of battledore and shuttlecock". It is the local authorities

---

[1] [1981] 1 All E.R. 601.
[2] [1981] 1 All E.R. 601 at 611.
[3] [1981] 1 All E.R. 601.

161

who are given sole responsibility for adjudicating whether people are homeless and whether they are to be housed in their area or not. Coupled with the powers to refer applicants to other local authorities (considered below), applicants are not entitled to be housed simply because they are citizens and simply because they are homeless. Rather the local nature of homelessness and the local responsibility for resolving the problem remains. In this context, there is little national co-ordination to resolve the problem. Similarly, no account is taken of the comparative capacity or willingness of different authorities to meet their obligations.

The Local Connection Provisions in Outline

11.04.   In circumstances where the authority to which the applicant applies believes that the applicant has no local connection with its district, the authority can refer the applicant to another authority with which it considers the applicant does have a local connection.

11.05.   Therefore, the local connection provisions potentially exempt the authority which refers the applicant on ("the notifying authority") from an obligation to house that applicant permanently. The authority receiving the referral ("the notified authority") then bears the burden of finding accommodation for the applicant's occupation. The circumstances in which this translation of duties arises is set out in detail below. In short, the applicant must have no local connection with the notifying authority; the applicant must have a local connection with the notified authority; and there must not be any risk of domestic violence in the district of the notified authority.

11.06.   Clearly, there will be disputes in many cases between authorities where resources are called upon in this manner. There is to be agreement between the notifying and notified authorities that the applicant and the duty to house the applicant be passed between them.[4] Where the authorities fail to reach any such agreement, the matter is referred to arbitration.

11.07.   In practice, many local authorities "sell" their homeless people to other local authorities where those latter authorities have resources to house more than their quotient of homeless people. Some proportion of the re-location expenditure is then met by the notifying authority. This means of referral is considered further below but it is this writer's opinion that this practice resembles the

---

[4] Housing Act 1996, s. 198(5).

slave trade more closely than the Poor Law. In the absence of a co-ordinated system for housing homeless people in suitable locations in suitable accommodation, this ad hoc system cannot be in the best interests of the individuals concerned.

The Meaning of "local connection"

The definition of "local connection" is set out in section 199 of **11.08.** the 1996 Act. A person has a local connection with the district of a local housing authority if he has a connection with it:

"(a) because he is, or in the past was, normally resident there, and that residence is or was of his own choice,
(b) because he is employed there,
(c) because of family associations, or
(d) because of special circumstances".

The four possibilities to establish local connection are exclusive. **11.09.** There are no other categories permissible. Therefore, the applicant must demonstrate that she falls within one of the four categories. In short they are:

normal residence;
employment;
family associations;
special circumstances.

The essential point about the structure of section 199 is that the term "local connection" has been held by the House of Lords in *R. v. Eastleigh B.C., ex p. Betts*[5] to be the most central component of the section. It overrides the four individual categories. Therefore, each of the four examples of local connection are not exclusive definitions in themselves, rather any individual applicant's circumstances must be weighed against the central term.

The core decision in this area is therefore that of the House of **11.10.** Lords in *R. v. Eastleigh B.C., ex p. Betts*.[6] The applicant had lived on a houseboat in the Southampton area after securing employment there. The applicant lived there with his family from August 1980. In October 1980, the applicant was given a house by Eastleigh Borough Council. The applicant subsequently lost his job and fell into arrears with the rent. He was evicted in February 1981. The applicant applied to Eastleigh Borough Council to be

[5] [1983] 2 A.C. 613.
[6] [1983] 2 A.C. 613.

rehoused. Eastleigh referred the matter to Blaby Council on the basis that the applicant had been resident in Eastleigh for less than six months. As a result of the short term of this occupation, Eastleigh Borough Council was of the view that the applicant was not normally resident within its district. The Court of Appeal held that the rigid application of the Local Authority Agreement (that residence must be for a term of more than six months to constitute "normal residence") was not the correct approach on these facts.

11.11.   However, the House of Lords held that the fundamental question was whether or not the applicant had a local connection with the authority's area. The application of the term "local connection" required a higher test than "normal residence": it required something more than mere normal residence. Therefore, the authority was required to consider whether or not the applicant had a local connection and as part of that whether he was also normally resident within its area. The four criteria set out in the section were subsidiary components of the central test whether or not an applicant had some local connection. Therefore, normal residence must be such as to constitute a local connection.

11.12.   Clearly this decision has a two-fold effect. The requirements of the definition of local connection within section 199 are shown to be more severe than might otherwise appear to be the case on a literal reading of the provision, and the test for local connection is less certain than the perimeters of the four criteria would appear to suggest.

11.13.   What is also important is that the local authority are required to consider each application on its own merits and that they do not seek to fetter their decision by applying a standard measure to all cases absolutely. The authority in *Betts* was criticised for this by the House of Lords. It was found that the authority had sought to apply the terms of the Local Authority Agreement without reference to the precise circumstances of the case before them.

11.14.   The length of occupation within an authority's district is still often of considerable importance in deciding the question of local connection. For example, in *Smith* it was held that a period of employment in the area for six months before occupying armed-forces accommodation in the area for the subsequent ten years would not be sufficient to constitute a local connection.

11.15.   In *R. v. Newham L.B.C., ex p. Smith*[7] deciding on the appropriate date at which the authority should assess whether or not the applicant had a local connection with its area, the correct date was

[7] *The Times*, April 11, 1996.

held to be the date on which the application for housing was made. This would be the case even in circumstances where there was some delay while the authority made inquiries under Part VII before reaching its decision whether or not the applicant was homeless. However, where such a delay did occur and the authority decided to refer the applicant to an authority with which the applicant had a local connection, the authority should always be ready to reconsider their decision.

Normal Residence

It is frequently local authority policy that "normal residence" **11.16.** will only be established by six-months residence within an authority's area. As discussed above, the law in this area is set out in the House of Lords in *Re Betts*. The term "local connection" itself is the core test, rather than the term "normal residence". Therefore, the applicant is required to demonstrate something more substantial than mere "normal residence". Whether or not there is a local connection is the anterior question. The four criteria set out in section 199 were subsidiary components of the central test whether or not an applicant had some local connection. Therefore, normal residence must be of such a quality as to constitute a local connection.

The test of "residence" is that set out by the House of Lords in **11.17.** *R. v. Barnet L.B.C., ex p. Shah*[8] and by the House of Lords in *Re Betts*. *Re Betts* approved the Local Authority Agreement which suggested that the requirement of local connection would be satisfied where there has been residence for six months in the previous 12 months or three years out of the previous five years. However, it is still necessary for local authorities to consider each case on its merits but these guidelines do offer some assistance.

Residence of Own Choice

It is an important part of the requirement that the applicant be **11.18.** resident in the requisite district and that residing there is out of the applicant's own choice. For the purposes of defining the term "residence of own choice", residence in a district is not of a person's own choice in the following situations:

> "(a) he becomes resident there because he, or a person who might reasonably be expected to reside with him, is serving in the regular armed forces of the Crown,[9] or

---

[8] [1983] 2 A.C. 309.
[9] Housing Act 1996, s. 199(3)(a).

(b) he, or a person who might reasonably be expected to reside with him, becomes resident there because he is detained under the authority of an Act of Parliament".[10]

Detention under an Act of Parliament would include being a prisoner, whether convicted or held on remand, and a person held under the terms of the Mental Health Act 1983.

11.19.   The issue of armed forces personnel was shown up most clearly in the appeals in Smith and Hay.[11] In both of these cases the armed forces' practice of allowing personnel to remain in forces married quarters for a period between discharge and recovery of those quarters, was contended on behalf of the applicants to demonstrate a period of local connection. It was held that the exclusion for personnel in forces quarters was intended to run from the commencement of the occupation of those quarters until cessation of occupation as a member of the armed forces. However, simply holding over the end of the period of commission in the forces would not be enough to constitute a local connection on these facts.

11.20.   By section 199(5), the Secretary of State may specify other circumstances in which residence in a district is not to be treated as of a person's own choice. As yet there have been no regulations passed which extend these categories.

Employment

11.21.   The terms of the Local Authority Agreement are that employment should be something of more than a casual nature. Therefore, the word "employment" is not to be given its simple meaning "being employed". Rather "employment" in this context will be required to denote some local connection beyond the superficial.

11.22.   It is suggested that the term "employment" might refer equally well to those who have been self-employed in the area for a sufficient length of time to generate a local connection. The term that might be better used to describe the relationship is "worked in an area for such a period as to develop a local connection". It is not clear why voluntary work or work that does not necessarily amount to employment (such as "meals on wheels" provision or voluntary healthcare) should not qualify as an activity which provides the applicant with a local connection. If links with a community are

---

[10] s. 199(3)(b).
[11] *R. v. White Horse D.C., ex p. Smith and Hay* (1984) 17 H.L.R. 160.

what are required by the Act, then there is no reason in principle why such activities should not be encompassed by the definition. This would appear to be more in line with the spirit of the House of Lords' decision in *Betts* than a straightforward test which looks simply at a period of paid employment.

The Local Authority Agreement suggests that the authority seek **11.23.** confirmation from an employer as to the applicant's status as an employee and also as to the nature of the employment. While this does not expressly exclude self-employed people or those working only part-time, it does seem to be slanted in favour of the traditional "nine-to-five" working environment which is not the reality for many of the people who apply for housing on grounds of homelessness: they are frequently part-time workers or those on short-term contracts. Therefore, it is suggested that the term "employment" be given a broader meaning to ensure that such people are not excluded under Part VII of the 1996 Act.

Re Betts approved the terms of the Local Authority Agreement **11.24.** which suggested that the requirement of "local connection" would be satisfied where there has been residence for six months out of the previous 12 months or three years out of the previous five years.

By section 199(5), the Secretary of State may specify other **11.25.** circumstances in which a person is not to be treated as employed in a district.

Family Associations

There is no definition of "family associations" and the case law **11.26.** is thin and the Code of Guidance offers no definition of it. The Local Authority Agreement views the expression "family associations" as encompassing applicants, members of the applicant's immediate family, parents, adult children and siblings residing within the area. According to the Agreement, those extended categories of persons must have been living in the area for a period of five years or more.

Of course, it may be that an applicant does not wish to be **11.27.** referred to an area which will keep her close to her family associations. Therefore, the applicant may object to such a referral. It would appear that the wishes of the applicant, while relevant, cannot override the words of the statute: (*R. v. McCall, ex p. Eastbourne B.C.*[12])

---

[12] (1981) 8 H.L.R. 48.

11.28.   In *R. v. Hammersmith and Fulham L.B.C., ex p. Avdic*[13] the
applicant was a Bosnian refugee who appealed against the authority's decision not to grant her a right to be housed. The applicant
lived in Yorkshire and therefore the authority argued that she had
no local connection with its area. The applicant contended that she
had a cousin who lived in the authority's district and therefore she
had a local connection with it under what is now section 199 of the
1996 Act. She contended further that she had special circumstances which should lead to her being found to have a local
connection.

11.29.   Tucker J. held that the authority were entitled to find that the
applicant had no local connection. Family connections could be
interpreted as extending only as far as parents, adult children,
brothers or sisters. In the opinion of Tucker J., if the applicant
could not demonstrate a family connection then she could show
that she had special circumstances. Therefore, on these facts, her
relationship to the area could not amount to having a local
connection.

Other Special Circumstances

11.30.   The "other special circumstances" are left undefined. There is
no suggestion in the statute that the term be defined strictly
ejusdem generis with the other categories of local connection in
section 199(1). Examples of the "other special circumstances"
given in the Local Authority Agreement include families returned
to the United Kingdom after serving in the armed forces overseas
and returning to an area where the applicant was brought up.

11.31.   Other arguments made in this area have been connected with
cultural factors. For example, it was argued in *Smith and Hay* that
family members wished to live near a church which they fre-
quented. It was held that the authority was correct in concluding
that this did not, of itself, amount to a local connection.

11.32.   On the issue of cultural factors, *R. v. Westminster C.C., ex p.
Benniche*[14] the Court of Appeal considered the case of an applicant
who sought judicial review of the authority's decision that he and
his family did not have a local connection with the authority's
district. The applicant was a Muslim who expressed a wish to visit
the Central London Mosque every day as he had done before

---

[13] *The Times*, June 11, 1996.
[14] *The Times*, April 15, 1996.

moving into the district of another authority. He also wished to send his children to a particular Muslim school in the area. Shiemann L.J., giving the opinion of the court, found that in accordance with the test in *Betts*, the authority was entitled to find that the applicant did not have sufficient local connection with the authority's district.

As discussed above, the decision of Tucker J. in *R. v. Ham-* **11.33.** *mersmith and Fulham L.B.C., ex p. Avdic*[15] had ramifications for the definition of "special circumstances". In the opinion of Tucker J., if the applicant could not demonstrate a family connection then she could show that she had special circumstances. Therefore, on these facts, her relationship to the area could not amount to having a local connection.[16]

In *R. v. Slough B.C., ex p. Khan*,[17] K and his family lived in **11.34.** Rochdale, before they went to live in Slough with a relation, B. B went to Pakistan, leaving K in occupation of his home to look after it in his absence. The authority obtained a possession order at which point K applied to be housed. Following inquiries, the authority accepted that the family was not intentionally homeless but were of the view that the family had no local connection with the authority's area. Therefore, the authority sought to refer the issue to Rochdale M.B.C. The issue arose whether Slough had considered the racial harassment which the family had suffered before quitting the accommodation. Roger Toulson Q.C. held that the family had sufficient family connections with the district and also that the referral decision dealt only with the question of residence and was therefore defective.

Services Personnel

In deciding whether an applicant has a local connection it is **11.35.** important to remember that a person is not employed in a district if he is serving in the regular armed forces of the Crown.[18] In this regard "regular armed forces of the Crown" means the Royal Navy, the regular armed forces as defined by section 225 of the Army Act 1955, the regular air force as defined by section 223 of the Air Force Act 1955 and Queen Alexandra's Royal Naval Nursing Service.

---

[15] *The Times*, June 11, 1996.
[16] See also *R. v. Slough B.C., ex p. Khan* (1995) 27 H.L.R. 492 in this regard.
[17] (1995) 27 H.L.R. 492.
[18] Housing Act 1996, s. 199(2).

Referrals to other Local Housing Authorities

Powers of the Notifying Authority

11.36.　　The provisions relating to local connection enable referrals of applicants from one authority to another in the manner outlined above. The means by which this is done are set out in section 198 of the 1996 Act. Those referral provisions come into operation where the notifying housing authority are satisfied that the applicant is homeless, in priority need, is not intentionally homeless and that the specific requirements set out below are satisfied.[19]

11.37.　　In short, where there is no local connection between the applicant and the authority's area, the authority is entitled to notify a second authority that it considers that the applicant has a local connection with that second authority's area. Therefore, the local connection provisions exempt the authority which refers the applicant on ("the notifying authority") from an obligation to provide permanent accommodation for that applicant. The authority receiving the referral ("the notified authority") bears the burden of finding permanent accommodation for the applicant. The requirements are as follows: the applicant must have no local connection with the notifying authority; the applicant must have a local connection with the notified authority; and there must not be any risk of domestic violence in the district of the notified authority.

11.38.　　As a result, the local authority need not necessarily have any responsibility for housing the homeless person within its district. If an applicant is successfully referred, the only obligations borne by the notifying authority will be those relating to temporary accommodation. Rather, the notifying authority discharge their functions under the 1996 Act where they pass their homeless people to the notified authority to be housed by that notified authority.

Threatened with Homelessness

11.39.　　The referral provisions apply only in circumstances where the applicant is in fact homeless. Where the applicant is simply threatened with homelessness, it appears that the provisions will not exclude the notifying authority from its obligations to provide housing in those circumstances.

11.40.　　In Williams v. Exeter C.C.[20] the applicant applied for housing after an order for possession had been granted against her, but before that order for possession was executed against her. The

---

[19] s. 198(1).
[20] (1981) LAG Bulletin 287.

court order had been validly obtained but not served on the applicant. Therefore, it was held that she was only threatened with homelessness and not actually homeless at the time of the application. The local authority's obligations to her were consequently those set out in the precursor to section 195. However, on the facts it was found that the authority were not able to rely on the local connection provisions to deny her right to accommodation under the 1985 legislation.

Under section 175(4) "a person is threatened with homelessness **11.41.** if it is likely that he will become homeless within 28 days". While this is the statutorily provided period of time, it would appear that prudent policy on behalf of local authorities would be to take action as early as possible in relation to persons becoming homeless, rather than allowing the situation to drift within the 28 day period.

Section 195 of the 1996 Act applies where the local housing **11.42.** authority is satisfied that an applicant is threatened with homelessness and is eligible for assistance.[21] The authority are required to take reasonable steps to secure that some accommodation continues to be available for her occupation.[22] If the authority are satisfied that she has a priority need,[23] but do not consider that she became threatened with homelessness intentionally,[24] they are required to take reasonable steps to ensure that accommodation continues to be available for her occupation. It should, however, be noted that section 195(2) takes effect subject to the duty under section 197, (where other suitable accommodation is available).

Importantly, section 195(2) does not affect any right of the **11.43.** authority, whether by virtue of a contract, enactment or rule of law, to secure vacant possession of any accommodation.[25] The authority is at liberty to commence proceedings to recover possession, in spite of the broader context of actions under section 195.

The Mechanics of Referral to Another Authority

The referral provisions under section 198 come into operation **11.44.** where the notifying housing authority is required to find accommodation for an applicant who is homeless, in priority need and is

---

[21] Housing Act 1996, s. 195(1).
[22] s. 195(2).
[23] s. 195(2)(a).
[24] s. 195(2)(b).
[25] s. 195(3).

not intentionally homeless.[26] The authority are able to consider a
referral where they consider that all the conditions in the referral
provisions are met.

11.45.   If the notifying authority consider that the conditions are met
for referral of the case to a notified local housing authority, the
notifying authority may "notify that other authority of their
opinion". Thus, the notifying authority have the power to reach a
view on the local connection of an applicant. There is no standard
or burden of proof required to shore up that view. A local housing
authority are always susceptible to judicial review on grounds of
irrationality where they makes such a decision in contravention of
the *Wednesbury* principles.

11.46.   Importantly, the notifying authority need not consider whether
for the purposes of section 197 there is other suitable accommodation available for the applicant's use before proceeding under
section 198.[27] That is so whether it be accommodation within or
without the authority's area.

11.47.   The conditions for referral to another authority are that:

neither the applicant (nor any person who might reasonably be
expected to reside with the applicant) has a local connection
with the district of the authority to which the application was
made,[28]
the applicant (or a person who might reasonably be expected to
reside with the applicant) has a local connection with the
district of the notified authority,[29] and
neither the applicant (nor any person who might reasonably be
expected to reside with the applicant) will run the risk of
domestic violence in that other district,[30] or
the applicant was placed in accommodation in the district of the
authority to which his application is now made under Part VII
on a previous application, and the previous application was
within a prescribed period before the present application.[31]

The categories of person who have a local connection with a
local authority district are considered above. The prescribed period
will be a period specified by regulations.[32]

---

[26] s. 198(1).
[27] s. 198(1).
[28] s. 198(2)(a).
[29] s. 198(2)(b).
[30] s. 198(2)(c).
[31] s. 198(4).
[32] s. 215(1).

The power to refer is a discretionary power vested in the **11.48.**
notifying authority. It is therefore for the notifying authority to
exercise that power reasonably in accordance with the *Wednesbury*
guidelines. The remedies for any failure in the authority to
exercise their power in this way are discussed in Judicial Review in
Chapter 7, above. For example, where an irrelevant consideration
is taken into account, the authority cannot be said to have
exercised its power in a reasonable way. In *R. v. Newham L.B.C., ex
p. Tower Hamlets L.B.C.*[33] the Court of Appeal held that it was not
reasonable for the notifying authority to compare the housing
situation in Bangladesh, where the applicant had lived previously,
with that in its own area as part of its decision. The authority were
required to consider whether the applicant was in priority need,
not intentionally homeless, and had a local connection. Com-
parisons of housing situations were irrelevant to a decision on the
element set out in the statute.

Domestic Violence

In deciding whether or not an individual "runs the risk of **11.49.**
domestic violence" for the purposes of section 198(2)(c), there is
deemed to be such a risk where:

> "(a) he runs the risk of violence from a person with whom he
> is associated, or
> (a) he runs the risk of threats of violence from such a person
> which are likely to be carried out.[34]

This definition of domestic violence mirrors that in section 177
discussed above In Chapters 8 and 9. For the purposes of defining
whether a person is "homeless", section 177(1) provides that it is
not reasonable for a person to continue to occupy accommodation
if it is probable that this will lead to domestic violence against that
person, or against categories of prescribed persons. Therefore,
where an individual is the victim of domestic violence it is
considered not reasonable for a person to continue to occupy
accommodation. The result is that such a person is considered
homeless having accommodation where the domestic violence will
probably occur. For this purpose "domestic violence", in relation
to a person, means violence from a person with whom she is
associated, or threats of violence from such a person which are
likely to be carried out.[35]

The test of reasonableness is extended beyond the individual **11.50.**
homeless person. It is not reasonable for that person to continue to
occupy the accommodation if it is probable that a person who

---

[33] s. (1990) 23 H.L.R. 62.
[34] Housing Act 1996, s. 198(3).
[35] s. 177(1).

normally lives with him as a member of his family,[36] or any other person who might reasonably be expected to reside with him, bears the same risk of domestic violence.[37]

11.51.   Section 177(1) provides that an applicant is not to be considered as having available accommodation where it is probable that continued occupation will lead to domestic violence against him. As mentioned, the definition of "domestic violence" includes threats which are likely to be carried out. Therefore, it would appear that an applicant can produce evidence or testimony of threats coupled with a real expectation that they will be put into practice.

11.52.   The distinction between becoming intentionally homeless and leaving accommodation because it is unreasonable to continue to occupy it on grounds of expected domestic violence, is consequently problematic. In *R. v. Purbeck D.C., ex p. Cadney*[38] the applicant was the joint owner of the matrimonial home. She left her husband due to his violence and went to live with another man, D. D asked her to leave after three months. The applicant did not seek to return to the matrimonial home because she was frightened that her husband would resume his violence towards her. The applicant sought judicial review of the authority's decision that she was not required to be rehoused. Nolan J. held that the applicant had not attempted to gain access to the matrimonial home and therefore there was no direct evidence that she would suffer violence if she did attempt to gain access to the property. It was necessary for her to attempt to gain access or to adduce some evidence that the violence would be re-commenced. Consequently, the local housing authority could not be said to have made an error in failing to find that she was homeless.

11.53.   The position with reference to domestic violence is complicated throughout the Part VII regime by court decisions which require concrete evidence of something which is often based on nothing more tangible than fear. Applicants can only be confident of satisfying the tests where they can demonstrate they are the victims of abuse at the time of their applications. In tandem with the provisions of the Family Law Act 1996 relating to domestic violence, there is a need for consistency in decision-making so that those who are able to rely on the provisions of the Family Law Act 1996 are also able to succeed in their applications under Part VII of the Housing Act 1996.

---

[36] s. 177(1)(a).
[37] s. 177(1).
[38] [1986] F.L.R. 158.

The issue arises who will be a person associated with the **11.54.**
applicant in this context. The applicant will be associated with
anyone with whom she is married, where they are cohabitants or
former cohabitants; they live or have lived in the same household;
they are relatives; they have agreed to marry one another; or each
of them is a parent of a child dependent upon them or has had
parental responsibility for such a child.[39]

The Local Authority Agreement

In deciding whether the conditions for referring a case to **11.55.**
another authority are satisfied, that decision shall be made by
agreement between the notifying authority and the notified authority.[40] Where there is no such agreement reached, the decision is to
be made in accordance with such arrangements as the Secretary of
State may order.[41] This scheme of provisions led to the formation
of the Local Authority Agreement under the 1985 legislation.
There is no such agreement created yet with reference to the 1996
legislation — but it is reasonable to assume that the local
authorities will continue to apply the agreement and policies set
out under the former legislation until such a new document were
created.

An order made by the Secretary of State under section 198(5) **11.56.**
may direct that the arrangements shall be the arrangements agreed
by any relevant authorities or associations of relevant authorities.
Alternatively they may be any other arrangements which the
Secretary of State considers to be suitable, after consultation with
appropriate persons.[42] In any event, no such order can be made
unless a draft of the order has been approved by a resolution of
each House of Parliament.[43]

The provisions discussed above for referral of applications to a **11.57.**
different local housing authority, and the duties owed to an
applicant whose case is considered for referral or actually referred,
apply to applications referred by a local authority in Scotland in
pursuance of sections 33 and 34 of the Housing (Scotland) Act
1987, and to people whose applications are so transferred, in the
same way that they apply to cases arising under Part VII of the
1996 Act.[44]

[39] Housing Act 1996, s. 178.
[40] s. 198(5).
[41] s. 198(5).
[42] s. 198(6).
[43] s. 198(7).
[44] s. 201(1).

Obligations of Notified Authority

11.58.   The notified authority is required to assist the notifying authority. Thus, it is theoretically possible for obligations to reach the
notified authority where the notifying authority is simply attempting to move the responsibility from themselves. The notifying
authority, however, will always bear the risk of being found to have
acted irrationally.

11.59.   The authority or body which is notified and requested to
accommodate the applicant must co-operate in giving such assistance in effecting the request as is reasonable in the circumstances.[45] This obligation arises for the first time when one local
housing authority request another relevant housing authority or
body, in England, Wales or Scotland, to assist them in the
discharge of their functions under Part VII of the 1996 Act.
Alternatively, the referral can be made by means of a request to a
social services authority, in England, Wales or Scotland, to exercise
any of their functions in relation to a case which the local housing
authority are dealing with under Part VII.

11.60.   For these purposes the term "relevant housing authority or
body" means (in England and Wales) a local housing authority, a
new town corporation, a registered social landlord or a housing
action trust. In Scotland the expression includes a local authority,
a development corporation, a registered housing association or
Scottish Homes. All the expressions used are provided to bear the
same meaning as in the Housing Act 1985 and as in the Housing
(Scotland) Act 1987 respectively.

11.61.   It is expressly provided in section 213(3), that this obligation
applies to a request by a local authority in Scotland under section
38 of the Housing (Scotland) Act 1987 in the same way that it
applies to a request by a local housing authority in England and
Wales. The references to Part VII of the 1996 Act are to be
construed, in relation to such a request, as being references to Part
II of the 1987 Act.

Notification Process

11.62.   When the authority notify the applicant that they are referring
the application to another authority, they cease to have obligations
under a number of provisions in Part VII. They cease to be subject

[45] s. 213(1).

to any duty under section 188 (which provides for an interim duty to accommodate in a case of apparent priority need). Further, they are not subject to "the main housing duty" under section 193. However, the authority are required to secure that accommodation is available for occupation by the applicant until he is notified of the decision whether the conditions for referral of his case are met. These exemptions apply further to section 200(1), where a local housing authority notify the applicant that they intend to notify or have notified another local housing authority of their opinion that the conditions are met for the referral of his case to that other authority.

When the notifying authority have decided whether the condi- **11.63.** tions for referral are met, that notifying authority shall notify the applicant of the decision and inform him of the reasons for it.[46] The notice must also inform the applicant of his right to request a review of the decision and of the time within which such a request must be made.

Obligation where Conditions for Referral are Not Met

If it is decided that the conditions for referral are not met, the **11.64.** notifying authority must ensure that accommodation is available for occupation by the applicant until the authority have considered whether other suitable accommodation is available for his occupation in their district.[47] If they are satisfied that other suitable accommodation is available for his occupation in their district, section 197(2) applies; and if they are not so satisfied, they are subject to the duty under section 193 (the main housing duty). Where section 197(2) does apply, the local housing authority are required to provide the applicant with such advice and assistance as the authority consider is reasonably required to enable the applicant to secure accommodation. Where section 193 applies, the local authority are required to ensure that accommodation is available for occupation by the applicant.[48] This obligation arises in circumstances where the local housing authority are satisfied under section 193(1) that an applicant is homeless, eligible for assistance, has a priority need, and are not satisfied that he became homeless intentionally.

Further to section 200(5) the duty owed to an applicant under **11.65.** section 200(3) ceases even if the applicant requests a review of the authority's decision (see section 202). The authority may continue

[46] s. 200(2).
[47] s. 200(3).
[48] s. 193(2).

to secure that accommodation is available for the applicant's occupation pending the decision on a review.

Obligation where Conditions for Referral are Met

11.66. If the authority decides that the conditions for referral are met, the notified authority must ensure that interim accommodation is available for the applicant's occupation until they have considered whether other suitable accommodation is available for his occupation in its district.[49] If they are satisfied that other suitable accommodation is available for his occupation in their district, section 197(2) applies (as set out above); and if they are not so satisfied, they are subject to the duty under section 193 (the main housing duty, as set out above). The notifying authority then begins the process of referral to the notified authority as set out above.

11.67. Further to section 200(5) the duty owed to an applicant under section 200(4) ceases even if the applicant requests a review of the authority's decision (see section 202). The authority may continue to secure that accommodation is available for the applicant's occupation pending the decision on a review.

11.68. Any notice required to be given to an applicant under section 200 must be given in writing and, if not received by the applicant, must be treated as having been given to him if it is made available at the authority's office for a reasonable period for collection by him or on his behalf.[50]

The Resolution of Disputes

11.69. The term "arrangements" as set out in the legislation is required to be those arrangements which are agreed by the local housing authorities, or associations of local authorities. Where there is no such agreement made, it falls to the Secretary of State to reach a decision as to the arrangements which will be suitable in this context.

11.70. Therefore, the provisions for the resolution of disputes in this area are expected to result in the formation of the Local Authority Agreement. The status of the Local Authority Agreement is then problematic. It is probably correct to say that it operates as a guide to authorities who are required to reach agree but who wish to do

---

[49] s. 200(4).
[50] s. 200(6).

so without the need for formal arbitration or court proceedings. The Local Authority Agreement was therefore conceived to provide such a scheme of rules. A second such scheme was devised to cover the arbitration situation in purely Scottish or in cross-border disputes.

The Local Authority Agreement

The old Local Authority Agreement was revised in June 1979 in **11.71.** the light of experience of the first 18 months of operation of the 1977 Act. It is expected that it will be revised in the light of the new Code of Guidance as is indicated in para. 16.12. The 1996 Act sets out the four categories of local connection. Those requirements and the *Betts* decision, concerning the interpretation of those provisions are considered above. The Local Authority Agreement in its early stages provides that it is the finding of any local connection within the statute that is significant. An authority in receipt of an application is therefore required to consider it in this light. This is the case even though there might appear to be a stronger local connection with the area of another authority. Therefore, the authority are not allowed to avoid their responsibilities where there is some connection with its own area — even though that authority may consider that there is another authority which bears some greater local connection.

The Local Authority Agreement requires that the notified **11.72.** authority are required to make inquiries in any case referred to it. This is so even where it might have considered that the application should be the responsibility of another authority or where the notified authority does not consider that they bear an obligation to the applicant or the applicant's associates. The inquiries which the notified authority then makes may be requests of or questions to another local authority. The Local Authority Agreement does urge that such inquiries, if they are to be made, are made as soon as possible.

These provisions of the Local Authority Agreement are designed **11.73.** to consider the common situation where the applicant appears to have local connections with more than one authority. The Agreement therefore provides that the notifying authority ought to give due consideration to all the pertinent circumstances when trying to decide which authority should receive referral of the application. Such consideration should clearly encompass the four statutory categories of local connection.

In *McCall*, it was held that where the considerations appear to be **11.74.** evenly balanced, an arbitrator between authorities should consider the applicant's personal preferences. The arbitrator was also considered to be entitled to take into account the provisions of the Local Authority Agreement but that the applicant's wishes may displace this in a situation where the considerations are equally matched. In the context of a balanced spread of circumstances it was considered both reasonable "and within the spirit of the statutory provisions", for the arbitrator to have regard to the wishes of the family. It is worth mentioning that the Code of Guidance also provides that the wishes of the applicant are something to be taken into account in determining the appropriate authority with which to fix the local connection.

11.75.   The mechanics of the procedure require that there is a system within each authority for the receipt and dissemination of referrals and opinions. The Local Authority Agreement suggests that there be a unit within each authority for this purpose. More contentiously, the Agreement suggests that authorities to some extent must accept all statements of the facts of the case as stated by the notifying authority. The exception would be in cases where the notified authority had factual evidence of its own which rebutted those facts asserted by the notifying authority. However, where the notified authority does contend that it has evidence of its own, it is incumbent on the notifying authority to reconsider its opinion.

11.76.   The matter of reconsideration is discretionary in any case. The spirit of the Agreement is that there be some re-consideration in such circumstances. On the basis of whether or not to refer the position is more straightforward. There is another situation in which there are doubts as to the authority's opinion on the homelessness, priority need or intention of the applicant.

11.77.   Where the provisions of the Local Authority Agreement resolves the issue, it is submitted that it is incumbent on the notified authority or the notifying authority (as applicable) to provide accommodation for the applicant in accordance with the provisions discussed below in Chapter 13 "Obligations to House". Under the Local Authority Agreement there is a 14-days grace period in which the authority can make such arrangements. Clearly, the longer this process takes, the greater is the hardship on the applicants. Similarly, the Agreement makes provision for the payment of expenses involved in the situation where one authority accepts responsibility for the applicant. The date from which the duty to defray expenses arises may depend on the reasonableness of the lapse of time in reaching the decision.

Arbitration

In many situations, authorities will not consider it to be in their **11.78.** interests or within their responsibilities to house particular applicants. Therefore, provision is made in the Local Authority Agreement for authorities to go to arbitration to seek a resolution of their dispute. It is provided that authorities have 21 days from the date of notification of the referral in which to agree the issue, or to appoint a person to resolve the issue between them. Where there is no such agreement between the authorities, the notifying authority is required to report on the issue to the selected proper officer for such referrals. It is possible for the notified authority to make such a report if appropriate. The proper officer must then appoint an arbitrator in accordance with the Agreement.

There are provisions as to the identity of the proper officer in **11.79.** these circumstances. In relation to a non-metropolitan district council, the proper officer will be the chairperson of the A.D.C. in relation to a London Borough Council or to the Common Council of the City of London, or to the chairperson of the L.B.A. Where the issue concerns any other housing authority, the proper officer will be the chairperson of the A.M.A. The proper officer may nominate someone else if he is incapacitated or absent. A referee will be drawn from a panel agreed for these purposes by the A.D.C., A.M.A. and L.B.A.

In the situation where both of the authorities decide to report **11.80.** the issue, it is necessary for there to be two proper officers. The proper officer for the notifying authority is required to forward a copy of the report to the proper officer for the notified authority. This is the case even if the notified authority have refused to report directly to such a person before that time. It then falls to the two proper officers to decide who shall be the referee. Where they are unable to reach agreement on this point, they nominate a person each from the panel to be referee, and the proper officer for the notifying authority has the privilege of deciding by lot between the two persons so nominated.

When an appointment has been made, the proper officer for the **11.81.** notifying authority is obliged to notify both the notifying and the notified authority of the identity of the person who has been appointed. It does remain open to the authorities to reach an agreement on this issue between them even after this arbitration process has been commenced.

The referee is not required to consider matters which arose **11.82.** before the local connection issue. Therefore the referee need not consider issues of homelessness, priority need or intentional homelessness. The referee is required to invite the person to whom the notification relates to provide him with information and also to take into account any relevant oral or written representations made by the notifying authority and the applicant. The referee is entitled to take into account any representation made by any person where they are relevant.

11.83.   The situation which might arise is the following.[51] Where the applicant's mother had been living with the applicant and her husband for a while, the applicant and her husband having lived in Islington for a large part of their time as a married couple and had moved to Sunderland for a mixture of family and employment reasons. The mother then joined them in Sunderland. They later moved to Easington, the authority which received the applications in the first place. It was in Easington that the applicant's husband acquired a job with some accommodation. The husband was dismissed from that employment, at which time the applicant and her husband applied to the authority for accommodation under Part VII of the 1996 Act. Two days later, the applicant's mother also applied to Easington council.

11.84.   Assuming that the authority decided that they were homeless, in priority need and not intentionally homeless, Easington might take the view that there was no local connection with their area. Rather, they might be of the view that there was a local connection with both Sunderland and Islington. Where Sunderland and Islington both disagree with this opinion and the applicability of the local connection provisions, they would consider that all three of the applicants had acquired local connections with Easington. The referee would ultimately decide that responsibility lay with Sunderland.[52]

11.85.   The issue would arise as to whether there had been one or two applications made by the family. Where the referee operates on the basis that there have been separate applications by the applicant and her husband on the one hand, and by the mother on the other, the referee would conclude that the husband and wife would have local connections with both Islington and Sunderland together with the mother. However, the mother applying on her own would appear to have no local connection with Islington at all. This might therefore influence the referee's final decision to place responsibility on Sunderland.

---

[51] The facts for the following example are taken from the unreported case of *R. v. McCall, ex p. Eastbourne B.C.* which is discussed at (1981) 8 H.L.R. 48.
[52] In accordance with the decision in *R. v. McCall, ex p. Eastbourne B.C.*

The further issue would arise whether the referee should rely on **11.86.** the definition of local connection set out in the Local Authority Agreement or on the statutory rules. It has been held that the Agreement must be irrelevant to the arbitration. Once agreement has failed to be reached, and the matter goes before the referee, it is for him to apply the statutory provisions only.[53]

The correct view must be that, whether applications are made **11.87.** individually or together, the statutory provisions require consideration not only of the particular applicant but also of any person who might reasonably be expected to reside with her. The mother would self-evidently fall within that category in respect of the applicant and therefore her lack of local connection with Islington would be irrelevant.

Importantly, the referee is not obliged to notify the applicant of **11.88.** the decision. It is for the notifying authority to discharge this responsibility. Any decision of the referee will be open to judicial review proceedings. The notifying and notified authorities must pay their own costs of the arbitration. Despite this general principle it is open to the referee may make an order as to costs. The referee is also empowered to direct that the notifying or notified authority, or both of them, pay the travelling expenses of any applicant who has provided information orally where invited to do so by the referee. The general power to make a costs order is wide enough to order one authority to pay the costs of another, or pay the costs of any person, not only those of an applicant.

[53] *Ibid.*

CHAPTER 12

Intentional Homelessness

Introduction

12.01. The intentional homelessness provisions were created to prevent people in accommodation from leaving their occupation deliberately so that they could be re-housed automatically, thus putting a huge strain on local authorities' resources. Therefore, where an applicant has left accommodation intentionally, there is no duty to provide that applicant with permanent accommodation. Rather there are only limited duties to provide temporary accommodation and to provide advice and assistance, as discussed at Chapter 13, below.

12.02. Much of the litigation in the area of homelessness revolves around this area. The reason why this corner of the legislation has attracted so much attention is that it has been used by the local authorities, in many circumstances, to cap the numbers of people for whom they are obliged to find permanent accommodation. As such, a large body of case law has developed setting out the perameters within which a person will be found to be intentionally homeless.

The Definition of "intentionally homeless"

12.03. The core of the definition of intentional homelessness is set out in section 191(1) of the 1996 Act:

> "A person becomes homeless intentionally if he deliberately does or fails to do anything in consequence of which he ceases to occupy accommodation which is available for his occupation and which it would have been reasonable for him to continue to occupy".

Therefore, the test revolves around the applicant ceasing to occupy accommodation which was both available and reasonable for her to occupy, where that cessation of occupation is caused by some deliberate action or omission on her part. It is a central requirement that this act or omission is deliberate. An act or omission in good faith on the part of a person who was unaware of any relevant fact shall not be treated as deliberate.[1]

The authority is required to satisfy itself that all of the require- **12.04.** ments of the statute are satisfied before reaching a decision that the applicant is intentionally homeless. There is a five stage test. For the applicant to be intentionally homeless, the authority must be satisfied that:—

the applicant had deliberately done some act or omitted to do some thing;
loss of the accommodation had been in consequence of that act or omission;
there had been cessation of occupation and not failure to take up accommodation;
accommodation was available for the applicant's occupation;
it was reasonable for the applicant to continue to occupy that accommodation.

What Conduct?

The first issue is therefore the type of conduct which will lead **12.05.** an applicant to be considered intentionally homeless. There are clearly a number of acts which a person could do which would lead to her becoming homeless or which might contribute to the ultimate result of homelessness. What is necessary is to divide those acts which are considered to be important in reaching that decision and those acts which can be overlooked as not contributing to the applicant becoming intentionally homeless.

Deliberate Act

Section 191 of the 1996 Act provides that the applicant becomes **12.06.** intentionally homeless as the result of some deliberate act or omission. In considering the type of deliberate act that is appropriate, the case law has developed the following categories of situation as satisfying the test.

It is not necessary that the actions of the applicant were **12.07.** deliberately directed at securing eviction from the premises. The local housing authority is required to demonstrate only that the act

---

[1] Housing Act 1996, s. 191(2).

itself was a voluntary and intentional act. There is no need to show an intention linking the act with being wishing to be evicted. Thus in *R. v. Slough B.C., ex p. Ealing L.B.C.*,[2] the Court of Appeal considered the situation in which the Lynch family had been evicted from accommodation on the basis that they were in rent arrears. Mr Lynch had applied to Slough for accommodation but Slough decided that the Lynch family were intentionally homeless. The Lynch family lived in Hillingdon with friends but the premises became overcrowded within the statutory definition of overcrowding. Hillingdon found that the Lynch family were not homeless but that they had no local connection with Hillingdon. Therefore, the matter was remitted to Slough. The Court of Appeal held that it was open to the authority to find that the applicant had become intentionally homeless without deliberately seeking to be made homeless. It is enough that the act resulting in homelessness was intended; there is no requirement that its purpose was to lead to homelessness.

12.08.   The approach which has been taken in many of the lower courts has been that of an objective view of whether or not the acts were deliberate. In *Robinson v. Torbay B.C.*,[3] H.H. Judge Goodhall held that the test for deciding whether or not acts were deliberate should be dealt with on the following lines:

> "I think that if a man has been evicted then . . . he became homeless intentionally if the fair-minded bystander could say to himself "He asked for it" . . . if his conduct is such as to drive his landlord to evict him, and if the fair-minded bystander could say of the person evicted, "Well I'm very sorry but he asked for it"."

12.09.   The Court of Appeal adopted this approach in *R. v. Salford C.C., ex p. Devenport.*[4] The applicants were council tenants. A petition was delivered to the council signed by 237 other tenants protesting that they be removed from the estate due to the assaults, vandalism and violence caused by their children. The council contended that the applicants were intentionally homeless as a result of failing to control their children. The applicants contended that the authority were required to show that the applicants had taken a deliberate decision not to control their children. The Court of Appeal held that the authority's decision had plainly been based on the parents' lack of control. Furthermore, the applicants had been issued with

---

[2] [1981] Q.B. 801.
[3] [1982] 1 All E.R. 726 at 730.
[4] (1983) 82 L.G.R. 89.

warnings that they would be evicted if they failed to exercise control over their children. Therefore, the parents were held to be intentionally homeless.

This solution is more problematic when it is applied to those **12.10.** applicants who have learning difficulties, or who are suffering from mental illness or disability. Using an objective test in these circumstances might fail to take into account the particular distinguishing factors of the applicant's own case. For example, a parent suffering from physical disability in facts similar to those in *Devenport* might be unable to restrain children despite any number of official warnings from the council. Applying the same objective criteria might work injustice in that circumstance and fail to tackle the real problem. Where there are criminal offences being committed by children, that is correctly a juvenile criminal justice matter more than a housing matter.

Involuntarily Deliberate Acts

One particularly acute example of the phenomenon of non- **12.11.** deliberate action would be the acts of drug addicts. This is particularly so where the actions complained of are failure to pay rent or mortgage arrears. Those addicted to controlled substances lose much of their self-control and self-determination. To an objective test, it might appear that a drug addict brings eviction upon himself by anti-social behaviour and failure to pay rent. However, this takes no account of the medical and potentially psychological needs of the occupant. The broader issue of taking a vulnerable and problematic member of the population and adding to their disadvantage by categorising them as intentionally homeless, does nothing to solve the root of the problem.

In the unreported case of *R. v. Westminster C.C., ex p. Fellowes*[5] a **12.12.** person addicted to heroin who used rent money to buy heroin was held to have performed a deliberate act in spending that money other than on rent and was therefore found to have become homeless intentionally. A distinction was drawn in that case between an action being performed deliberately and there being some fault. In the High Court's opinion, the applicant's act was deliberate — it was not necessary to demonstrate fault for the "authority to conclude rationally that the applicant has deliberately put herself in such circumstances that . . . she could not pay her rent".

---

[5] Unreported (July 19, 1994).

Examples of such Deliberate Acts

12.13.   "Nuisance or annoyance". The first category is where the applicant (or some person connected with the applicant) causes some nuisance or annoyance leading to her losing the accommodation. In circumstances where the applicant's actions have provoked or caused eviction from the accommodation, the applicant has been held to have become intentionally homeless (see for example *R. v. Hammersmith and Fulham L.B.C. ex p. P*[6]; *Afan B.C. v. Marchant.*[7] In *ex p. P*, the applicant had become subject to IRA death threats as a result of his continued actions. This led to his loss of the accommodation. The High Court found that he had become intentionally homeless on the basis that his deliberate actions had caused his loss of the accommodation.

12.14.   Anti-social behaviour, as in the *Devenport* case, will tend to point towards a deliberate act which leads to loss of accommodation. In such a case there would generally be evidence of such behaviour in the proceedings to recover possession of the accommodation occupied formerly by the applicant.

12.15.   "Spending rent/mortgage money". The most common head of "deliberate act" is failure to pay the rent or the mortgage arrears. Particularly in cases of alcoholism or drug addiction where there is a compulsion to spend the money properly owed in rent, the issue arises whether that action is deliberate. There is a conceptual distinction to be made between those who are unable to pay and those who simply refuse to pay rent or mortgage payments.[8]

12.16.   As set out above, for an act to be deliberate it does not need to be performed by someone in full possession of their faculties. Therefore, in the unreported case of *R. v. Westminster C.C., ex p. Fellowes*[9] a person addicted to heroin who used rent money to buy heroin was held to have performed a deliberate act in spending that money otherwise than on the rent. Consequently, she was found to have become intentionally homeless. In the High Court's opinion, it was open to the "authority to conclude rationally that the applicant has deliberately put herself in such circumstances that . . . she could not pay her rent".

12.17.   A distinction is drawn in the Code of Guidance between a person who is forced to sell their home because they are unable to keep paying the rent or because they get into mortgage arrears, and

---

[6] (1989) 22 H.L.R. 21.
[7] (1980) January LAG Bulletin 15.
[8] This approach was approved in *R. v. Wandsworth L.B.C., ex p. Hawthorne* (1994) 27 H.L.R. 59.
[9] Unreported (July 19, 1994).

a person who sells a home in circumstances where there is no real risk of losing that home.

Alternatively, the central distinction is probably to be drawn 12.18. with a person whose wilful refusal to pay rent or mortgage instalments and a person who is genuinely unable to make those payments, and is therefore forced to leave the home. Many cases will fall into a category where the applicant did not deliberately withhold payments with a view to being made homeless. A liberal view was taken of this issue by Lord Denning in obiter remarks in *R. v. Slough B.C., ex p. Ealing L.B.C.*[10] Lord Denning held that the applicants fell into arrears with their rent, however while "[t]heir non-payment of rent was deplorable . . . it may not have been deliberate in the sense required by [section 191]. The family did not do it deliberately so as to get turned out . . ."

The authorities subsequently have taken a stricter line in this 12.19. area. The word "deliberate" has been held to exclude only accidental acts or omissions (as in *Held and Robinson v. Torbay B.C.*[11]). Consequently, the applicants cannot argue that, because they did not set out to become homeless, their act was not "deliberate" within section 191.

In *Devenport*, the Court of Appeal held that it was not necessary 12.20. to demonstrate that the applicant acted deliberately so as to be evicted from the former accommodation. In *Robinson*, it was held that an applicant is deemed to be homeless where he:

"deliberately does an act the reasonable result of which is his eviction, and the act is in fact the cause of his eviction . . . even though he did not appreciate that it would be the cause. Similarly, if a person deliberately does an act and eviction is the likely result of what he deliberately does, then he becomes threatened with homelessness intentionally, even though he may not have appreciated that it would be the likely result. . . It is not necessary to show that the tenant deliberately did something intending to get himself turned out. That seems to me contrary to the language of [section 191]. The word deliberately . . . governs only the act or omission . . ."

The decision of Kennedy J. in *R. v. Hillingdon L.B.C., ex p.* 12.21. *Tinn*[12] sets out a potentially liberal principle that it cannot be reasonable for a person to continue to occupy accommodation

[10] [1981] Q.B. 801.
[11] [1982] 1 All E.R. 726.
[12] (1988) 20 H.L.R. 305.

which is beyond her financial means. Thus, if an applicant would have been required to suffer some deprivation to their normal standard of living, it is not unreasonable to quit that accommodation. The types of deprivation which were envisaged included going without food, clothing, heating, transport and other such essentials. Further, it has been held in *R. v. Wandsworth L.B.C., ex p. Hawthorne*[13] that the authority as part of their inquiries must ask an applicant whether loss of the accommodation was caused by financial hardship leading to failure to pay rent. The authority is then entitled to come to a decision on the basis of these facts: (*R. v. Shrewsbury B.C., ex p. Griffiths*[14]; *R. v. Islington L.B.C, ex p. Bibi*,[15] as above).

12.22.   Persistent non-payment of rent and persistent failure to pay mortgage arrears have been held to be deliberate in the circumstance of non-payment of rent: (*R. v. Eastleigh B.C., ex p. Beattie (No. 2))*.[16] However, where the applicant mistakenly believed that such payments were in fact being met, then he was not intentionally homeless: (White v. Exeter C.C.).[17]

12.23.   It is incumbent on the authority to attempt to find out why the arrears of rent or mortgage payments have arisen. Failure to consider a relevant explanation will lead to a decision being quashed: (*R. v. Wyre B.C., ex p. Joyce).*[18]

12.24.   **"Moving accommodation".** Moving from settled accommodation into unsettled accommodation is something which might lead to the applicant being found to be intentionally homeless. The issue of mistake in this context is clearly important. Where an applicant mistakenly believes that she had a further period of one year to run on her tenancy, she will not be homeless intentionally when she is evicted from that accommodation: (*R. v. Christchurch, ex p. Conway).*[19] There is a distinction between an honest belief and reckless belief (such as turning a blind eye to the facts). Only the former will exclude the applicant from being intentionally homeless: (*R. v. Hammersmith and Fulham L.B.C., ex p. Lusi*[20]; *R. v. City of Westminster, ex p. Ali and Bibi).*[21] This issue is discussed further below.

[13] (1994) 27 H.L.R. 59.
[14] (1993) 25 H.L.R. 613.
[15] *The Times*, July 10, 1996.
[16] (1984) 17 H.L.R. 168.
[17] (1981) December LAG Bulletin 287.
[18] (1983) 11 H.L.R. 73.
[19] (1987) 19 H.L.R. 238.
[20] (1991) 23 H.L.R. 460.
[21] (1992) 25 H.L.R. 109.

"Pregnancy". There is no suggestion that becoming pregnant **12.25.** can constitute a means by which a person becomes intentionally homeless. It is possible for a pregnant woman to be intentionally homeless but the pregnancy, of itself, cannot be the cause. For example, where accommodation is unsuitable for a pregnant woman, the fact of pregnancy cannot be the factor which makes that woman intentionally homeless: (see, *Re Islam*[22]; also *R. v. Eastleigh B.C., ex p. Beattie (No. 1)*[23]).

"Loss of tied accommodation". In circumstances where the **12.26.** applicant has some employment which provides accommodation, the difficult issue arises whether the applicant is intentionally homeless in circumstances where that employment comes to an end.

There is a preliminary question as to whether or not the **12.27.** accommodation was lost as a "consequence" of the loss of employment. This is factual matter which would depend on the link between employment and occupation. The issue of the causal link between the act and loss of accommodation is discussed above.

One good example of this problem is the case of *R. v. Thurrock* **12.28.** *B.C., ex p. Williams*[24] where a publican was dismissed by his employer for irregularities connected to stock control and secret profits. The publican denied all of these charges. He was resident at the public house which he managed as part of his employment. The publican pursued the dismissal appeal procedure with the assistance of his union representative. Part way through the proceedings, his employer offered him the choice between resigning and being dismissed. The publican chose to resign. He therefore lost his accommodation. Then, he applied for accommodation on the grounds that he was homeless. The authority took the view that he had become homeless intentionally. The authority decided that the accommodation was reasonable for the publican to continue to occupy and that it had been available for his occupation. The authority viewed the letter of resignation as causing intentional homelessness but also considered that the publican would have been intentionally homeless in any event if he was dismissed.

A distinction was made between situations in which the appli- **12.29.** cant loses his job as a result of incompetence spread over a period of time and the situation where the applicant loses his job because

[22] [1983] 1 A.C. 688.
[23] (1983) 10 H.L.R. 134.
[24] (1982) 1 H.L.R. 129.

of a one-off deliberate act such as resignation. Where someone's action is spread over a period of time in cases such as incompetence, it is said by the court to lack the quality of a deliberate act because there is a lack of the necessary intention.

12.30.   In *R. v. Thanet D.C., ex p. Reeve*[25] the employee worked for a car-hire firm and lived over the premises. She lived with a man whom she told her employers was not disqualified from driving. In fact he had been disqualified from driving and therefore her employers sacked her. She applied to the authority to be rehoused on grounds of homelessness. The authority reached the decision that she had become homeless as a result of a deliberate act: the mis-statement to her employers. The authority's investigation had concluded that she had been dismissed as a result of a deliberate act of misconduct—although this was still in doubt at the time of the hearing. Nevertheless the court held that this case came close to borderline of intentional homelessness. The acid test for the authority would be whether the employment was lawfully terminated and therefore there must be some conduct on the part of the applicant which made it reasonable for the employer to terminate the employment.

12.31.   *Jennings v. Northavon D.C.*[26] concerned a family which quit secure council accommodation let to the applicant to move into accommodation in connection with his employment. Subsequently, the applicant gave notice terminating his employment. He applied to the authority for housing. The authority decided that he was intentionally homeless on the basis that he left secure accommodation for less secure accommodation. The intentional homelessness here was held to exist as a result of the combination of moving to less secure accommodation and resigning from employment.[27]

12.32.   Where a woman leaves a relationship and moves in with another man, and then leaves the second relationship when it breaks down, the issue arises whether or not she is intentionally homeless. In *Hunt*[28] it was held that her decision to leave secure accommodation and move into less secure accommodation constituted a deliberate act which made her intentionally homeless. This was despite her contention that the second relationship constituted an intervening act because she had intended to live there permanently. The court

---

[25] (1981) 6 H.L.R. 31.
[26] (1981) December LAG Bulletin 287.
[27] See also *Goddard v. Torridge D.C.*, (1981) December LAG Bulletin 287.
[28] *R. v. East Herts D.C., ex p. Hunt* (1986) 18 H.L.R. 51, Q.B.D.

held that the authority was entitled to apply an objective view of the circumstances and take the view that the arrangement was a transient and intermediary one.

In *R. v. Portsmouth C.C., ex p. Knight*[29] the applicant had **12.33.** occupied accommodation as part of his employment with a wine merchant. He was dismissed and left the accommodation before his employer obtained a possession order. The authority argued that he was intentionally homeless. Woolf J. held that the applicant had become a trespasser from the time he lost his employment and therefore it was not reasonable for the authority to decide that he was intentionally homeless.

There is some reason to think that in making inquiries where a **12.34.** member of the family unit is claiming not to have been part of that decision to become intentionally homeless, there is a need for the applicant to discharge a presumption of involvement in the decision (see *R. v. North Devon D.C., ex p. Lewis*).[30] However, the authority will be required to examine the circumstances of each relationship in turn to see whether or not the applicant in fact had any option but to acquiesce (see *R. v. Tower Hamlets L.B.C., ex p. Khatun*[31]).

"Emergency". In *R. v. Walsall M.B.C., ex p. Price*[32] P was **12.35.** served with an order for possession on grounds of non-payment of rent and non-compliance with tenancy conditions. The council wished to demolish the houses in P's street and therefore demolished the properties either side of P's accommodation. P's accommodation was therefore exposed to damp, rodent infestation and an accumulation of sewerage. P was evicted and applied to be housed on grounds of homelessness. P was found not to be homeless. Judicial review was sought on the basis that insufficient inquiries were made and that the council should have considered what caused P to become homeless in the first place. P contended that his situation should have been considered to be an emergency. Harrison J. held that the officer had failed to inquire into the demolition and therefore had failed to make adequate inquiries.[33] The term "emergency" must refer to something urgent and not an accumulation of events over time. Therefore, the gradual accretion of events in this case could not constitute an emergency.

[29] (1983) 10 H.L.R. 115.
[30] [1981] 1 W.L.R. 328.
[31] (1993) 27 H.L.R. 344.
[32] Unreported (September 7, 1996).
[33] See in this context *Bayani* [1991] C.L.Y. 1987.

Omission

12.36.   Section 191 of the 1996 Act provides that the applicant becomes intentionally homeless as the result of some deliberate act or omission. In considering the type of deliberate act that is appropriate, the case law has developed the following categories of situation as satisfying the test.

12.37.   **"Failure to pay rent or mortgage interest".**   As set out above under "Spending the Rent Money", the attitude of the courts and of the authorities in bringing litigation is that the applicants have performed a deliberate act in circumstances where the rent money or the mortgage interest has been frittered away on other things. This activity has not generally been dealt with by the courts as an omission to pay the rent. Contending that it fell within the category omission would remove the need to argue that it was a deliberate choice to act but rather a decision not to do something.

Mistake as to Relevant Fact

12.38.   Where the applicant was ignorant of the outcome of her actions or of a set of circumstances, then she will not be intentionally homeless. There is clearly a narrow line between a mistake as to fact and a mistake as to law. In circumstances where a woman believed her husband's assertions that they would be re-housed under a union agreement, she was found to have been labouring under a mistake of fact rather than law: (*R. v. Mole Valley D.C., ex p. Burton*).[34] Such a mistake must be in good faith to escape the categorisation of intentional homelessness.[35]

12.39.   In *R. v. Christchurch B.C., ex p. Conway*,[36] a woman believed that she had 12 months within which to decide whether or not to renew her shorthold tenancy. In fact, she did not have this 12 month period in which to decide. It was held that her mistake in thinking she had this time meant that she was not intentionally homeless when she was forced to leave her accommodation at the end of the shorthold tenancy. It was held that her mistake was a mistake of fact, as to the time in which she could decide to extend the tenancy, rather than a mistake as to the legal effect of the tenancy agreement.

12.40.   Where there has been legal advice given to the applicant that failure to pay mortgage instalment would not be a deliberate act, persistent failure to do so was held to be a deliberate act. Under

[34] (1988) 20 H.L.R. 479.
[35] Housing Act 1996, s. 191(2).
[36] (1987) 19 H.L.R. 238.

section 60(3) of the 1985 Act, ignorance of a material fact did not cover ignorance of the law and therefore the applicant was intentionally homeless, as in *R. v. Eastleigh B.C., ex p. Beattie (No. 2)*.[37] There is no reason to suppose that that interpretation should not subsist.

The issue of good faith is important here. The applicant must be **12.41.** able to show that she genuinely believed her account of the facts. A genuine belief, even in the face of direct evidence to the contrary, which had been presented to the applicant personally, will be sufficient.[38] A distinction must be drawn between a genuine belief and a mere hope. In *R. v. Ealing L.B.C., ex p. Sukhija*,[39] where the applicant had come to England in the hope of finding work and accommodation, it was held that she was intentionally homeless. On the authorities it appears to be the difference between Dorothy in the *Wizard of Oz* knowing she has a home in Kansas and simply following the Yellow Brick Road. Similarly, being incompetent or a fool will not make an applicant intentionally homeless, provided it is done in good faith.[40] However, acting so recklessly as to be unreasonable will lead to a finding of intentional homelessness. Therefore, where the applicant has made misrepresentations on the acquisition of a mortgage, she will not be found to have acted in good faith and therefore will have became homeless intentionally.[41]

There is a distinction between an honest belief and reckless **12.42.** belief (such as turning a blind eye to the facts). Only the former will exclude the applicant from being intentionally homeless.[42] For example, where an applicant genuinely believes that accommodation will still be available for her occupation after three years absence, then she will not be intentionally homeless.[43]

Mistake as to Legal Effect

Where there has been legal advice given to the applicant that **12.43.** failure to pay mortgage instalment would not be a deliberate act, persistent failure to do so was held to be a deliberate act. Ignorance

---

[37] (1984) 17 H.L.R. 168 (see also *R. v. Croydon L.B.C., ex p. Toth* (1988) 20 H.L.R. 576)

[38] *Wincentzen v. Monklands D.C.* 1988 S.L.T. 259.

[39] (1994) 26 H.L.R. 726.

[40] *R. v. Winchester C.C., ex p. Ashton* (1991) 24 H.L.R. 48; *R. v. Exeter C.C., ex p. Tranckle* (1993) 26 H.L.R. 244; *R. v. Westminster C.C., ex p. Obeid, The Times*, July 16, 1996.

[41] *R. v. Wandsworth L.B.C., ex p. Onwudiwe* (1994) 26 H.L.R. 302. As in *R. v. Barnet L.B.C., ex p. Rughooputh* (1993) 25 H.L.R. 607.

[42] *R. v. Hammersmith and Fulham L.B.C., ex p. Lusi* (1991) 23 H.L.R. 460; *R. v. City of Westminster, ex p. Ali and Bibi* (1992) 25 H.L.R. 109.

[43] *R. v. Tower Hamlets L.B.C., ex p. Rouf* (1991) 23 H.L.R. 460.

of a material fact did not cover ignorance of the law and therefore the applicant was intentionally homeless: (*Beattie (No. 2)* as above).

12.44. **"Failure to exercise remedy".** As part of making a mistake as to the legal effect of a set of circumstances, there is the possibility that the applicant does not realise that there is a remedy available for her use which she fails to use, leading to her becoming homeless. For example, where a tenant fails to take proceedings to enable her to re-enter leased premises or where a spouse (or other co-habitee) does not use family law legislation remedies which are available to her.

12.45. In the former category, a person is homeless in circumstances where she cannot secure entry to property which is available for her occupation. Most commonly this is property which was occupied by persons who have become the victims of unlawful eviction. Similarly, there might be a risk of violence to the applicant where she attempts to re-enter property from which she has been unlawfully evicted.

12.46. The issue is, therefore, whether the applicant is required to exhaust these remedies before she is found to be homeless. It would appear that the answer would depend upon the circumstances of any case. Where a spouse faces a real risk of continued domestic violence, it would appear to be unreasonable to require her to effect re-entry to the premises given those risks. However, it might be reasonable for her to take action to exclude the abusive spouse from the property.

Arrangements

12.47. The alteration in the definition of intentional homelessness to include arrangements whereby a person becomes homeless is the major change in this area of the legislation from the 1985 Act. The purpose of the legislation is to capture arrangements which are intended to make a person fit within the definition of homeless, so that a housing authority acquires some duty towards them under Part VII. The test set out above is extended by section 191(3) to include further situations in which a person is to be treated as becoming homeless intentionally. The two situations are where:

> the applicant enters into an arrangement under which he is required to cease to occupy accommodation which it would have been reasonable for him to continue to occupy, and
> the purpose of the arrangement is to enable him to become entitled to assistance under this Part VII.

It is a further requirement that there is no other good reason why she is homeless.[44] As set out above, this is aimed to preclude

[44] Housing Act 1996, s. 191(3).

deliberate abuse of the obligations imposed on local authorities under the 1996 Act.

The statute intends to prevent the situation in which an applicant engineers a situation in which she is homeless. Thus an applicant might enter into some arrangement whereby accommodation is no longer made available for her occupation, with the result that she appears to be homeless within the meaning of Part VII. **12.48.**

Failure to Find Accommodation

The issue arises where someone applies for housing and is given assistance in finding other accommodation but fails to do so. The approach of the statute is that an applicant is to be considered intentionally homeless if she fails to find suitable accommodation after being given advice. Therefore, under section 191(4) an applicant who has been given advice or assistance to find accommodation,[45] but fails to secure suitable alternative accommodation will be considered to be homeless intentionally where it was reasonable to expect that she would find such accommodation. **12.49.**

This provision is a new inclusion in the 1996 Act which was not present in the 1985 Act. The authority must be satisfied that there is other suitable accommodation in its area which is available for her occupation. **12.50.**

What is not expressed anywhere in Part VII is the extent to which the advice provided by the authority must have been useful. In penalising an applicant for having received advice or assistance and then failing to find accommodation, this would appear to involve some logically anterior question that the advice or assistance was conducive to the applicant finding accommodation at all. Section 191(4) provides that the circumstances must be such that it could reasonably be expected that the applicant would have found accommodation. Therefore, an applicant could contend that unsatisfactory advice or assistance did not lead to the applicant being intentionally homeless under section 191(4). **12.51.**

The issue arises how the homeless person is to find accommodation. What is also unclear is the set of circumstances in which an applicant is then entitled to make a further application for housing under Part VII, or how far the "stigma" of this failure to find **12.52.**

---

[45] *E.g.*, under s. 197 (duty where other suitable alternative accommodation available).

accommodation is said to attach to the applicant. The issue of the possibility of future application is considered.

Conduct by Whom?

12.53.   The issue arises, by whom the conduct must be done. While concentration has focused on the applicant thus far, it is open under the 1996 Act for those with whom the applicant might reasonably be expected to reside to apply for housing also. Therefore, the question arises whether the people with whom the applicant could reasonably be expected to reside could be the ones who commit those acts which lead to the finding of intentional homelessness. There is also the question of multiple applications from one family where the first applicant is found to be intentionally homeless. It would appear that all the family have a theoretical right to apply for housing where the family loses accommodation.

Acquiescence

12.54.   The doctrine of acquiescence is problematical in this context. In what circumstances will one person allowing another to behave in a particular way impact upon a finding that they are intentionally homeless themselves? Where a couple cease to live together and the husband seeks a surrender of the accommodation, to which his wife had always objected, then his wife will not be considered to be intentionally homeless with regard to that shared accommodation: (*R. v. Penwith D.C., ex p. Thomas*).[46] In *R. v. Cardiff C.C., ex p. Thomas*,[47] a man was held to have acquiesced in conduct by his partner which caused annoyance and nuisance. As a result of her conduct, they lost their accommodation. The man did not attend the hearing nor had he attempted to stop his wife's conduct. Woolf J. held that he had therefore acquiesced in it.

12.55.   Circumstances in which co-habitees will not have acquiesced are cases where the applicant did not know of the circumstances leading to loss of the accommodation (as in *R. v. East Northamptonshire D.C., ex p. Spruce*[48]), or were not living with their partner at the time of the action (as in *R. v. Penwith D.C., ex p. Thomas*[49]). This will be the case unless there is evidence that the

---

[46] (1983) 9 H.L.R. 64.
[47] (1983) 9 H.L.R. 64.
[48] (1988) 20 H.L.R. 508.
[49] (1983) 9 H.L.R. 64.

applicant has in fact had some knowledge of the conduct and either connived in it or ignored it.[50] The court will be required to examine the circumstances of each relationship in turn to see whether or not the applicant in fact had any option but to acquiesce.[51]

It is not solely circumstances of marriage where these rules **12.56.** apply. Parent are also liable for the acts of their children.[52] Where the acts of children cause the eviction of the whole family, the authority is required to consider the responsibility of each parent individually in that circumstance.[53]

In a further context, a licensor may be held liable for the actions **12.57.** of a licensee and thereby to have acquiesced in becoming intentionally homeless. In *R. v. Cardiff C.C., ex p. John*[54] the applicant had given permission to a third party to occupy her accommodation. That third party had caused such nuisance at times when she was out of the premises that she was evicted. The court held that she had acquiesced in this behaviour by not removing the licensee from the premises.

Multiple Applications

Where there are applications from a number of people who are **12.58.** members of the same family, the authority are required to consider each application separately. The issue of multiple applications was considered in *R. v. North Devon D.C., ex p. Lewis*[55] where a man lost his employment and therefore lost the tied employment which came with it at the same time. The authority considered that they needed only to consider the single application on behalf of the entire family unit rather than separate applications from individual family members. The issue revolved, in the opinion of the court, around the question whether or not each of those separate applicants were parties to the decision to quit the tied accommodation. Where a family member was not a party to the decision to become intentionally homeless, she would not be intentionally homeless herself.

---

[50] *R. v. Barnet L.B.C., ex p. O'Connor* (1990) 22 H.L.R. 486; *R. v. Ealing L.B.C., ex p. Salmons* (1990) 23 H.L.R. 272.

[51] *R. v. Tower Hamlets L.B.C., ex p. Khatun* (1993) 27 H.L.R. 344.

[52] *R. v. Salford C.C., ex p. Devenport* (1983) 8 H.L.R. 54; *R. v. Southampton C.C., ex p. Ward* (1984) 14 H.L.R. 114; *Smith v. Bristol C.C.* ((1981) December LAG Bulletin 287).

[53] *R. v. East Hertfordshire D.C., ex p. Bannon* (1986) 18 H.L.R. 515.

[54] (1982) 9 H.L.R. 56.

[55] [1981] 1 W.L.R. 328.

12.59. There may be factual situations in which the court is entitled to consider that the applicant has agreed to the conduct which has led to the loss of accommodation and the intentional homelessness.[56] For example, where a wife takes no action to prevent her husband from spending all of the rent money on drink, the Court of Appeal has held that she too was intentionally homeless.[57] Even where the couple had continued to live together, but the applicant played no part in the course of action which led to the loss of accommodation, the applicant would not be considered to become homeless intentionally.[58] Where the couple have ceased to live together at the time of the conduct, it is possible that the applicant spouse will be considered not to have been a party to the conduct which led to the loss of accommodation (as held in *R. v. London Borough of Ealing, ex p. Sidhu*[59]; and also *R. v. Penwith D.C., ex p. Thomas*[60]).

In Consequence

12.60. It is a requirement of section 191 that the homelessness must be "in consequence" of the applicant becoming homeless intentionally. There is, therefore, a requirement for a causal link between the deliberate act or omission and the ensuing homelessness. The question may therefore be linking an act which occurs before the homelessness results and deciding, as a matter of fact, whether the two are joined.

12.61. The notion of consequence was considered in cases such as *Dyson v. Kerrier D.C.*[61] and *Din v. Wandsworth L.B.C.*[62] The most common problem is satisfying those cases' requirement of "cause and effect" in the case of homelessness. There is often a time lag between the deliberate action which caused the homelessness and the time of the application. The applicant will seek to demonstrate that the stigma of intent has been removed by some intervening action.

---

[56] *R. v. Woodspring D.C., ex p. Walters* (1984) 16 H.L.R. 73; *R. v. Reigate and Banstead D.C., ex p. Paris* (1984) H.L.R. 103.
[57] *R. v. Nottingham C.C., ex p. Caine* (1995) 28 H.L.R. 374.
[58] *R. v. Eastleigh B.C., ex p. Beattie (No.2)* (1984) 17 H.L.R. 168. See also *R. v. West Dorset D.C., ex p. Phillips* (1985) 17 H.L.R. 336; *R. v. Mole Valley D.C., ex p. Burton* (1988) 20 H.L.R. 479.
[59] (1982) 2 H.L.R. 45 applying *Lewis*.
[60] (1983) 9 H.L.R. 64.
[61] [1980] 1 W.L.R. 1206.
[62] [1983] 1 A.C. 657.

The Statutory Test

Section 191 provides that "A person becomes homeless inten- **12.62.** tionally if he deliberately does or fails to do anything in consequence of which he ceases to occupy accommodation which is available for his occupation and which it would have been reasonable for him to continue to occupy".[63]

It should perhaps be noted that the statute provides that all the **12.63.** verbs are expressed in the present tense, except for the test of reasonableness. Therefore, intentional homelessness is expressed as a process of evolution, of "becoming homeless". This suggests that a person can alter their status (that is: becoming intentionally homeless) as a result of an accumulation of circumstances where she fails to do something and ceases to occupy accommodation. At the time of the cessation, the occupation must be available for her occupation. However, the test of reasonableness is phrased in the conditional: "would have been". This suggests that it need not have been reasonable at the time of cessation of occupation on a literal reading of the words.

The issue is whether the applicant is able to occupy accommo- **12.64.** dation between the time when the intention arose and the homelessness occurred. The use of the words "a person becomes homeless intentionally" in section 191 suggests that the homelessness need not occur contemporaneously with the formation of the intention. However, the use of the present tense ". . . if he deliberately does or fails to do anything in consequence of which he ceases to occupy accommodation . . ." simply implies that the deliberate act or omission and the cessation of occupation happen at some time after the act and the consequential cessation of occupation. The words suggest only that the act/omission and the cessation of occupation are conditions for the test of intentional homelessness and not that there is any specific sequence of events which must be followed.

Common Law Intention

The case law has found intention in a number of instances. It is **12.65.** always a matter of fact in any case. Similarly, it is a matter of fact whether the homelessness is in consequence of the deliberate act or omission. In *Davis v. Kingston-upon-Thames R.L.B.*,[64] a family of former travellers acquired a caravan while in council accommodation. The family surrendered the council accommodation and

---

[63] Author's emphasis.
[64] *The Times*, March 27, 1981.

began their previous lifestyle of living on the road in the caravan. The family found the caravan and a successor caravan became unusable and therefore applied to the authority on the basis that they were homeless. The Court of Appeal held that the family had become intentionally homeless when it surrendered the council-owned accommodation in favour of the caravan.

12.66.   Similarly, in *Smith v. Wokingham D.C.*[65] the applicant's family had lived in a caravan on land owned by an adjoining local authority. The applicant and his family did not have any formal permission to occupy that land in the way they had been occupying it. It was held that a new period of homelessness began when they quit the land with the caravan. That they had no right to occupy the land did not make them continuously homeless during the period when they did occupy the land in this way.

12.67.   In *R. v. Harrow L.B.C., ex p. Holland*[66] a couple, one of whom was disabled, left a caravan site on which they had been living. The couple asserted that they had had intervening accommodation between leaving the site and making an application to the authority. It was held that the couple could not rely on the argument that they had such intervening accommodation because they had not disclosed such information to the authority.

Intervening Period of Accommodation

12.68.   The time lag between the intentional action giving rise to the homelessness and the time of the application may cause the intentional homelessness to be disregarded. The applicant will seek to demonstrate that the stigma of intent has been removed by some intervening action. That intervening action will only exist where the applicant has had some "settled accommodation" during that time lag as held in *Din* by Lord Wilberforce.[67] Conversely, if the applicant became homeless validly and then occupied settled accommodation, the applicant may be intentionally homeless on leaving that settled accommodation.

12.69.   Settled accommodation will include a Rent Act protected tenancy, an assured shorthold tenancy (*R. v. Rochester-upon-Medway C.C., ex p. Williams,*[68] *R. v. Wandsworth L.B.C., ex p. Crooks*[69]). In

---

[65] (1980) LAG Bulletin 92.

[66] (1980) 4 H.L.R. 108.

[67] However, since the speech of Lord Hoffmann in *Awua* which held that accommodation need not be "settled" to satisfy the local authority's obligation, it cannot now be certain that the period of accommodation required to break the stigma of intentional homelessness must be "settled".

[68] (1994) 26 H.L.R. 588.

[69] (1995) 27 H.L.R. 660.

short, the accommodation must be available and reasonable to occupy (*R. v. Wandsworth L.B.C., ex p. Wingrove*[70]). Settled accommodation will not include premises occupied by persons in the country illegally (*R. v. Croydon L.B.C., ex p. Easom*[71]) nor a mere licence obtained by deception (*R. v. Exeter C.C., ex p. Gliddon*[72]).

Lord Hoffmann in *Awua v. Brent L.B.C.*[73] did cast some doubt **12.70.** on whether settled accommodation would break the happening of intentional homelessness. It is submitted that this cannot have been his Lordship's intention. If it were impossible for intentional homelessness to be displaced by settled accommodation, then it would be impossible for the applicant ever to be housed under Part VII. Rather, his Lordship was considering the issue whether the term "accommodation" could be qualified by any words not in the statute. Therefore, the issue is the nature of settled accommodation necessary to displace intentional homelessness.

The case law suggests that there is an absence of any set order in **12.71.** which the events leading up to intentional homelessness must occur. Therefore, in *De Falco, Silvestri v. Crawley B.C.*[74] the court looked behind a period of some months during which the family of the applicant had lived with relatives, to a time when the family had voluntarily left accommodation in Italy. It was held that in those circumstances, the applicant and his family had become intentionally homeless. The time spent living with relatives did not constitute "settled accommodation".

This case should be read in conjunction with the decision of the **12.72.** Court of Appeal in *Dyson v. Kerrier D.C.*,[75] where the applicant had taken an out-of-season let to enable her to live closer to her sister. She surrendered accommodation to take up this letting. When the letting came to an end she applied to the local authority for housing on grounds of homelessness. The court held that she had voluntarily surrendered accommodation to take up the short-term let and therefore was intentionally homeless throughout the period after she surrendered her prior accommodation. The acquisition of the short let was held part of the deliberate surrender of previous accommodation. Losing the short term let did not constitute a *novus actus interveniens* for this purpose.

[70] (1996) 28 H.L.R. 7.
[71] (1992) 25 H.L.R. 262.
[72] (1984) 14 H.L.R. 103.
[73] [1995] 3 All ER 493.
[74] [1980] Q.B. 460.
[75] [1980] 3 All ER 313.

12.73.   However, in his dissenting speech, Lord Lowry in *Din v. Wandsworth L.B.C.*,[76] was of the view that the temporary nature of the out-of-season let meant that the applicant had been homeless throughout that period.

12.74.   The issue of causation is complicated in this instance. It must be a deliberate act of the applicant which caused the homelessness for the applicant to be found to have become homeless intentionally. Therefore, where a man was violent towards his wife, and consequently became subject to an ouster order, it was held that the homelessness resulted from the ouster order (*R. v. Islington L.B.C., ex p. Hinds.*[77] Where an applicant received a grant of £20,000 from the authority to live in Columbia, it was held that she would not have left her secure tenancy but for that grant. Therefore, the matters relied upon by the authority in giving the grant caused the homelessness: (*R. v. Camden L.B.C., ex p. Aranda*[78]).

Commencement of Intentional Homelessness

12.75.   The issue of when the intentional homelessness commenced was part of the Court of Appeal's consideration in *Davis v. Kingston-upon-Thames R.L.B.*[79] In that circumstance, the time at which the family left the accommodation they had previously occupied, was considered by the authority to be the time at which the family became intentionally homeless. The Court of Appeal held that it was a matter for the authority when the family became homeless intentionally. Therefore, the court would not substitute the date when either the family were unable to use their first or the second caravan. The conclusion reached by the authority was considered to be reasonable in all of the circumstances. The question is one for the authority in any case.

12.76.   The case of *Lambert v. Ealing L.B.C.*[80] was similar to *Davis*. A family gave up accommodation in France in favour of a caravan in England and subsequently took up holiday lettings in England. At the end of the holiday lettings, the family applied to the authority to be housed. The authority took the view, and the court held, that the family had become intentionally homeless at the time when they had left the accommodation in France.

12.77.   In *R. v. Islington L.B.C., ex p. Hassan*,[81] an order for possession was obtained against the applicant. The applicant was found to be homeless by the authority. The landlord informed him that the

---

[76] [1981] 3 All ER 881.
[77] (1995) 28 H.L.R. 302.
[78] (1996) 28 H.L.R. 7.
[79] *The Times*, March 27, 1981.
[80] [1981] 1 W.L.R. 550.
[81] (1995) 27 H.L.R. 485.

order would not have been enforced if he agreed to have housing benefit paid directly to the landlord. The authority found him intentionally homeless because he knew of his landlord's offer after the accommodation was lost. It was held that the authority could not rely on events which happened after the authority had found that the applicant was homeless.

Ceasing to Occupy

Section 191 provides that "A person becomes homeless inten- **12.78.** tionally if he deliberately does or fails to do anything in consequence of which he ceases to occupy accommodation which is available for his occupation and which it would have been reasonable for him to continue to occupy."

At the time of the cessation, the occupation must be available for **12.79.** her occupation. However, the test of reasonableness is phrased in the conditional: "would have been". This suggests that it need not have been reasonable at the time of cessation of occupation on a literal reading of the words.

The authority are required to consider accommodation at the **12.80.** time at which the applicant ceased to occupy it (*R. v. Reigate, ex p. Paris*).[82] The authority cannot refuse to accommodate the applicants by relying on the argument that the applicants had failed to secure permanent accommodation was available for their occupation in the United Kingdom when they ceased to occupy accommodation in Italy: (*De Falco*[83]).

"Ceasing to occupy" does not equate to "failing to take up **12.81.** occupation". Therefore, where an authority made an offer of accommodation to an applicant and that applicant refused to occupy the accommodation, the authority could not contend that the applicant had ceased to occupy it (*R. v. Westminster C.C., ex p. Chambers*[84]).

Ceasing to be Available

Section 191 provides that: "A person becomes homeless inten- **12.82.** tionally if he deliberately does or fails to do anything *in consequence of which he ceases to occupy accommodation* which is available for his

---

[82] (1984) 17 H.L.R. 103.
[83] [1980] Q.B. 460.
[84] (1982) 6 H.L.R. 24.

occupation and which *it would have been reasonable for him to continue to occupy.*[85] Therefore, the above arguments relate to accommodation which is no longer available for the applicant, in the same way as the applicant stops occupying it. The issue is the applicant's role in securing that the accommodation was no longer available.

Reasonable to Occupy

12.83.   Section 191 provides that: "A person becomes homeless intentionally if he deliberately does or fails to do anything in consequence of which he ceases to occupy accommodation which is available for his occupation and which it would have been reasonable for him to continue to occupy."

12.84.   At the time of the cessation, the occupation must be available for her occupation. However, the test of reasonableness is phrased in the conditional: "would have been". This suggests that it need not have been reasonable at the time of cessation of occupation on a literal reading of the words.

Circumstances in which it is not Reasonable to Continue to Occupy

12.85.   The issues in this area fall into three categories:
The condition of the property
It may be that the property is overcrowded or unsuitable for an infant child, or unsuitable for a person who suffers from a particular medical condition.
Other circumstances related to the property
The test for "reasonable to continue to occupy" in this context has covered prison-like estate accommodation (*R. v. Brent L.B.C., ex p. Omar*[86]) as well as being located where there was a strong possibility of racist attacks (*R. v. Southwark L.B.C., ex p. Holder*[87]).
The applicant's own personal circumstances
Personal circumstances would cover situations like domestic violence or relationship breakdown.

The Condition of the Property

12.86.   There is no specific guidance is given in Part VII as to what will constitute "reasonable" in these circumstances. For example, none of the categories from the 1985 Act are incorporated into Part VII,

---

[85] Author's emphasis.
[86] (1991) 23 H.L.R. 446.
[87] Unreported (February 10, 1993).

such as unfitness for human habitation, to constitute situations in which it would be reasonable to give up accommodation.

The Code of Guidance suggests that the local authority is 12.87. required to carry out a balancing exercise between the applicant's reasons for quitting the accommodation and "whether there is a housing shortage or whether there are many people living in the area in worse conditions than the applicant" (*R. v. Westminster C.C., ex p. Ali*[88]; *R. v. Reigate and Banstead B.C., ex p. Paris*[89]). It should be borne in mind that this type of information is unlikely to be available to the applicants.

Overcrowding. Overcrowding is considered in greater detail 12.88. above in Chapter 8 "Suitable Accommodation". It is worth considering some of the principles as set out in the case law here. A local housing authority is required to consider the condition of the housing which is available to the applicant currently, as well as any accommodation which the applicant has left. For example, the failure of a housing authority to consider whether it was reasonable for a family of six to continue to live in a two-bedroomed house led to their decision being quashed in *R. v. Eastleigh B.C., ex p. Beattie.*[90]

Conditions which are grossly overcrowded will not be accepted 12.89. as reasonable, as where an applicant lived with this wife and five young children in one room measuring 12ft by 10ft. Simply because there had been two rooms 12ft by 12ft available for sole occupation by the applicant and his family in Bangladesh did not necessarily mean such accommodation continued to be so available. There must be proper investigation of claims of overcrowding — where an applicant left accommodation which was stated to be overcrowded but where the dimensions of the accommodation and which members of the family were occupying it were not clarified at interview, it could not be said that it would have been reasonable to continue to occupy such accommodation.[91]

Unfit accommodation. The authority will generally have 12.90. regard to the statutory definitions of unfitness for human habitation in considering this ground. This ground will enable the applicant to remain outside the definition of intentional homelessness. In the case of *Lester*, set out above, the court did suggest that

[88] (1984) 11 H.L.R. 72.
[89] (1984) 11 H.L.R. 103.
[90] (1983) 10 H.L.R. 134.
[91] *Beattie, supra.*

the authority should reconsider the position of an applicant whose infant son had been hospitalised due to the alleged damp housing conditions. The question of unfitness is considered in detail in Chapter 8, above.

12.91. It would appear that in deciding whether or not accommodation is overcrowded, the authority must consider whether the number of people occupying the property is reasonable — the authority cannot simply rely on the statutory definitions of what will and will not constitute overcrowding (*R. v. Westminster C.C., ex p. Alouat*[92]).

12.92. In circumstances where the property is unsafe because the lift did not operate, there was only one internal staircase and there was no fire escape, the Court of Appeal held that the authority could provide for a structured solution with the owner of the property without being found to be either irrational or perverse: (*R. v. Kensington and Chelsea R.L.B.C., ex p. Ben-el-Mabrouk*[93]). Consequently, the authority's director of environmental health could put proposals for improvements to the owner of the property, rather than accept an obligation to accommodate or assist the applicant.

12.93. **Unsuitable Accommodation.** The question of what constitutes unsuitable accommodation is the subject of Chapter 8, above. Some outline of the principles is of use here. The authority bears a responsibility to inquire into specific allegations concerning the state of council accommodation which is considered unsuitable for the applicant: (*R. v. Westminster C.C., ex p. Bishop*[94]).

12.94. An all-too-typical example of the issue involved is set out in *R. v. Brent L.B.C., ex p. Yusuf.*[95] The applicant was a Somalian who had been granted exceptional leave to remain in the United Kingdom on her application for asylum. She began living with a man who had already been resident at the address where they cohabited and she became pregnant. The relationship ended. Conditions at the house were not suitable for bringing up a child, in the applicant's opinion. The house was dirty and frequently full of her former partner's drunken friends. The applicant left the house and went to stay with a friend. She applied to the authority for housing. The authority considered that the applicant was intentionally homeless. The applicant contended that the authority

---

[92] (1989) 21 H.L.R. 47.
[93] (1995) 27 H.L.R. 564.
[94] (1993) 25 H.L.R. 459.
[95] Unreported (November 8, 1995).

should have considered that she was pregnant when they made their decision.

Turner J. applied the rule in *Din v. Wandsworth L.B.C.*[96] He held **12.95.** that the decision whether or not an applicant was homelessness must be based on the conditions at the time of the application and not on what might happen in the future. The applicant's contention that she would not be able to live in the accommodation when her child was born was not relevant at the time when the application was made. There was four months of the pregnancy left to run at the time when the applicant left the accommodation and therefore it was not a current event at that time.

In the case of *R. v. Kensington and Chelsea R.L.B.C., ex p. Ben-el-* **12.96.** *Mabrouk*[97] the Court of Appeal took a constructive approach to the manner in which local authorities could ensure that accommodation is suitable. The applicant had contended that accommodation was not suitable because it is not safe. He lived with his wife and child on the fifth floor of a building in multiple occupation. The lift did not operate, there was only one internal staircase and there was no fire escape. Sir Thomas Bingham M.R. held that it was not irrational for the authority to seek to solve the problem by approaching the owner of the property to see whether or not improvements could be made to the property. In his view, the court must look to the problems faced by the authority with 4,500 properties under its control. In the circumstances of those problems, seeking a structured solution with the owner of the property was neither irrational nor perverse.

In *R. v. Westminster C.C., ex p. Obeid*[98] the applicant sought **12.97.** judicial review of the authority's decision that she was intentionally homeless. She and her family were housed by the authority in temporary accommodation and were then offered permanent accommodation which they accepted, although with reservations on health grounds about the property's suitability. Before moving in they found private rented accommodation which they judged more suitable and moved in after ascertaining that housing benefit would be payable. They subsequently discovered, however, that their housing benefit was subject to a reduction because the rent on that property was deemed by the rent officer to be unreasonably high in comparison with rent payable for suitable alternative accommodation and they were unable to pay the shortfall. An

---

[96] [1983] 1 A.C. 657.
[97] (1995) 27 H.L.R. 564.
[98] *The Times*, July 16, 1996.

application was made to the authority for housing, which the local authority refused finding instead that the applicant was intentionally homeless.

12.98.   The issue to be determined was whether the applicant's assumption that the rent would be covered by housing benefit meant that she was "unaware" of a "relevant fact" within the meaning of the statute. Carnwath J. held that the authority ought to have found that O did not become homeless intentionally. There was no question that the applicant had acted in good faith and her genuine misapprehension concerning her housing benefit entitlement amounted to being unaware of a relevant fact.[99]

Other Circumstances Related to the Property

12.99.   **Violence or intimidation from non-partners.**   The issue of intimidation causing the applicant to leave the property is considered in detail above in Chapter 8 "Suitable Accommodation". It is in the area of intentional homelessness that it is most applicable. One example of an applicant not being found to be intentionally homeless in circumstances where he was intimidated was in *R. v. Hillingdon L.B.C., ex p. H.*[1] A former serviceman serving in Northern Ireland had received threats on his home and therefore left it. As a result, he quit the accommodation and sought to be rehoused. The question according to the court was: "whether the accommodation was accommodation which it would have been reasonable for him to continue to occupy. In considering the question I can find nothing in the Act which would entitle the local authority to disregard harassment simply because it was not domestic".

12.100.   In *R. v. Northavon D.C., ex p. Smith*[2] the issue arose between the duty to provide housing under what is now Part VII of the 1996 Act and that under section 27 of the Children Act 1989 to provide for the welfare of children in the local authority's district. The applicant and his wife had five children under the age of ten. They left accommodation as a result of violence and harassment. The local authority accepted that they were homeless and in priority need but considered that they were homeless intentionally. Therefore, the local authority provided them with temporary bed and breakfast accommodation. The applicant and his wife approached the county council to seek accommodation from them in line with

[99] *R. v. Exeter C.C., ex p. Tranckle* (1994) 26 H.L.R. 244; and *R. v. Ealing L.B.C., ex p. Sukhija* (1994) 26 H.L.R. 726 considered.
[1] (1988) 20 H.L.R. 554, at 560.
[2] [1993] 4 All ER 731.

their obligations under section 27 of the 1989 Act. Further to that provision the county council requested the local authority to provide accommodation on the basis that they were held not to be entitled under the 1985 Act.

It was held by the Court of Appeal that, in accordance with **12.101.** section 27(2) of the 1989 Act, the county council was required to protect the welfare of the children and empowered to make a request of another authority. This obligation obtained even in circumstances where the local authority had lawfully decided that it was not obliged to house the applicant and his family permanently under the 1985 Act. These duties were held not to be inconsistent because the requirements of section 27 of the 1989 Act referred to the needs of the children and not the accommodation and priority need of the applicant. The local authority had not responded lawfully to the request made by the county council because it had not given reasons for its decision in this context. As Sir Thomas Bingham M.R. held "Reading these two statutory codes side by side, I find a clear parliamentary intention that children in need should not fall between them".[3]

In *R. v. Newham L.B.C., ex p. Begum*[4] B entered the United **12.102.** Kingdom from Bangladesh in 1990. She sought to appeal against her offer of accommodation under the 1985 Act following the authority's decision that she was not intentionally homeless and in priority need. She refused to move into the premises on the basis that she had suffered racial abuse on visiting the premises for the first time. The authority decided that there were no exceptional circumstances and therefore they had carried out their duty to B. B sought judicial review of this decision on the basis that there were exceptional circumstances justifying B refusing the accommodation on this occasion.

Richards J. held that although earlier letters had failed to consider whether there was an exceptional circumstance by taking into account the relevant facts, the subsequent letter from the Director of Housing demonstrated that the matter had been reconsidered with full knowledge of the facts and he was entitled to decide that it was nevertheless reasonable for B to move into the property. Further, Richards J. held that under the true construction of the authority's procedure once it had been decided that exceptional circumstances did not apply, then the applicant should be given the opportunity to move into the property in order to exercise her right of appeal, following *R. v. Wycombe D.C., ex p.*

---

[3] *Ibid.* at 740.
[4] Unreported (February 5, 1996).

Hazeltine.[5] In this case the judge exercised his discretion against B as she had not shown any intention of moving into the property in order to appeal and the property had already been let to someone else.

12.103. In *R. v. Swansea C.C., ex p. Evans*[6] the applicants contended that they had Rent Act protected accommodation available to them after they left council accommodation. They ceased to occupy the private sector accommodation they moved to as a result of threats of violence from their landlord. The authority's decision that they became intentionally homeless on leaving their council accommodation was quashed because the authority failed to consider whether the private accommodation had been "settled accommodation" in the context of the threats of violence.

12.104. **Accommodation too costly.** It has generally been held by the courts to be unreasonable to continue to occupy accommodation where the cost of that accommodation is excessive. The court took the view in *R. v. Hillingdon L.B.C., ex p. Tinn*[7] that:

> "it cannot be reasonable for a person to continue to occupy accommodation when they can no longer discharge their fiscal obligations in relation to that accommodation, that is to say, pay the rent and make the mortgage repayments, without so straining their resources as to deprive themselves of the ordinary necessities of life, such as food, clothing, heat, transport and so forth."

12.105. In *R. v. Wandsworth L.B.C., ex p. Hawthorne*[8] the applicant ran up arrears of rent in excess of £600 with the authority. The authority obtained an order for possession subject to the applicant paying her current rent plus an extra weekly amount to reduce the arrears of rent. She was reliant entirely on welfare benefits and was a single parent with young children. Therefore, she claimed that she could not even afford to pay the rent, let alone the extra amounts. The applicant was evicted and sought re-housing from the authority. The authority decided that she was intentionally homeless as a result of her persistent refusal to pay rent and to comply with rent agreements. The authority contended that "deliberate act" included the choice between action and inaction — on these facts the decision not to pay rent and other amounts.

Nourse L.J., in giving the judgment of the Court of Appeal, held that the authority were bound to take into account the financial

[5] (1993) 25 H.L.R. 313.
[6] (1990) 22 H.L.R. 467.
[7] (1988) 20 H.L.R. 305.
[8] [1995] 2 All ER 331.

resources of an applicant who was found intentionally homeless on grounds of persistent and deliberate failure to pay rent. Where the authority found that the applicant had to maintain a family alone and was having trouble making ends meet, this could not be said to be a deliberate act causing her to become intentionally homeless. The council had not considered the central question posed by Nourse L.J. "in deciding whether the applicant's failure to pay rent was deliberate, were the council bound to consider whether it was caused by the inadequacy of her resources to cover both the rent and the maintenance of her children?"[9]

In the Court of Appeal in *R. v. Brent L.B.C., ex p. Grossett*[10] the **12.106.** issue arose whether or not the applicant was intentionally homeless in circumstances where the rent and other such payments was so high that it would have led to deprivation of necessities of life for the applicant if it was paid. The applicant was evicted from council accommodation for non-payment of an amenity charge. The applicant argued that she could not have afforded to meet the payments. The authority decided after making inquiries that she could have met the payments and was therefore intentionally homeless. Dillon L.J. held that it was properly a matter for the local authority whether or not the applicant could have met the payments without depriving herself of "the ordinary necessities of life". He considered the judgment in *Tinn* and continued that it could not be said that the authority had acted unfairly in this circumstance nor that the decision reached was so unreasonable that no reasonable authority could have come to it.

In *R. v. Islington L.B.C., ex p. Bibi*,[11] B who came to England **12.107.** from Bangladesh with eight members of her family claiming she was unable to feed them there, applied for judicial review of Islington's decision that she had become homeless intentionally. It was held that a finding on whether it was reasonable for a homeless applicant to cease to occupy accommodation had to be made by reference to that person's ability to pay for such accommodation.[12] An inability to afford the basic necessities of life was a relevant consideration in assessing whether the decision to leave was reasonable, and there was no evidence that Islington had addressed that question in determining whether B was intentionally homeless.[13]

---

[9] Ibid at 335.
[10] (1996) 28 H.L.R. 9.
[11] *The Times,* July 10, 1996.
[12] *R. v. Hillingdon L.B.C., ex p. Tinn* (1988) 20 H.L.R. 305 was applied in this regard.
[13] *R. v. Northampton B.C., ex p. Clarkson* (1992) 24 H.L.R. 529 should be considered in this context.

The applicant's own personal circumstances

12.108.   Domestic violence.   The Code of Practice provides that people who are the victims of domestic violence are not to be regarded as having become homeless intentionally on the basis that it could not be considered reasonable to require such a person to continue living with a violent partner. Just because a victim of domestic violence has secured accommodation away from a violent partner does not mean that this accommodation will always remain safe: (*R. v. Tynedale D.C., ex p. McCabe*[14]). Similarly it would seem unreasonable to consider a woman who has exercised her rights under the matrimonial homes legislation, such as the Family Law Act 1996, as having become homeless intentionally solely for that reason.[15]

12.109.   Non-violent relationship difficulties.   The issue arises whether or not it is reasonable for the applicant to quit accommodation where her relationship with a partner is breaking down. This category is distinct from the cases of domestic violence considered above. It would appear that the issue of reasonableness will turn on the applicant's personal circumstances. More specifically there might be an issue relating to the possibility of the applicant pursuing some legal remedy under matrimonial or other law to retain occupation of the relationship home.

12.110.   The problems with requiring applicants to exhaust all potential legal remedies are plain. It is not obvious to the applicant or the authority which forms of legal redress are available, let alone whether there is sufficient possibility of success to justify pursuing them. The issue of seeking appeals against lost litigation and so forth also arises. There have been occasions where authorities have seised on judicial dicta in some cases and have expected applicants to remain in domestic arrangements which seem to be quite unrealistic because of the potential of bringing legal actions (see for example: *R. v. Eastleigh B.C., ex p. Evans*[16] and *R. v. Purbeck D.C., ex p. Cadney*[17]).

12.111.   In *R. v. Wandsworth L.B.C., ex p. Nimako-Boateng*[18] a pregnant mother left her husband in Ghana and returned to the United Kingdom where she stayed in temporary accommodation with relatives. She was forced to leave that accommodation and therefore applied to the respondent housing authority for housing as a

[14] (1991) 24 H.L.R. 384.
[15] The Scottish Code of Guidance provides for this expressly.
[16] (1984) 17 H.L.R. 515.
[17] (1985) 17 H.L.R. 534.
[18] (1984) 11 H.L.R. 95.

homeless person. The authority determined that she had become homeless intentionally because she had come to the United Kingdom without securing accommodation for her occupation beforehand. The applicant explained that she had left Ghana because her marriage had broken down. She cited her husband's mistreatment of her as a factor in this process. However, he had not been violent towards her. The issue which arose for the court's determination was, therefore, whether in these circumstances it would have been reasonable for the applicant to have continued to live in the matrimonial home. Woolf J. held that they were entitled to reach that conclusion:

> "In considering the matrimonial home, what was relevant was the marital conduct to which the applicant was subjected by her husband whilst she was living there. Of course, there could be conduct on the part of the husband, who could not be prevented from entering the home, which could make it quite impossible for the wife to continue to occupy that accommodation . . . The conclusion that [the council] came to was that there was no fear of any violence and, on that basis, he formed the opinion that it would be reasonable for the applicant to remain in the accommodation provided by the matrimonial home . . . that is a conclusion to which the authority were fully entitled to come".[19]

These dicta disposed of the application. However, Woolf J. continued that in the context where English law afforded "all sorts of protection that a woman can get if her husband misbehaves", it is possible for an authority to decide that it is reasonable for a wife to continue to live in the matrimonial home with her husband and to rely on the wife to seek legal redress. He continued:

> "The local authority could perfectly properly in many cases in this country take the view that it would be reasonable for the wife to continue to occupy accommodation and to say to the wife, if she thinks it right: æIf you are having trouble with your husband, go to the appropriate authority, be it a magistrates' court of the Family Division, and get protection against your husband'. If the woman does not take that course and chooses to leave, the authority could then take the view that it was reasonable for the lady to remain".[20]

Therefore, there is pressure on spouses and co-habitees to seek **12.112.** to exercise their legal remedies. Woolf J. does not require that all potential forms of redress are pursued to their absolute conclusion. However, it is necessary for such an applicant to take some action.

---

[19] *Ibid.* at 102.
[20] *Ibid.* at 103.

Where there are alternatives to staying in the matrimonial home

12.113.   The remarks made by Woolf J. in *R. v. Wandsworth L.B.C., ex p. Nimako-Boateng,*[21] as set out above, are probably *obiter* in the context of the decision. It is submitted that it would be unfortunate if those remarks were to be applied in the case of a woman who was the victim of domestic violence. While there are remedies under the Family Law Act 1996 with reference to the status of the relationship and the right to occupy the property, it would create great hardship for such women if those dicta were strictly applied. There is some difficulty in requiring people undergoing such stress to commence legal proceedings immediately in those circumstances, rather than simply quitting the property.

12.114.   The term "reasonable to continue to occupy" was considered in a similar context in *R. v. Basingstoke and Deane B.C., ex p. Bassett.*[22] In this case a couple whose marriage was foundering decided to emigrate to Canada. Consequently, they surrendered the tenancy of their council flat and went to stay with relatives in Canada while the husband sought employment. However, their application to stay in Canada permanently was refused and some months later the family were deported.

12.115.   On returning to the United Kingdom they stayed with relatives briefly before their marriage disintegrated. They separated a month later. Divorce proceedings were initiated and a year later Mrs Bassett obtained a decree nisi against her husband on the ground of his unreasonable behaviour. Within two months, the applicant was required to quit the accommodation she had been occupying. The applicant therefore approached the authority for assistance under the homelessness legislation. The authority, as they had done on a previous occasion, decided that the applicant had become homeless intentionally when she and her husband voluntarily terminated the tenancy of their council property before moving to Canada. Taylor J. held that the decision was capable of being quashed on the basis that the authority had failed to consider the personal circumstances of the applicant at the time when the accommodation was given up:

> "The authority failed in this case to take into account the human element; the human situation of a marriage which was in danger of foundering and the human situation of a wife doing

---

[21] (1984) 11 H.L.R. 95.
[22] (1983) 10 H.L.R. 125.

her best to follow her husband and hold the marriage together. I find it quite impossible to say that any reasonable authority could have regarded what she did as being unreasonable, or would have regarded it in the circumstances as reasonable if she had continued to stay whilst her husband departed for Canada".[23]

In contrast with the decision of Woolf J. in *R. v. Wandsworth* **12.116.** *L.B.C., ex p. Nimako-Boateng*,[24] Taylor J.'s decision sets out a different test. In certain circumstances it may be reasonable for an applicant to give up accommodation which was available for her occupation in an attempt to deal with marital difficulties such as, in this case, the avoidance of marital breakdown.

It would appear that there is no hard and fast rule here. Rather, **12.117.** each case will turn on its individual circumstances. In *R. v. Eastleigh B.C. ex p. Evans*[25], McNeill J. decided that a female applicant had become homeless intentionally where she left her husband after an attempt to salvage their relationship had failed. McNeill J. considered that the decision of Taylor J. in *Bassett* could be considered as the furthest point in which the courts will seek to find for such applicants. In the absence of matrimonial violence or severe emotional stress as outlined in the Code, McNeill J. held that the authority were entitled to find that such an applicant had become homeless intentionally because she failed to accept their advice and exercise her legal remedies in respect of the matrimonial home.

The attempts made during the passage of the Family Law Bill **12.118.** 1996 to provide for a system of compulsory attempts towards reconciliation between partners and co-habitees, might be seen as a movement towards rewarding those partners who have attempted to keep their relationship in tact. On the basis of *Evans*, people who seek counselling, guidance or take their own independent action to preserve a marriage will prejudice their position with reference to the Housing Act 1996. It might be better to say that the applicant has a duty to take some action, including surveying all the possible legal remedies, but where some action has been taken which does not solve the relationship breakdown, it may be reasonable to leave the accommodation.

Employment-related issues. The applicants in *R. v. Ham-* **12.119.** *mersmith and Fulham L.B.C., ex p. Duro-Rama*,[26] had lived in the United Kingdom from 1964 until 1979 when they returned to

---

[23] (1983) 10 H.L.R. 125 at 132.
[24] (1984) 11 H.L.R. 95.
[25] (1984) 11 H.L.R. 515.
[26] (1983) 81 L.G.R. 702.

Spain to care for a relative. The family returned to the United Kingdom when the husband's entitlement to Spanish social security benefits expired. The husband obtained work and a flat to rent. Later the family were evicted from their accommodation and applied for housing. The council, however, held that they were intentionally homeless because they had voluntarily left accommodation in Spain which it would have been reasonable to continue to occupy.

12.120.   The applicants contended that the council should have considered the unavailability of social security benefits in Spain. The authority argued that it was only matters directly related to the housing which were relevant. Woolf J. rejected the authority's contention and observed that section 17(4) of the 1977 Act was drafted in a way that would allow other considerations to be taken into account. Consequently, the local housing authority must have regard to the applicant's employment prospects and the lack of social security benefits available in the country he left.

12.121.   This leaves the applicant with the difficulty of verifying her claims about her employment position. Thus, while the principle laid down in *Duro-Rama*, that employment prospects are a relevant matter to be considered by a housing authority has been accepted as valid, later cases show that in practice the result is variable. For example, in *Mazzaccherini v. Argyll and Bute D.C.*,[27] Lord Jauncey rejected the contention that it was incumbent on the authority in reaching its decision to make exhaustive inquiries into the labour market in two different towns for a person with the applicant's qualification.

12.122.   In *R. v. Kensington and Chelsea Royal London B.C., ex p. Cunha*,[28] Otton J. stated that to require the housing authority to inquire into employment conditions in Brazil would be to place an unwarranted burden on them. More recently in *R. v. Winchester C.C., ex p. Ashton*[29] a middle-aged woman was offered a one-year contract in Winchester which she hoped would lead to more permanent employment. She had been unemployed for six years prior to living in private rented accommodation in Tunbridge Wells. She obtained a non-secure tenancy in a council flat in Winchester which she lost when she was made redundant after 11 months. The council considered that she had become homeless intentionally because she had given up private rented accommodation to move

---

[27] 1987 S.C.L.R. 475.
[28] (1988) 21 H.L.R. 16.
[29] (1992) 24 H.L.R. 520.

to take up the job. It was held by the Court of Appeal that the applicant was entitled to "grasp the opportunity for employment that had come her way after six years" without being considered to be intentionally homeless.

General circumstances in the area. The question of the 12.123. availability of required medical services is one which appears regularly in this context. While it would appear reasonable to deal with this issue as falling within the judgment in *Duro-Rama* (set out above) that the court should look beyond factors which are related solely and directly to housing. In determining the reasonableness of accommodation, authorities may have regard to the general circumstances prevailing in relation to housing in their area.

This issue has been considered by the House of Lords. The 12.124. question of whether or not a person has to wait until a possession order is granted before leaving accommodation depended, in the view of Lord Fraser, in *Din v. Wandsworth L.B.C.*,[30] on overall housing conditions and prevailing demand for accommodation in the area of the housing authority. In this case the Din family quit accommodation linked to Mr Din's employment and began to live with relatives to avoid incurring further rent and rate arrears. Observing that accommodation in the area of Inner London is scarce, the House of Lords suggested that it was not reasonable for the Dins to quit their accommodation.

However, if the same issue had arisen in another part of the 12.125. country, where accommodation was under less pressure, the position might have been different, in the opinion of Lord Fraser. It is noteworthy that in their affidavits in judicial review cases that authorities are wont to give detailed information of the extent, turnover and demand on the housing stock. The issue is one that is measured on the facts in any case and in any local authority's area.

In Ali[31], McCullough J. expressed the view that it was astonish- 12.126. ing that anyone should regard it as reasonable that a family of seven should continue to live in one room measuring 12ft by 10 ft. He added that in the absence of the evidence that the general housing circumstances in the area were so desperate that it would be reasonable to accept such gross overcrowding, he was driven to the conclusion that the question of reasonableness had not been properly determined by the authority.

[30] [1983] 1 A.C. 657, at 671.
[31] (1983) 11 H.L.R. 83.

Responsibilities of the Authority in Making Inquiries

12.127.   Some attention should be paid to the position of the local authorities in this area. It is often the case the local authorities will look for some evidence that the applicant has become homeless intentionally. Similarly, they will often re-confirm decisions that have already been made with reference to that applicant.

Inquiries

12.128.   The issue of inquiries is considered in Chapter 4, above. There are some decisions which are specific to the highly litigious area of intentional homelessness. The drift of the cases in this area is that the local authority is the body which bears both the power and the responsibility of deciding what inquiries should be made in any given situation.

12.129.   For example, in *R. v. Tower Hamlets L.B.C., ex p. Khatun*[32] the Court of Appeal considered a case of intentional homeless where the applicant had come from Bangladesh to England to marry. She lived with her parents-in-law for five years before the family went to Bangladesh on holiday and stayed for two years. She returned to England to live with her parents-in-law again. She was told to leave by her mother-in-law because the house was overcrowded. The applicant wife therefore applied to the authority to be housed on grounds of homelessness. The applicant was interviewed twice and 11 reasons given by the authority why she was considered intentionally homeless.

Neill L.J. held that she had only a reasonable expectation that she would be housed when she returned to the United Kingdom. Furthermore, the judge at first instance had held that the interviews were inherently flawed on the basis that they were conducted by an employee of the authority. Neill L.J. found that it was for the authority to decide on the method for appropriate inquiries.

12.130.   There is some reason to think that in making inquiries where a member of the family unit is claiming not to have been part of that decision to become intentionally homeless, there is a need for the applicant to discharge a presumption of involvement in the decision: (see *R. v. North Devon D.C., ex p. Lewis*[33]). However, the authority will be required to examine the circumstances of each

---

[32] (1995) 27 H.L.R. 465.
[33] [1981] 1 W.L.R. 328.

relationship in turn to see whether or not the applicant in fact had any option but to acquiesce.[34]

In any event, it falls to the authority to consider each case on its **12.131.** merits and not simply to rubber stamp the decision of any other public body: (*R. v. South Herefordshire D.C., ex p. Miles*[35]).

Notifications

The question of the duties borne by the authority to make **12.132.** notifications is considered in detail in Chapter 5, above. In *Gloucester v. Miles*[36], the Court of Appeal held that notifications of intentional homelessness should state four things:

that the authority are satisfied that the applicant is homeless;
the time at which the authority decides the applicant became homeless;
the reason why they became homeless; and
that it would have been reasonable to continue to occupy the accommodation in question.

Decisions

While the scope of inquiries are a matter for the authorities, the **12.133.** scope of the decision-making power is something which the courts will often be more astute to review. The authority will be restricted to the consideration of relevant issues. Thus, in *R. v. Islington L.B.C., ex p. Hassan*[37], an order for possession was obtained against the applicant. The applicant was found to be homeless by the authority. The landlord informed him that the order would not have been enforced if he agreed to have housing benefit paid directly to the landlord. The authority found him intentionally homeless because he knew of his landlord's offer after the accommodation was lost. It was held that the authority could not rely on events which happened after the authority had found that the applicant was homeless.

In *R. v. Westminster C.C., ex p. Ermakov*[38] the applicant and his **12.134.** family had left Uzbekistan to move to Greece due to the political situation and to care for a sick relative. The family then moved to

---

[34] See *R. v. Tower Hamlets L.B.C., ex p. Khatun* (1993) 27 H.L.R. 344.
[35] (1983) 17 H.L.R. 82.
[36] (1985) 17 H.L.R. 292.
[37] (1995) 27 H.L.R. 485.
[38] [1996] 2 All E.R. 302.

the United Kingdom and sought housing from the authority. The authority sought information from Greece to corroborate the applicant's story but received none. Instead, the authority found that the applicant had become homeless intentionally. The reasons given for the decision were that the authority did not believe the applicant's version of events. The authority's officer swore an affidavit that these were not the real reasons and that the applicant had been denied permanent housing because it was believed that he had become homeless intentionally. The applicant sought judicial review and challenged the district judge's decision to allow the affidavit evidence to be admitted.

12.135.   In applying *R. v. Tynedale D.C., ex p. Shield*[39], Hutchison L.J. held that the statute required that the reasons for the decision were more than procedural. Indeed, unacceptable reasons would be subject to prima facie judicial review, whether or not the applicant had suffered any prejudice from that decision. Further, the court would be reluctant to admit evidence by affidavit in the way it had been admitted here. However, where the decision letter can be shown to have been flawed, as in this case, exceptionally affidavit evidence of the real reasons could be adduced.[40] On these facts, the district judge had not admitted the evidence on the exceptional basis of substituted reasons and therefore the decision of the housing authority would be quashed.

Conflicting Statutory Obligations

12.136.   The obligations which weigh on local authorities appear to conflict in some circumstances. The clearest example in the area of homelessness is the inter-action between Part VII of the Housing Act 1996 and the Children Act 1989.

12.137.   In *R. v. Northavon D.C., ex p. Smith*[41], the question of where the line lies between the duty to provide accommodation (under what is now Part VII of the 1996 Act) and that under section 27 of the Children Act 1989 (to provide for the welfare of children in the local authority's district) arose directly. The applicant and his wife had five children under the age of ten. They left accommodation as a result of violence and harassment. The local authority accepted that they were homeless and in priority need but that they were homeless intentionally. Therefore, the local authority provided

[39] (1987) 22 H.L.R. 144.
[40] See in this context *R. v. Croydon L.B.C., ex p. Graham* (1993) 26 H.L.R. 286; and *R. v. Northampton B.C., ex p. Carpenter* (1992) 25 H.L.R. 349.
[41] [1993] 4 All E.R. 731.

them with temporary bed and breakfast accommodation. The applicant and his wife approached the county council to seek accommodation from them in line with their obligations under section 27 of the 1989 Act. Further to that provision the county council requested the local authority to provide accommodation on the basis that they were held not to be entitled under the 1985 Act.

It was held by the Court of Appeal that where in accordance **12.138.** with section 27(2) the county council was required to protect the welfare of the children and empowered to make a request of another authority. This obligation obtained even in circumstances where the local authority had lawfully decided that it was not obliged to house the applicant and his family permanently under the 1985 Act. These duties were held not to be inconsistent because the requirements of section 27 of the 1989 Act referred to the needs of the children and not the accommodation and priority need of the applicant. The local authority had not responded lawfully to the request made by the county council because it had not given reasons for its decision in this context. As Sir Thomas Bingham M.R. held "Reading these two statutory codes side by side, I find a clear parliamentary intention that children in need should not fall between them".[42]

---

[42] [1993] 4 All E.R. 731 at 740.

CHAPTER 13

Statutory Obligations to the Homeless

13.01. The purpose of this chapter is to set out in one coherent section the obligations which are placed on local authorities by the 1996 Act. The manner in which authorities carry out their obligations under the Act is clearly the most important issue confronting the homeless applicant. Therefore, this chapter considers the different duties owed to the applicant and the different categories that applicant falls into within the terms of Part VII. Also discussed are the ways in which the authorities validly discharge their housing functions. There is also some discussion of the other specific obligations which are imposed by the statute. In this last, short section there is some overlap with other chapters (as set out) but its inclusion enables a full survey of local authority obligations here.

The Obligations to Provide Accommodation

13.02. The obligations that are placed on the local housing authorities by Part VII of the 1996 Act are somewhat complicated. There is no straightforward duty to provide permanent accommodation. Rather, the applicant is required to comply with all of the entry qualifications to the procedure before there is an obligation to provide any accommodation. For some applicants who do not satisfy all of the Part VII requirements, the obligations owed to them are less than a right to be provided with more than temporary accommodation. Those qualifications are:

Homelessness (discussed at Chapter 8, above);
Priority need (discussed at Chapter 10, above);
Local connection (discussed at Chapter 11, above);
Non-intentional homeless (discussed at Chapter 12, above).

These provisions are set out in the introductory section in outline. However, it is possible that the local authority will bear obligations to provide some interim housing to the applicant in some other circumstances, as set out below.

The primary duties imposed on authorities, as discussed below, **13.03.** are:

the duties to provide advice and assistance;
the duties to provide temporary accommodation;
the duty to provide permanent accommodation

Introductory: Obligation to House the Homeless

Part VII of the 1996 Act sets out the circumstances in which **13.04.** local housing authorities are required to act with respect to those people who are homeless.[1] The statute also sets out the obligations and powers of the Secretary of State to make provisions in relation to the treatment of homeless people (as discussed at the end of this chapter).

Local Connection and Power to Refer

Before considering the obligation to provide accommodation, it **13.05.** is worth considering briefly the system of "shuttlecock and battledore"[2] that is the referral mechanism between local authorities. While the local authority may well bear obligations to house homeless people, at this stage it is important to remember that the local connection provisions may exempt the housing authority from that duty altogether. Where the authority to which the applicant applies considers that there is no local connection between the applicant and its district, it is open to that authority to refer the applicant to a district where the applicant does have a local connection.

Therefore, the local connection provisions exempt the authority **13.06.** which refers the applicant on ("the notifying authority") from an obligation to house that applicant. The authority receiving the referral ("the notified authority") then bears the burden of securing accommodation for the applicant. The circumstances in which this translation of duties arises is set out in some detail below. In short, the applicant must have no local connection with the notifying authority; the applicant must have a local connection with the notified authority; and there must not be any risk of domestic violence in the district of the notified authority.[3]

[1] As set out in Chapter 8, above.
[2] In the words of Lord Denning in *R. v. Slough B.C., ex p. Ealing L.B.C., op cit.*
[3] This procedure is considered in detail above in Chapter 11 "Local Connection".

The Obligations on Local Housing Authorities

Obligation to Provide Free Advice

13.07. The 1996 Act provides for a scheme of assistance for applicants by way of advice to all people in their district relating to homelessness. It is important to remember that "homelessness" in this context extends beyond street homelessness to a number of situations in which citizens require advice on the potential or actual impact of homelessness.

13.08. There is an obligation on every local housing authority to secure that free advice and information is available to any person in their district.[4] This provision is new to the 1996 Act. The advice and information that must be provided is "advice and information about homelessness and the prevention of homelessness".[5]

13.09. For example, where property-owners or -occupiers voluntarily give up their property, they will then seek to be re-housed by the local housing authority. However, the provisions relating to intentional homelessness (discussed above at Chapter 12) will exempt the local housing authority from an obligation to secure accommodation is available for such an applicant.

13.10. Similarly, there are those applicants who require advice where they are in occupation of accommodation which is unsuitable or which places them in a category of person which falls within the definition of homeless in section 175 of the 1996 Act. The purpose of advice provision by the local housing authority must therefore be to educate these people as to their rights and to enable them to locate housing for their needs. Although there is no definition of the form that advice must take in the statute, in the case of intentional homelessness, in this writer's opinion, such advice should warn the applicant about the risks of ceasing to occupy permanent accommodation voluntarily.

13.11. It may be that the advice or assistance is provided by some agency other than the local housing authority. The local housing authority are empowered to give assistance by way of grant or loan, to any person giving such advice and information on behalf of the authority.[6] It is therefore possible for the authority to provide real assistance to such an agency. The local housing authority may also assist any such person in a number of ways set out in the statute:[7]

---

[4] Housing Act 1996, s. 179(1).
[5] s. 179(1).
[6] s. 179(2).
[7] s. 179(3).

"(a) by permitting him to use premises belonging to the authority,[8]
(b) by making available furniture or other goods, whether by way of gift, loan or otherwise,[9] and
(c) by making available the services of staff employed by the authority."[10]

The voluntary sector clearly fulfils a very significant role in the **13.12.** provision of advice and assistance to people who are homeless or threatened with homelessness. Therefore, provision is made in the 1996 Act to enable local authorities to support the voluntary sector in this work.[11] The Secretary of State or a local housing authority may give assistance to voluntary organisations concerned with homelessness or matters relating to homelessness.[12] The assistance may be given by way of grant or loan.[13] Powers are also given to local housing authorities to assist any such organisation in a number of different ways under section 180(2). The powers given are:

"(a) by permitting them to use premises belonging to the authority,[14]
(b) by making available furniture or other goods, whether by way of gift, loan or otherwise,[15] and
by making available the services of staff employed by the authority."[16]

For these purposes a "voluntary organisation" is a body whose activities are not carried on for profit.[17] The voluntary organisation cannot be a public or local authority.[18]

The Nature of the Advice and Assistance

Part VII does not clearly set out the assistance which the local **13.13.** housing authority is required to give to the applicants. Rather, the statute provides for an ad hoc system of giving advice and

---

[8] s. 179(3)(a).
[9] s. 179(3)(b).
[10] s. 179(3)(c).
[11] It is not clear how wide the term "voluntary organisations" will be in this context. It might encompass housing associations and social landlords not making profits, as set out in *Goodman v. Dolphin Square Trust Ltd* (1979) 38 P. & C.R. 257, C.A.
[12] Housing Act 1996, s. 180(1).
[13] s. 180(1).
[14] s. 180(2)(a).
[15] s. 180(2)(b).
[16] s. 180(2)(c).
[17] s. 180(3).
[18] s. 180(3).

assistance. Section 181 sets out the terms and conditions on which assistance is given under section 179 or section 180[19]. Under section 181(2), assistance is to be "on such terms, and subject to such conditions, as the person giving the assistance may determine". The section refers, in terms, to the giving of financial or similar assistance. Such assistance to be given on the terms set out under the section. Similarly, the statute reserves the power to recover the assistance given where those conditions are not complied with.

13.14.   Therefore, it is for the advice-giver to set out the terms of the relationship and to police them. For example, where assistance is given by way of provision of furniture or household equipment, the advice-giver is able to control the means for which that equipment or furniture is used. There are conditions placed on the pre-requisites for giving assistance, under section 181(3). No assistance is to be given unless the person to whom assistance is given undertakes the following two things:

"(a) to use the money, furniture or other goods or premises for a specified purpose,[20] and

(b) to provide such information as may reasonably be required as to the manner in which the assistance is being used."[21]

13.15.   Where the applicant is required to provide information to the advice-giver (for example about family members or specific personal requirements) further to section 181(3)(b), the person giving the assistance may require such information by notice in writing.[22] If there is a requirement of providing information by notice in writing, that requirement shall be complied with within the period of 21 days: such period starting from the date on which the notice is served.

13.16.   There are further mandatory conditions to the giving of assistance under section 181. The conditions under which assistance is to be given, must always include the conditions set out in section 181(4):

"(a) to keep proper books of account and have them audited in such manner as may be specified,[23]

(b) to keep records indicating how he has used the money, furniture or other goods or premises,[24] and

---

[19] s. 181(1).
[20] s. 181(3)(a).
[21] s. 181(3)(b).
[22] s. 181(3).
[23] s. 181(4)(a).
[24] s. 181(4)(b).

(c) to submit the books of account and records for inspection by the person giving the assistance."[25]

The aim of these provisions is therefore to cut down on waste and to provide safeguards against the mis-use of resources in this casualised system.

Where it appears to the person giving the assistance, that the **13.17.** person to whom the assistance was given has failed to carry out her undertakings as to the purpose for which the assistance was to be used, she shall take all reasonable steps to recover from that person an amount equal to the amount of the assistance.[26] The person giving the assistance must first serve on the person to whom the assistance was given a notice specifying the amount which in her opinion is recoverable and the basis on which that amount has been calculated.[27] The advice-giver is therefore required to scrupulous in the controls for giving advice and assistance, given the powers to recover those assets.

Obligation to Observe Statutory Guidance

Local housing authorities and social services authorities arc **13.18.** required to have regard to the Code of Guidance issued by the Secretary of State in the exercise of their functions relating to homelessness and the prevention of homelessness.[28] The Secretary of State is empowered to give guidance generally or to give guidance to specified descriptions of authorities. [29]

It is important to note that the precise terms of the Code of **13.19.** Guidance do not have legal effect. Rather it is to guide the authority in the operation of their policies and in the way in which they deal with individual applications. It is important to note that local housing and other authorities are not able to ignore the detail of individual cases and apply blanket policies, as discussed above in Chapter 7. This would be to fetter the authority's discretion and therefore would leave them open to having their decision quashed in proceedings for judicial review.

Further, the Code does not itself create legal rules as to the **13.20.** application of Part VII. Therefore, it is possible that an authority could be acting unreasonably where it is observing the Code.

---

[25] s. 181(4)(c).
[26] s. 181(5).
[27] s. 181(6).
[28] s. 182(1).
[29] s. 182(2).

However, it is unlikely that anything in the Code would be taken to be unreasonable in itself. What may be unreasonable is failing to consider the precise circumstances of the applicant's own case. The authority is therefore required by statute to have regard to the Code as a benchmark of reasonable operation of the statutory requirements.

13.21. It is envisaged by section 182 that the Secretary of State will give guidance generally as to the operation of Part VII. These guidances are themselves open to judicial review, in the manner discussed above. It is, therefore, possible for the Secretary of State to give guidance other than in a central Code of Guidance. This guidance may be general or it may be directed at "specified descriptions of authorities". Therefore, it may be applied, for example, to geographically organised authorities or it may be directed, for example, at social security authorities specifically.

Obligation on Receiving an Application for Housing

13.22. Section 183 deals with the situation where a local housing authority receives an application for accommodation on the grounds of homelessness, or for assistance in obtaining accommodation.[30] (The term "applicant" is defined as meaning "a person making such an application" as referred to in section 183.) The section applies where the local housing authority have reason to believe that the applicant is or may be homeless or threatened with homelessness. The definition of whether a person is "homeless" or not is contained in section 175 and discussed above in Chapter 8.

13.23. The provisions of section 183 and subsequent provisions do not affect a person's entitlement to advice and information under section 179 (duty to provide advisory services).[31]

Making Inquiries

13.24. There is an obligation on the local housing authority to make inquiries where they have reason to believe that an applicant may be homeless or threatened with homelessness.[32] The inquiries that the local housing authority are required to make are those which are necessary to satisfy itself of the following[33]:

whether the applicant is eligible for assistance,[34] and if so

---

[30] s. 183(1).
[31] s. 183(3).
[32] s. 184(1).
[33] s. 184(1).
[34] s. 184(1)(a).

whether any duty is owed to him under the following provisions
of this Part,[35] and if so
what duty is owed to him.[36]

The local housing authority may also make inquiries as to **13.25.**
whether the applicant has a local connection with the district of
another local housing authority in England, Wales or Scotland.[37]
The provisions relating to local connection are discussed above in
Chapter 11.

On completing their inquiries, the authority is required to notify **13.26.**
the applicant of their decision.[38] The local housing authority is
required to inform the applicant of the reasons for their decision if
there is any issue making up that decision is decided against the
interests of the applicant.[39] If the authority have notified, or intend
to notify, another local housing authority under section 198
(referral of cases), they are required to notify the applicant of that
decision and inform him of the reasons for it at the same time.[40]

Any notice made under subsection (3) or (4) must also inform **13.27.**
the applicant of her right to request a review of the decision and of
the time within which such a request for a review must be made.[41]

A notice which is required to be given to a person under section **13.28.**
184 shall be given in writing.[42] If the notice is not received by her,
it shall be treated as having been given to her if it is made available
at the authority's office for a reasonable period for collection by her
or on her behalf.[43]

"Advice and assistance"

References to "assistance under this Part" in the statute mean **13.29.**
the benefit of any function under section 183 and the following
provisions of Part VII of the 1996 Act relating to accommodation,
or assistance in obtaining accommodation. References to being
"eligible for assistance" refers to an applicant not excluded from
such assistance by section 185 (persons from abroad not eligible for
housing assistance) or section 186 (asylum seekers and their
dependents).

[35] s. 184(1)(b).
[36] s. 184(1)(b).
[37] s. 184(2).
[38] s. 184(3).
[39] s. 184(3).
[40] s. 184(4).
[41] s. 184(5).
[42] s. 184(6).
[43] *Ibid.*

13.30.   The statute does not require that the authority undertake all the provision of accommodation. Rather, the authority is able to sub-contract out the work of advice and assistance. Nor is there anything in the statute to require a minimum level of service to the recipient of the advice or assistance. Therefore, the obligation can be delegated to advice agencies. It is then for those agencies to decide what advice and assistance is appropriate.

13.31.   The expression that the authority procure advice and assistance "such that the applicant secures accommodation from another" seems wide enough to cover advice and assistance leading to house purchase by an applicant who is financially able to undertake such a step. Some other person, in this context, may be a person (or authority) abroad. In *Browne*, a woman with no local connection with Bristol (but who had suffered domestic violence there), and no local connection with the area of any other housing authority, was offered assistance to return to her home town of Tralee in the Republic of Ireland. The authorities in Tralee were prepared to ensure that she was housed. It was held that the authority did not need to know the exact details of the accommodation which was to be made available to her. The arrangement was only found to be appropriate on the basis that the authority could demonstrate that the woman ran no risk of domestic violence in Tralee.

13.32.   When the applicant is only threatened with homelessness at the time that a finding of intentionality is made, the authority's duty is to furnish her with advice and such assistance as they consider appropriate in any attempts she may make to secure that accommodation does not cease to be available for her occupation. This may include financial advice, or advice on the powers of the court to suspend an order. It would seem that when homelessness itself occurs, the applicant appears to be entitled to a period of temporary accommodation.

Enforcing the Duty to Make Inquiries

13.33.   The means of enforcement are considered in Chapters 6 and 7, above. Local authorities bear duties to make inquiries with reference to those applying for housing on the basis of homelessness. The issue arises as to the type and scope of inquiries which the authority is required to make. There is a line to be drawn between the obligation of local authorities to conduct original research and to rely on information gleaned from other sources or from information already known to the authority.

13.34.   The authority will be required to comply with the *Wednesbury* principles in reaching a decision. Clearly the Code of Guidance has a part to play in making decisions as to what will and will not be required to be investigated. The role of the Code in judicial review proceedings is potentially important. The Code sets out best practice in some areas and guidance in others. Therefore, deviance from the suggested course in the Code would be prima facie evidence of irrational or unreasonable procedures or decision-making on the part of the local authority.

Given that the Code does not have the effect of law itself, it **13.35.** would be difficult to argue that ignorance of the code was necessarily a misdirection in law. However, it would be a contributory factor alongside an analysis of what the law in fact requires the local authority to do.

The Interim Obligation to House Homeless Persons

A local housing authority has an obligation to secure that **13.36.** accommodation is available for the applicant's occupation pending a decision as to the duty they owe to the applicant in the following circumstances:[44]

The local housing authority must have reason to believe that the **13.37.** applicant:

may be homeless,
is eligible for assistance, and
has a priority need.

This is the core obligation to house homeless persons within Part VII of the 1996 Act. This obligation to secure that accommodation is available pending a decision as to the duty (if any) owed to him under Part VII of the 1996 Act.[45]

The core duty under section 188 arises irrespective of any **13.38.** possibility of the referral of the applicant's case to another local housing authority under sections 198 to 200 of the 1996 Act.[46] The core duty ceases when the authority's decision is notified to the applicant, even if the applicant requests a review of the decision, as under section 202 of the 1996 Act.[47]

The obligation is to secure that accommodation becomes available **13.39.** able for the applicant's occupation, which by definition means that accommodation is available for her and anyone with whom she is reasonably expected to reside. The duty is usually perceived as one

[44] s. 188(1).
[45] s. 188(1).
[46] s. 188(2).
[47] s. 188(3).

requiring the authority to have accommodation available once homelessness itself actually occurs, as distinct from an obligation to take steps to defend the current home. An applicant is not threatened with homelessness until 28 days before it is likely that she will become homeless.

13.40.   The authority may seek co-operation from other bodies, including a registered housing association, or a request may be made to social service or social work authorities to discharge the obligation on behalf of the housing authority. The authority is able to provide accommodation either by making available its own accommodation, or by securing that the applicant obtains accommodation from some other person, or by giving such advice and assistance that secures that accommodation is obtained from some other person. Reasonable charges may be made for accommodation, or a contribution sought towards payments the authority makes to another.

13.41.   A further problem is posed by "local authority policies". In particular the frequency with which all kinds of applicants receive identical offers of 28 days' accommodation suggests that many authorities operate some sort of policy under this provision. If such a policy is rigidly applied in decision-making, it can be set aside. However, if the 28-day rule is merely a guideline, which is reconsidered in each case, it might not be possible to set it aside as *ultra vires*. The Code suggests that 28 days would be adequate to discharge this duty but warns that "authorities should take account of local circumstances, including how readily other accommodation is in practice available in the area".

Duties to Persons Found to be Homeless Intentionally

13.42.   If the local housing authority are satisfied that the applicant has a priority need, the obligations set out in section 190 have effect, as provided in section 190(2).[48] As discussed above at chapter 12, the intentional homelessness code was created to prevent people in accommodation from leaving their occupation deliberately so that they could be re-housed automatically, putting a huge strain on local authorities. Therefore, where an applicant has left accommodation intentionally, there is no duty to provide that applicant with permanent accommodation. Rather there are only limited duties to provide temporary accommodation and to provide advice and assistance, as discussed below.

---

[48] The requirements for priority need are set out at s. 189 and are discussed in detail in Chapter 10, above.

Section 190 applies only where the local housing authority are **13.43.** satisfied:

first, that an applicant is homeless, and
secondly, that the applicant is eligible for assistance, but
thirdly, that the applicant became homeless intentionally.[49]

The definition of "homeless intentionally" in outline. The **13.44.** core of the definition of intentional homelessness is set out in section 191(1) of the 1996 Act:

"A person becomes homeless intentionally if he deliberately does or fails to do anything in consequence of which he ceases to occupy accommodation which is available for his occupation and which it would have been reasonable for him to continue to occupy".

Therefore, the test revolves around the applicant ceasing to occupy accommodation which was both available and reasonable for her to occupy, where that cessation of occupation is caused by some deliberate action or omission on her part. It is a central requirement that this act or omission is deliberate. An act or omission in good faith on the part of a person who was unaware of any relevant fact shall not be treated as deliberate.[50]

The nature of the interim obligations on the local author- 13.45. ity. The local housing authority is required to perform both of the following actions. First, to secure that some accommodation is available for the applicant's occupation for a period to enable the applicant to find accommodation.[51] This provision of accommodation is required to be for a period which the local housing authority consider will give the applicant a reasonable opportunity of securing accommodation for his occupation.[52] Secondly, to provide the applicant with such advice and assistance as the local housing authority consider appropriate in relation to any attempts the applicant may make to secure that accommodation becomes available for his occupation.[53]

Therefore, the authority is required to provide that some **13.46.** temporary accommodation is available. Then the authority is required to advise and assist the applicant to procure permanent accommodation. The duty incumbent on the local housing authority to provide that permanent accommodation itself, is considered below.

[49] s. 190(1).
[50] s. 191(2).
[51] s. 190(2).
[52] s. 190(2)(a)
[53] s. 190(2)(b).

13.47.   Obligation where applicant is intentionally homeless and in priority need.   Section 190(2) provides that the authority bear the following obligation where the applicant is in priority need and is homeless intentionally:—

> "(2) If the authority are satisfied that the applicant has a priority need, they shall—
> (a) secure that accommodation is available for his occupation for such period as they consider will give him a reasonable opportunity of securing accommodation for his occupation, and
> (b) provide him with advice and such assistance as they consider appropriate in the circumstances in any attempts he may make to secure that accommodation becomes available for his occupation."

In deciding whether or not a person is homeless, regard should be had to section 175 and the core definition of homelessness, as discussed at Chapter 8, above. The definition of becoming intentionally homeless is set out in section 191 an discussed in detail at Chapter 12, above.

13.48.   The obligation on the authority is therefore to enable the applicant to find some accommodation by the provision of advice and assistance. It does not extend to providing accommodation itself.

13.49.   Obligation where applicant is not in priority need and homeless intentionally.   If the local housing authority believe that the applicant is not in priority need, it is required to provide her with the advice and assistance which it considers appropriate in relation to any attempts the applicant may make to secure that accommodation becomes available for her occupation.[54] Therefore, there is a duty to give advice and assistance in circumstances where the applicant does not satisfy the priority need test in section 189.

13.50.   Where the applicant is homeless intentionally and not in priority need, section 190(3) provides for the following obligation:—

> "(3) If they are not satisfied that he has a priority need, they shall provide him with advice and such assistance as they consider appropriate in the circumstances in any attempts he may make to secure that accommodation becomes available for his occupation".

[54] s. 190(3).

The nature of the obligation. As discussed above, the duty to **13.51.**
provide advice and assistance is a flexible one. The authority is
able to sub-contract the work of advice and assistance. There is
nothing in the statute to ensure a minimum level of service to the
recipient of the advice or assistance. Similarly, it is for those
agencies to decide what advice and assistance is appropriate. The
agency then has the power to decide whether or not the applicant
ought to have been able to secure accommodation on the basis of
that advice and assistance. There is little input into that statutory
code for the applicant to object to the quality of the service
provided. The introduction of charters for local authority service is
the closest that the applicant can come. Alternatively, the applicant
is thrown back on judicial review proceedings or claims for breach
of statutory duty on the basis that the statutory obligation has not
been fully complied with.

The authority should interview everyone for whom they have a **13.52.**
duty to provide advice and should counsel them on the local
accommodation options open to them, where appropriate referring
them to other specialist agencies. This right must include advice
on rights of accommodation—both in the public and in the private
sector. When the authority's findings fall in this class, they also
have a duty to notify the applicant of their decision and of the
reasons for it. In *Gillespie*, in this context, a rule restricting
registration on the waiting list of certain classes of applicant was
declared unlawful on the ground that the authority had to consider
each applicant for registration.

One issue which arises here is when the obligation to provide **13.53.**
accommodation commences. In *Dyson*, the applicant was told on
May 21 that she would be provided with one month's accommodation from May 25 (the date on which her homelessness would
actually occur). This decision appears to have been taken by an
official, and appears to have required ratification by a committee.
In the event, the time was subsequently extended to July 6, but it
was not until July 3 that the committee's ratification was communicated to the applicant. It was held that time could run from the
earlier notification by the official, as the letter of July 3 was merely
confirmation of that decision.

An alternative view was taken in *De Falco* where only four days **13.54.**
had been allowed between notification of decision and the expiry
of the interim accommodation. The Court of Appeal considered
that this period was probably adequate, having regard to the
several weeks in accommodation provided by the authority, prior
to its decision. *De Falco* was the hearing of an interlocutory appeal
for an interlocutory injunction to house until trial and therefore

that matter was conclusive on the exercise of judicial discretion. Bridge L.J. held that time prior to the communication of the local authority's decision was wholly irrelevant. In his opinion, only time which had elapsed after the decision had been communicated was relevant. The aim of the legislation was to facilitate a period of time within which the applicant could find somewhere else to live after the decision on entitlement to permanent accommodation had been made.

Obligation where Applicant not in Priority Need and not Homeless Intentionally

13.55. An obligation arises, where an applicant is not in priority need and not homeless intentionally, where the local housing authority satisfy themselves as follows:[55]

> that the applicant is homeless and eligible for assistance,[56] and
> that the applicant has not become homeless intentionally[57]; and
> that the applicant has a priority need.[58]

The authority are then required to provide the applicant with the advice and assistance they consider appropriate in the circumstances in relation to any attempts the applicant may make to find accommodation. The advice and assistance is to be given to the extent the authority considers to be appropriate to assist the applicant in attempts she may make in ensuring that such accommodation becomes available for her occupation.[59]

Obligation where Applicant in Priority Need and not Homeless Intentionally

13.56. Unless the local housing authority refer the application to another local housing authority (see section 198), they are required to secure that accommodation is available for occupation by the applicant.[60] This obligation arises in circumstances where the local housing authority are satisfied under section 193(1) that an applicant is:

> homeless,
> eligible for assistance,
> has a priority need, and
> not homeless intentionally.

---

[55] s. 192(1).
[56] s. 192(1)(a).
[57] s. 192(1)(b).
[58] s. 192(1).
[59] s. 192(2).
[60] s. 193(2).

Section 193 takes effect subject to section 197, which provides for the duty of a local housing authority where there is other suitable accommodation available.

The scope of the obligation. The local housing authority are **13.57.** subject to the duty under section 193 for a period of two years ("the minimum period"). This is subject to the remaining provisions of section 193. After the end of that period, the authority is empowered to continue to secure that accommodation is available for occupation by the applicant, but are not obliged to do so.[61]

The minimum period begins at different times depending on the **13.58.** circumstances in which the applicant comes to occupy the property. If the applicant was occupying accommodation made available under section 188 (interim duty to accommodate), the minimum period begins of the day on which she was notified of the authority's decision that the duty under this section was owed to her.[62]

If the applicant was occupying accommodation made available to **13.59.** her under section 200(3) (which provides for an interim duty where the applicant's case is considered for referral but not referred), the minimum period begins on the date on which she was notified under subsection (2) of that section of the decision that the conditions for referral were not met.[63] In any other case, the minimum period begins on the day on which the accommodation was first made available to her in pursuance of the duty under section 193.[64]

The authority are bound to have regard to slum clearance, **13.60.** overcrowding and so forth. The duty generally is to take reasonable steps to secure that accommodation does not cease to be available for the applicant's occupation.

The meaning of "accommodation" in these circum- **13.61.** **stances.** The Court of Appeal in *R. v. Wandsworth L.B.C., ex p. Wingrove* and *R. v. Wandsworth L.B.C., ex p. Mansoor*[65] considered the meaning of "accommodation" in this circumstance. It upheld the remarks of Lord Hoffmann in *Awua* in this regard as being correct in the context of what is now section 193. Accommodation was to be understood as meaning somewhere to live rather than

---

[61] s. 193(3) and further s. 194.
[62] s. 193(4)(a).
[63] s. 193(4)(b).
[64] s. 193(4)(c).
[65] [1996] 3 All ER 913.

property provided permanently. The term "accommodation" must be qualified by a concept of being "somewhere tolerable to live" (in the words of Sir Thomas Bingham M.R.). It would only be possible to challenge an offer of accommodation on the basis that it was not permanent enough on the basis of the *Wednesbury* principles. Thus, the authority's decision is required to be proportionate in the circumstances of the case, in line with administrative law principles.

13.62.   In *Wingrove*, the applicant, W, and another, who were unintentionally homeless and in priority need, appealed against the dismissal of their applications for judicial review of the authority's decision to offer them accommodation. The authority had made an offer of accommodation by way of arranging for a private landlord to grant them assured shorthold tenancies which had a reasonable likelihood of renewal. W argued that the authorities had failed to discharge their duty under section 65(2) of the 1985 Act, as the accommodation offered was not permanent.

13.63.   The authority relied on the decision in *R. v. Brent L.B.C., ex p. Awua*.[66] The local authority contended that they had discharged their duty satisfactorily provided that the accommodation offered was suitable and that the tenure was not likely to expire within 28 days without alternative accommodation being available. Furthermore, there was no requirement that the accommodation offered be settled or permanent. W contended that Lord Hoffman's speech in *Awua* was *obiter* on this point and that his interpretation of the term "accommodation" differed from that adopted in previous cases and legislation.

13.64.   The Court of Appeal did hold that it was unlikely that Lord Hoffman's interpretation of the word "accommodation" was *obiter* in *Awua* but was in any event of great persuasive authority and correct in principle. There was nothing to conflict with this interpretation of the term in any event in the legislation or in the Code of Guidance. In the wake of *Awua* it was clearly possible for a local authority to discharge its statutory duty by arranging for an assured shorthold tenancy to be offered, provided the accommodation offered was suitable.

This issue is considered in greater detail in Chapter 9, above.

13.65.   **Cessation of the obligation.** The local housing authority ceases to be subject to the duty under section 193 if the applicant refuses an offer of accommodation which the authority are satisfied

---

[66] [1996] 1 A.C. 55.

is suitable for him.[67] The authority is then required to notify the applicant that they regard themselves as having discharged their duty under this section.[68] This is in circumstances where the applicant has been informed by the authority of the possible consequence of refusal.[69]

The local housing authority ceases to be subject to the duty **13.66.** under section 193 if the applicant:

"(a) ceases to be eligible for assistance,[70]
(b) becomes homeless intentionally from the accommodation made available for his occupation,[71]
(c) accepts an offer of accommodation under Part VI (allocation of housing),[72] or
(d) otherwise voluntarily ceases to occupy as his only or principal home the accommodation made available for his occupation."[73]

Further, the local housing authority ceases to be subject to the **13.67.** duty under section 193 if:

the applicant refuses an offer of accommodation under Part VI, after being informed of the possible consequence of refusal,[74] and
the authority are satisfied that the accommodation was suitable for the applicant and that it was reasonable for the applicant to accept it and notify the applicant accordingly within 21 days of the refusal.[75]

In this context, the applicant may reasonably be expected to **13.68.** accept an offer of accommodation under Part VI even though she is under contractual or other obligations in respect of his existing accommodation.[76] This is so provided the applicant is able to terminate those obligations before she is required to take up the offer.[77]

A person, who ceases to be owed the duty set out in section 193, **13.69.** may make a fresh application to the authority for accommodation or assistance in obtaining accommodation.[78] Therefore, for the

---

[67] Housing Act 1996, s. 193(5).
[68] *Ibid.*
[69] *Ibid.*
[70] s. 193(6)(a).
[71] s. 193(6)(b).
[72] s. 193(6)(c).
[73] s. 193(6)(d).
[74] s. 193(7)(a).
[75] s. 193(7)(b).
[76] s. 193(8).
[77] *Ibid.*
[78] s. 193(9).

purposes of making an application, the section 193 obligation is capable of extinction, and the process begins again.

13.70.   There is a body of case law around this area, restricting the obligation of the local authority's offer of accommodation. The offer cannot be deferred for a reason which is not bound up with the Part VII decision-making process.[79] In this vein, a conditional offer of accommodation will not satisfy the obligation. The offer is to remain open for a reasonable period of time.[80]

13.71.   The question of whether the duty has been properly discharged may be qualified by a number of principles. Where an applicant accepts the accommodation for a limited period, this may not absolve the authority from a claim that the accommodation is not suitable.[81] An authority cannot require the applicant to move into property before entertaining a claim that it is not suitable,[82] particularly where such a policy is rigidly applied.[83] Similarly, where the property is occupied by squatters, there cannot be an adequate discharge of the obligation.[84]

Power Exercisable with Reference to Minimum Period

13.72.   It is open to a local housing authority, subject to section 194, to continue to secure that accommodation is available for the applicant's occupation in circumstances where that authority was subject to the duty to provide accommodation under section 193 until the end of the minimum period.[85] The word "secure" in this regard would seem to include not only the authority providing accommodation directly but also a situation in which the authority give the applicant such advice and information that results in another person providing that accommodation.

13.73.   The local housing authority shall not continue to provide accommodation in these circumstances unless they are satisfied on a review carried out under the terms of section 194 that a number of criteria are satisfied.[86] Those criteria are:

---

[79] *R. v. Tower Hamlets L.B.C., ex p. Khalique* (1991) 26 H.L.R. 517; *R. v. Newham L.B.C., ex p. Miah* (1995) 28 H.L.R. 279.

[80] *Parr v. Wyre B.C.* (1982) 2 H.L.R. 71, C.A.; *R. v. Wandsworth L.B.C., ex p. Lindsay* (1986) 18 H.L.R. 502.

[81] *R. v. Wycombe D.C., ex p. Hazeltine* (1993) 25 H.L.R. 313.

[82] *R. v. Newham L.B.C., ex p. Gentle* (1993) 26 H.L.R. 466.

[83] *R. v. Brent L.B.C., ex p. Baruwa* (1995) 28 H.L.R. 361; *R. v. Newham L.B.C., ex p. Laronde* (1994) 27 H.L.R. 215.

[84] *R. v. Ealing L.B.C., ex p. Denny* (1995) 27 H.L.R. 424.

[85] Housing Act 1996, s. 194(1).

[86] s. 194(2).

the applicant has a priority need,[87]
there is no other suitable accommodation available for occupation by the applicant in the authority's district,[88]
the applicant wishes the authority to continue securing that accommodation is available for her occupation,[89] and
the authority shall not continue to provide accommodation in these circumstances for more than two years at a time, unless they are satisfied on a further review under section 194 in these circumstances.[90]

The review under section 194 must be carried out, under section **13.74.** 194(2), "towards the end of the minimum period, or subsequent two year period" with a view to enabling the authority to make an assessment of the likely situation at the end of that period. The authority must cease to provide accommodation in these circumstances if events occur such that, by virtue of section 193(6) or (7), they would cease to be subject to any duty under that section.[91]

In circumstances where a local housing authority carry out a **13.75.** review under section 194, the local housing authority is required to make such inquiries as the authority consider appropriate to determine whether they are satisfied as to the matters mentioned in subsection (2)(a) to (c) (set out above) and whether any of the events referred in subsection (3) has occurred.[92] On completing the review, the authority must notify the applicant of their determination and of whether they propose to exercise, or continue to exercise, their power under section 194.[93]

The authority may at any time give notice to the person **13.76.** concerned that they propose to cease exercising their power under section 194 in the applicant's case.[94] This may be in consequence of a review or otherwise.[95] Such a notice must specify both the day on which the authority will cease exercising their power under this section, and any action that the authority intend to take as a result.[96] The notice must be given not less than the prescribed period before the day specified in the notice.[97]

---

[87] s. 194(2)(a).
[88] s. 194(2)(b).
[89] s. 194(2)(c).
[90] s. 194(2).
[91] s. 194(3).
[92] s. 194(4).
[93] *Ibid.*
[94] s. 194(5).
[95] *Ibid.*
[96] s. 194(6).
[97] *Ibid.*

13.77.   Section 195 applies where the local housing authority are satisfied that an applicant is threatened with homelessness and is eligible for assistance.[98] The authority are required to take reasonable steps to secure that accommodation does not cease to be available for his occupation.[99] If the authority are satisfied that she has a priority need,[1] and are not satisfied that she became threatened with homelessness intentionally[2] they are required to take reasonable steps to secure that accommodation does not cease to be available for her occupation. Section 195(2) takes effect subject to section 197 (which sets out the duty where there is other suitable accommodation available for the applicant).

13.78.   Importantly, section 195(2) does not affect any right of the authority, whether by virtue of a contract, enactment or rule of law, to secure vacant possession of any accommodation.[3] The authority is at liberty to commence proceedings to recover possession, in spite of the broader context of actions under section 195.

13.79.   In furthering the duty set out under section 195(2), the authority are required to secure that some accommodation is available for occupation by her.[4] This accommodation is required to be accommodation other than that occupied by the applicant when she made her application.[5]

13.80.   The provisions of section 193(3) to (9) (which set out the period for which the duty is owed) and section 194 (which creates the power in the authority to continue to provide such accommodation after the effluxion of the minimum period of duty) apply in relation to the duty under section 195 in the same way that they apply in relation to the duty under section 193.

13.81.   If the authority are not satisfied that the applicant has a priority need,[6] or are satisfied that she has a priority need but are also satisfied that she became threatened with homelessness intentionally,[7] they must provide her with the advice and assistance which they consider appropriate in the circumstances in any attempts the applicant may make to secure that accommodation does not cease to be available for her occupation.[8]

[98] s. 195(1).
[99] s. 195(2).
[1] s. 195(2)(a).
[2] s. 195(2)(b).
[3] s. 195(3).
[4] s. 195(4).
[5] *Ibid.*
[6] s. 195(5)(a).
[7] s. 195(5)(b).
[8] s. 195(5).

Obligations under Part III of the Children Act 1989

In considering the question of young people's vulnerability, the **13.82.**
authority should have regard to section 20 and Part III of the
Children Act 1989. Section 20 requires local authorities to provide
accommodation for children "in need" within their districts.
Children in need are to be found accommodation by an authority
where there is no person having parental responsibility for them;
where they have been lost or abandoned; or where the person who
has been caring for them, can no longer care for them. Local
authorities are required to provide accommodation where children
who have reached the age of 16 and whose welfare the authority
consider likely to be seriously prejudiced if they do not provide
them with accommodation.

Section 20 of the Children Act 1989, provides for the accommo-   **13.83.**
dation of children by local authorities in certain circumstances.
Every local authority is required to provide accommodation for
any child in need within their area who appears to them to require
accommodation. That need must arise as a result of:[9]

> there being no person who has parental responsibility for her;
> her being lost or having been abandoned; or
> the person who has been caring for her being prevented
> (whether or not permanently) from providing her with suitable
> accommodation or care.

In circumstances where a local authority provide accommo-   **13.84.**
dation for a child who is ordinarily resident in the area of another
local authority, that other local authority may take over the
provision of accommodation for the child.[10]

Every local authority is required to provide accommodation for   **13.85.**
any child in need within its area who has reached the age of
sixteen and whose welfare the authority consider is likely to be
seriously prejudiced if they do not provide her with accommodation.[11] A local authority is empowered, but not obliged, to
provide accommodation for any child in need within their area
(even though a person who has parental responsibility for her is
able to provide her with accommodation) if they consider that to
do so would safeguard or promote the child's welfare.[12] A local

---

[9] s. 20(1) of the 1989 Act.
[10] s. 20(2).
[11] s. 20(3).
[12] s. 20(4).

authority may provide accommodation for any person who has reached the age of 16 but is under 21 in any community home which takes children who have reached the age of 16 if they consider that to do so would safeguard or promote her welfare.[13]

13.86. There is a further obligation on local authorities to consider the child's wishes regarding the provision of accommodation and to give due consideration (given the child's comparative age and understanding) to such of her wishes as they have been able to ascertain.[14]

13.87. A local authority may not provide accommodation for the child in these circumstances if the person who has parental responsibility for the child objects. That person must be willing and able to

provide accommodation for the child or be willing and able to arrange for accommodation to be provided for the child.[15] Any person who has parental responsibility for a child may at any time remove the child from accommodation provided by or on behalf of the local authority.[16]

13.88. Every local authority is required to "make provision for the reception and accommodation of children" who are removed or kept away from home under Part V of the Children Act. This is so where the authority is the designated authority with reference to children in police protection; on remand; or the subject of a supervision order which imposes a residence requirement.[17]

13.89. It is then the duty of a local authority looking after any child to safeguard and promote her welfare, and to make use of any services available for children cared for by their own parents as appears to the authority reasonable in any case.[18] The local authority is required to consider the wishes and feelings of (1) the child; (2) her parents; (3) any person who is not a parent of his but who has parental responsibility for him; or (4) any other person whose wishes and feelings the authority consider to be relevant.[19] The local authority shall give due consideration to the child's age and understanding, to such wishes and feelings of the child as they have been able to ascertain, and to the child's religious persuasion, racial origin and cultural and linguistic background.[20]

[13] s. 20(5).
[14] s. 20(6).
[15] s. 20(7).
[16] s. 20(8).
[17] s. 21.
[18] s. 22(3).
[19] s. 22(4).
[20] s. 22(5).

Availability of Other Suitable Accommodation

The qualification to the definition of "homeless" is to the **13.90.** definition of "accommodation". Under section 175(3) "a person shall not be treated as having accommodation unless it is accommodation which it would be reasonable for him to continue to occupy". The issue is therefore what type of accommodation is not reasonable for an individual to occupy. This issue is considered generally in Chapter 9, above, but the salient issues with reference to the obligation on the local authority are set out below.

Duty where other suitable accommodation available. The **13.91.** duty on a local housing authority to provide accommodation where there is suitable accommodation available is set out in section 197. This section enables the local housing authority to avoid a duty to provide housing itself in circumstances where there is other accommodation which the applicant could occupy. There is a two-step introduction to this "get-out" for the authority and that is a requirement that the accommodation be:

available to the applicant,
suitable for the applicant, and
is within the authority's district.

Where the get-out is applicable, the local housing authority are required to provide the applicant with such advice and assistance as the authority consider is reasonably required to enable her to secure such accommodation for her occupation.[21]

The scope for the applicability of this get-out is set out in **13.92.** section 197(1). It applies where the local housing authority is under a duty under Part VII of the 1996 Act. In that case, the local authority are required to secure that accommodation is available for occupation by an applicant,[22] or to secure that accommodation does not cease to be available for her occupation.[23] This applies where the authority are not satisfied that other suitable accommodation is available for occupation by her in their district.

There are a number of areas in which this duty is expressly **13.93.** provided not to apply. Section 197(6) provides the complete list. The areas covered are — section 188 (which sets out the interim duty to accommodate an applicant in case of apparent priority need), section 190(2)(a) (which creates the limited duty of an

[21] s. 197(2).
[22] s. 197(1)(a).
[23] s. 197(1)(b).

authority to a person becoming homeless intentionally), or section 200(1), (3) or (4) (which create interim duties where a case is considered for referral or is actually referred).

13.94.   The duty on the authority ceases in circumstances where the applicant fails to take reasonable steps to secure that accommodation is available for her occupation.[24]

13.95.   The scope of the duty.   The issue arises as to the sort of advice and assistance that the local authority are required to provide. The authority must have regard to all the circumstances.[25] Some of the factors which the authority are required to look to as part of their duty are the characteristics and personal circumstances of the applicant,[26] and the state of the local housing market and the type of accommodation available.[27]

13.96.   In the circumstances of this particular duty, accommodation is not regarded as available for occupation by the applicant if it is available only with assistance beyond what the authority consider is reasonable in the circumstances.[28] The ambit of this subsection is therefore to discount accommodation which would require, in effect, unreasonable levels of assistance to procure for the applicant's benefit.

Duties to House Pending Referral to Another Authority

13.97.   There is a scheme for the referral of applicants from one authority to another. In circumstances where the authority to which the applicant applies are of the opinion that there is no local connection between the applicant and its district, it is open to the authority to refer the applicant to a district with which the applicant does have a local connection.

13.98.   Therefore, the local connection provisions exempt the authority which refers the applicant on ("the notifying authority") from an obligation to house that applicant. The authority receiving the referral ("the notified authority") then bear the burden of finding permanent accommodation for the applicant. The circumstances in which this translation of duties arises is set out in some detail below. In short, the applicant must have no local connection with the notifying authority; the applicant must have a local connection

---

[24] s. 197(3).
[25] s. 197(4).
[26] s. 197(4)(a).
[27] s. 197(4)(b).
[28] s. 197(5).

with the notified authority; and there must not be any risk of domestic violence in the district of the notified authority.

Notification process. When the authority notify the applicant **13.99.** that they are referring the application to another authority, they cease to have obligations under a number of provisions in Part VII. They cease to be subject to any duty under section 188 (interim duty to accommodate in case of apparent priority need). Further, they are not subject to any duty under section 193 (the main housing duty). However, the authority is required to secure that accommodation is available for occupation by the applicant until she is notified of the decision whether the conditions for referral of her case are met. These exemptions apply further to section 200(1), where a local housing authority notify the applicant that they intend to notify or have notified another local housing authority of their opinion that the conditions are met for the referral of her case to that other authority.

When the notifying authority have decided whether the condi- **13.100.** tions for referral are met, that notifying authority shall notify the applicant of the decision and inform her of the reasons for it.[29] The notice must also inform the applicant of her right to request a review of the decision and of the time within which such a request must be made.

The intricacies of the referral process are considered in Chapter 11, above.

Obligation where conditions for referral are not met. If it is **13.101.** decided that the conditions for referral are not met, the notifying authority must ensure that accommodation is available for occupation by the applicant until the authority have considered whether other suitable accommodation is available for her occupation in their district.[30] If they are satisfied that other suitable accommodation is available for her occupation in their district, section 197(2) applies; and if they are not so satisfied, they are subject to the duty under section 193 (the main housing duty).

Further to section 200(5) the duty owed to an applicant under **13.102.** section 200(3) ceases even if the applicant requests a review of the authority's decision (see section 202). The authority may continue to secure that accommodation is available for the applicant's occupation pending the decision on a review.

Obligation where conditions for referral are met. If the **13.103.** authority decide that the conditions for referral are met, the notified authority must ensure that accommodation is available for

[29] s. 200(2).
[30] s. 200(3).

the applicant's occupation until they have considered whether or not other suitable accommodation is available for her occupation in their district.[31] If they are satisfied that other suitable accommodation is available for his occupation in their district, section 197(2) applies; and if they are not so satisfied, they are subject to the duty under section 193 (the main housing duty).

13.104.   Further to section 200(5) the duty owed to an applicant under section 200(4) ceases even if the applicant requests a review of the authority's decision.[32] The authority may continue to secure that accommodation is available for the applicant's occupation pending the decision on a review.

13.105.   Any notice required to be given to an applicant under section 200 must be given in writing and, if not received by the applicant, must be treated as having been given to him if it is made available at the authority's office for a reasonable period for collection by her or on her behalf.[33]

Discharge of Housing Functions

13.106.   The following section governs the manner in which all of the above obligations are to be carried into effect. The 1996 Act makes specific provision for the ways in which the local housing authority is deemed to discharge its functions under Part VII. The only three ways in which they can achieve this discharge are set out in section 206(1):

> where the authority secures that suitable accommodation provided by them is available,[34]
> where the authority secures that the applicant obtains suitable accommodation from some other person,[35] or
> where the authority secures that she is given such advice and assistance as will secure that suitable accommodation is available from some other person.[36]

13.107.   There are requirements which can be imposed on the applicant or another person in relation to whom the authority are discharging such functions.[37] For example, a local housing authority may

---

[31] s. 200(4).
[32] See the discussion of s. 202 in Chapter 5, above.
[33] s. 200(6).
[34] s. 206(1)(a).
[35] s. 206(1)(b).
[36] s. 206(1)(c).
[37] s. 206(2).

require such a person to meet the costs of finding accommodation for her. This includes reasonable charges as determined by the authority. Those charges may be connected to accommodation which the authority secure for her occupation whether it is accommodation provided by the authority or by some other body or person.

In discharging the functions under section 206, the local author- **13.108.** ity is required to provide particular types of accommodation as set out in section 207(1). The accommodation must be one of the following types:

accommodation in a hostel within the meaning of section 622 of the Housing Act 1985,[38] or
accommodation leased to the authority.[39]

Furthermore, that accommodation must be provided for more than two years in any period of three years. This time period of two years need not be continuous — it is enough that that the two years are an aggregate two years out of the three.[40] This rule applies irrespective of the number of applications for accommodation, or assistance in obtaining accommodation, which the applicant makes.

The type of leased accommodation provided to the authority **13.109.** must comply with all three of the criteria in section 207(2). The accommodation must be leased to the authority with vacant possession for use as temporary housing accommodation. That lease may include terms which enable the lessor to recover vacant possession either on a specified date or at such time as the lessor requires. The second criterion is that the lessor is not an authority or body falling within the definition in section 80(1) of the Housing Act 1985 (being a landlord under a secure tenancy). The final condition is that the authority have no interest other than under the lease in question or as a mortgagee.

The exceptions from the authority's obligation to act under **13.110.** section 207 do not apply in relation to an applicant who normally resides with another person as a member of his family.[41] Alternatively, there is no obligation to fulfil this duty where the applicant resides (or may reasonably be expected to reside with) another person, where that other person would fall outside section 207(1).

---

[38] s. 207(1)(a).
[39] s. 207(1)(b).
[40] s. 207(1).
[41] s. 207(3).

13.111.   Further, the Secretary of State may, where a local housing authority ask, exclude or modify the operation of section 207(1) in relation to that authority if it appears to her that the authority will not otherwise be able reasonably to discharge their housing functions under Part VII.[42] Any such direction by the Secretary of State has effect only with respect to applicants specified for the period specified. Such a period cannot exceed one year in any event. The direction may be expressed to have effect subject to any other express conditions.[43]

Discharge of Functions with Reference to Out-of-District Placements

13.112.   There is the question then of the authority's performance of its obligations when an applicant is placed for accommodation outside the authority's own district. Section 208(1)provides that the local housing authority must secure that accommodation is available for the occupation of the applicant in their district. This obligation is circumscribed by the words "so far as reasonably practicable" in discharging their housing functions.

13.113.   If the authority secure that accommodation is available for the occupation of the applicant outside their district, the first authority must give notice to the local housing authority in whose district the accommodation is situated.[44] The notice must state the name of the applicant; the number and description of other persons who normally reside with her as a member of his family or might reasonably be expected to reside with her, the address of the accommodation; the date on which the accommodation was made available to her; and which function under Part VII the authority was discharging in securing that the accommodation is available for her occupation.[45] The notice must be in writing, and must be given before the end of the period of 14 days beginning with the day on which the accommodation was made available to the applicant.[46]

Arrangements with Private Landlords

13.114.   Much of local authority policy revolves around out-sourcing housing to private-sector landlords rather than maintaining a public housing stock. The issue therefore arises, how the authority discharges their obligations under the 1996 Act in this context.

[42] s. 207(1).
[43] s. 207(5).
[44] s. 208(2).
[45] s. 208(3).
[46] s. 208(4).

Section 209(1) expressly deals with this situation. In this area, a "private landlord" is defined as being a landlord who does not fall within section 80(1) of the Housing Act 1985 (the landlord condition for secure tenancies under that Act). The applicant in this circumstance is defined as being "a person specified by the authority".

In the first instance,[47] the section considers the situation where **13.115.** the authority's obligations arise under the interim duties provisions.[48] If a tenancy is granted in circumstances arising out of those duties, the tenancy cannot become an assured tenancy within 12 months. The start of the 12 month period is settled in one of two ways. It is usually the date on which the applicant was notified of the authority's decision under section 184(3) or 198(5). Alternatively, where there is a review of the authority's decision under section 202 (or an appeal to the court under section 204), the 12 months begins on the date on which the applicant is notified of the decision on review or the appeal is finally determined. The exception to this alternative provision is where, before or during the period, the tenant is notified by the landlord that the tenancy is to be regarded as an assured shorthold or an assured tenancy. It should be noted that a registered social landlord cannot serve such a notice making such a tenancy an assured tenancy other than an assured shorthold tenancy.[49]

In any other circumstances where a tenancy is granted in **13.116.** pursuance of arrangements under section 209 by a registered social landlord to the applicant ("a person specified by the authority") the tenancy cannot be an assured tenancy unless it is an assured shorthold tenancy, and the landlord cannot convert the tenancy to an assured tenancy.[50] The tenancy can be converted to an assured tenancy where the accommodation is allocated to the tenant under Part VI of the 1996 Act.

Discharge of Duties in Other Ways

The authority is entitled to call for assistance from other bodies **13.117.** including registered housing associations. Alternatively, they may arrange for social services or other similar departments to discharge those functions on their behalf. This requirement calls on some action by the authority. In *Sidhu*,[51] the accommodation was

---

[47] s. 209(2).
[48] Being ss. 188, 190, 200, or 204(4).
[49] s. 209(2).
[50] s. 209(3).
[51] (1982) 2 H.L.R. 45.

provided by a women's refuge — an organisation which was not even a public body. The authority contended that this constituted a discharge of its responsibilities. The accommodation in that case was not within the authority's district — nevertheless the authority contended that it discharged its obligations to house the applicant satisfactorily.

13.118.   There are a number of refuges which are provided by local authorities. In these circumstances there are a number of reasons why the authority may become susceptible to challenge by or on behalf of the applicant. The refuge is not independent of the authority and the provision of funds may be construed to constitute the provision of advice or assistance by the authority itself. Where the authority does provide the accommodation itself, the issue arises as to the time at which the applicant becomes a secure tenant of the authority.

The Right given to the Applicant

13.119.   The issue arises whether the applicant is a licensee or a tenant under the terms of the provision of the accommodation. A number of cases concerned with the 1977 Act considered whether or not such provision could amount to a secure tenancy (see for example *Family Housing Association v. Miah*[52] in this regard). Under the terms of Part IV of the 1985 legislation and to Schedule 1 paragraph 4 of that legislation, the House of Lords in *Walsh*[53] found that where temporary accommodation was provided under this duty, that provision of accommodation was held to amount to a secure tenancy. The authority contended that the provision of accommodation in such circumstances could only be said to amount to a licence.

13.120.   The test propounded by Lords Templeman and Oliver in *A.-G. Securities v. Vaughan*[54] and *Street v. Mountford*[55] decided that an occupant will have a tenancy where there is exclusive possession for a term at a rent. Therefore, a licence would have to be a permission to occupy which did not grant exclusive possession for a term at a rent. Indeed, it was accepted in *A.-G. Securities v. Vaughan* that there does not necessarily even need to be a rent to have a tenancy. The position of the local authority in this situation, is, therefore, that there is a tenancy granted under the operation of these statutory obligations to provide temporary accommodation.

[52] (1982) 5 H.L.R. 97.
[53] Eastleigh B.C. v. Walsh [1985] 1 W.L.R. 525
[54] [1990] 1 A.C. 417.
[55] [1985] A.C. 809.

For example, in *Family Housing Association v. Jones*[56] where a **13.121.** local authority purportedly licensed properties for the temporary accommodation of homeless people. The association entered into an agreement with the respondent Mrs Jones for her occupation and that of her son in a self-contained flat. The agreement described her and her son as licensees. The agreement also provided that she did not have exclusive possession: the association retained a key to the premises. The Court of Appeal held that Mrs Jones and her son were the only people who were to occupy the property, with the result that they had exclusive possession of it. Further, she paid a weekly sum to the authority. Therefore she was properly described as a tenant.

Occupation of temporary hostel accommodation is likely to be **13.122.** regarded as being occupied under the terms of a licence. In hostel situations, the occupant does not have exclusive possession of any part of the property — other than a bed or bedroom. There are communal kitchen and washing facilities — therefore there is not a complete occupation of the dwelling space required by the occupant so as to establish exclusive possession.

The authority is required to notify the applicant of its decision, **13.123.** whether or not it is favourable to the applicant. The authority is also required to provide reasons for its decision. The decision must be notified, as discussed in Chapter 6, above, at the completion of inquiries at the point in time when the decision is taken. The issue for the applicant is then to demonstrate the point in time at which notification ought to have taken place.

As to the quality of temporary accommodation, the decided cases **13.124.** relate to the position with reference to those who become intentionally homeless. In *Gliddon*[57] the local authority was alleged to have been in breach of its temporary duty because the accommodation provided was in substantial disrepair, requiring work under section 190 of the 1985 Act to prevent it becoming unfit. It was held that an authority is entitled to have regard to the time for which accommodation is likely to be occupied when determining what quality of accommodation is appropriate. The court accepted that some quality of accommodation would fall below the line of acceptable discharge of even a temporary duty, but the accommodation provided under the terms of section 190 did not necessarily do so. Even accommodation which is so unfit that it is not even capable of being repaired at a reasonable expense within the terms

---

[56] [1990] 1 W.L.R. 779.
[57] *Exeter C.C., ex p. Gliddon* [1985] 1 All ER 493.

of the 1985 Act, may well be suitable for a temporary purpose as a result of the decision in *Pulhofer* and subsequent decisions.

13.125.   In *Ward*,[58] accommodation in a mobile home on a caravan site was described in the evidence of a social worker as being in appalling condition. However, it was held that using that accommodation for the occupation of an applicant on a temporary basis was an adequate discharge of the duty to provide temporary accommodation. This was so on the facts in the light of the family's request to live in the temporary structure rather than in a permanent structure.

13.126.   Under the terms of the Code of Guidance, hotels are not considered suitable for use by families as long-term accommodation. In practice, bed and breakfast hotels are used for the accommodation of a very large number of families despite this guidance. Hotels are to be used in place of permanent accommodation only where it is considered absolutely necessary. In *Thrasyvoulou* the local authority tried to cease the use of low-grade bed and breakfast accommodation as temporary housing. The court accepted their rebuttal of the hotelier's argument that such accommodation should be considered to be suitable.

The Obligation to make Decisions

Obligation not to Fetter own Decision-Making Power

13.127.   A decision reached without making the proper inquiries will be an invalid decision. The most obvious examples of this principle occur where an authority seeks to give effect to a blanket policy without considering the precise circumstances of the case before them. For example, where an entire family is treated as intentionally homeless where they fall into arrears of rent constitute an invalid decision in relation to such family because no inquiries are made as to the reason for the rent arrears.

13.128.   Where the inquiries suggest that the applicant has become homeless intentionally but there is doubt or uncertainty in the matter, it should be resolved in favour of the applicant.[59] In *Barry v. Newham L.B.C.*[60] a decision to evict a tenant for arrears was

---

[58] *R. v. Southampton C.C., ex p. Ward* (1984) 14 H.L.R. 114.
[59] *R. v. North Devon D.C., ex p Lewis* [1981] 1 W.L.R. 328, *R. v. Gravesham B.C., ex p. Winchester; R. v. Thurrock D.C., ex p. Williams* (1981) 1 H.L.R. 128.
[60] (1980) L.A.G. Bulletin 142. See, however, the decision in *Zold v. Bristol C.C.* (1981) December L.A.G. Bulletin 287.

accompanied by notification that they were considered to have become homeless intentionally. The court did not uphold the validity of either the decision or the notification on the basis that it preceded the application itself. Where an authority fails to take into account information and material which had come to its attention between the time of a decision to evict the applicant and a decision made under the 1977 Act.[61] All circumstances up until the decision must be taken into account.[62] Thus, while a possession order is relevant no finding of intentionality can automatically follow.[63]

The authority must not seek to impose policies without any flexibility. So, in *R. v. Gateshead M.B.C., ex p Lauder*[64] L sought judicial review of two decisions of G to the effect that L's points for being overcrowded under G's letting policy would be suspended for a year. Potts J. held that the 1985 Act provided for a discretion exercisable by local authorities dealing with a provision of accommodation to those suffering overcrowding. The inclusion of the word "will" in its policy meant that it would not be flexible in the operation of that policy — therefore its discretion was being unlawfully fettered in relation to any decision made as a result of that policy. **13.129.**

While the obligation to reach a decision generally is not spelled out, it is implied in the legislation. An authority may not defer the obligation in the hope or expectation of a change where that change might reduce their duties (such as loss of priority need status). However, it may be that in an appropriate case a short-term deferral may be permissible where there is a valid reason for the authority to believe that there will be a material change in the applicant's circumstances. **13.130.**

Functions of the Secretary of State

A Code of Guidance on the operation of the statute, while yet to be completed at the time of going to press, has been prepared by the Secretary of State, and is set out in the Appendices below. Local housing authorities and social services authorities are required to have regard to guidance issued by the Secretary of State **13.131.**

[61] *Barry v. Newham L.B.C.* (1980) L.A.G. Bulletin 142; *Zold v. Bristol C.C.* (1981) December L.A.G. Bulletin 287. See also *Devenport, supra.*
[62] *Devenport v. Salford C.C.* (1983) 8 H.L.R. 54, C.A. and *R. v. Swansea C.C., ex p. John* (1982) 9 H.L.R. 56.
[63] *Ibid.*
[64] Unreported (May 16, 1996).

in the exercise of their functions relating to homelessness and the prevention of homelessness.[65] The Secretary of State is empowered to give guidance generally or to give guidance to specified descriptions of authorities.[66]

Asylum-Seekers and Immigration Matters

13.132.   The Secretary of State has obligations to local housing authorities with reference to asylum-seekers and immigration matters under section 187(1). The Secretary of State shall, at the request of a local housing authority, provide the authority with such information as they may require in connection with a number of matters, as set out below[67]:

> as to whether a person is or has become an asylum-seeker, or a dependent of an asylum-seeker,[68] and
> to enable them to determine whether such a person is eligible for assistance under Part VII under section 185 (persons from abroad not eligible for housing assistance).[69]

Where information under section 187 is given otherwise than in writing, the Secretary of State shall confirm it in writing if a written request is made to him by the authority.[70] If it appears to the Secretary of State that any application, decision or other change of circumstances has affected the status of a person about whom information was previously provided by him to a local housing authority under section 187, the Secretary of State is required to inform the authority in writing of that fact, the reason for it and the date on which the previous information became inaccurate.[71]

---

[65] Housing Act 1996, s. 182(1).
[66] s. 182(2).
[67] s. 187(1).
[68] s. 187(1)(a).
[69] s. 187(1)(b).
[70] s. 187(2).
[71] s. 187(3).

PART 4

OTHER LAW AFFECTING HOMELESS PEOPLE

CHAPTER 14

Adverse Possession

In considering the question of the homeless, it is easy to concen- **14.01.** trate exclusively on the provisions of Part VII of the 1996 Act. However, this book has aspirations towards being a more comprehensive account of the law on homelessness: that is, the law as it typically affects homeless people. An important part of homelessness is the struggle to find some sort of housing or shelter. This often leads to hostels, or to squatting. The occupation of hostels is a matter of licence with the (usually) charitable organisation which provides the shelter. There is little legal inter-action in that circumstance. More common is the situation where a homeless person gains access to property which she has no entitlement to occupy.

Trespass

The law on trespass is a complicated topic covering a number of **14.02.** areas from squatting to the law on landlord and tenant, to straightforward unlawful entry to land. There is no space in this book for a comprehensive account of the subject. What is intended is a brief summary of the law as it applies to homeless people or those who become homeless.

There are two main categories of factual situation: **14.03.**

Homeless people seeking shelter.
People who become homeless as a result of some act causing trespass.

The law is considered in a way which straddles both of these issues. The second is potentially more problematic. It is possible that people in suitable accommodation come to the end of their permitted period of occupation but seek to remain in the property, thus committing a trespass. Alternatively, people in accommodation may do some act which contravenes their right to occupy and thus makes them homeless. The issue might therefore arise whether they are intentionally homeless within the meaning of Part VII of the Housing Act 1996.

Who can Sue?

14.04.   The action in trespass is an action which seeks to protect those in possession of land. It is not a doctrine which aims to protect the rights of those who have rights in land. Thus, an action in trespass can be brought only by a person who is in possession of property. Thus a lessor who is not in possession cannot sue for trespass — rather the action is at the suit of the lessee in occupation.

14.05.   An action can only be brought by someone who is in possession unless the plaintiff has some relation to the property. Such plaintiff is required to have a right to possession of the property. Once such a person has acquired lawful possession of the land, she is entitled to commence an action for trespass.

14.06.   The occupant of property will, therefore, need to demonstrate that she has better title to the property than the homeless person who has sought access to it. Such a person will not include a licensee, as a person with only a permission to occupy, but will include a tenant or a freeholder.

14.07.   A more complicated issue is where one co-owner seeks to sue another co-owner for trespass. Clearly, there will be issues of mixed law and fact here as to whether the parties do or do not have the rights which they claim to have. The question might arise at law generally as to the rights that each of the co-owners has to the property. In the context of homelessness, it might be that one co-owner seeks to exclude the other from the property as a result of some infringement of the use of the property, such as causing damage.

What Constitutes a Trespass?

14.08.   It has been said ever since Blackstone J., in *Scott v. Shepherd*,[1] that it is only direct harm which can be actionable by trespass. Therefore, it is only damage caused by the trespasser to property which can be recovered in damages for trespass. Some consequential damage would not be similarly recoverable. Therefore, there is

[1] (1773) Blackstone 892.

still some requirement to plead trespass and other torts in the alternative.

There is a need for the defendant to have intended the trespass. **14.09.** However, the test has been extended beyond deliberate acts to negligent and reckless trespass onto land. Therefore, a person causing damage recklessly while gaining access to land will be liable in an action for trespass for such actions. However, the defendant must have intended the act which resulted in the trespass — while not necessarily intending that it would constitute a trespass (*League Against Cruel Sports; Letang v. Cooper*[2]).

Mistake as to the rights which a person has in the property will **14.10.** only be a defence to an action for trespass to the extent that such mistake removes the intention from the act causing the trespass. Where the act is mistaken but deliberate, it will still constitute a trespass. An applicant could be mistaken as to her ability to go into possession of property but still intend to force the lock on the door so as to secure access to it and therefore have committed a trespass.

It should be noted that there is no defence to entering property **14.11.** on the grounds that the trespasser was homeless at the time (*Carter v. Thomas*).[3] While there is a potential defence of necessity for those who trespass, it is not open to the homeless.[4]

Unlawful Entry of Land

The unlawful entry to land is the most common kind of trespass **14.12.** to occur in the area of homelessness. For example, where the homeless person breaks into property without authorisation, where that property is in the possession of another person, and thus commits a trespass. Each entry to the premises without permission constitutes a separate trespass. The question arises whether entry to unoccupied premises falls outside the rules against trespass.

Similarly, where the defendant ousts another from occupation of **14.13.** land while entering land herself, she will commit a trespass. Such dispossession might include the physical removal of another person from lawful possession of land or be restricted to preventing re-entry by the lawful possessor of the land.

---

[2] [1965] 1 Q.B. 232.
[3] [1893] 1 Q.B. 673.
[4] *Southwark L.B.C. v. Williams* [1971] Ch. 734, *per* Lord Denning.

Remaining after Effluxion of Right to Occupy

14.14.   Actions of unlawful entry could be caused by someone who had previously been a tenant on the property just as much as a person who breaks onto property to occupy it as a straightforward squatter. Therefore, a tenant at sufferance of land after the valid termination of the tenancy will commit a trespass every time she enters the land in those circumstances.

14.15.   It is conceivable that a person can commit a trespass if she exceeds the terms of the permission which she has to occupy the property. Therefore, where a person is allowed to occupy land during weekday evenings, she commits a trespass if she enters the property at the weekend. It is possible that she is a trespasser *ab initio* where she has always intended to occupy the property in excess of her permission.

Remedies for Trespass: Damages

14.16.   The plaintiff is entitled to nominal damages for any trespass. Entitlement to substantial damages requires some proof of loss resulting from the trespass.

14.17.   Where the trespass causes no harm to the property itself, the landowner is entitled to recover mesne profits from the trespasser. This will be in part a restitutionary remedy, as well as a specific action in trespass in itself (*Ministry of Defence v. Ashman.*)[5] An action for mesne profits will recover the benefit which the unlawful occupier enjoyed during the occupation. The plaintiff is entitled to recover an amount representing the value of the property during the period of the occupation (*Stoke-on-Trent C.C. v. W. & J. Wass Ltd*).[6] The amount taken to represent this value might be the rent on that property unless some other amount can be proved by the plaintiff to be appropriate (*Clifton Securities Ltd v. Huntley*).[7] However, the court may seek to reach the value of the property to the trespasser where that is considered to be a more appropriate measure (*Thompson*).[8]

14.18.   Where there has been actual damage to the property, the plaintiff will be able to recover the diminution in value of that land (*C.P. Taylor (Wholesale) Ltd v. Hepworths Ltd*[9]), together with the

---

[5] (1993) 25 H.L.R. 513.
[6] [1988] 1 W.L.R. 1406.
[7] [1948] 2 All E.R. 283.
[8] (1993) 25 H.L.R. 552.
[9] [1977] 1 W.L.R. 659.

costs of any necessary repairs (*Farmer Giles Ltd v. Wessex Water Authority*[10]). The aim, in any event, is to achieve a *restituto in integrum* with respect to that property. The plaintiff may wish to recover amounts for loss of enjoyment of the property, which would not be available on a straightforward diminution of the property measure. Such damages would appear to be available where the plaintiff intends to sell the property — it is not clear whether or not they would be available otherwise (*Taylor v. Hepworths*).[11]

Remedies for Trespass: Recovery of Possession

There are two means of recovering possession for the landowner **14.19.** in an action for trespass: in the county court under Order 24 of the County Court Rules and in the High Court under Order 113 of the Rules of the Supreme Court. The plaintiff is required to demonstrate that she has a superior title to the defendant and that she has a right to possession of the property as at the date of the commencement of the proceedings. The ability of a local authority landlord to obtain possession of property is tempered by conflicting obligations under on such authorities the housing legislation generally.

The county court has jurisdiction to hear any action relating to **14.20.** possession of land.[12] The action must be commenced in the court covering the district in which the land (or any part of it) is located.[13] The proceedings must be commenced by summons in the appropriate form or, occasionally, by originating application supported by affidavit.[14]

Summary proceedings for possession of land. These rules are **14.21.** set out in Order 113 of the Rules of the Supreme Court and Order 24 of the County Court Rules respectively. The aim is to facilitate an action where the defendant is not expected to mount a significant defence. They do not apply in the circumstance of a lessee remaining in property after the termination of the lease.

Commencement in the High Court is by means of a specified **14.22.** form of Originating Summons which requires no acknowledgement. The defendant, even if their name is unknown, must be served with the proceedings and made aware of the date of the

---

[10] [1990] 1 E.G.L.R. 177.
[11] [1977] 1 W.L.R. 659.
[12] County Courts Act 1984, s.21.
[13] C.C.R. Ord. 4, r.3.
[14] Pleadings must follow the requirements set out in C.C.R Ord. 6, rr.5, *et seq.*

hearing. Service is by one of the means set out in Order 113. These include posting through the letter-box, affixing a copy of the summons to the door, placing the summons on a stake on the land or by some other method ordered by the court.

14.23.   There is a requirement that five days pass between service and the hearing, unless the case is considered to be an emergency. Frequently, the defendant will not be present at the hearing when the final order is made on a summary basis. The provisions enable a summary trial of the action leading to a final order. It is often the case that orders are obtained against defendants whose names are not known. Therefore, the occupant of property is liable to be subject to a court order without having been present at the hearing and without the plaintiff finding out her name. The automatic directions do not apply to these proceedings.

14.24.   The order to be made under the Order 113 of the Rules of the Supreme Court procedure is in the form specified that the plaintiff "do recover possession". Under the County Court Rules, the equivalent procedure is found in Order 24, where the requirements for grant of possession are the same as in the High Court.

14.25.   In the High Court there is also the potential to bring an action *ex parte* under the emergency procedure in rule 6 of Order 113 of the Supreme Court Rules where there is some risk of damage to life, limb or property. It has been held that there is a power in the High Court to enjoin the unlawful occupier of land from causing damage to that land and also to make a final order for possession where travellers had occupied a sports field and have partially vandalised buildings on that land (*Ealing L.B.C. v. Persons Unknown*).[15]

14.26.   **Interim possession orders.** Interim possession orders are available in the county court to those who are entitled to claim possession under Order 24 of the County Court Rules: that is, on the basis that the defendant is not a tenant and has not been a tenant in the past. The order compels the defendant to vacate the premises within 24 hours of the service of the order on her. The order will then specify a return date at which time the court will do a combination of three things: make a final order, discharge the interim possession order, or allow the proceedings to continue under Part I of Order 24.

---

[15] Unreported (April 15, 1996).

The applicant for an interim possession order must not be **14.27.**
seeking any remedy other than possession of land and the proceedings must be commenced within 28 days of the date when the
applicant first knew of (or ought to have known) the respondents
were in occupation.

The proceedings are commenced by originating application in **14.28.**
the form specified by Form N130. As part of this, a standard form
of affidavit is to be sworn by the applicant. The applicant must
then procure service on the respondents of a notice of the
proceedings. Notice is achieved by fixing a copy of the originating
application to the front door of the property or by some other
method sufficient to bring the proceedings to the notice of the
respondents. Enforcement of the interim possession order is then
achieved by police action rather than by use of bailiffs).[16]

Sections 75 and 76 of the Criminal Justice and Public Order Act **14.29.**
1994, provide for offences related to interim possession orders
obtained against people who were trespassers from the out set or
licensees staying on after their licence was terminated. Where such
an order is made, it is a criminal offence not to quit the property
within 24 hours. This is issue is discussed in detail in Chapter 15,
below.

Remedies for Trespass: Injunctions

Injunctions are available on an interlocutory basis[17] to prevent **14.30.**
occupation while the issue comes on to trial (on the principles set
out in *American Cyanamid*[18]). Permanent injunctions are available
to restrain the unlawful occupier from seeking re-entry at any
point in the future. The law on injunctions is too complicated an
issue to consider here in detail. The application of the principles in
American Cyanamid are well known and dependent, in any event,
on the facts of every case.

It is possible that mandatory injunctions will be issued to **14.31.**
require the unlawful occupier of land to remove property from
land or to take some action to return the land to its former
condition. Such mandatory injunctions are at the discretion of the
court but the court will not generally be astute to exercise its
discretion in this way (*Redland Bricks Ltd v. Morris*).[19]

---

[16] C.C.R. Ord. 24, r.13.
[17] R.S.C. Ord. 29.
[18] [1975] A.C. 396.
[19] [1970] A.C. 652.

Nuisance and Unlawful Interference with Land

14.32.   The law on nuisance is a complicated topic covering a number of areas from escape of animals or toxic substances, to the relationship of landlord and tenant, to noise caused by neighbours. There is no space in this book for a comprehensive account of the subject. What is intended is a brief summary of the law as it applies to homeless people or those who become homeless.

14.33.   There are two main categories of factual situation:

Homeless people seeking shelter constituting a nuisance.
People who become homeless as a result of some act causing nuisance.

The law is considered in a way which straddles both of these issues. The second is potentially more problematic in this context. It is possible that people in suitable accommodation cause a nuisance thus terminating their ability to occupy the property. The issue might therefore arise whether they are intentionally homeless within the meaning of Part VII of the Housing Act 1996. Alternatively, a person who seeks accommodation might cause a nuisance themselves.

14.34.   The law on nuisance with respect to land concerns "hurt or annoyance" to land (Blackstone's definition of nuisance, Bl. Comm. III, c. 13, p. 216) in respect of a person who has some right in the land damaged by the nuisance. The plaintiff must have some right in the property and not be a mere licensee: (*Malone v. Laskey*).[20] Simply being in occupation of land will not constitute sufficient interest to found an action in nuisance.[21]

Remedies for Nuisance: Abatement

14.35.   The plaintiff is in some circumstances entitled to abate the nuisance by taking some action on the land to stop it. Much action in this context concerning occupation of land by squatters does run the risk of constituting a criminal offence as discussed below in Chapter 16.

Remedies for Nuisance: Damages

14.36.   Damages for nuisance are available on normal tortious principles to recover out-of-pocket loss caused by nuisance.

---

[20] [1907] 2 K.B. 144.
[21] *Ibid.*

Remedies for Nuisance: Injunction

Injunctions are available on an interlocutory basis[22] to prevent **14.37.** occupation while the issue comes on to trial (on the principles set out in *American Cyanamid*[23]). As discussed above, the law on injunctions is too complex to consider here in great detail.

Permanent injunctions are available to restrain the unlawful **14.38.** occupier from seeking re-entry at any point in the future. It is possible that mandatory injunctions will be issued to require the unlawful occupier of land to remove property from land or to take some action to return the land to its former condition. Such mandatory injunctions are at the discretion of the court but the court will not generally be astute to exercise its discretion in this way (*Redland Bricks Ltd v. Morris*).[24]

[22] R.S.C. Ord. 29.
[23] [1975] A.C. 396.
[24] [1970] A.C. 652.

CHAPTER 15

Homelessness and the Criminal Law

15.01. One of the facts of everyday life for homeless people is crime. Frequently homeless people are the victims of criminal assaults and other similar offences. Street homeless people occasionally become involved in crime in stealing food and so forth. There is, however, a specific raft of criminal law dealing with those who do not have permanent accommodation. In advising the homeless person it is necessary to consider the Criminal Justice Act 1977 and the Criminal Justice and Public Order Act 1994 in particular. The purpose of this chapter is to analyse the criminal law relating specifically to people without permanent accommodation.

15.02. It is in keeping with the history of the law affecting homeless people that there is a large amount of criminal law aimed at them specifically. Ever since the Poor Law of 1530 through to the Vagrancy Acts, the law has victimised those who are without homes. Section 4 of the Vagrancy Act 1824, as amended by the Vagrancy Act 1935, made being homeless and begging a criminal offence. While part of section 4 was removed by the Criminal Attempts Act 1981 relating to the "sus" laws, the provisions relating to vagrancy appear to have remained on the statute book and some commentators feel that this has not interfered with the offence under section 1 of the 1935 Vagrancy Act.[1]

Offences Related to Applications under the Housing Act 1996

There are two offences specified by Part VII of the 1996 Act.

---

[1] See *e.g. Hoath* (1983) at p.20.

False Statements or Omissions

The statute sets out a number of criminal offences committed in **15.03.**
connection with the provision of accommodation to homeless
people. The first offence is set out in section 214, to deal with false
statements made to the housing authority. The offence deals
specifically with knowingly or recklessly making false statements
or withholding information with the intention of making the
authority believe that the applicant is entitled to accommodation
under Part VII.

Therefore, under section 214(1). **15.04.**

"(1) It is an offence for a person, with intent to induce a local
housing authority to believe in connection with the
exercise of their functions under this Part that he or
another person is entitled to accommodation or assistance
in accordance with the provisions of this Part, or is
entitled to accommodation or assistance of a particular
description—

(a) knowingly or recklessly to make a statement which is
false in a material particular, or

(b) knowingly to withhold information which the authority have reasonably required him to give in connection with the exercise of those functions".

It is an offence for an applicant to mislead a local housing **15.05.**
authority as to her entitlement to be assisted under Part VII. The
offence requires an intention on the part of the applicant that the
local authority come to believe that either the applicant or another
person is entitled to assistance under Part VII. Therefore, an
offence can be committed by a person who makes such a statement
on behalf of another.

The actions which are the subject of the offence are then: **15.06.**

making a statement which is false in a material particular;
withholding information reasonably required by the authority.

It is significant that the offender need not know that the
statement was false: it is enough that the offender was reckless as
to whether or not the statement was false in a material particular.
Therefore, where an applicant tells the local authority officer what
she thinks that officer wants to hear, she will commit an offence
where that involves recklessness in giving information she knows
might well be false.

Where information is withheld, that information must be know- **15.07.**
ingly withheld by the applicant to constitute an offence. Therefore,
an applicant will not commit an offence where she innocently fails

to disclose a fact which would have been important: for example, some factor which might cause her to be considered intentionally homeless. However, if an applicant were asked a direct question but recklessly withheld the information at that stage, it would be possible that this withholding would constitute a statement which was false in a material particular.

Continuing Obligation

15.08.   There is a continuing obligation on the applicant under section 214(2) not to omit to inform the authority of a change in her circumstances. Consequently, if before an applicant receives notification of the local housing authority's decision on her application, there is any change of facts material to her case, she must notify the authority as soon as possible. Any person who fails to comply with this obligation commits an offence under section 214(3).

15.09.   The authority shall explain to every applicant, in ordinary language, the duty imposed on her by subsection (2) and the effect of subsection (3). There are two statutory defences to section 214(2) set out in section 214(3). The first is that the applicant must show that she was not given the explanation required. The second is that the applicant had some other reasonable excuse for non-compliance. A person guilty of such an offence is liable on summary conviction to a fine not exceeding level 5 on the standard scale.[2]

Offences under the Criminal Law Act 1977 and the Criminal Justice and Public Order Act 1994

15.10.   This book aims to consider the whole of the law dealing with homeless people. Therefore the provisions dealing with the criminalisation of squatting are dealt with briefly below as a potentially important component of the law affecting those who are without permanent accommodation available to them.

15.11.   The civil law on adverse possession is considered above in Chapter 14 "Adverse Possession". The ability of the owner of land to recover that land or to sue the squatter in trespass are considered there in detail. The aim of this section is to provide an overview of the criminal law in this area.

---

[2] Housing Act 1996, s. 214(4).

Violence to Secure Entry

It is an offence to secure entry to property by violence. Under **15.12.** section 6 of the 1977 Act (as amended by the 1994 Act) any person who, without lawful authority, uses or threatens violence to gain entry to any premises for herself or for any other person is guilty of an offence. The use of violence must be performed without lawful authority. There are two provisos to the offence. First, there must be someone present on those premises at the time who is opposed to the entry which the violence is intended to secure[3] and secondly, the person using or threatening the violence knows that that is the case.[4] It should be noted that having an interest in the property, or a right to possession of it, does not constitute lawful authority for the use or threat of the use of violence to secure entry to the premises.[5]

This offence was amended by the Criminal Justice and Public **15.13.** Order Act 1994. Under section 6(1A) of the 1977 Act, the offence does not apply to a person who is either a "displaced residential occupier"[6] of the premises or a "protected intending occupier"[7] of the premises in question. Alternatively, that person may be acting on behalf of such an occupier and consequently be excluded from commission of the offence. The burden of proof is specifically altered. Where the accused produces sufficient evidence that she was either such an occupier herself or acting on behalf of such an occupier, it is presumed that she did occupy the property in that capacity. It is then for the prosecution to prove the contrary.

In the commission of the offence under section 6, it is imma- **15.14.** terial whether the violence in question is directed against the person occupying the property or against the property itself.[8] It is also of no importance whether the entry which the violence is intended to secure is for the purpose of acquiring possession of the premises in question or for any other purpose.[9]

The penalty accruing to a person guilty of an offence under this **15.15.** section is that they shall be liable on summary conviction to imprisonment for a term not exceeding six months or to a fine not exceeding level 5 on the standard scale or both.[10] There is a power

---

[3] Criminal Law Act 1977, s. 6(1)(a)
[4] s. 6(1)(b).
[5] s. 6(2).
[6] As discussed below at para. 15.16
[7] As discussed below at para. 15.17.
[8] Criminal Law Act 1977, s. 6(4)(a).
[9] s. 6(4)(b).
[10] s. 6(5).

of arrest in a constable in uniform who may arrest without warrant anyone who is, or whom he, with reasonable cause, suspects to be, guilty of an offence under section 6.[11]

"Premises" is defined as meaning any building or part of a building under separate occupation, and its surrounding site.[12] "Access" is defined as meaning any part of the premises which is usually used for access to the premises.[13]

"Displaced residential occupier"

15.16.   A "displaced residential occupier" will be any person who "was occupying any premises as a residence" immediately before being excluded from occupation by anyone who has gained access to the premises as a trespasser. The person continues to be a displaced residential occupier for so long as she is excluded from the premises in that way.

"Protected intending occupier"

15.17.   There are three situations in which an individual will be a protected intending occupier of property.

15.18.   First, an individual is a protected intending occupier of any premises in the cumulation of the following circumstances:[14]

she has a freehold interest, or a leasehold interest with not less than two years still to run, in those premises; and
she requires the premises for her own occupation as a residence; and
she is excluded from occupation of the premises by a person who entered them, or has any access to them, as a trespasser; and
she (or a person acting on her behalf) holds a written statement which specifies her interest in the premises and states that she requires the premises for occupation as a residence for herself.

The statement referred to must be signed by the person whose interest is specified in it in the presence of a justice of the peace or commissioner for oaths; and that the justice of the peace or commissioner for oaths must have subscribed her name as a witness to the signature.[15]

15.19.   Secondly, an individual is also a protected intending occupier of any premises where she has a tenancy of those premises or a licence to occupy those premises. The tenancy must not be a local

---

[11] s. 6(6).
[12] s. 12(1)(a).
[13] s. 12(1)(b).
[14] s. 12A(2).
[15] s. 12A(3).

authority tenancy, as set out below. The licence to occupy must have been granted by a person with a freehold interest, or a leasehold interest with not less than two years still to run in the premises. Further, she must require the premises for her own occupation as a residence; have been excluded from occupation of the premises by a person who entered them, or who has gained any access to them, as a trespasser; and she or a person acting on his behalf holds a written statement.[16]

That statement must state that she has been granted a tenancy of those premises or a licence to occupy those premises; specify the interest in the premises of the person who granted that tenancy or licence to occupy ("the landlord"); and state that she requires the premises for occupation as a residence for herself. Furthermore, the statement must be signed by the landlord and by the tenant or licensee in the presence of a justice of the peace or commissioner for oaths and the justice of the peace or commissioner for oaths has subscribed his name as a witness to the signatures.[17]

Thirdly, an individual is also a protected intending occupier of **15.20.** any premises if:[18]

she has a tenancy of those premises or a licence to occupy those premises granted by an authority;
she requires the premises for her own occupation as a residence;
she is excluded from occupation of the premises by a person who entered the premises, or any access to them, as a trespasser;
there is a certificate on behalf of the authority which states that she has been granted a tenancy of those premises or a licence to occupy those premises as a residence by the authority.

The authority which granted that tenancy or licence to occupy **15.21.** must: (1) be any body mentioned in section 14 of the Rent Act 1977 (landlord's interest belonging to local authority etc.); (2) the Housing Corporation; (3) Housing for Wales; and (4) a registered housing association within the meaning of the Housing Association Act 1985.

It is an offence if she makes a statement for these purposes **15.22.** which the person making it either knows it to be false in a material particular or makes that statement recklessly as to its potential falsehood.[19] The penalty for this offence on summary conviction is imprisonment for a term not exceeding six months, or a fine not exceeding level 5 on the standard scale, or to both.[20]

---

[16] s. 12A(4).
[17] s. 12A(5).
[18] s. 12A(6).
[19] s. 12A(8).
[20] s. 12A(10).

15.23.   It should be noted that a protected intending occupier of any premises is also expressly deemed to be a protected intending occupier of any access to those premises.[21]

Squatting

15.24.   Section 7 of the 1977 Act creates a criminal offence in the area of adverse occupation of residential premises. In short, any person who is on any premises as a trespasser after having entered as such is guilty of an offence if she fails to leave those premises when asked to do so by or on behalf[22] of a displaced residential occupier of the premises[23] or an individual who is a protected intending occupier of the premises.[24]

15.25.   There are a number of defences created in the statute. It is a defence for the accused to prove that she believed that the person requiring her to leave the premises was not a displaced residential occupier or protected intending occupier of the premises.[25] Similarly, it is a defence to demonstrate that she believed that the person requiring her to leave was not a person acting on behalf of a displaced residential occupier or protected intending occupier.[26] It is also a defence where the accused can prove that the premises in question are or form part of premises used mainly for non-residential purposes; and that she was not on any part of the premises used wholly or mainly for residential purposes.[27] These defences extend expressly to any access to the premises.[28]

15.26.   The penalty for this offence is imprisonment for a term not exceeding six months or to a fine not exceeding level 5 on the standard scale, or to both.[29] The power of arrest in this instance is vested in a constable in uniform who may arrest anyone without warrant who that constable, with reasonable cause, suspects to be guilty of the offence.[30]

15.27.   Under section 12A(9) the accused has one further defence where she was requested to leave the premises by a person claiming to be or to act on behalf of a protected intending occupier of the

---

[21] s. 12A(11).
[22] s. 7(1).
[23] s. 7(1)(a), as defined above.
[24] s. 7(1)(b), as defined above.
[25] s. 7(2).
[26] *Ibid.*
[27] s. 7(3).
[28] s. 7(4).
[29] s. 7(5).
[30] s. 7(6).

premises. It is a defence for her to prove that at the time the accused was requested to leave, that person asking her to leave failed at that time to produce to the accused the statement required.[31] Any document purporting to be a certificate under section 7(6)(d) is to be received in evidence and, unless the contrary is proved, deemed to have been issued by or on behalf of the authority stated in the certificate.

Trespass with an Offensive Weapon

Under section 8 there is an offence of trespassing with a **15.28.** "weapon of offence". A person who is on any premises as a trespasser (where she entered the premises as such) is guilty of an offence if she has with him on the premises any weapon of offence, without lawful authority or reasonable excuse.[32]

The term "weapon of offence" is defined to mean any article **15.29.** which is made or adapted for use for causing injury to or incapacitating a person. [33] Alternatively, it is sufficient that the article is intended by the person having it with her for use for causing injury to or incapacitating a person.[34]

The penalty attaching to the offence is imprisonment for a term **15.30.** not exceeding three months or to a fine not exceeding level 5 on the standard scale or both.[35] The concomitant power of arrest is for a constable in uniform to arrest without warrant anyone whom she, with reasonable cause, suspects to be in the act of committing an offence under this section.[36]

Trespassing on the Premises of Foreign Missions

There is a raft of provisions which, prima facie, make it an **15.31.** offence to enter a diplomatic or consular mission as a trespasser. This area is perhaps a little abstruse in the context of homelessness and, therefore, it is given only cursory consideration here. However, it is an offence aimed specifically at those trespassing on the premises of overseas missions and may therefore cover the homeless trespasser with social aspirations. A person who enters or is on the premises of a diplomatic mission or consular premises as a trespasser is guilty of an offence.[37] It is a defence for the accused

[31] As set out at para. 15.25
[32] Criminal Law Act 1977, s. 8(1).
[33] s. 8(2).
[34] s. 8(2).
[35] s. 8(3).
[36] s. 8(4).
[37] s. 9(1).

to prove that she believed that the premises in question were not premises to which the provision applies.[38] A person guilty of this offence is liable to imprisonment for a term not exceeding six months or a fine not exceeding level 5 on the standard scale or both.[39] However, no proceedings for this offence can be instituted against any person except by or with the consent of the Attorney General.[40]

Obstruction of Court Officers

15.32.   Under section 10 there is a further offence where a person obstructs court officers who are executing process to obtain possession against unauthorised occupiers.

15.33.   The offence is expressly without prejudice to section 8(2) of the Sheriffs Act 1887. A person is guilty of an offence if she resists or intentionally obstructs any persons who is in fact an officer of a court engaged in executing any specified process issued by the High Court or by any county court.[41] The specified processes are proceedings to enforce any judgment or order for the recovery of any premises or for delivery of possession of any premises.[42] It is a defence for the accused to prove that she believed that the person she was resisting or obstructing was not an officer of the court.[43]

15.34.   There is a proviso that the proceedings must have been brought under a rule of court concerned solely with obtaining possession of any premises on an allegation that the premises in question are occupied solely by a person or persons (not being a tenant or tenants holding over after the termination of the tenancy) who entered into or remained in occupation of the premises without the licence or consent of the person claiming possession.[44]

15.35.   The penalty for this offence is imprisonment for a term not exceeding six months or to a fine not exceeding level 5 on the standard scale or to both.[45] A constable in uniform or any officer of a court is granted a power to arrest without warrant anyone whom she suspects, with reasonable cause, to be guilty of the offence.[46]

---

[38] s. 9(3).
[39] s. 9(5).
[40] s. 9(6).
[41] s. 10(1).
[42] *Ibid.*
[43] s. 10(3).
[44] s. 10(2).
[45] s. 10(4).
[46] s. 10(5).

An "officer of a court" is defined to mean any sheriff, under **15.36.**
sheriff, deputy sheriff, bailiff or officer of a sheriff; and any bailiff
or other person who is an officer of a county court within the
meaning of the County Courts Act 1959.[47]

Powers to Remove Trespassers from Land

The Criminal Justice and Public Order Act 1994 creates powers **15.37.**
to remove trespassers from land. This will impact on those without
settled accommodation who are trespassing on land. The concept
of trespass is discussed above in Chapter 14. Section 61 of the
Criminal Justice and Public Order Act 1994 sets out the scope of
the powers to remove trespassers from land.

The provision is aimed at trespassers who move onto land in **15.38.**
groups, seeking to occupy that land. Section 61(1) provides that the
powers come into effect where the senior police officer present at
the scene reasonably believes that the following factors are
present[48]:

two or more persons are trespassing on land;
those persons are present on that land with the common
purpose of residing there for any period of time;
reasonable steps have been taken by or on behalf of the occupier
to ask them to leave; and
either any of those persons has caused damage to the land or to
property on the land or used threatening, abusive or insulting
words or behaviour towards the occupier, a member of his
family or an employee or agent of his, or
those persons have between them six or more vehicles on the
land.

The senior police officer present is then empowered to direct **15.39.**
those people, or any of them, to leave the land and to remove any
vehicles or other property they have with them on the land.[49] The
term "vehicle" includes any vehicle, whether or not it is in a fit
state for use on roads. It also includes within the term "vehicle"
any chassis or body, whether with or without wheels, which
appears to have formed part of such a vehicle. The term also
encompasses any load carried by, and anything attached to, such a
vehicle.[50]

It should also be noted that a person may be regarded for the **15.40.**
purposes of this section as having a purpose of residing in a place
notwithstanding that he has a home elsewhere.[51]

---

[47] s. 10(6).
[48] Criminal Justice and Public Order Order Act 1994, s. 61(1).
[49] s. 61(1).
[50] s. 61(9). "Caravans" are as defined in s. 29(1) of the Caravan Sites and Control
of Development Act 1960.
[51] Criminal Justice and Public Order Order Act 1994, s. 61(9).

15.41.   In circumstances where the alleged trespassers are reasonably believed by the senior police officer not to have been trespassers when they entered the land originally, but is of the view that they have become trespassers on the land, the senior officer must reasonably believe that all of the other conditions set out above are satisfied, once those persons became trespassers. If the senior officer is not so satisfied, she cannot exercise the power conferred by section 61(1) to remove the trespassers.

15.42.   There is a criminal offence committed by any person who ignores an instruction to leave the land. The direction may be communicated to the trespassers by any constable at the scene.[52] If a person knows that they have been directed to leave the land, she commits an offence if she does any of the following[53]:

> fails to leave the land as soon as reasonably practicable, or
> having left again enters the land as a trespasser within the period of three months beginning with the day on which the direction was given.

> Trespassing on common land attracts the same penalty as if a trespass against the occupier or an infringement of the commoners' rights.[54]

15.43.   It is a defence for the accused to show that he was not trespassing on the land, or that he had a reasonable excuse for failing to leave the land as soon as reasonably practicable or, as the case may be, for again entering the land as a trespasser.[55]

15.44.   The penalty is imprisonment for a term not exceeding three months or a fine not exceeding level 4 on the standard scale, or both.[56] A constable in uniform who reasonably suspects that a person is committing this offence, is empowered to arrest that person without a warrant.[57]

Further Powers of Seizure

15.45.   Section 62 of the 1994 Act provides for supplementary powers of seizure. A constable is given the power to seize and remove a vehicle in the following circumstances. Where a direction is given under section 61,[58] and a constable reasonably suspects that a

---

[52] s. 61(3).
[53] s. 61(4).
[54] s. 61(7).
[55] s. 61(6).
[56] *Ibid.*
[57] s. 61(5).
[58] As set out above.

person to whom the direction applies has done the following without reasonable excuse:

> failed to remove any vehicle on the land which appears to the constable to belong to her or to be in her possession or under her control; or
> entered the land as a trespasser with a vehicle within the period of three months beginning with the day on which the direction was given.[59]

Retention and Charges for Seized Property

Section 67 of the 1994 Act provides for the retention of seized **15.46.** property and charges connected to seized property. Where vehicles have been seized and removed by a constable under section 62(1) above, they may be retained in accordance with regulations made by the Secretary of State.[60] The Secretary of State is empowered to make regulations which regulate the retention and safe keeping and the disposal and the destruction in prescribed circumstances of vehicles.[61] The Secretary of State can also make regulations to prescribe charges in respect of the removal, retention, disposal and destruction of vehicles.[62] Those regulations may make different provisions for different classes of vehicles or for different circumstances.[63]

Similarly, any authority is entitled to recover from a person from **15.47.** whom a vehicle has been seized such charges as may be prescribed in respect of the removal, retention, disposal and destruction of the vehicle by the same authority.[64] These charges are recoverable as a simple contract debt.[65] Until the charges are paid, the authority which has custody of the vehicles under those regulations, is entitled to retain custody of the vehicles.

Aggravated Trespass

The 1994 Act sought to criminalise the actions of disruptive **15.48.** trespassers. Section 68 therefore creates the offence of aggravated trespass. The aim of the offence is to prevent the activities of hunt saboteurs. However, it is drafted more broadly than that. It would appear to cover a trespasser who enters land to prevent others carrying out a lawful purpose on it. Therefore, occupation of land

---

[59] Criminal Justice and Public Order Order Act 1994, s. 62(1).
[60] s. 67(1).
[61] s. 67(3)(a).
[62] s. 67(3)(b).
[63] s. 67(5).
[64] s. 67(4).
[65] s. 67(6).

by travellers which prevents some lawful activity would appear to fall within the offence. A person commits the offence of aggravated trespass if she trespasses on land in the open air.[66] Further, in relation to any lawful activity which other people are engaging in (or are about to engage in) on that or adjoining land in the open air, does there anything which is intended by her to have the effect of:

> intimidating those persons or any of them so as to deter them or any of them from engaging in that activity,
> obstructing that activity, or
> disrupting that activity.[67]

15.49.   Adverse possession of land with tents or mobile homes might fall within this offence where it disrupts the lawful activity of the landowner. An activity on land is considered to be "lawful" if the people engaging in it are able to engage in the activity on the land on that occasion without committing an offence or trespassing on the land.[68]

15.50.   The penalty is imprisonment for a term not exceeding three months or a fine not exceeding level 4 on the standard scale, or both.[69] A constable in uniform who reasonably suspects that a person is committing an offence under this section may arrest her without a warrant.[70]

Powers of Removal

15.51.   Further there are powers to remove persons committing or participating in aggravated trespass under section 69 of the 1994 Act. The senior police officer present at the scene may direct people to leave the land where she reasonably believes[71]:

> that a person is committing, had committed or intends to commit the offence of aggravated trespass on land in the open air; or
> that two or more persons are trespassing on land in the open air and are present there with the common purpose of intimidating persons so as to deter them from engaging in a lawful activity or of obstructing or disrupting a lawful activity.

15.52.   An offence is committed by a person who knows that a direction has been given which applies to her and yet fails to leave the land as soon as practicable, or enters the land as a trespasser within the

---

[66] s. 68(1).
[67] s. 68(1).
[68] s. 68(2).
[69] s. 68(3).
[70] s. 68(4)
[71] s. 69(1).

period of three months beginning with the day on which the direction was given.[72] The available defence is that the defendant was not trespassing on the land, or that she had a reasonable excuse for failing to leave the land as soon as practicable or, as the case may be, for entering the land as a trespasser again.[73] A constable in uniform who reasonably suspects that a person is committing an offence under this section may arrest him without a warrant.

Offences Relating to Interim Possession Orders

The provisions relating to interim possession orders are dis- 15.53. cussed above in Chapter 14. The 1994 Act sets out situations in which an offence is committed with reference to obtaining such an order. In terms of homelessness, this covers the homeless person who is excluded from land. It is also a situation relating to the person who is homeless because she is excluded from accommodation which is subject to adverse possession at the time. Under section 75 of the 1994 Act there are potentially offences committed by the person seeking the order and the person resisting the order.

Where a person is seeking an interim order for possession, she 15.54. commits an offence if, in order to obtain an interim possession order, she:

"(a) makes a statement which he knows to be false or mislead-
       ing in a material particular; or
 (b) recklessly makes a statement which is false or misleading
       in a material particular."[74]

An offence is also committed by a person who is attempting to 15.55. resist the making of an interim possession order in the following circumstances where she:

"(a) makes a statement which he knows to be false or mislead-
       ing in a material particular; or
 (b) recklessly makes a statement which he knows to be false or
       misleading in a material particular."[75]

The penalty is, on conviction on indictment, to imprisonment for a term not exceeding two years or a fine or both; or on summary conviction, to imprisonment for a term not exceeding six months or a fine not exceeding the statutory maximum or both.[76]

---

[72] s. 69(3).
[73] s. 69(4).
[74] s. 75(1).
[75] s. 75(2).
[76] s. 75(3).

15.56. An "interim possession order" is defined as an interim possession order made under rules of court for the bringing of summary
proceedings for possession of premises which are occupied by
trespassers.[77] A "statement" in this context is any written or oral
statement, either of fact or belief, which is made in or for the
purposes of the proceedings.[78]

15.57. If there is a person on the premises as a trespasser at any time
during the currency of an interim possession order, she commits
an offence under section 76.[79] However, no offence is committed
under section 76(2) if she leaves the premises within 24 hours of
the time of service of the order and does not return; or a copy of
the order was not fixed to the premises in accordance with the
rules of the court.

15.58. A person who was in occupation of the premises at the time of
service of the order, but leaves them when the order is served, will
commit an offence if she re-enters the premises as a trespasser (or
attempts to do so) after the expiry of the order but within the
period of one year beginning with the day on which the order was
served.[80] A person who is in occupation of the premises at the time
of service of the order shall be treated for the purposes of this
section as being present as a trespasser.[81]

*Powers of Local Authority to Direct Unauthorised Campers to
Leave Land*

15.59. Local authorities are empowered to direct unauthorised campers
to leave land under section 77 of the 1994 Act. The authority is
empowered to give a direction that specified people leave land and
remove any vehicles and any other property they have with them
on the land.[82] This power exists where a local authority considers
that those people are residing in a vehicle or vehicles within that
authority's area on any land in the open air[83] which forms part of a
highway, or any other unoccupied land in the open air, or on any
occupied land without the consent of the occupier.[84]

15.60. The authority must serve notice of the direction on the persons
to whom the direction applies. It is sufficient that the direction
specifies the land concerned and is addressed to all occupants of

[77] s. 75(4).
[78] *Ibid.*
[79] s. 76(2).
[80] s. 76(4).
[81] s. 76(6).
[82] s. 77(1).
[83] s. 77(6).
[84] *Ibid.*

the vehicles on the land, without necessarily needing to name them.[85] It is usual to provide that these notices are "to whom it may concern" and that proceedings are commenced against "persons unknown". It is advisable that the authority take some action to attempt to discover the identity of the people unknown.

There is another offence committed where a person, who knows **15.61.** that a direction has been given which applies to her and yet fails, as soon as practicable, to leave the land or remove from the land any vehicle or other property which is the subject of the direction, or, having removed any such vehicle or property, again enters the land with a vehicle within the period of three months beginning with the day on which the direction was given.[86]

It is a defence for the accused to show that her failure to leave or **15.62.** to remove the vehicle or other property as soon as practicable or that her re-entry with a vehicle was due to illness, mechanical breakdown or other immediate emergency.[87]

The term "vehicle" includes any vehicle, whether or not it is in **15.63.** a fit state for use on the roads. It also includes any chassis or body, whether with or without wheels, which appears to have formed part of such a vehicle. The term also encompasses any load carried by, and anything attached to, such a vehicle.[88] A person may be regarded for the purposes of this section as residing on any land notwithstanding that he has a home elsewhere.[89]

Orders for the Removal of Persons and Vehicles Unlawfully on Land

Where a local authority makes a complaint, a magistrates' court **15.64.** may make an order requiring the removal of any vehicle or other property which is so present on the land and any person residing in it. The court can make such an order if satisfied that persons and vehicles in which those people are residing are present on land within that authority's area in contravention of a direction given under section 77.[90]

The form of the order may take a number of forms. It may **15.65.** authorise the local authority to take such "reasonably necessary" steps to ensure that the order is complied with.[91] It may authorise

---

[85] s. 77(2).
[86] s. 77(4).
[87] s. 77(5).
[88] s. 77(6).
[89] *Ibid.*
[90] s. 78(1).
[91] s. 78(2).

the authority's officers to enter the land specified in the order and to take such steps for securing entry and the removal of any vehicle or property in pursuance of the order.[92]

15.66.   In any event, the local authority cannot enter any occupied land unless they have given to the owner and occupier at least 24-hours notice of their intention to do so.[93] Where it is not possible to find such an owner, the local authority is entitled to enter after having conducted reasonable inquiries if they are unable to ascertain their names and addresses.[94]

15.67.   It is an offence to wilfully obstruct any person in the exercise of any power conferred on him by such a court order.[95]

15.68.   Where it is impracticable to serve a relevant document on a person named in it, the document shall be treated as duly served on him if a copy of it is fixed in a prominent place to the vehicle concerned.[96] Where a relevant document is directed to the unnamed occupants of vehicles, it shall be treated as duly served on those occupants if a copy of it is fixed in a prominent place to every vehicle on the land in question at the time when service is thus effected.[97]

15.69.   It is the responsibility of the local authority to take all steps which are reasonably practicable to ensure that a copy of any relevant document is displayed on the land in a manner designed to ensure that it is likely to be seen by any person camping on the land.[98] Furthermore, notice of any relevant document shall be given by the local authority to the owner of the land in question and to any occupier of that land unless, after reasonable inquiries, the authority is unable to ascertain the name and address of the owner or occupier; and the owner of any such land and any occupier of such land shall be entitled to appear and to be heard in the proceedings.[99]

---

[92] *Ibid.*
[93] s. 78(3).
[94] *Ibid.*
[95] s. 78(4).
[96] s. 79(2).
[97] *Ibid.*
[98] s. 79(3).
[99] s. 79(4).

APPENDICES

MATERIALS

APPENDIX ONE

Housing Act 1996

PART VII

"HOMELESSNESS"

HOMELESSNESS AND THREATENED HOMELESSNESS

175.—(1) A person is homeless if he has no accommodation available for his occupation, in the United Kingdom or elsewhere, which he—

(a) is entitled to occupy by virtue of an interest in it or by virtue of an order of a court,

(b) has an express or implied licence to occupy, or

(c) occupies as a residence by virtue of any enactment or rule of law giving him the right to remain in occupation or restricting the right of another person to recover possession.

(2) A person is also homeless if he has accommodation but—

(a) he cannot secure entry to it, or

(b) it consists of a moveable structure, vehicle or vessel designed or adapted for human habitation and there is no place where he is entitled or permitted both to place it and to reside in it.

(3) A person shall not be treated as having accommodation unless it is accommodation which it would be reasonable for him to continue to occupy.

(4) A person is threatened with homelessness if it is likely that
he will become homeless within 28 days.

Meaning of accommodation available for occupation

176.[1]—Accommodation shall be regarded as available for a
person's occupation only if it is available for occupation by him
together with—

(a) any other person who normally resides with him as a
member of his family, or
(b) any other person who might reasonably be expected to
reside with him.

References in this Part to securing that accommodation is
available for a person's occupation shall be construed accordingly.

Whether it is reasonable to continue to occupy

177.[2]—(1) It is not reasonable for a person to continue to occupy
accommodation if it is probable that this will lead to domestic
violence against him, or against—

(a) a person who normally resides with him as a member of his
family, or

---

[1] Cut from s.176:
   (X) Accommodation shall not be regarded as available for a person's occupa-
      tion if —
        (a) he cannot secure entry to it, or
        (b) it consists of a moveable structure, vehicle or vessel designed or
            adapted for human habitation and there is no place where he is
            entitled or permitted both to place it and to reside in it.
   (Y) Accommodation shall not be regarded as available for a person's occupa-
      tion unless it is accommodation which it would be reasonable for him to
      continue to occupy.
[2] (1) . . . from some other person residing in it or to threats of violence from some
other person residing in it and likely to carry out the threats.
   (2) In determining whether it would be, or would have been, reasonable for a
person to continue to occupy accommodation, regard may be had to the general
circumstances prevailing in relation to housing in the district of the local housing
authority to whom he has applied for accommodation or for assistance in obtaining
accommodation.
   (3) The Secretary of State may by order specify —
      (a) other circumstances in which it is to be regarded as reasonable or not
        reasonable for a person to continue to occupy accommodation, and
      (b) other matters to be taken into account or disregarded in determining
        whether it would be, or would have been, reasonable for a person to
        continue to occupy accommodation."

(b) any other person who might reasonably be expected to reside with him.

For this purpose "domestic violence", in relation to a person, means violence from a person with whom he is associated, or threats of violence from such a person which are likely to be carried out.

(2) In determining whether it would be, or would have been, reasonable for a person to continue to occupy accommodation, regard may be had to the general circumstances prevailing in relation to housing in the district of the local housing authority to whom he has applied for accommodation or for assistance in obtaining accommodation.

(3) The Secretary of State may by order specify—

(a) other circumstances in which it is to be regarded as reasonable or not reasonable for a person to continue to occupy accommodation, and

(b) other matters to be taken into account or disregarded in determining whether it would be, or would have been, reasonable for a person to continue to occupy accommodation.

Meaning of associated person

178.—For the purposes of this Part, a person is associated with another person if—

(a) they are or have been married to each other;
(b) they are cohabitants or former cohabitants;
(c) they live or have lived in the same household;
(d) they are relatives;
(e) they have agreed to marry one another (whether or not that agreement has been terminated);
(f) in relation to a child, each of them is a parent of the child or has, or has had, parental responsibility for the child.

(2) If a child has been adopted or has been freed for adoption by virtue of any of the enactments mentioned in section 16(1) of the Adoption Act 1976, two persons are also associated with each other for the purposes of this Part if—

(a) one is a natural parent of the child or a parent of such a natural parent, and
(b) the other is the child or a person—

    (i) who has become a parent of the child by virtue of an adoption order or who has applied for an adoption order, or

   (ii) with whom the child has at any time been placed for adoption.

(3) In this section—

"adoption order" has the meaning given by section 72(1) of the Adoption Act 1976;

"child" means a person under the age of 18 years;

"cohabitants" means a man and a woman who, although, not married to each other, are living together as husband and wife, and "former cohabitants" shall be construed accordingly;

"parental responsibility" has the same meaning as in the Children Act 1989; and

"relative", in relation to a person, means—

   (a) the father, mother, stepfather, stepmother, son, daughter, stepson, stepdaughter, grandmother, grandfather, grandson or granddaughter of that person or of that person's spouse or former spouse, or

   (b) the brother, sister, uncle, aunt, niece or nephew (whether of the full blood or of the half blood or by any affinity) of that person or of that person's spouse or former spouse,

and includes, in relation to a person who is living or has lived with another person as husband and wife, a person who would fall within paragraph (a) or (b) if the parties were married to each other.

Duty of local housing authority to provide advisory services

179.—(1) Every local housing authority shall secure that advice and information about homelessness, and the prevention of homelessness, is available free of charge to any person in their district.

(2) The authority may give to any person by whom such advice and information is provided on behalf of the authority assistance by way of grant or loan.

(3) A local housing authority may also assist any such person—

   (a) by permitting him to use premises belonging to the authority,

(b) by making available furniture or other goods, whether by way of gift, loan or otherwise, and

(c) by making available the services of staff employed by the authority.

Assistance for voluntary organisations

180.—(1) The Secretary of State or a local housing authority may give assistance by way of grant or loan to voluntary organisations concerned with homelessness or matters relating to homelessness.

(2) A local housing authority may also assist any such organisation—

(a) by permitting them to use premises belonging to the authority,

(b) by making available furniture or other goods, whether by way of gift, loan or otherwise, and

(c) by making available the services of staff employed by the authority.

(3) A "voluntary organisation" means a body (other than a public or local authority) whose activities are not carried on for profit.

Terms and conditions of assistance

181.—(1) This section has effect as to the terms and conditions on which assistance is given under section 179 or 180.

(2) Assistance shall be on such terms, and subject to such conditions, as the person giving the assistance may determine.

(3) No assistance shall be given unless the person to whom it is given undertakes—

(a) to use the money, furniture or other goods or premises for a specified purpose, and

(b) to provide such information as may reasonably be required as to the manner in which the assistance is being used.

The person giving the assistance may require such information by notice in writing, which shall be complied with within 21 days beginning with the date on which the notice is served.

(4) The conditions subject to which assistance is given shall in all cases include conditions requiring the person to whom the assistance is given—

(a) to keep proper books of account and have them audited in such manner as may be specified,

(b) to keep records indicating how he has used the money, furniture or other goods or premises, and
(c) to submit the books of account and records for inspection by the person giving the assistance.

(5) If it appears to the person giving the assistance that the person to whom it was given has failed to carry out his undertaking as to the purpose for which the assistance was to be used, he shall take all reasonable steps to recover from that person an amount equal to the amount of the assistance.

(6) He must first serve on the person to whom the assistance was given a notice specifying the amount which in his opinion is recoverable and the basis on which that amount has been calculated.

Guidance by the Secretary of State

182.—(1) In the exercise of their functions relating to homelessness and the prevention of homelessness, a local housing authority or social services authority shall have regard to such guidance as may from time to time be given by the Secretary of State.

(2) The Secretary of State may give guidance either generally or to specified descriptions of authorities.

Application for assistance

183.—(1) The following provisions of this Part apply where a person applies to a local housing authority for accommodation, or for assistance in obtaining accommodation, and the authority have reason to believe that he is or may be homeless or threatened with homelessness.

(2) In this Part—

"applicant" means a person making such an application,
"assistance under this Part" means the benefit of any function under the following provisions of this Part relating to accommodation or assistance in obtaining accommodation, and
"eligible for assistance" means not excluded from such assistance by section 185 (persons from abroad not eligible for housing assistance) or section 186 (asylum seekers and their dependants).

(3) Nothing in this section or the following provisions of this Part affects a person's entitlement to advice and information under section 179 (duty to provide advisory services).

Inquiry into cases of homelessness or threatened homelessness

184.—(1) If the local housing authority have reason to believe that an applicant may be homeless or threatened with homelessness, they shall make such inquiries as are necessary to satisfy themselves—

(a) whether he is eligible for assistance, and
(b) if so, whether any duty, and if so what duty, is owed to him under the following provisions of this Part.

(2) They may also make inquiries whether he has a local connection with the district of another local housing authority in England, Wales or Scotland.

(3) On completing their inquiries the authority shall notify the applicant of their decision and, so far as any issue is decided against his interests, inform him of the reasons for their decision.

(4) If the authority have notified or intend to notify another local housing authority under section 198 (referral of cases), they shall at the same time notify the applicant of that decision and inform him of the reasons for it.

(5) A notice under subsection (3) or (4) shall also inform the applicant of his right to request a review of the decision and of the time within which such a request must be made (see section 202).

(6) Notice required to be given to a person under this section shall be given in writing and, if not received by him, shall be treated as having been given to him if it is made available at the authority's office for a reasonable period for collection by him or on his behalf.

Persons from abroad not eligible for housing assistance

185.—(1) A person is not eligible for assistance under this Part if he is a person from abroad who is ineligible for housing assistance.

(2) A person not subject to immigration control within the meaning of the Asylum and Immigration Act 1996 is not eligible for housing assistance unless he is of a class prescribed by regulations made by the Secretary of State.

(3) The Secretary of State may make provision by regulations as to the other descriptions of persons who are to be treated for the purposes of this Part as persons from abroad who are ineligible for housing assistance.

(4) A person from abroad who is not eligible for housing assistance shall be disregarded in determining for the purposes of this Part whether another person—

(a) is homeless or threatened with homelessness, or
(b) has a priority need for accommodation.

Asylum-seekers and their dependents

186.—(1) An asylum-seeker, or a dependent of an asylum-seeker who is not by virtue of section 185 a person from abroad who is ineligible for housing assistance, is not eligible for assistance under this Part if he has any accommodation in the United Kingdom, however temporary, available for his occupation.

(2) For the purposes of this section a person who makes a claim for asylum—

(a) becomes an asylum-seeker at the time when his claim is recorded by the Secretary of State as having been made, and
(b) ceases to be an asylum-seeker at the time when his claim is recorded by the Secretary of State as having been finally determined or abandoned.

(3) For the purposes of this section a person—

(a) becomes a dependent of an asylum-seeker at the time when he is recorded by the Secretary of State as being a dependent of the asylum-seeker, and
(b) ceases to be a dependent of an asylum-seeker at the time when the person whose dependent he is ceases to be an asylum-seeker or, if it is earlier, at the time when he is recorded by the Secretary of State as ceasing to be a dependent of the asylum-seeker.

(4) In relation to an asylum-seeker, "dependent" means a person—

(a) who is his spouse or a child of his under the age of eighteen, and
(b) who has neither a right of abode in the United Kingdom nor indefinite leave under the Immigration Act 1971 to enter or remain in the United Kingdom.

(5) In this section a "claim for asylum" means a claim made by a person that it would be contrary to the United Kingdom's obligations under the Convention relating to the Status of Refugees done at Geneva on 28th July 1951 and the Protocol to that Convention for him to be removed from, or required to leave, the United Kingdom.

Provision of information by Secretary of State

187.—(1) The Secretary of State shall, at the request of a local
housing authority, provide the authority with such information as
they may require—

    (a) as to whether a person is or has become an asylum-seeker,
or a dependent of an asylum-seeker, and
    (b) to enable them to determine whether such a person is
eligible for assistance under this Part under section 185
(persons from abroad not eligible for housing assistance).

(2) Where that information is given otherwise than in writing,
the Secretary of State shall confirm it in writing if a written request
is made to him by the authority.

(3) If it appears to the Secretary of State that any application,
decision or other change of circumstances has affected the status of
a person about whom information was previously provided by him
to a local housing authority under this section, he shall inform the
authority in writing of that fact, the reason for it and the date on
which the previous information became inaccurate.

Interim duty to accommodate in case of apparent priority need

188.—(1) If the local housing authority have reason to believe
that an applicant may be homeless, eligible for assistance and have
a priority need, they shall secure that accommodation is available
for his occupation pending a decision as to the duty (if any) owed
to him under the following provisions of this Part.

(2) The duty under this section arises irrespective of any
possibility of the referral of the applicant's case to another local
housing authority (see sections 198 to 200).

(3) The duty ceases when the authority's decision is notified to
the applicant, even if the applicant requests a review of the
decision (see section 202).

Priority need for accommodation

189.—(1) The following have a priority need for
accommodation—

    (a) a pregnant woman or a person with whom she resides or
might reasonably be expected to reside;
    (b) a person with whom dependent children reside or might
reasonably be expected to reside;

(c) a person who is vulnerable as a result of old age, mental illness or handicap or physical disability or other special reason, or with whom such a person resides or might reasonably be expected to reside;

(d) a person who is homeless or threatened with homelessness as a result of an emergency such as flood, fire or other disaster.

(2) The Secretary of State may by order—

(a) specify further descriptions of persons as having a priority need for accommodation, and

(b) amend or repeal any part of subsection (1).

(3) Before making such an order the Secretary of State shall consult such associations representing relevant authorities, and such other persons, as he considers appropriate.

(4) No such order shall be made unless a draft of it has been approved by resolution of each House of Parliament.

Duties to persons becoming homeless intentionally

190.—(1) This section applies where the local housing authority are satisfied that an applicant is homeless and is eligible for assistance but are also satisfied that he became homeless intentionally.

(2) If the authority are satisfied that the applicant has a priority need, they shall—

(a) secure that accommodation is available for his occupation for such period as they consider will give him a reasonable opportunity of securing accommodation for his occupation, and

(b) provide him with advice and such assistance as they consider appropriate in the circumstances in any attempts he may make to secure that accommodation becomes available for his occupation.

(3) If they are not satisfied that he has a priority need, they shall provide him with advice and such assistance as they consider appropriate in the circumstances in any attempts he may make to secure that accommodation becomes available for his occupation.

Becoming homeless intentionally

191.—(1) A person becomes homeless intentionally if he deliberately does or fails to do anything in consequence of which he ceases to occupy accommodation which is available for his occupation and which it would have been reasonable for him to continue to occupy.

(2) For the purposes of subsection (1) an act or omission in good faith on the part of a person who was unaware of any relevant fact shall not be treated as deliberate.

(3) A person shall be treated as becoming homeless intentionally if—

(a) he enters into an arrangement under which he is required to cease to occupy accommodation which it would have been reasonable for him to continue to occupy, and
(b) the purpose of the arrangement is to enable him to become entitled to assistance under this Part,

and there is no other good reason why he is homeless.

(4) A person who is given advice or assistance under section 197 (duty where other suitable alternative accommodation available), but fails to secure suitable alternative accommodation in circumstances in which it was reasonably to be expected that he would do so, shall, if he makes a further application under this Part, be treated as having become homeless intentionally.

Duty to persons not in priority need who are not homeless intentionally

192.—(1) This section applies where the local housing authority—

(a) are satisfied that an applicant is homeless and eligible for assistance, and
(b) are not satisfied that he has become homeless intentionally,

but are not satisfied that he has a priority need.

(2) The authority shall provide the applicant with advice and such assistance as they consider appropriate in the circumstances in any attempts he may make to secure that accommodation becomes available for his occupation.

Duty to persons with priority need who are not homeless intentionally

193.(1) This section applies where the local housing authority are satisfied that an applicant is homeless, eligible for assistance and has a priority need, and are not satisfied that he became homeless intentionally.

This section has effect subject to section 197 (duty where other suitable accommodation available).

(2) Unless the authority refer the application to another local housing authority (see section 198), they shall secure that accommodation is available for occupation by the applicant.

(3) The authority are subject to the duty under this section for a period of two years ('the minimum period'), subject to the following provisions of this section.

After the end of that period the authority may continue to secure that accommodation is available for occupation by the applicant, but are not obliged to do so (see section 194).

(4) The minimum period begins with—

(a) if the applicant was occupying accommodation made available under section 188 (interim duty to accommodate), the day on which he was notified of the authority's decision that the duty under this section was owed to him;

(b) if the applicant was occupying accommodation made available to him under section 200(3) (interim duty where case considered for referral but not referred), the date on which he was notified under subsection (2) of that section of the decision that the conditions for referral were not met;

(c) in any other case, the day on which the accommodation was first made available to him in pursuance of the duty under this section.

(5) The local housing authority shall cease to be subject to the duty under this section if the applicant, having been informed by the authority of the possible consequence of refusal, refuses an offer of accommodation which the authority are satisfied is suitable for him and the authority notify him that they regard themselves as having discharged their duty under this section.

(6) The local housing authority shall cease to be subject to the duty under this section if the applicant—

(a) ceases to be eligible for assistance,

(b) becomes homeless intentionally from the accommodation made available for his occupation,

(c) accepts an offer of accommodation under Part VI (allocation of housing), or

(d) otherwise voluntarily ceases to occupy as his only or principal home the accommodation made available for his occupation.

(7) The local housing authority shall also cease to be subject to the duty under this section if—

(a) the applicant, having been informed of the possible consequence of refusal, refuses an offer of accommodation under
Part VI, and

(b) the authority are satisfied that the accommodation was
suitable for him and that it was reasonable for him to accept
it and notify him accordingly within 21 days of the refusal.

(8) For the purposes of subsection (7) an applicant may reasonably be expected to accept an offer of accommodation under Part
VI even though he is under contractual or other obligations in
respect of his existing accommodation, provided he is able to bring
those obligations to an end before he is required to take up the
offer.

(9) A person who ceases to be owed the duty under this section
may make a fresh application to the authority for accommodation
or assistance in obtaining accommodation.

Power exercisable after minimum period of duty under s.193

194.—(1) Where a local housing authority have been subject to
the duty under section 193 in relation to a person until the end of
the minimum period, they may continue to secure that accommodation is available for his occupation.

(2) They shall not do so unless they are satisfied on a review
under this section that—

(a) he has a priority need,

(b) there is no other suitable accommodation available for
occupation by him in their district, and

(c) he wishes the authority to continue securing that accommodation is available for his occupation;

and they shall not continue to do so for more than two years at a
time unless they are satisfied on a further review under this section
as to those matters.

The review shall be carried out towards the end of the minimum
period, or subsequent two year period, with a view to enabling the
authority to make an assessment of the likely situation at the end
of that period.

(3) They shall cease to do so if events occur such that, by virtue
of section 193(6) or (7), they would cease to be subject to any duty
under that section.

(4) Where an authority carry out a review under this section
they shall make such inquiries as they consider appropriate to
determine—

(a) whether they are satisfied as to the matters mentioned in subsection (2)(a) to (c), and
(b) whether any of the events referred in subsection (3) has occurred;

and on completing the review they shall notify the applicant of their determination and of whether they propose to exercise, or continue to exercise, their power under this section.

(5) The authority may at any time, whether in consequence of a review or otherwise, give notice to the person concerned that they propose to cease exercising their power under this section in his case.

(6) The notice must specify—

(a) the day on which they will cease exercising their power under this section, and
(b) any action that they intend to take as a result,

and must be given not less than the prescribed period before the day so specified.

Duties in case of threatened homelessness

195.—(1) This section applies where the local housing authority are satisfied that an applicant is threatened with homelessness and is eligible for assistance.

(2) If the authority—

(a) are satisfied that he has a priority need, and
(b) are not satisfied that he became threatened with homelessness intentionally,

they shall take reasonable steps to secure that accommodation does not cease to be available for his occupation.

This subsection has effect subject to section 197 (duty where other suitable accommodation available).

(3) Subsection (2) does not affect any right of the authority, whether by virtue of a contract, enactment or rule of law, to secure vacant possession of any accommodation.

(4) Where in pursuance of the duty under subsection (2) the authority secure that accommodation other than that occupied by the applicant when he made his application is available for occupation by him, the provisions of section 193(3) to (9) (period for which duty owed) and section 194 (power exercisable after minimum period of duty) apply, with any necessary modifications,

in relation to the duty under this section as they apply in relation to the duty under section 193.

(5) If the authority—

(a) are not satisfied that the applicant has a priority need, or
(b) are satisfied that he has a priority need but are also satisfied that he became threatened with homelessness intentionally,

they shall furnish him with advice and such assistance as they consider appropriate in the circumstances in any attempts he may make to secure that accommodation does not cease to be available for his occupation.

Becoming threatened with homelessness intentionally

196.—(1) A person becomes threatened with homelessness intentionally if he deliberately does or fails to do anything the likely result of which is that he will be forced to leave accommodation which is available for his occupation and which it would have been reasonable for him to continue to occupy.

(2) For the purposes of subsection (1) an act or omission in good faith on the part of a person who was unaware of any relevant fact shall not be treated as deliberate.

(3) A person shall be treated as becoming threatened with homelessness intentionally if—

(a) he enters into an arrangement under which he is required to cease to occupy accommodation which it would have been reasonable for him to continue to occupy, and
(b) the purpose of the arrangement is to enable him to become entitled to assistance under this Part,

and there is no other good reason why he is threatened with homelessness.

(4) A person who is given advice or assistance under section 197 (duty where other suitable alternative accommodation available), but fails to secure suitable accommodation in circumstances in which it was reasonably to be expected that he would do so, shall, if he makes a further application under this Part, be treated as having become threatened with homlessness intentionally.

Duty where other suitable accommodation available

197.—(1) This section applies if the local housing authority would be under a duty under this Part—

(a) to secure that accommodation is available for occupation by an applicant, or

(b) to secure that accommodation does not cease to be available for his occupation,

but are not satisfied that other suitable accommodation is available for occupation by him in their district.

(2) In that case, their duty is to provide the applicant with such advice and assistance as the authority consider is reasonably required to enable him to secure such accommodation.

(3) The duty ceases if the applicant fails to take reasonable steps to secure such accommodation.

(4) In deciding what advice and assistance to provide under this section, and whether the applicant has taken reasonable steps, the authority shall have regard to all the circumstances including—

(a) the characteristics and personal circumstances of the applicant, and

(b) the state of the local housing market and the type of accommodation available.

(5) For the purposes of this section accommodation shall not be regarded as available for occupation by the applicant if it is available only with assistance beyond what the authority consider is reasonable in the circumstances.

(6) Subsection (1) does not apply to the duty of a local housing authority under—

section 188 (interim duty to accommodate in case of apparent priority need),

section 190(2)(a) (limited duty to person becoming homeless intentionally), or

section 200(1), (3) or (4) (interim duties where case is considered for referral or referred).

Referred to another local housing authority

198.—(1) If the local housing authority would be subject to the duty under section 193 (accommodation for those with priority need who are not homeless intentionally) but consider that the conditions are met for referral of the case to another local housing authority, they may notify that other authority of their opinion.

The authority need not consider under section 197 whether other suitable accommodation is available before proceeding under this section.

(2) The conditions for referral of the case to another authority are met if—

   (a) neither the applicant nor any person who might reasonably be expected to reside with him has a local connection with the district of the authority to whom his application was made,

   (b) the applicant or a person who might reasonably be expected to reside with him has a local connection with the district of that other authority, and

   (c) neither the applicant nor any person who might reasonably be expected to reside with him will run the risk of domestic violence in that other district.

(3) For this purpose a person runs the risk of domestic violence—

   (a) if he runs the risk of violence from a person with whom he is associated, or

   (b) if he runs the risk of threats of violence from such a person which are likely to be carried out.

(4) The conditions for referral of the case to another authority are also met if—

   (a) the applicant was on a previous application made to that other authority placed (in pursuance of their functions under this Part) in accommodation in the district of the authority to whom his application is now made, and

   (b) the previous application was within such period as may be prescribed of the present application.

(5) The question whether the conditions for referral of a case are satisfied shall be decided by agreement between the notifying authority and the notified authority, or, in default of agreement, in accordance with such arrangements as the Secretary of State may direct by order.

(6) An order may direct that the arrangements shall be—

   (a) those agreed by any relevant authorities or associations of relevant authorities, or

   (b) in default of such agreement, such arrangements as appear to the Secretary of State to be suitable, after consultation with such associations representing relevant authorities, and such other persons, as he thinks appropriate.

(7) No such order shall be made unless a draft of the order has been approved by a resolution of each House of Parliament.

Local connection

199.—(1) A person has a local connection with the district of a local housing authority if he has a connection with it—

(a) because he is, or in the past was, normally resident there, and that residence is or was of his own choice,
(b) because he is employed there,
(c) because of family associations, or
(d) because of special circumstances.

(2) A person is not employed in a district if he is serving in the regular armed forces of the Crown.

(3) Residence in a district is not of a person's own choice if—

(a) he becomes resident there because he, or a person who might reasonably be expected to reside with him, is serving in the regular armed forces of the Crown, or
(b) he, or a person who might reasonably be expected to reside with him, becomes resident there because he is detained under the authority of an Act of Parliament.

(4) In subsections (2) and (3) "regular armed forces of the Crown" means the Royal Navy, the regular armed forces as defined by section 225 of the Army Act 1955, the regular air force as defined by section 223 of the Air Force Act 1955 and Queen Alexandra's Royal Naval Nursing Service.

(5) The Secretary of State may by order specify other circumstances in which—

(a) a person is not to be treated as employed in a district, or
(b) residence in a district is not to be treated as of a person's own choice.

Duties to applicant whose case is considered for referral or referred

200.—(1) Where a local housing authority notify an applicant that they intend to notify or have notified another local housing authority of their opinion that the conditions are met for the referral of his case to that other authority—

(a) they cease to be subject to any duty under section 188 (interim duty to accommodate in case of apparent priority need), and

(b) they are not subject to any duty under section 193 (the main housing duty),

but they shall secure that accommodation is available for occupation by the applicant until he is notified of the decision whether the conditions for referral of his case are met.

(2) When it has been decided whether the conditions for referral are met, the notifying authority shall notify the applicant of the decision and inform him of the reasons for it.

The notice shall also inform the applicant of his right to request a review of the decision and of the time within which such a request must be made.

(3) If it is decided that the conditions for referral are not met, the notifying authority shall secure that accommodation is available for occupation by the applicant until they have considered whether other suitable accommodation is available for his occupation in their district.

If they are satisfied that other suitable accommodation is available for his occupation in their district, section 197(2) applies; and if they are not so satisfied, they are subject to the duty under section 193 (the main housing duty).

(4) If it is decided that the conditions for referral are met, the notified authority shall secure that accommodation is available for occupation by the applicant until they have considered whether other suitable accommodation is available for his occupation in their district.

If they are satisfied that other suitable accommodation is available for his occupation in their district, section 197(2) applies; and if they are not so satisfied, they are subject to the duty under section 193 (the main housing duty).

(5) The duty under subsection (1), (3) or (4) ceases as provided in that subsection even if the applicant requests a review of the authority's decision (see section 202).

The authority may continue to secure that accommodation is available for the applicant's occupation pending the decision on a review.

(6) Notice required to be given to an applicant under this section shall be given in writing and, if not received by him, shall be treated as having been given to him if it is made available at the authority's office for a reasonable period for collection by him or on his behalf.

Application of referral provisions to cases arising in Scotland

201.—(1) Sections 198 and 200 (referral of application to another local housing authority and duties to applicant whose case is considered for referral or referred) apply—

(a) to applications referred by a local authority in Scotland in pursuance of sections 33 and 34 of the Housing (Scotland) Act 1987, and

(b) to persons whose applications are so transferred,

as they apply to cases arising under this Part (the reference in section 198 to this Part being construed as a reference to Part II of that Act).

Right to request review of decision

202.—(1) An applicant has the right to request a review of—

(a) any decision of a local housing authority as to his eligibility for assistance,

(b) any decision of a local housing authority as to what duty (if any) is owed to him under sections 190 to 193 and 195 to 197 (duties to persons found to be homeless or threatened with homelessness),

(c) any decision of a local housing authority to notify another authority under section 198(1) (referral of cases),

(d) any decision under section 198(5) whether the conditions are met for the referral of his case,

(e) any decision under section 200(3) or (4) (decision as to duty owed to applicant whose case is considered for referral or referred), or

(f) any decision of a local housing authority as to the suitability of accommodation offered to him in discharge of their duty under any of the provisions mentioned in paragraph (b) or (e).

(2) There is no right to request a review of the decision reached on an earlier review.

(3) A request for review must be made before the end of the period of 21 days beginning with the day on which he is notified of the authority's decision or such longer period as the authority may in writing allow.

(4) On a request being duly made to them, the authority or authorities concerned shall review their decision.

Procedure on a review

203.—(1) The Secretary of State may make provision by regulations as to the procedure to be followed in connection with a review under section 202.

Nothing in the following provisions affects the generality of this power.

(2) Provision may be made by regulations—

    (a) requiring the decision on review to be made by a person of appropriate seniority who was not involved in the original decision, and

    (b) as to the circumstances in which the applicant is entitled to an oral hearing, and whether and by whom he may be represented at such a hearing.

(3) The authority, or as the case may be either of the authorities, concerned shall notify the applicant of the decision on the review.

(4) If the decision is—

    (a) to confirm the original decision on any issue against the interests of the applicant, or

    (b) to confirm a previous decision—

        (i) to notify another authority under section 198 (referral of cases), or

        (ii) that the conditions are met for the referral of his case,

they shall also notify him of the reasons for the decision.

(5) In any case they shall inform the applicant of his right to appeal to a county court on a point of law, and of the period within which such an appeal must be made (see section 204).

(6) Notice of the decision shall not treated as given unless and until subsection (5), and where applicable subsection (4), is complied with.

(7) Provision may be made by regulations as to the period within which the review must be carried out and notice given of the decision.

(8) Notice required to be given to a person under this section shall be given in writing and, if not received by him, shall be treated as having been given if it is made available at the authority's office for a reasonable period for collection by him or on his behalf.

Right of appeal to county court on point of law

204.—(1) If an applicant who has requested a review under section 202—

    (a) is dissatisfied with the decision on the review, or

    (b) is not notified of the decision on the review within the time prescribed under section 203, he may appeal to the county court on any point of law arising from the decision or, as the case may be, the original decision.

(2) An appeal must be brought within 21 days of his being notified of the decision or, as the case may be, of the date on which he should have been notified of a decision on review.

(3) On appeal the court may make such order confirming, quashing or varying the decision as it thinks fit.

(4) Where the authority were under a duty under section 188, 190 or 200 to secure that accommodation is available for the applicant's occupation, they may continue to secure that accommodation is so available—

(a) during the period for appealing under this section against the authority's decision, and
(b) if an appeal is brought, until the appeal (and any further appeal) is finally determined.

Supplementary Provisions

205.—(1) The following sections have effect in relation to the discharge by a local housing authority of their functions under this Part to secure that accommodation is available for the occupation of a person—

section 206 (general provisions),
section 207 (provision of accommodation by authority),
section 208 (out-of-area placements),
section 209 (arrangements with private landlord).

(2) In those sections those functions are referred to as the authority's "housing functions under this Part'.

Discharge of functions by local housing authorities

206.—(1) A local housing authority may discharge their housing functions under this Part only in the following ways—

(a) by securing that suitable accommodation provided by them is available,
(b) by securing that he obtains suitable accommodation from some other person, or
(c) by giving him such advice and assistance as will secure that suitable accommodation is available from some other person.

(2) A local housing authority may require a person in relation to whom they are discharging such functions—

    (a) to pay such reasonable charges as they may determine in respect of accommodation which they secure for his occupation (either by making it available themselves or otherwise), or

to pay such reasonable amount as they may determine in respect of sums payable by them for accommodation made available by another person.

Discharge of functions: provision of accommodation by the authority

207.—(1) A local housing authority shall not under section 206(1)(a) discharge their housing functions under this Part by providing accommodation other than—

    (a) accommodation in a hostel within the meaning of section 622 of the Housing Act 1985, or
    (b) accommodation leased to the authority as mentioned in subsection (2) below,

for more than two years (continuously or in aggregate) in any period of three years.

This applies irrespective of the number of applications for accommodation or assistance in obtaining accommodation made by the person concerned.

(2) The accommodation referred to in subsection (1)(b) is accommodation—

    (a) leased to the authority with vacant possession for use as temporary housing accommodation on terms which include provision for the lessor to obtain vacant possession from the authority on the expiry of a specified period or when required by the lessor,
    (b) the lessor of which is not an authority or body within section 80(1) of the Housing Act 1985 (the landlord condition for secure tenancies), and
    (c) in which the authority have no interest other than under the lease in question or as a mortgagee.

(3) The authority shall not discharge such functions in relation to a person who—

    (a) normally resides with another person as a member of his family, or

    (b) might reasonably be expected to reside with another person,

in such a way that subsection (1) would be contravened if the functions were discharged in relation to that other person.

(4) The Secretary of State may, on the application of a local housing authority, by direction exclude or modify the operation of subsection (1) in relation to that authority if it appears to him that the authority will not otherwise be able reasonably to discharge their housing functions under this Part.

(5) Any such direction shall have effect only—

    (a) with respect to applicants of a description specified in the direction, and

    (b) for a period specified in the direction, which shall not exceed one year,

and may be expressed to have effect subject to any conditions specified in the direction.

(6) Where the Secretary of State gives or has given a direction under subsection (4), he may give the authority such directions as he considers appropriate as to the discharge of their housing functions under this Part in cases affected by the direction having or ceasing to have effect.

Discharge of functions: out-of-area placements

208.—(1) So far as reasonably practicable a local housing authority shall in discharging their housing functions under this Part secure that accommodation is available for the occupation of the applicant in their district.

(2) If they secure that accommodation is available for the occupation of the applicant outside their district, they shall give notice to the local housing authority in whose district the accommodation is situated.

(3) The notice shall state—

    (a) the name of the applicant,

    (b) the number and description of other persons who normally reside with him as a member of his family or might reasonably be expected to reside with him,

(c) the address of the accommodation,

(d) the date on which the accommodation was made available to him, and

(e) which function under this Part the authority was discharging in securing that the accommodation is available for his occupation.

(4) The notice must be in writing, and must be given before the end of the period of 14 days beginning with the day on which the accommodation was made available to the applicant.

Discharge of functions: arrangements with private landlord

209.—(1) This section applies where in pursuance of any of their housing functions under this Part a local housing authority make arrangements with a private landlord to provide accommodation.

For this purpose a "private landlord" means a landlord who is not within section 80(1) of the Housing Act 1985 (the landlord condition for secure tenancies).

(2) If the housing function arises under section 188, 190, 200, or 204(4) (interim duties), a tenancy granted in pursuance of the arrangements to a person specified by the authority cannot be an assured tenancy before the end of the period of twelve months, beginning with—

(a) the date on which the applicant was notified of the authority's decision under section 184(3) or 198(5), or

(b) if there is a review of that decision under section 202 or an appeal to the court under section 204, the date on which he is notified of the decision on review or the appeal is finally determined,

unless, before or during that period, the tenant is notified by the landlord (or, in the case of joint landlords, at least one of them) that the tenant is to be regarded as an assured shorthold tenancy or an assured tenancy other than an assured shorthold tenancy.

A registered social landlord cannot serve such a notice making such a tenancy an assured tenancy other than an assured shorthold tenancy.

(3) Where in any other case a tenancy is granted in pursuance of the arrangements by a registered social landlord to a person specified by the authority—

(a) the tenancy cannot be an assured tenancy unless it is an assured shorthold tenancy, and

(b) the landlord cannot convert the tenancy to an assured tenancy unless the accommodation is allocated to the tenant under Part VI.

Suitability of accommodation

210.—(1) In determining for the purposes of this Part whether accommodation is suitable for a person, the local housing authority shall have regard to Parts IX, X and XI of the Housing Act 1985 (slum clearance; overcrowding; houses in multiple occupation).
(2) The Secretary of State may be order specify—

(a) circumstances in which accommodation is or is not to be regarded as suitable for a person, and
(b) matters to be taken into account or disregarded in determining whether accommodation is suitable for a person.

Protection of property of homeless persons and persons threatened with homelessness

211.—(1) This section applies where a local housing authority have reason to believe that—

(a) there is danger of loss of, or damage to, any personal property of an applicant by reason of his inability to protect or deal with it, and
(b) no other suitable arrangements have been or are being made.

(2) If the authority have become subject to a duty towards the applicant under—

section 188 (interim duty to accommodate)
section 190, 193, or 195 (duties to persons found to be homeless or threatened with homelessness), or
section 200 (duties to applicant whose case is considered for referral or referred),

then, whether or not they are still subject to such a duty, they shall take reasonable steps to prevent the loss of the property or prevent or mitigate damage to it.
(3) If they have not become subject to such a duty, they may take any steps they consider reasonable for that purpose.

(4) The authority may decline to take action under this section except upon such conditions as they consider appropriate in the particular case, which may include conditions as to—

    (a) the making and recovery by the authority of reasonable charges for the action taken, or

    (b) the disposal by the authority, in such circumstances as may be specified, of property in relation to which they have taken action.

(5) References in this section to personal property of the applicant include personal property of any person who might reasonably be expected to reside with him.

(6) Section 212 contains provisions supplementing this section.

Protection of property: supplementary provisions

212.—(1) The authority may for the purposes of section 211 (protection of property of homeless persons or persons threatened with homelessness)—

    (a) enter, at all reasonable times, any premises which are the usual place of residence of the applicant or which were his usual last place of residence, and

    (b) deal with any personal property of his in any way which is reasonably necessary, in particular by storing it or arranging for its storage.

(2) Where the applicant asks the authority to move his property to a particular location nominated by him, the authority—

    (a) may, if it appears to them that his request is reasonable, discharge their responsibilities under section 211 by doing as he asks, and

    (b) having done so, have no further duty or power to take action under that section in relation to that property.

If such a request is made, the authority shall before complying with it inform the applicant of the consequence of their doing so.

(3) If no such request is made (or, if made, is not acted upon) the authority cease to have any duty or power to take action under section 211 when, in their opinion, there is no longer any reason to believe that there is a danger of loss of or damage to a person's personal property by reason of his inability to protect it or deal with it.

But property stored by virtue of their having taken such action may be kept in store and any conditions upon which it was taken into store continue to have effect, with any necessary modifications.

(4) Where the authority—

(a) cease to be subject to a duty to take action under section 211 in respect of an applicant's property, or
(b) cease to have power to take such action, having previously taken such action,

they shall notify the applicant of that fact and of the reason for it.

(5) The notification shall be given to the applicant—

(a) by delivering it to him, or
(b) by leaving it, or sending it to him, at his last known address.

(6) References in this section to personal property of the applicant include personal property of any person who might reasonably be expected to reside with him.

Co-operation between relevant housing authorities and bodies

213.—(1) Where a local housing authority—

(a) request another relevant housing authority or body, in England, Wales or Scotland, to assist them in the discharge of their functions under this Part, or
(b) request a social services authority, in England, Wales or Scotland, to exercise any of their functions in relation to a case which the local housing authority are dealing with under this Part,

the authority or body to whom the request is made shall co-operate in rendering such assistance in the discharge of the functions to which the request relates as is reasonable in the circumstances.

(2) In subsection (1)(a) "relevant housing authority or body" means—

(a) in relation to England and Wales, a local housing authority, a new town corporation, a registered social landlord or a housing action trust;

(b) in relation to Scotland, a local authority, a development corporation, a registered housing association or Scottish Homes.

Expressions used in paragraph (a) have the same meaning as in the Housing Act 1985; and expressions used in paragraph (b) have the same meaning as in the Housing (Scotland) Act 1987.

(3) Subsection (1) applies to a request by a local authority in Scotland under section 38 of the Housing (Scotland) Act 1987 as it applies to a request by a local housing authority in England and Wales (the references to this Part being construed, in relation to such a request, as references to Part II of that Act).

False statements, withholding information and failure to disclose change of circumstances

214.—(1) It is an offence for a person, with intent to induce a local housing authority to believe in connection with the exercise of their functions under this Part that he or another person is entitled to accommodation or assistance in accordance with the provisions of this Part, or is entitled to accommodation or assistance of a particular description—

(a) knowingly or recklessly to make a statement which is false in a material particular, or
(b) knowingly to withhold information which the authority have reasonably required him to give in connection with the exercise of those functions.

(2) If before an applicant receives notification of the local housing authority's decision on his application there is any change of facts material to his case, he shall notify the authority as soon as possible.

The authority shall explain to every applicant, in ordinary language, the duty imposed on him by this subsection and the effect of subsection (3).

(3) A person who fails to comply with subsection (2) commits an offence unless he shows that he was not given the explanation required by that subsection or that he had some other reasonable excuse for non-compliance.

(4) A person guilty of an offence under this section is liable on summary conviction to a fine not exceeding level 5 on the standard scale.

Regulations and orders

215.—(1) In this Part "prescribed" means prescribed by regulations of the Secretary of State.

(2) Regulations or an order under this Part may make different provision for different purposes, including different provision for different areas.

(3) Regulations or an order under this Part shall be made by statutory instrument.

(4) Unless required to be approved in draft, regulations or an order under this Part shall be subject to annulment in pursuance of a resolution of either House of Parliament.

Transitional and consequential matters

216.—(1) The provisions of this Part have effect in place of the provisions of Part III of the Housing Act 1985 (housing the homeless) and shall be construed as one with that Act.

(2) Subject to any transitional provision contained in an order under section 232(4) (power to include transitional provision in commencement order), the provisions of this Part do not apply in relation to an applicant whose application for accommodation or assistance in obtaining accommodation was made before the commencement of this Part.

(3) The enactments mentioned in Schedule 17 have effect with the amendments specified there which are consequential on the provisions of this Part.

Minor definitions: Part VII

217.—(1) In this Part, subject to subsection (2)—

"relevant authority" means a local housing authority or a
    social services authority; and
"social services authority" means a local authority for the
    purposes of the Local Authority Social Services Act 1970, as
    defined in section 1 of that Act.

(2) In this Part, in relation to Scotland—

(a) "local housing authority" means a local authority within
    the meaning of the Housing (Scotland) Act 1988, and
(b) "social services authority" means a local authority for the
    purposes of Social Work (Scotland) Act 1968.

(3) References in this Part to the district of a local housing authority—

(a) have the same meaning in relation to an authority in England or Wales as in the Housing Act 1985, and

(b) in relation to an authority in Scotland, mean the area of the local authority concerned.

APPENDIX TWO

Criminal Law Act 1977

PART II (ss.6–12A)

(as amended by Criminal Justice and Public Order Act 1994,
Part V; (ss.72–76))

Violence for securing entry

6.—(1) Subject to the following provisions of this section, any person who, without lawful authority, uses or threatens violence for the purpose of securing entry into any premises for himself or for any other person is guilty of an offence, provided that—

(a) there is someone present on those premises at the time who is opposed to the entry which the violence is intended to secure; and

(b) the person using or threatening the violence knows that that is the case.

(1A) Subsection (1) does not apply to a person who is a displaced residential occupier or a protected intending occupier of the premises in question or who is acting on behalf of such an occupier; and if the accused adduces sufficient evidence that he was, or was acting on behalf of, such an occupier he shall be presumed to be, or to be acting on behalf of, such an occupier unless the contrary is proved by the prosecution.

(2) Subject to subsection (1A) above, the fact that a person has any interest in or right to possession or occupation of any premises shall not for the purposes of subsection (1) above constitute lawful authority for the use of threat of violence by him or anyone else for the purposes of securing his entry into those premises.

(4) It is immaterial for the purposes of this section—

(a) whether the violence in question is directed against the person or against property; and
(b) whether the entry which the violence is intended to secure is for the purpose of acquiring possession of the premises in question or for any other purpose.

(5) A person guilty of an offence under this section shall be liable on summary conviction to imprisonment for a term not exceeding six months or to a fine not exceeding level 5 on the standard scale or both.

(6) A constable in uniform may arrest without warrant anyone who is, or whom he with reasonable cause, suspects to be, guilty of an offence under this section.

(7) Section 12 below contains provisions which apply for determining when any person is to be regarded for the purposes of this Part of this Act as a displaced residential occupier of any premises or of any access to any premises and section 12A below contains provisions which apply for determining when any person is to be regarded for the purposes of this Part of this Act as a protected intending occupier of any premises or of any access to any premises.

Adverse occupation of residential premises

7.—(1) Subject to the following provisions of this section and to section 12A(9) below, any person who is on any premises as a trespasser after having entered as such is guilty of an offence if he fails to leave those premises on being required to do so by or on behalf of—

(a) a displaced residential occupier of the premises; or
(b) an individual who is a protected intending occupier of the premises.

(2) In any proceedings for an offence under this section it shall be a defence for the accused to prove that he believed that the person requiring him to leave the premises was not a displaced residential occupier or protected intending occupier of the premises or a person acting on behalf of a displaced residential occupier or protected intending occupier.

(3) In any proceedings for an offence under this section it shall be a defence for the accused to prove—

(a) that the premises in question are or form part of premises used mainly for non-residential purposes; and

(b) that he was not on any part of the premises used wholly or mainly for residential purposes.

(4) Any reference in the preceding provisions of this section to any premises includes a reference to any access to them, whether or not any such access itself constitutes premises, within the meaning of this Part of this Act.

(5) A person guilty of an offence under this section shall be liable on summary conviction to imprisonment for a term not exceeding six months or to a fine not exceeding level 5 on the standard scale or to both.

(6) A constable in uniform may arrest without warrant anyone who is, or whom he, with reasonable cause, suspects to be, guilty of an offence under this section.

(7) Section 12 below contains provisions which apply for determining when any person is to be regarded for the purposes of this Part of this Act as a displaced residential occupier of any premises or of any access to any premises and section 12A below contains provisions which apply for determining when any person is to be regarded for the purposes of this Part of this Act as a protected intending occupier of any premises or of any access to any premises.

Trespassing with a weapon of offence

8.—(1) A person who is on any premises as a trespasser, after having entered as such, is guilty of an offence if, without lawful authority or reasonable excuse, he has with him on the premises any weapon of offence.

(2) In subsection (1) above "weapon of offence" means any article made or adapted for use for causing injury to or incapacitating a person, or intended by the person having it with him for such use.

(3) A person guilty of an offence under this section shall be liable on summary conviction to imprisonment for a term not exceeding three months or to a fine not exceeding level 5 on the standard scale or both.

(4) A constable in uniform may arrest without warrant anyone who is, or whom he, with reasonable cause, suspects to be, in the act of committing an offence under this section.

Trespassing on premises of foreign missions, etc.

9.—(1) Subject to subsection (3) below, a person who enters or is on any premises to which this section applies as a trespasser is guilty of an offence.

(2) This section applies to any premises which are or form part of—

    (a) the premises of a diplomatic mission within the meaning of the definition in Article 1(i) of the Vienna Convention on Diplomatic Relations signed in 1961 as the Article has effect in the United Kingdom by virtue of section 2 and Schedule 1 of the Diplomatic Privileges Act 1964;

    (aa) the premises of a closed diplomatic mission;

    (b) consular premises within the meaning of the definition in paragraph 1(j) of Article 1 of the Vienna Convention on Consular Relations signed in 1963 as the Article has effect in the United Kingdom by virtue of section 1 and Schedule 1 of the Consular Relations Act 1968;

    (bb) the premises of a closed consular post;

    (c) any other premises in respect of which any organisation or body is entitled to inviolability by or under any enactment; and

    (d) any premises which are the private residence of a diplomatic agent (within the meaning of Article 1(e) mentioned in paragraph (a) above) or of any other person who is entitled to inviolability of residence by or under any enactment.

(2A) In subsection (2) above—

    "the premises of a closed diplomatic mission" means premises which fall within Article 45 of the Convention mentioned in subsection (2)(a) above (as that Article has effect in the United Kingdom by virtue of the section and Schedule mentioned in that paragraph); and

    "the premises of a closed consular post" means premises which fall within Article 27 of the Convention mentioned in subsection (2)(b) above (as that Article has effect in the United Kingdom by virtue of the section and Schedule mentioned in that paragraph).

(3) In any proceedings for an offence under this section it shall be a defence for the accused to prove that he believed that the premises in question were not premises to which this section applies.

(4) In any proceedings for an offence under this section a certificate issued by or under the authority of the Secretary of State stating that any premises were or formed part of premises of any description mentioned in paragraphs (a) to (d) of subsection (2) above at the time of the alleged offence shall be conclusive

evidence that the premises were or formed part of premises of that description at that time.

(5) A person guilty of an offence under this section shall be liable on summary conviction to imprisonment for a term not exceeding six months or a fine not exceeding level 5 on the standard scale or both.

(6) Proceedings for an offence under this section shall not be instituted against any person except by or with the consent of the Attorney General.

(7) A constable in uniform may arrest without warrant anyone who is, or whom he, with reasonable cause, suspects to be, in the act of committing an offence under this section.

Obstruction of court officers executing process for possession against unauthorised occupiers

10.—(1) Without prejudice to section 8(2) of the Sheriffs Act 1887 but subject to the following provisions of this section, a person is guilty of an offence if he resists or intentionally obstructs any persons who is in fact an officer of a court engaged in executing any process issued by the High Court or by any county court for the purpose of enforcing any judgment or order for the recovery of any premises or for delivery of possession of any premises.

(2) Subsection (1) above does not apply unless the judgment or order in question was given or made in proceedings brought under any provisions of rules of court applicable only in circumstances where the person claiming possession of any premises alleges that the premises in question are occupied solely by a person or persons (not being a tenant or tenants holding over after the termination of the tenancy) who entered into or remained in occupation of the premises without the licence or consent of the person claiming possession or any predecessor in title of his.

(3) In any proceedings for an offence under this section it shall be a defence for the accused to prove that he believed that the person he was resisting or obstructing was not an officer of the court.

(4) A person guilty of an offence under this section shall be liable on summary conviction to imprisonment for a term not exceeding six months or to a fine not exceeding level 5 on the standard scale or to both.

(5) A constable in uniform or any officer of a court may arrest without warrant anyone who is, or whom he, with reasonable cause, suspects to be, guilty of an offence under this section.

(6) In this section "officer of a court" means—

    (a) any sheriff, under sheriff, deputy sheriff, bailiff or officer of a sheriff; and

(b) any bailiff or other person who is an officer of a county court within the meaning of the County Courts Act 1959.

Protected intending occupiers: supplementary provisions

12A.—(1) For the purposes of this Part of this Act an individual is a protected intending occupier of any premises at any time if at that time he falls within subsection (2), (4) or (6) below.

(2) An individual is a protected intending occupier of any premises if—

(a) he has in those premises a freehold interest or a leasehold interest with not less than two years still to run;
(b) he requires the premises for his own occupation as a residence;
(c) he is excluded from occupation of the premises by a person who entered them, or any access to them, as a trespasser; and
(d) he or a person acting on his behalf holds a written statement—
   (i) which specifies his interest in the premises;
  (ii) which states that he requires the premises for occupation as a residence for himself; and
 (iii) with respect to which the requirements in subsection (3) below are fulfilled.

(3) The requirements referred to in subsection (2)(d)(ii) above are—

(a) that the statement is signed by the person whose interest is specified in it in the presence of a justice of the peace or commissioner for oaths; and
(b) that the justice of the peace or commissioner for oaths has subscribed his name as a witness to the signature.

(4) An individual is also a protected intending occupier of any premises if—

(a) he has a tenancy of those premises (other than a tenancy falling within subsection (2)(a) above or (6)(a) below) or a licence to occupy those premises granted by a person with a freehold interest or a leasehold interest with not less than two years still to run in the premises;
(b) he requires the premises for his own occupation as a residence;

(c) he is excluded from occupation of the premises by a person who entered them, or any access to them, as a trespasser; and

(d) he or a person acting on his behalf holds a written statement—

    (i) which states that he has been granted a tenancy of those premises or a licence to occupy those premises;

    (ii) which specifies the interest in the premises of the person who granted that tenancy or licence to occupy ("the landlord");

    (iii) which states that he requires the premises for occupation as a residence for himself; and

    (iv) with respect to which the requirements in subsection (5) below are fulfilled.

(5) The requirements referred to in subsection (4)(d)(iv) above are—

(a) that the statement is signed by the landlord and by the tenant or licensee in the presence of a justice of the peace or commissioner for oaths;

(b) that the justice of the peace or commissioner for oaths has subscribed his name as a witness to the signatures.

(6) An individual is also a protected intending occupier of any premises if—

(a) he has a tenancy of those premises (other than a tenancy falling within subsection (2)(a) or (4)(a) above) or a licence to occupy those premises granted by an authority to which this subsection applies;

(b) he requires the premises for his own occupation as a residence;

(c) he is excluded from occupation of the premises by a person who entered the premises, or any access to them, as a trespasser; and

(d) there has been issued to him by or on behalf of the authority referred to in paragraph (a) above a certificate stating that—

    (i) he has been granted a tenancy of those premises or a licence to occupy those premises as a residence by the authority; and

    (ii) the authority which granted that tenancy or licence to occupy is one to which this subsection applies, being of a description specified in the certificate.

(7) Subsection (6) above applies to the following authorities—

(a) any body mentioned in section 14 of the Rent Act 1977 (landlord's interest belonging to local authority etc.);
(b) the Housing Corporation;
(c) Housing for Wales; and
(d) a registered housing association within the meaning of the Housing Association Act 1985.

(8) A person is guilty of an offence if he makes a statement for the purposes of subsection(2)(d) or (4)(d) above which he knows to be false in a material particular or if he recklessly makes such a statement which is false in a material particular.

(9) In any proceedings for an offence under section 7 of this Act where the accused was requested to leave the premises by a person claiming to be or to act on behalf of a protected intending occupier of the premises—

(a) it shall be a defence for the accused to prove that, although asked to do so by the accused at the time the accused was requested to leave, that person failed at that time to produce to the accused such a statement as is referred to in subsection (2)(d) or (4)(d) above or such a certificate as is referred to in subsection (6)(d) above; and
(b) any document purporting to be a certificate under subsection (6)(d) above shall be received in evidence and, unless the contrary is proved, shall be deemed to have been issued by or on behalf of the authority stated in the certificate.

(10) A person guilty of an offence under subsection (8) above shall be liable on summary conviction to imprisonment for a term not exceeding six months or to a fine not exceeding level 5 on the standard scale or to both.

(11) A person who is a protected intending occupier of any premises shall be regarded for the purposes of this Part of this Act as a protected intending occupier also of any access to those premises.

APPENDIX THREE

Criminal Justice and Public Order Act 1994

Powers to remove trespassers from land

61.—(1) If the senior police officer present at the scene reasonably believes that two or more persons are trespassing on land and are present there with the common purpose of residing there for any period, that reasonable steps have been taken by or on behalf of the occupier to ask them to leave and—

    (a) that any of those persons has caused damage to the land or to property on the land or used threatening, abusive or insulting words or behaviour towards the occupier, a member of his family or an employee or agent of his, or

    (b) that those persons have between them six or more vehicles on the land,

he may direct those persons, or any of them, to leave the land and to remove any vehicles or other property they have with them on the land.

(2) Where the persons in question are reasonably believed by the senior police officer to be persons who were not originally trespassers but have become trespassers on the land, the officer must reasonably believe that the other conditions specified in subsection (1) are satisfied after those persons became trespassers before he can exercise the power conferred by that subsection.

(3) A direction under subsection (1) above, if not communicated to the persons referred to in subsection (1) by the police officer giving the direction, may be communicated to them by any constable at the scene.

(4) If a person knowing that a direction under subsection (1) above has been given which applies to him—

(a) fails to leave the land as soon as reasonably practicable, or
(b) having left again enters the land as a trespasser within the period of three months beginning with the day on which the direction was given,

he commits an offence and is liable on summary conviction to imprisonment for a term not exceeding three months or a fine not exceeding level 4 on the standard scale, or both.

(5) A constable in uniform who reasonably suspects that a person is committing an offence under this section may arrest him without a warrant.

(6) In proceedings for an offence under this section it is a defence for the accused to show—

(a) that he was not trespassing on the land, or
(b) that he had a reasonable excuse for failing to leave the land as soon as reasonably practicable or, as the case may be, for again entering the land as a trespasser.

(7) In its application in England and Wales to common land this section has effect as if in the preceding subsections of it—

(a) references to trespassing or trespassers were references to acts and persons doing acts which constitute either a trespass as against the occupier or an infringement of the commoners' rights; and
(b) references to "the occupier" included the commoners or any of them or, in the case of common land to which the public has access, the local authority as well as any commoner.

(8) Subsection (7) above does not—

(a) require action by more than one occupier; or
(b) constitute persons trespassers as against any commoner or the local authority if they are permitted to be there by the other occupier.

(9) In this section—

"common land" means common land as defined in section 22 of the Commons Registration Act 1965;
"commoner" means a person with rights of common as defined in section 22 of the Commons Registration Act 1965;

"land" does not include—
(a) buildings other than—
    (i) agricultural buildings within the meaning of, in England and Wales, paragraphs 3 to 8 of Schedule 5 to the Local Government Finance Act 1988 or, in Scotland, section 7(2) of the Valuation and Rating (Scotland) Act 1956, or
    (ii) scheduled monuments within the meaning of the Ancient Monuments and Archaeological Areas Act 1979;
(b) land forming part of—
    (i) a highway unless it falls within the classifications in section 54 of the Wildlife and Countryside Act 1981 (footpath, bridleway or byway open to all traffic or road used as a public path) or is a cycle track under the Highways Act 1980 or the Cycle Tracks Act 1984; or
    (ii) a road within the meaning of the Roads (Scotland) Act 1984 unless it falls within the definitions in section 151(2)(a)(ii) or (b) (footpaths and cycle tracks) of that Act or is a bridleway within the meaning of section 47 of the Countryside (Scotland) Act 1967;

"the local authority", in relation to common land, means any local authority which has powers in relation to the land under section 9 of the Commons Registration Act 1965;

"occupier" (and in subsection (8) "the other occupier") means—
(a) in England and Wales, the person entitled to possession of the land by virtue of an estate or interest held by him; and
(b) in Scotland, the person lawfully entitled to natural possession of the land;

"property", in relation to damage to property on land, means—
(a) in England and Wales, property within the meaning of section 10(1) of the Criminal Damage Act 1971; and
(b) —

and "damage" includes the deposit of any substance capable of polluting the land;

"trespass" means, in the application of this section—
(a) in England and Wales, subject to the extensions effected by subsection (7) above, trespass as against the occupier of the land;

(b) —; and

"trespassing" and "trespasser" shall be construed accordingly;

"vehicle" includes—
(a) any vehicle, whether or not it is in a fit state for use on roads, and includes any chassis or body, with or without wheels, appearing to have formed part of such a vehicle, and any load carried by, and anything attached to, such a vehicle; and
(b) a caravans defined in section 29(1) of the Caravan Sites and Control of Development Act 1960;
and a person may be regarded for the purposes of this section as having a purpose of residing in a place notwithstanding that he has a home elsewhere.

Supplementary powers of seizure

62.—(1) If a direction has been given under section 61 and a constable reasonably suspects that any person to whom the direction applies has, without reasonable excuse—

(a) failed to remove any vehicle on the land which appears to the constable to belong to him or to be in his possession or under his control; or
(b) entered the land as a trespasser with a vehicle within the period of three months beginning with the day on which the direction was given,

the constable may seize and remove that vehicle.
(2) In this section, "trespass" and "vehicle" have the same meaning as in section 61.

Retention and charges for seized property

Retention and charges for seized property

67.—(1) Any vehicles which have been seized and removed by a constable under section 62(1) or 64(4) may be retained in accordance with regulations made by the Secretary of State under subsection (3) below.
(2) Any sound equipment which has been seized and removed by a constable under section 64(4) may be retained until the conclusion of proceedings against the person from whom it was seized for an offence under section 63.

(3) The Secretary of State may make regulations—

(a) regulating the retention and safe keeping and the disposal and the destruction in prescribed circumstances of vehicles; and

(b) prescribing charges in respect of the removal, retention, disposal and destruction of vehicles.

(4) Any authority shall be entitled to recover from a person from whom a vehicle has been seized such charges as may be prescribed in respect of the removal, retention, disposal and destruction of the vehicle by the same authority.

(5) Regulations under subsection (3) above may make different provisions for different classes of vehicles or for different circumstances.

(6) Any charges under subsection (4) above shall be recoverable as a simple contract debt.

(7) Any authority having custody of vehicles under regulations under subsection (3) above shall be entitled to retain custody until any charges under subsection (4) are paid.

(8) The power to make regulations under subsection (3) above shall be exercisable by statutory instrument which shall be subject to annulment in pursuance of a resolution of either House of Parliament.

(9) In this section—

"conclusion of proceedings" against a person means—
(a) his being sentenced or otherwise dealt with for the offence or for his acquittal;
(b) the discontinuance of the proceedings; or
(c) the decision not to prosecute him,
whichever is the earlier;
"sound equipment" has the same meaning as in section 64; and
"vehicle" has the same meaning as in section 61.

Disruptive trespassers

Offence of aggravated trespass

68.—(1) A person commits the offence of aggravated trespass if he trespasses on land in the open air and, in relation to any lawful activity which persons are engaging in or are about to engage in on that or adjoining land in the open air, does there anything which is intended by him to have the effect—

(a) of intimidating those persons or any of them so as to deter them or any of them from engaging in that activity,

(b) of obstructing that activity, or

(c) of disrupting that activity.

(2) Activity on any occasion on the part of a person or persons on land is "lawful" for the purposes of this section if he or they may engage in the activity on the land on that occasion without committing an offence or trespassing on the land.

(3) A person guilty of an offence under this section is liable on summary conviction to imprisonment for a term not exceeding three months or a fine not exceeding level 4 on the standard scale, or both.

(4) A constable in uniform who reasonably suspects that a person is committing an offence under this section may arrest him without a warrant.

(5) In this section "land" does not include—

(a) the highways and roads excluded from the application of section 61 by paragraph (b) of the definition of "land" in subsection (9) of that section; or

(b) a road within the meaning of the Roads (Northern Ireland) Order 1993.

Powers to remove persons committing or participating in aggravated trespass

69.—(1) If the senior police officer present at the scene reasonably believes—

(a) that a person is committing, had committed or intends to commit the offence of aggravated trespass on land in the open air; or

(b) that two or more persons are trespassing on land in the open air and are present there with the common purpose of intimidating persons so as to deter them from engaging in a lawful activity or of obstructing or disrupting a lawful activity,

he may direct that person or (as the case may be) those persons (or any of them) to leave the land.

(2) A direction under subsection (1) above, if not communicated to the persons referred to in subsection (1) by the police officer giving the direction, may be communicated to them by any constable at the scene.

(3) If a person knowing that a direction under subsection (1) above has been given which applies to him—

(a) fails to leave the land as soon as practicable, or
(b) having left again enters the land as a trespasser within the period of three months beginning with the day on which the direction was given,

he commits an offence and is liable on summary conviction to imprisonment for a term not exceeding three months or a fine not exceeding level 4 on the standard scale, or both.

(4) In proceedings for an offence under subsection (3) it is a defence for the accused to show—

(a) that he was not trespassing on the land, or
(b) that he had a reasonable excuse for failing to leave the land as soon as practicable or, as the case may be, for again entering the land as a trespasser.

(5) A constable in uniform who reasonably suspects that a person is committing an offence under this section may arrest him without a warrant.

(6) In this section "lawful activity" and "land" have the same meanings as in section 68.

Interim possession orders: false or misleading statements

75.—(1) A person commits an offence if, for the purpose of obtaining an interim possession order, he—

(a) makes a statement which he knows to be false or misleading in a material particular; or
(b) recklessly makes a statement which is false or misleading in a material particular.

(2) A person commits an offence if, for the purpose of resisting the making of an interim possession order, he—

(a) makes a statement which he knows to be false or misleading in a material particular; or
(b) recklessly makes a statement which he knows to be false or misleading in a material particular.

(3) A person guilty of an offence under this section shall be liable—

(a) on conviction on indictment, to imprisonment for a term not exceeding two years or a fine or both;

(b) on summary conviction, to imprisonment for a term not exceeding six months or a fine not exceeding the statutory maximum or both.

(4) In this section—

"interim possession order" means an interim possession order (so entitled) made under rules of court for the bringing of summary proceedings for possession of premises which are occupied by trespassers;

"premises" has the same meaning as in Part II of the Criminal Law Act 1977 (offences relating to entering and remaining on property); and

"statement", in relation to an interim possession order, means any statement, in writing or oral and whether as to fact or belief, made in or for the purposes of the proceedings.

Interim possession orders: trespassing during currency of order

76.—(1) This section applies where an interim possession order has been made in respect of any premises and served in accordance with rules of court; and references to "the order" and "the premises" shall be construed accordingly.

(2) Subject to subsection (3), a person who is present on the premises as a trespasser at any time during the currency of the order commits an offence.

(3) No offence under subsection (2) is committed by a person if—

(a) he leaves the premises within 24 hours of the time of service of the order and does not return; or

(b) a copy of the order was not fixed to the premises in accordance with rules of court.

(4) A person who was in occupation of the premises at the time of service of the order but leaves them commits an offence if he re-enters the premises as a trespasser or attempts to do so after the expiry of the order but within the period of one year beginning with the day on which it was served.

(5) A person guilty of an offence under this section shall be liable on summary conviction to imprisonment for a term not exceeding six months or a fine not exceeding level 5 on the standard scale, or both.

(6) A person who is in occupation of the premises at the time of service of the order shall be treated for the purposes of this section as being present as a trespasser.

(7) A constable in uniform may arrest without a warrant anyone who is, or whom he reasonably suspects to be, guilty of an offence under this section.

(8) In this section—

"interim possession order" has the same meaning as in section 75 above and "rules of court" is to be construed accordingly; and

"premises" has the same meaning as in that section, that is to say, the same meaning as in Part II of the Criminal Law Act 1977 (offences relating to entering and remaining on property).

Powers of local authority to direct unauthorised campers to leave land

Power of local authority to direct unauthorised campers to leave land

77.—(1) If it appears to a local authority that persons are for the time being residing in a vehicle or vehicles within that authority's area—

(a) on any land forming part of a highway
(b) on any other unoccupied land; or
(c) on any occupied land without the consent of the occupier,

the authority may give a direction that those persons and any others with them are to leave the land and remove the vehicle or vehicles and any other property they have with them on the land.

(2) Notice of a direction under subsection (1) must be served on the persons to whom the direction applies, but it shall be sufficient for this purpose for the direction to specify the land and (except where the direction applies to only one person) to be addressed to all occupants of the vehicles on the land, without naming them.

(3) If a person knowing that a direction under subsection (1) above has been given which applies to him—

(a) fails, as soon as practicable, to leave the land or remove from the land any vehicle or other property which is the subject of the direction, or
(b) having removed any such vehicle or property again enters the land with a vehicle within the period of three months beginning with the day on which the direction was given,

he commits an offence and is liable on summary conviction to a fine not exceeding level 3 on the standard scale.

(4) A direction under subsection (1) operates to require persons who re-enter the land within the said period with vehicles or other property to leave and remove the vehicles or other property as it operates in relation to the persons and vehicles or other property on the land when the direction was given.

(5) In proceedings for an offence under this section it is a defence for the accused to show that his failure to leave or to remove the vehicle or other property as soon as practicable or his re-entry with a vehicle was due to illness, mechanical breakdown or other immediate emergency.

(6) In this section—

"land" means land in the open air;
"local authority" means—
  (a) in Greater London, a London borough or the Common Council of the City of London;
  (b) in England outside Greater London, a county council, a district council or the Council of the Isles of Scilly;
  (c) in Wales, a county council or a county borough council;

"occupier" means the person entitled to possession of the land by virtue of an estate or interest held by him;
"vehicle" includes—
  (a) any vehicle, whether or not it is in a fit state for use on the roads, and includes any body, with or without wheels, appearing to have formed part of such a vehicle, and any load carried by, and anything attached to, such a vehicle; and
  (b) a caravan as defined in section 29(1) of the Caravan Sites and Control of Development Act 1960;

and a person may be regarded for the purposes of this section as residing on any land notwithstanding that he has a home elsewhere.

(7) Until 1st April 1996, in this section "local authority" means, in Wales, a county council or a district council.

Orders for removal of persons and their vehicles unlawfully on land

78.—(1) A magistrates' court may, on a complaint made by a local authority, if satisfied that persons and vehicles in which they are residing are present on land within that authority's area in contravention of a direction given under section 77, make an order requiring the removal of any vehicle or other property which is so present on the land and any person residing in it.

(2) An order under this section may authorise the local authority to take such steps as are reasonably necessary to ensure that the order is complied with and, in particular, may authorise the authority, by its officers and servants—

(a) to enter upon the land specified in that order; and
(b) to take, in relation to any vehicle or property to be removed in pursuance of the order, such steps for securing entry and rendering it suitable for removal as may be so specified.

(3) The local authority shall not enter upon any occupied land unless they have given to the owner and occupier at least 24 hours notice of their intention to do so, or unless after reasonable inquiries they are unable to ascertain their names and addresses.

(4) A person who wilfully obstructs any person in the exercise of any power conferred on him by an order under this section commits an offence and is liable on summary conviction to a fine not exceeding level 3 on the standard scale.

(5) Where a complaint is made under this section, a summons issued by the court requiring the person or persons to whom it is directed to appear before the court to answer to the complaint may be directed—

(a) to the occupant of a particular vehicle on the land in question; or
(b) to all occupants of vehicles on the land in question, without naming him or them.

(6) Section 55(2) of the Magistrates' Courts Act 1980 (warrant for arrest of defendant failing to appear) does not apply to proceedings on a complaint made under this section.

(7) Section 77(6) of this Act applies also for the interpretation of this section.

Provisions as to directions under s.77 and orders under s.78

79.—(1) The following provisions apply in relation to the service of notice of a direction under section 77 and of a summons under section 78, referred to in those provisions as a "relevant document".

(2) Where it is impracticable to serve a relevant document on a person named in it, the document shall be treated as duly served on him if a copy of it is fixed in a prominent place to the vehicle

concerned; and where a relevant document is directed to the unnamed occupants of vehicles, it shall be treated as duly served on those occupants if a copy of it is fixed in a prominent place to every vehicle on the land in question at the time when service is thus effected.

(3) A local authority shall take such steps as may be reasonably practicable to secure that a copy of any relevant document is displayed on the land in question (otherwise than by being fixed to a vehicle) in a manner designed to ensure that it is likely to be seen by any person camping on the land.

(4) Notice of any relevant document shall be given by the local authority to the owner of the land in question and to any occupier of that land unless, after reasonable inquiries, the authority is unable to ascertain the name and address of the owner or occupier; and the owner of any such land and any occupier of such land shall be entitled to appear and to be heard in the proceedings.

(5) Section 77(6) applies also for the interpretation of this section.

APPENDIX FOUR

Children Act 1989

Provision of accommodation for children: general

20.—(1) Every local authority shall provide accommodation for any child in need within their area who appears to them to require accommodation as a result of—

(a) there being no person who has parental responsibility for him;
(b) his being lost or having been abandoned; or
(c) the person who has been caring for him being prevented (whether or not permanently, and for whatever reason) from providing him with suitable accommodation or care.

(2) Where a local authority provide accommodation under subsection (1) for a child who is ordinarily resident in the area of another local authority, that other local authority may take over the provision of accommodation for the child within—

(a) three months of being notified in writing that the child is being provided with accommodation; or
(b) such other longer period as may be prescribed.

(3) Every local authority shall provide accommodation for any child in need within their area who has reached the age of sixteen and whose welfare the authority consider is likely to be seriously prejudiced if they do not provide him with accommodation.

(4) A local authority may provide accommodation for any child in need within their area (even though a person who has parental

responsibility for him is able to provide him with accommodation) if they consider that to do so would safeguard or promote the child's welfare.

(5) A local authority may provide accommodation for any person who has reached the age of sixteen but is under twenty-one in any community home which takes children who have reached the age of sixteen if they consider that to do so would safeguard or promote his welfare.

(6) Before providing accommodation under this section, a local authority shall, so far as is reasonably practicable and consistent with the child's welfare—

(a) ascertain the child's wishes regarding the provision of accommodation; and
(b) give due consideration (having regard to his age and understanding) to such wishes of the child as they have been able to ascertain.

(7) A local authority may not provide accommodation under this section for any child if any person who—

(a) has parental responsibility for him; and
(b) is willing and able to-
    (i) provide accommodation for him; or
    (ii) arrange for accommodation to be provided for him,
objects.

(8) Any person who has parental responsibility for a child may at any time remove the child from accommodation provided by or on behalf of the local authority under this section.

(9) Subsections (7) and (8) do not apply while any person—

(a) in whose favour a residence order is in force with respect to the child; or
(b) who has care of the child by virtue of an order made in the exercise of the High Court's inherent jurisdiction with respect to children,

agrees to the child being looked after in accommodation provided by or on behalf of the local authority.

(10) Where there is more than one such person as is mentioned in subsection (9), all of them must agree.

(11) Subsections (7) and (8) do not apply where a child who has reached the age of sixteen agrees to being provided with accommodation under this section.

Provision of accommodation for children in police protection or detention or on remand, etc.

21.—(1) Every local authority shall make provision for the reception and accommodation of children who are removed or kept away from home under Part V.

(2) Every local authority shall receive, and provide accommodation for, children—

(a) in police protection whom they are requested to receive under section 46(3)(f);

(b) whom they are requested to receive under section 38(6) of the Police and Criminal Evidence Act 1984;

(c) who are—

  (i) on remand under section 16(3A) or 23(1) of the Children and Young Persons Act 1969; or

  (ii) the subject of a supervision order imposing a residence requirement under section 12AA of that Act,

and with respect to whom they are the designated authority.

(3) Where a child has been-

(a) removed under Part V; or

(b) detained under section 38 of the Police and Criminal Evidence Act 1984,

and he is not being provided with accommodation by a local authority or in a hospital vested in the Secretary of State or otherwise made available pursuant to arrangements made by a District Health Authority, and any reasonable expenses of accommodating him shall be recoverable from the local authority in whose area he is ordinarily resident.

General duty of local authority in relation to children looked after by them

22.—(1) In this Act, any reference to a child who is looked after by a local authority is a reference to a child who is—

(a) in their care; or

(b) provided with accommodation by the authority in the exercise of any functions (in particular those under this Act) which stand referred to their social services committee under the Local Authority Social Services Act 1970.

(2) In subsection (1) "accommodation" means accommodation which is provided for a continuous period of more than 24 hours.

(3) It shall be the duty of a local authority looking after any child—

(a) to safeguard and promote his welfare; and
(b) to make such use of services available for children cared for by their own parents as appears to the authority reasonable in his case.

(4) Before making any decision with respect to a child whom they are looking after, or proposing to look after, a local authority shall, so far as reasonably practicable, ascertain the wishes and feelings of—

(a) the child;
(b) his parents;
(c) any person who is not a parent of his but who has parental responsibility for him; or
(d) any other person whose wishes and feelings the authority consider to be relevant,

regarding the matter to be decided.

(5) In making any such decision a local authority shall give due consideration—

(a) having regard to his age and understanding, to such wishes and feelings of the child as they have been able to ascertain;
(b) to such wishes and feelings of any person mentioned in subsection (4)(b) to (d) as they have been able to ascertain; and
(c) to the child's religious persuasion, racial origin and cultural and linguistic background.

(6) If it appears to a local authority that it is necessary, for the purpose of protecting members of the public from serious injury, to exercise their powers with respect to a child whom they are looking after in a manner which may not be consistent with their duties under this section, they may do so.

(7) If the Secretary of State considers it necessary, for the purpose of protecting members of the public from serious injury, to give directions to a local authority with respect to the exercise of their powers with respect to a child whom they are looking after, he may give such directions to the authority.

(8) Where any such directions are given to an authority they shall comply with them even though doing so is inconsistent with their duties under this section.

APPENDIX FIVE

Family Law Act 1996

The general principles underlying Parts II and III

1.—The court and any person, in exercising functions under or in consequence of Parts II and III, shall have regard to the following general principles —

(a) that the institution of marriage is to be supported;
(b) that the parties to a marriage which may have broken down are to be encouraged to take all practicable steps, whether by marriage counselling or otherwise, to save the marriage;
(c) that a marriage which has irretrievably broken down and is being brought to an end should be brought to an end —
   (i) with minimum distress to the parties and to the children affected;
   (ii) with questions dealt with in a manner designed to promote as good a continuing relationship between the parties and any children affected as is possible in the circumstances; and
   (iii) without costs being unreasonably incurred in connection with the procedures to be followed in bringing the marriage to an end; and
(d) that any risk to one of the parties to a marriage, and to any children, of violence from the other party should, so far as reasonably practicable, be removed or diminished.

APPENDIX SIX

Department of the Environment
Department of Health

CODE OF GUIDANCE ON PARTS VI AND VII OF THE HOUSING ACT 1996

ALLOCATION OF LOCAL AUTHORITY HOUSING HOMELESSNESS

(October 1996)

Contents

10. Dealing with Homelessness Applications under Part VII of the 1996 Act

11. Carrying out Enquiries

12. Eligible for Assistance

To follow

13. Homeless or Threatened with Homelessness

14. Priority Need

1. Introduction

Why a Code of Guidance?

1.1. The Secretary of State for the Environment and the Secretary of State for Health are issuing this Code of Guidance jointly to local housing authorities in England under s. 169 and s. 182 of the Housing Act 1996 (the 1996 Act). In exercising their functions under Parts VI and VII of the 1996 Act, such authorities must have regard to this guidance. The Code is not, however, a substitute for the legislation; it gives guidance on how local authorities should discharge their functions and apply the various statutory criteria in practice.

1.2. The Secretary of State for Wales is issuing a separate Code of Guidance to local housing authorities in Wales under the same provisions of the 1996 Act.

Who is the Code for?

1.3. The guidance is specifically for members and staff of local housing authorities in England. In exercising their functions relating to homelessness and the prevention of homelessness, social services authorities are also required under s. 182(1) of the 1996 Act to have regard to the guidance.

1.4. The guidance is also of direct relevance to registered social landlords, including those who have or are to acquire stock transferred to them by local authorities, who have a duty in the 1996 Act to co-operate to such extent as is reasonable with local housing authorities. Many of the provisions in Parts VI and VII require joint planning and operational co-operation between local housing authorities and social services departments, health authorities, other referral agencies, voluntary sector organisations and the diverse range of bodies working in the rented sectors.

1.5. The Secretary of State for the Environment is aware that a number of local authorities in England have already delegated the operation of their allocations and homelessness functions either voluntarily or under compulsory competitive tendering. Where such contracts have already been awarded to external contractors (including delegations to Tenant Management Organisations), the contractor must be made aware of the provisions of Parts VI and VII and advised how the legislation and this guidance may apply to them. Functions of an operational or administrative nature may also have been delegated or contracted out to transfer landlords or registered social landlords; they, too, must be made aware of these provisions and of the guidance.

Structure of the Code

1.6. The Code follows the sequence of the sections in Parts VI and VII, explaining the policy context and the general legislative framework. It also contains (at **Annex B**) a list of useful references which may assist in developing this guidance into practice.

PART VI OF THE HOUSING ACT 1996

2. The New Framework for Allocations

The policy context: Part VI of the Housing Act 1996

2.1. The new framework for the allocation of local authority housing is a key policy change in that, to date, there has not been a *duty* to hold a housing register. Local authorities have had considerable discretion over the allocation of their housing stock. **Section 22 of the Housing Act 1985** (the 1985 Act) merely required that certain categories of people be given "reasonable preference" in the allocation process, leaving it to each authority to devise their own system for ensuring that this was done.

The new legislative framework

2.2. Part VI of the 1996 Act repeals **s. 22 of the 1985 Act** and introduces a new legislative regime which, for the first time, places a duty on local housing authorities to set up and maintain a housing register and to make most allocations from their housing register to "qualifying persons" through an allocations scheme. The scheme must operate within parameters laid down in the 1996 Act. All allocations made after commencement of Part VI must be made in accordance with the 1996 Act.

2.3. A local authority secure tenancy or an assured periodic tenancy with a registered social landlord (RSL) is, in many cases, a guarantee of social housing for life. It is therefore important that authorities should take a long term view of applicants' circumstances, to ensure that such housing, and nominations to registered social landlords, go to those households with the greatest underlying needs.

2.4. Part VI of the 1996 Act ensures that all applicants will have their long term needs assessed on a consistent basis. Apart from a few exceptional cases, the local authority's housing register will be the sole route by which people may be allocated a local authority secure tenancy, or be nominated by the authority to an assured tenancy with a RSL.

When does Part VI (the allocation scheme) apply?

2.5. **Section 159** of the 1996 Act (allocation of housing accommodation) sets the scene. Under that section local housing authorities must comply with the provisions of the 1996 Act in "allocating housing accommodation". This is defined in **s. 159(2)** as when a local housing authority:

a) select someone to be a secure or introductory tenant of housing held by the authority;
b) nominate someone to be a secure or introductory tenant of housing held by another person; or
c) nominate someone to be an assured tenant of housing held by a registered social landlord.

2.6. These terms are defined in **s. 159(3)** and **s. 159(4)** is including:

— exercising any power to notify an existing tenant or licensee that his/her tenancy or licence is to be a secure tenancy (a) above only); and
— nominating a person in pursuance of any arrangements (whether legally enforceable or not) to require that housing is made available to a person (or one of a number of people) nominated by the authority (b) and c) above only).

What discretion do local authorities have?

2.7. **Section 159(7)** allows a local housing authority to allocate housing as they consider appropriate, subject to the provisions of Part VI of the 1996 Act.

When does Part VI (the allocation scheme) not apply?

2.8. Under **s. 159(5)** the provisions of Part VI do not apply to someone who is already:

— a secure or introductory tenant;
— an assured tenant (other than an assured shorthold tenant) of housing which is owned by a RSL; or
— an assured tenant of housing which is allocated by a local housing authority.

Thus the allocation scheme does not apply to transfers and mutual exchanges within the RSL's stock or between local authorities and RSLs, for example through the Housing Organisations Mobility and Exchange Services (HOMES) schemes.

2.9 If someone is already a secure, introductory or assured tenant, and the authority want to allocate housing jointly to that person and another person they may do so under **s. 159(6)** without having to go through the housing register and the allocations process, provided that the other person is not excluded from being a qualifying person by **s. 161(2)** or by regulations made under **s. 161(3)**. **Annex C, which replaces DoE Circular 7/96 'Local Authority Joint Tenancies',** gives advice on the use of joint tenancies.

Specific cases where Part VI does not apply

2.10. **Section 160** of the 1996 Act (cases where provisions about allocation do not apply) exempts from the provisions of Part VI cases where a secure tenancy:

a) vests under **s. 89 of the 1985 Act** (succession to periodic secure tenancy on death of tenant);

b) remains a secure tenancy by virtue of **s. 90 of the 1985 Act** (devolution of term certain of secure tenancy on death or tenant);

c) is assigned under **s. 92 of the 1985 Act** (assignment of secure tenancy by way of exchange);

d) is assigned to someone who would be qualified to succeed to the tenancy if the secure tenant died immediately before the assignment; or

e) vests or is otherwise disposed of in pursuance of an order made under:

— **s. 24 of the Matrimonial Causes Act 1973** (property adjustment orders in connection with matrimonial proceedings);

— **s. 17(1) of the Matrimonial and Family Proceedings Act 1984** (property adjustment orders after overseas divorce); or

— **paragraph 1 of Schedule 1 to the Children Act 1989** (orders for financial relief against parents).

2.11. The provisions of Part VI also do not apply where an introductory tenancy:

a) becomes a secure tenancy on ceasing to be an introductory tenancy;

b) vests under **s. 133(2)** of the 1996 Act (succession to an introductory tenancy on death of tenant); or

c) is assigned to someone who would be qualified to succeed the introductory tenancy if the introductory tenant died immediately before the assignment; or

d) meets the criteria in paragraph 2.10(e) above.

Further exemptions prescribed in regulations

2.12. Under **s. 160(4)** the Secretary of State may prescribe other exemptions to the provisions of Part VI in regulations. The Secretary of State has made Regulations which provide that Part VI does not apply in the following cases:

— to the allocation of housing accommodation by a local housing authority to a person who is already:

a) a secure tenant under **Part II of the Housing (Northern Ireland) Order 1983** (secure tenants), where the estate of the landlord belongs to the Northern Ireland Housing Executive;
b) a secure tenant under **Part III of the Housing (Scotland) Act 1987** (rights of public order tenants);
c) an assured tenant of accommodation under **Part II of the Housing (Scotland) Act 1988** (otherwise than under a short assured tenancy within the meaning given by **s. 32** of that Act), where the interest in the landlord belongs to:
   i) a housing association registered by Scottish Homes under **s. 3 of the Housing Associations Act 1985** (the register); or
   ii) a person who acquired the accommodation (otherwise than under **Part III of the Housing (Scotland) Act 1987**) from a district council or islands council constituted under **s. 2 of the Local Government (Scotland) Act 1973** (constitution of councils of regions, islands areas and districts), a council constituted under **s. 2 of the Local Government etc. (Scotland) Act 1994** (constitution of councils), or Scottish Homes;

— where a local housing authority secure the provision of suitable alternative accommodation under **s. 39 of the Land Compensation Act 1973** (duty to rehouse residential occupiers); or
— in relation to the grant of a secure tenancy under **s. 554** or **s. 555 of the 1985 Act** (grant of a tenancy to a former owner-occupier or statutory tenant of defective dwelling-house).

2.13. Local Housing authorities should ensure that their allocations schemes reflect the variety of housing needs and circumstances of vulnerable individuals, including those who require support or care services. The legislation governing allocations is designed to enable applications from such individuals to be considered through an integrated allocation scheme, and the priority categories encompass the key issues which arise in assessing their need for social housing. There is ample scope to operate discretionary elements within the scheme to give the flexibility required to respond to individuals' particular needs. It is envisaged that, in general, authorities should be able to consider the needs of individuals referred to the housing authority by other agencies, for example, social services departments, through the allocation scheme. As a complementary measure, the Department of the Environment is currently considering ways in which authorities might make a certain number of their allocations to such individuals outside the allocation scheme: *Regulations and further guidance on this issue will follow.*

Joint working with social services departments and other agencies

2.14. Under the **National Health Service and Community Care Act 1990** (the 1990 Act), social services departments are required to carry out an assessment for any individual who may have a need for community care services. It is the intention of that legislation that the planning and assessment processes should identify the full range of needs, including housing needs. **Section 47 of the 1990 Act** requires social service authorities to notify the housing authority if there appears to be a housing need when the assessment is carried out. The housing need may be for alternative accommodation, or for renovation or adaption of the accommodation in which the individual is currently living.

2.15. A joint approach should be agreed between local housing and social services and health authorities, to include:

— mechanisms and triggers for referral between housing, health and social services authorities in relation to housing and community care issues, and alerting relevant agencies to any difficulties;
— co-ordination between housing and social services assessments;
— communication and follow-up once a care plan has been implemented, for example between community psychiatric nurses, social workers or care managers, and housing officers;
— the assessment of individuals who require emergency accommodation; and
— identification of those clients with inter-dependent health, housing and social services needs.

2.16. Local authority housing, social services and health authorities should liaise over the best solution for each client, recognising, for example, that the provision of more appropriate housing may assist in the delivery of social services; and/or that increased support or care services may allow a person to remain in his/her current home rather than moving to new accommodation. Where clients' needs warrant varying levels of priority for different services, procedures should be in place for reaching agreement on how clients' needs should be addressed.

2.17. The Government is particularly keen to ensure the delivery of a full spectrum of care for people suffering from severe mental illness. Research has shown that provision of suitable, stable housing is essential if community care is to be a reality for this vulnerable group of clients. A key element in the spectrum of care is the development of a care plan under the Government's care programme approach (CPA). The initial assessment under the CPA must include an assessment of an individual's housing needs. It is essential that housing authorities liaise closely with social services authorities so that any housing allocation is appropriate to the needs of the individual, and meshes in with the social and health care support that may be a part of the patient's care programme.

2.18. Timing can be critical when people have to move from long stay institutions, or from temporary accommodation. Again, procedures should be agreed between the local housing authority and the referring agencies, incorporating criteria for and the timing of referrals, and the action to be taken on them.

2.19. Under **s. 20 of the Children Act 1989**, a local social services authority must provide accommodation for a child in need in their area who requires it as a result of:

— there being no person who has parental responsibility for him/her;
— his/her being lost or having been abandoned; or
— the person who has been caring for him/her being prevented (whether or not permanently, and for whatever reason) from providing him/her with suitable accommodation.

In the Government's view, social services authorities should not accommodate children in public care as a result of his/her family's homelessness. This would separate children from their parents, and cut across the Government's objective, that family breakdown should be avoided wherever possible.

2.20. If the child who is accommodated under this duty is ordinarily resident in the area of another local authority, the latter authority may take over the provision of accommodation for the child within three months of being notified in writing that the child is being accommodated. Local authorities are also required to provide accommodation for a child in need who has reached the age of 16 if his/her welfare is otherwise likely to be seriously prejudiced. **Section 20(4)** of the 1989 Act empowers a local authority to provide accommodation for any child in their area if it would safeguard or promote his/her welfare.

2.21. Under **s. 27 of the Children Act 1989**, a local social services authority can ask a local housing authority to help in delivering services for children in need, and the housing authority must comply with such a request to the extent that it is compatible with their own statutory or other duties and other obligations, and does not unduly prejudice the discharge of any of their own functions.

3. The Housing Register

The new housing register

3.1. **Section 162 of the 1996 Act** requires every local housing authority to establish and maintain a register of qualifying persons, to be called their "housing register". **Subsection (2)** allows authorities to keep the register in any appropriate form. Local authorities will wish to consider how to make the register sensitive to applicants' preferences for specific areas or estates and how to match households' needs with appropriately sized accommodation. Some applicants may be seeking specialised housing, provided either by the authority or by a RSL. Local housing authorities may set up sub-registers and sub-lists, for example for specialised accommodation such as sheltered housing or different numbers of bedrooms as well as for geographical areas and neighbourhoods within their district.

3.2. **Section 162(3)** allows local authorities to keep their housing register as part of a larger register which is maintained for other housing purposes or is maintained in common by the authority and one or more other landlords, provided that the authority's housing register kept under **s. 162** can be distinguished separately.

3.3. The reference to "other housing purposes" allows authorities to operate combined allocations and transfer lists, and to include on their register other sources of accommodation for households who are seeking accommodation but who are outside the provisions of Part VI. It also allows comprehensive housing management information systems to continue and to develop, and permits authorities to keep their housing register on the same database, or as part of the same computer or administrative system as, for example, their tenant, property and rent accounts systems. Local authorities may therefore wish to consider whether their housing register should be kept as part of a register maintained for other housing purposes directly related to the allocation of housing (such as transfers, exchanges and warden assisted accommodation) and/or whether it should form part of a wider and more comprehensive housing database.

What about common housing registers?

3.4. The reference in **s. 162(3)** to maintaining the register with other landlords enables the development of common housing registers between local housing authorities, RSLs and other landlords. If a local authority already operate a common housing register, or are in the process of introducing one, they must ensure that the entries for "qualifying persons" on the housing register are identified separately (for example, by an asterisk) from people on the common housing register who are not "qualifying persons" for local authority accommodation under Part VI. Local authorities may wish to refer to the good practice guide on common housing registers, published jointly by the Chartered Institute of Housing and the Housing Corporation, and to the Housing Corporation's evaluation and analysis of current practice.

What information must be on the housing register?

3.5. **Section 162(4)** requires an authority's register to contain whatever information is prescribed by the Secretary of State in regulations about the people appearing on it and any other relevant matters. Regulations provide that the register shall contain, in relation to each qualifying person:

a) the name of the qualifying person;
b) the number of other persons who normally reside with him/her as a member of his/her family, or who might reasonably be expected to reside with him/her;
c) the number of persons falling within a) and b) above who are:
    i) under the age of 10 years;
    ii) expecting a child;
    iii) over the age of 60 years;
d) the address of the qualifying person;
e) the date on which the qualifying person was put on the register; and
f) the most recent date on which an entry on the register was amended.

3.6. Subject to any regulations under **s. 162(4)** a local authority may decide under **s. 162(5)**, what information is to be contained on their housing register. This will generally be the information that the authority require to determine the priority to be given to that applicant in accordance with their allocation scheme.

3.7. It is good practice that all applications for housing are made on a standard form, and not by letter or verbal request, other than requests for referrals from recognised agencies. The application form(s) should be accompanied by guidance notes which are easy to understand and in plain language. Translations of all forms and notes should be available for applicants whose first language is not English. Audio tapes of the notes or braille copies should be available for people who have a visual impairment. Help should be available from trained staff to complete application forms.

What is the position of local authorities which have completed a large scale voluntary transfer or are setting up a local housing company?

3.8. Local housing authorities which have transferred all or part of their housing stock, or are in the process of transferring their stock, are still required, under Part VI, to set up and maintain a housing register and allocations scheme. *On October 21, 1996, the Department of the Environment issued for consultation a draft Order which would enable local authorities to contract out certain of their allocations and homelessness functions.*

Maintaining and monitoring the housing register

3.9. Housing registers, like waiting lists, will not be static and will change on a day-to-day basis. applicants may find accommodation (either through the local authority or a RSL or by an alternative means), or they may no longer require housing, or their circumstances and needs may have changed, or they may simply have moved on. Consequently, the register should be reviewed regularly to keep it up to date and so help to maximise the effectiveness of the allocations system.

3.10. Local housing authorities must comply with statutory requirements applying to equal opportunities, and relevant codes of practice including the Commission for Racial Equality's 'Code of Practice in Rented Housing' (see paragraphs 6.1.–6.4.). Authorities should also consider having in place a formal equal opportunities policy relating to all aspects of the allocation process with the aim of ensuring equality of treatment for all applicants.

4. Operating the Housing Register

The requirement to allocate only to qualifying persons

4.1. **Section 161** of the 1996 Act (allocation only to qualifying persons) requires a local housing authority to allocate housing only to people who are defined as "qualifying persons". The Secretary of State may prescribe classes of persons who are, or are not, qualifying persons for these purposes.

4.2. **Section 161(2)** provides that people who are subject to immigration control within the meaning of the **Asylum and Immigration Act 1996** do not qualify to be allocated local authority housing in England and Wales, unless regulations made by the Secretary of State prescribe otherwise.

4.3. Regulations under s. 161(3) may prescribe classes of persons who are, or are not, qualifying persons either in respect of local housing authorities generally or for a particular local housing authority.

4.4. Subject to these statutory requirements, a local housing authority may decide the classes of people who are, or are not, qualifying persons (see paragraphs 4.6. *et seq.* below).

4.5. In the case of the allocation of housing to two or more persons jointly, at least one of the persons must be a qualifying person, and the other person(s) cannot be a non-qualifying person by virtue of **s.161(2)** or regulations made under **s. 161(3)**.

Who must be allowed to appear on the housing register?

4.6. The following are the classes of person prescribed in regulations as qualifying persons in relation to a local housing authority for the purposes of **s. 161(3)**:

a) a person over the age of 18 years who is owed a duty by the authority under:
 i) **s. 193** (duty to persons with priority need who are not homeless intentionally); or
 ii) **s. 195(2)** (duties in case of threatened homelessness) where, in pursuance of the duty under that subsection, the authority secure that accommodation other than that occupied by that person when s/he made the application for assistance under Part VII is available for his/her occupation;

b)
 i) subject to (ii) below, a person over the age of 18 years who is owed a duty by that authority under **s. 192(2)** or **197(2)** of the 1996 Act (duty to persons not in priority need who are not homeless intentionally and duty where other suitable accommodation available);
 ii) subject to (iii) below, she is also a qualifying person for a period of two years beginning on the day on which she ceases to be owed a duty by that authority under **s. 192(2)** or **197(2)** of the 1996 Act;
 iii) s/he shall cease to be a qualifying person if the authority notify him/her under **s. 184(3)** of the 1996 Act (enquiry into cases of homelessness or threatened homelessness) that s/he has become homeless intentionally.

Who is not allowed to appear on the housing register?

4.7. *Guidance to follow on the categories of persons from abroad who will not be eligible to appear on the register.*

What discretion do authorities have in defining "qualifying persons"?

4.8. Local housing authorities have discretion about who is a qualifying person, subject to **s. 161(2)** or any regulations made under **s. 161(3)**. Local authorities may wish to consider whether people who are owed a duty under **s. 193** and are placed in their area by another authority should be given the opportunity to register with the authority in whose area they have been placed, as they may establish a connection with that area.

4.9. There is a considerable range of practice among local authorities in the use of minimum age limits for acceptance on to a waiting list. In deciding whether, and if so where, to set an age limit, local authorities will want to bear in mind the needs of vulnerable young single people, such as some care leavers, who may need a long-term tenancy.

4.10. Local authorities are entitled to determine that certain groups of people are not qualifying persons provided that such groups do not conflict with classes prescribed by regulations under s. 161 and the primary legislation in s. 161(2). Such groups might include people with a history of anti-social behaviour, people who have attacked housing department staff, or tenants with a record of rent arrears. Authorities could impose other qualifications, such as those related to residency in the authority's district or ownership of a property, although they may wish to consider the implications of excluding all members of such groups, *e.g.* elderly owner-occupiers.

4.11. Whatever general rules local authorities use to define who can appear on the register, they are encouraged to make provision to enable others to appear on the register if their individual circumstances merit it. This is especially important for vulnerable people with a particular need for settled housing, but there could be exceptional cases across the whole range of potential applicants.

Applying to appear on the housing register

4.12. **Section 163** (operation of housing register) entitles a person to be on a housing register if s/he applies to be put on it and s/he appears to the authority to be a "qualifying person". Under **s. 163(3)**, if an authority put an applicant on their register they must notify him/her that they have done so.

4.13. The notification required under **s. 163(3)** may be delegated to an appropriate officer who may, in the name of the responsible chief officer, inform the applicant that s/he has been put on the register. In reviewing their forms, letters and the paperwork associated with the allocations process as part of introducing the new statutory arrangements, authorities should aim to adopt high customer care standards. Authorities will wish to ensure that applicants are made aware of any steps that they are expected to take (for example, to notify the authority of a change of address) and of the circumstances in which they may be removed from the register.

4.14. Under **s. 163(2)** a local housing authority may put someone on their housing register without any application, if s/he appears to be a qualifying person. If they do so, they must notify the person concerned to confirm their action. This might be appropriate in cases of referrals by social services authorities, citizens advice bureau, or other bodies and for some people owed a homeless duty under **s. 193**.

Amending entries on the housing register

4.15. **Section 163(4)** allows an authority to amend an entry on their housing register in such circumstances as they think fit. Where they do so, the authority must notify the person concerned of the amendment.

Removing people from the housing register

4.16. **Section 163(5)** allows a local authority to remove someone from their housing register in such circumstances as they see fit. Such circumstances may include, for example, cases where an applicant fails to reply to a request for further information, or to confirm that s/he still wishes to be considered for rehousing. The local authority must first comply with requirements in Regulations under **s. 163(7)** (see paragraph 4.17. below). They may also remove people who are rehoused by an authority or a RSL.

4.17. Local authorities are required, under **s. 163(6)**, to remove a person from their register if it appears to them that s/he has never been, or is no longer, a qualifying person, or if s/he asks them to do so, provided that s/he is not owed a duty under **s. 193** or **s. 195(2)** (main housing duties owed to persons who are homeless or threatened with homelessness).

4.18. Before exercising their discretion to remove someone from their register, under **s. 163(5)** a local authority must comply with any requirements prescribed in regulations made by the Secretary of State under s.163(7). The Regulations require an authority to give notice which shall:

a) require the person to provide the authority with such information as they reasonably require to enable them to decide whether to remove him/her from the register,

b) specify a period of not less than 28 days beginning with the day on which the person receives the notice, within which the information must be provided, and

c) inform the person that the authority may decide to remove him/her from their register if:

    i) they do not receive the information within the specified period, or

    ii) they consider that in the light of the information they receive within that period there are reasons why s/he should be removed.

The notice to a person under these regulations must be in writing, and if it is not received by him/her, it shall be treated as having been given if it is made available at the authority's office for a reasonable period for his/her collection.

The right to review

4.19. **Section 164** (notification of adverse decision and right to review) details the local housing authority's obligations if they decide:

— not to put someone on their housing register who has applied to be put on it; or
— to remove someone from their register other than at his/ her own request.

A local authority are required to notify the person of their decision and the reasons for it. Housing authorities should also inform social services of their decision in cases where, for example, the housing application is part of a care plan and social services are involved.

4.20. The notice must, as required by **s. 164(2)**, also inform the person of his/her right to request a review of the decision and of the time within which such a request must be made. **Section 164(3)** specifies that the request must be made within 21 days from the day on which the applicant is notified of the authority's decision and reasons for the decision. Local authorities have discretion to allow a longer period. The applicant must be informed in writing of the time allowed in which to request a review. Information on the right to review will need to be easy to understand and in plain language, with translations available for those whose first language is not English. Advice should also be available on audio tape and/or in braille for those people with a visual impairment.

4.21. Local authorities are required, under **s. 164(5)**, to review their decision once a request has been made to them. **Section 164(4)** makes it clear that an applicant has no right to request a review of a decision reached on a previous review.

The procedure for reviews

4.22. *REGULATIONS AND GUIDANCE TO FOLLOW.*

Information on the housing register

4.23. **Section 166** of the 1996 Act (information about housing register) describes an applicant's entitlement to see information on the register and the requirement for that information not to be disclosed to a member of the public. A person on the housing register of a local authority is entitled, under **s. 166(1)(a)** to see his/ her own entry on the register and to receive a copy of it free of charge.

4.24. **Section 166(2)** prohibits the disclosure to any other member of the public that someone is on the housing register and the disclosure of information about him/her held on the register.

4.25. **The Data Protection Act 1984** gives members of the public the right to see information about them which is held by a local authority in a computerised format. The person has to make the request in writing, and pay any fee required. The authority must, within 40 days of receiving the request, inform the person whether they hold any data about him/her, and, if so, provide a copy of the data. **The Access to Personal Files Act 1987** gives any applicant for housing from a local authority the right to see any personal information, held about him/herself in any format (on paper as well as computerised); this includes information held about his/her applications for housing whether as an existing or prospective tenant.

4.26. There may be occasions where disclosure is necessary, for example, to housing officers, doctors, social workers, or staff of RSLs — where the sharing of such information is sensible and can expedite the allocation process. **Section 166** should not preclude this, although authorities will wish to preserve confidentiality and supply information only on a "need to know" basis. There may also be other reasons for sharing information, for example where tenants have particular needs for support, without which they may be unable to maintain their tenancy. In such cases, housing managers should be made aware of those needs, to enable continued support to be given and to alert the appropriate support agencies of the tenants' needs.

Giving applicants information about when an offer is likely to be made

4.27. **Section 166(1)(b)** entitles a person on a housing register to be given general information to enable him/her to assess how much time is likely to elapse before accommodation appropriate to his/her needs becomes available to him/her. The intention is to provide applicants with sufficient information to enable them to form a view of when they are likely to be made an offer. Local authorities are not required to give their own estimate, although there is nothing to prevent them from doing so. What counts as sufficient information will depend on local housing conditions and the authority's own allocation scheme. At a minimum, the authority should give an applicant an indication of his/her position in the queue and of the likely supply of appropriate properties over the coming year.

4.28. An authority could also consider giving an indication of the demand for a particular area or estate, or for accommodation of a particular size, for example, 3-bedroomed flats below the fifth floor, or, in rural areas, 4-bedroomed houses in the centre of a village. The yardsticks could be the annual turnover of such properties, the number of points at which people are currently being made offers, or how long people currently being housed have waited. The applicant should be told of any likely changes in his/her position, or in the supply of appropriate housing.

5. The Allocation Scheme

The policy context

5.1. **Section 167** of the 1996 Act is intended to ensure that social housing meets long term needs but it should also be seen in a wider context. The allocation of housing is not just about meeting housing need. It embraces other objectives such as using stock effectively, reducing the number of empty and under-occupied properties, improving the turnround time for void properties, maximising rental income, and, where possible, creating balanced communities.

The allocation scheme

5.2. **Section 167** (allocation in accordance with allocation scheme) requires every local housing authority to have an allocation scheme which determines the authority's priorities and the procedure to be followed in allocating housing. "Procedure" is defined to include all aspects of the allocation process, including the people, or descriptions of people, by whom decision are taken.

The priority categories

5.3. **Section 167(2)** requires that, in framing their allocation scheme, an authority shall ensure that **reasonable preference** is given to:

   a) people occupying insanitary or overcrowded housing or otherwise living in unsatifactory housing conditions;
   b) people occupying housing accommodation which is temporary or occupied on insecure terms;
   c) families with dependent children;
   d) households consisting of or including someone who is expecting a child;
   e) households consisting of or including someone with a particular need for settled accommodation on medical or welfare grounds; and
   f) households whose social or economic circumstances are such that they have difficulty in securing settled accommodation.

It also requires that **additional preference** be given to households within the definition at e) consisting of someone with a particular need for settled accommodation on medical or welfare grounds, who cannot reasonably be expected to find settled accommodation for themselves in the foreseeable future.

What does "reasonable preference" means?

5.4. The concept of reasonable preference has been used to articulate how authorities should prioritise different indicators of need ever since the term appeared in **s. 51 of the Housing Act 1935**. Its use in the 1996 Act represents a continuation of the existing principles of housing allocation. It means that authorities should give due weight to the factors listed in **s. 167(2)**, but it does not restrict authorities to taking only such factors into account. Authorities could add other factors of their own, such as housing key workers coming into the area, whose presence is essential for economic growth. However, an authority should not allow their own secondary criteria to dominate their allocations sheme at the expense of factors in the statutory list.

5.5. Other considerations also apply to allocations. Authorities have a general duty to manage the resources at their disposal prudently. They may wish to take into account the characteristics of the people they select as tenants, both individually (as potentially good tenants) and collectively. This could extend to selecting tenants for property on a new estate in such a way as to ensure a viable social mix on the estate. There may also be cases where the only way an authority can ensure full use of all vacant stock is by giving some preference to categories of person whose characteristics are not reflected in **s. 167(2)**. For example, some authorities have to adopt special strategies on hard-to-let property, granting tenancies to whoever is willing to take the property, regardless of housing need; this would not conflict with the principles in **s. 167(2)**, provided that there is no other way of letting the property reasonably, and that those accorded a reasonable preference are given the opportunity to consider the property. When nominating to bodies such as RSLs, local authorities should recognise that those bodies will also wish to ensure that they are able to manage their own stock effectively.

5.6. It is for each authority to consider how to reflect the categories set out in **s. 167(2)** in the allocation scheme which they devise. A number of possible indicators are given in Annex A to this Guidance. There is no requirement for authorities to give equal weight to each of the factors listed in **s. 167(2)**. Generally, authorities will wish to ensure that their allocation schemes give greter preference to the more severe cases of need, whether manifested singly or through a spread of indicators. For example, an authority may wish to give greater priority to a household which includes a woman who is both pregnant (attracting reasonable preference under **s. 167(2)(d)**) and living in insanitary conditions (**s. 167(2)(a)**) than to a household which includes a woman who is only pregnant. However, the fact that a household includes a woman who is both pregnant and has a dependent child (attracting reasonable preference under both **s. 167(2)(c) and (d)**) should not of itself give that household greater preference over a family which has two dependent children (and therefore only attracts preference under **s. 167(2)**). Each authority should have arrangements for determining priority in allocation between two households with similar levels of need. It would be quite legitimate to employ some indicator that reflects the time spent waiting at a particular level of need. Whatever indicators are used, they should be set out clearly in the allocation scheme.

5.7. The flexibility inherent in the provisions of **s. 167** means that an authority should not operate on a purely formulaic basis. Authorities must behave rationally, taking into acocunt all considerations relevant to housing and social needs, and ignoring irrelevant factors. It would be open to an authority to establish, as part of their allocation scheme, a procedure for dealing with special cases on an exceptional basis. For example if a household on the register has a reasonable expectation of being offered accommodation within three months but suddenly lose their existing home as a result of a disaster, it would be open to the authority to make an immediate offer of accommodation through the register.

What does "additional preference" mean?

5.8. In order to secure that "additional preference" is given, an allocation scheme would have to ensure that proper priority is accorded to a person with a particular need for settled accommodation on medical or welfare grounds who cannot reasonably be expected to find accommodation for him/herself in the future.

5.9. The provision is aimed at individuals who are particularly vulnerable, for example as a result of old age, physical or mental illness, and/or because of a learning or physical disability. These are people who could live independently with the necessary support, but who could not be expected to secure accommodation on their own initiative. The provision does not require authorities to allocate the first available property of any sort in such cases, but it does assume that people meeting this description will have first call on suitable vacancies.

5.10. An authority should take into account: the availability of suitable accommodation, whether a package of care and support services is required in order to enable the applicant to take up an offer of accommodation, as well as decisions by social services or health agencies about how the applicant's support, care or health needs should be met. Close and effective working between housing, social services and health authorities will be critical in order to deliver the most appropriate solution to the housing, support and care needs of people who come into this category.

5.11. There is a great deal of guidance issued to social services authorities to help them assess people with community care needs. See, for example: 'Caring for People: Community Care in the Next Decade and Beyond', Department of Health, 1989, Cmd. 849; Department of Health Circular 12/70 on 'The Chronically Sick and Disabled Persons Act 1970' (Disabled Persons); 'Community Care in the Next Decade and Beyond: Policy Guidance', 1990 HMSO; 'Care Management and Assessment Practitioners' Guide', SSI/ SWSG, HMSO, 1991; and Department of Health/Department of the Environment Circular 10/92 — joint circular on 'Housing and Community Care'. In view of the need for housing departments to work with and inform social services about the operation of the allocations system, local authorities should also have regard to the Department of Health/Department of the Environment joint guidance 'Housing and Community Care; Establishing a Strategic Framework' (due to be published in November 1996).

What is "settled accommodation"?

5.12. **Section 167(2)(e)** and **(f)** introduces the concept of "settled" accommodation. This suggests accommodation that can provide a long-term home, rather than transient or short-term accommodation.

What are "medical or welfare grounds"?

5.13. Local housing authorities will usually take into account advice from medical professionals in considering whether an applicant has "medical grounds" which are relevant to his/her application for rehousing. The term "welfare grounds" is intended to encompass not only care or support needs, but also other social needs which do not require ongoing care and support, such as the need to provide a secure base from which a care leaver or other vulnerable person can build a stable life. It could include vulnerable people with care and support needs, who could be expected to find accommodation on their own initiative but have a need for a secure base; or vulnerable people who do not have care and support needs, but do have a need for a secure base.

Children and "medical or welfare grounds"

5.14. Households may include a child with a need for settled accommodation on medical or welfare grounds. Under **s. 27 of the Children Act 1989,** local housing authorities are required to liaise closely with social services authorities, who have duties towards children under that Act. **Section 17 of the Children Act 1989** imposes a general duty on social services authorities "to safeguard and promote the welfare of children within their area who are in need; and so far as is consistent with that duty, to promote the upbringing of such children by their families, by providing a ranged and level of services appropriate to those children's needs". Section 27 of that Act enables the local authority to request help from another authority (including the local housing authority) or person in order to meet the needs of children in need, and that other authority must comply with the request if it is compatible with their own statutory duties and obligations.

5.15. A child in need is defined in the **Children Act 1989** as a person who "is unlikely to achieve or maintain, or to have the opportunity of achieving or maintaining, a reasonable standard of health or development without the provision . . . of services by a local authority; (a person whose) health or development is likely to be significantly impaired, or further impaired, without the provision . . . of such services; or (a person who) is disabled". A child in need may be a person with a need for settled accommodation on medical or welfare grounds; housing authorities are unlikely to be able to reach a decision on the level of priority to accord in such cases without taking into account the views of the social services authority.

Which needs groups are included in the priority categories?

5.16. The first of the new priority, or reasonable preference categories ((a) in paragraph 5.3) is self-explanatory. The second ((b) in paragraph 5.3), is designed to ensure that the needs of households who are at risk of losing their present accommodation, but who are otherwise housed adequately, are considered alongside the needs of other households seeking social housing. This category would cover instances where it is known that the present tenure is about to end, for example where a household is required to leave tied accommodation. Local authorities will also be able to give preference to applicants where it is uncertain whether the present accommodation will continue. It is open to authorities to apply the test more broadly, but on a graduated basis; for instance, an authority might give limited preference to someone living in an assured shorthold tenancy and a higher weighting to anyone whose lack of security is more acute.

5.17. Categories (c), (d) and (e) in paragraph 5.3 reflect the underlying social characteristics of households who warrant preference for settled accommodation over other households living in similar conditions. Recognising the importance of a stable home environment to a child's development, local authorities should give reasonable preference to families with dependent children or those who are expecting a child.

5.18. Category (e) in paragraph 5.3. embraces households whose circumstances mean that a settled home is required to ensure that other needs are adequately met. Households within this category may need social housing to give or receive care, or because their personal circumstances make stability particularly important. Such households may include someone with a physical or learning disability, or someone who is elderly or mentally ill, or people with progressive conditions such as Multiple Sclerosis, and people with addictive behaviour or behavioural difficulties. Again, local housing authorities should involve social services and health authorities in assessing whether a household has a particular need for settled accommodation and whether this warrants providing long term social housing.

5.19. The sixth reasonable preference category, (f), reflects the particular difficulties that some households on a low income may have in obtaining settled accommodation for themselves in the private sector. Local authorities should consider both the household's immediate circumstances and its longer-term prospects.

What factors may an authority not use as part of an allocations scheme?

5.20. Ministers have no immediate plans to make regulations under **s. 167(4)**, about factors which a local housing authority must not take into account in allocating housing, but will monitor local authority practices and review the position as required.

What discretion do local authorities have in devising their allocations schemes?

5.21. By virtue of **s. 167(6)** a local housing authority is free to decide the structure of their allocations scheme (for example, whether it is points-based, date order or quota based, or any combination of these), what indicators to use, and what weighting to give to the categories listed in **s. 167(2)**, provided, of course, that reasonable preference is still given to those categories when allocating housing. Discretion rests with the authority, as it did previously, although the scheme may be devised and operated by the director of housing, or the appropriate chief officer, under delegated powers. The Secretaries of State would encourage local authorities to exercise this discretion to ensure that first priority should be the provision of housing for married couples with children, and for vulnerable individuals, who a reliving in unsuit able accommodation.

The requirement to consult registered social landlords on the allocations scheme

5.22. **Section 167(7)** requires local housing authorities, before adopting an allocation scheme, or altering their existing scheme to reflect a major change of policy, to:

> — send a copy of the draft scheme, or proposed alteration, to every registered social landlord with which they have nomination arrangements, and

— ensure that those registered social landlords have a reasonable opportunity to comment on the proposals.

No timetable is specified in the Act for receipt of comments: six weeks should allow sufficient time for RSLs to consider the proposals fully and to comment to the authority.

Information about the allocations scheme

5.23. **Section 168(1)** requires local housing authorities to publish a summary of their scheme and to provide a copy of the summary free of charge to any member of the public who requests one. An authority is also required, under **s. 168(2)**, to make the scheme available for inspection at their principal office and to provide a copy of the scheme, on payment of a reasonable fee, to any member of the public who requests one.

5.24. Local housing authorities have considerable experience of producing leaflets and other publicity material aimed at informing their customers of the authority's policies and practices in a wide range of activities. Few authorities charge customers for copies of their existing allocation schemes and copies of summary leaflets are invariably free. Authorities may wish to consider providing customers with an information pack about the allocation scheme. If they do so it should be written in jargon-free, plain language and presented in a clear, attractive design and format. It should also be available in all the local community languages and be accessible to people who have a visual impairment through large print, audiotape and braille versions.

5.25. Copies of the allocation scheme (or information pack) must be available at a local authority's principal office. Authorities may also wish to have copies of it and/or the summary available at all housing and council offices (including libraries and leisure facilities) which are open to members of the public, as well as advice centres, citizens advice bureau, post offices and agencies used by the local community.

5.26. Local authorities are encouraged to maintain lists of properties in their stock which are suitable for disabled people and other special needs groups on their housing register. These lists may be published but there is no obligation to do so and they may be retained for internal management purposes only. The list might include all accessible or significantly adapted local authority stock, RSL properties and private sector properties to which authorities nominate tenants. The list would show, for example, those properties built or fully adapted for a wheelchair user, including level access to and within the property, and with an adapted bathroom or kitchen. It would also show other properties suited to people with limited mobility, and the level of accessibility. Premises with only minor adaptations (*e.g.* bath rails) and with very restricted access should not be included.

Consulting on changes to an allocations scheme

5.27. Under **s. 168(3)**, an authority must notify everyone on the housing register, within a reasonable period, of any change in their scheme reflecting a major change of policy and explain, in general terms, the effect of the change. **Section 168** replaces parts of **s. 106 of the 1985 Act** (information about housing allocation). Local authorities should be aware that there is still a duty under **s. 106** for them to provide information about their allocation scheme for transfer applicants, and for other allocations which they make outside the housing register (*e.g.* referrals). Although it is not a statutory requirement, local housing authorities will wish to consider consulting social services departments, health authorities, registered social landlords, voluntary sector organisations and other recognised referral bodies. Authorities may also wish to consider informing or consulting their existing tenants through their current consultation arrangements.

5.28. Only where authorities are adopting a major policy change should each applicant on the housing register be informed personally by letter; allocation schemes can be subject to frequent amendment and refinement to reflect changing local circumstances and national requirements, it is recognised that to inform every applicant of every policy change would entail disproportionate costs.

6. Equal Opportunities within the Allocations Process

Sex Discrimination Act 1975

6.1. The **Sex Discrimination Act 1975** makes it unlawful to discriminate against a person on the grounds of gender by treating him/her less favourably than others. **Section 20** of that Act makes specific provision about the management and disposal of accommodation. It is unlawful to discriminate:

— in the terms on which accommodation is offered;
— by refusing applications;
— in the treatment of applications in relation to any other people on the register in need of such accommodation.

Race Relations Act 1976

6.2. Local housing authorities will be familiar with their obligations under the **Race Relations Act 1976** not to discriminate on racial grounds in the provision of their housing services, including the allocation and letting of their properties. Authorities should have regard to the Commission for Racial Equality's 'Code of

Practice in Rented Housing'. Although the Code imposes no legal obligations, it is admissible as evidence in court proceedings.

6.3. **Section 71 of the 1976 Act** places a general duty on local authorities to "make appropriate arrangements with a view to securing that their various functions are carried out with due regard to the need to eliminate unlawful discrimination, and to promote equality of opportunity and good relations between persons of different racial groups". More specifically with regard to allocating housing, **s. 21** makes it unlawful to discriminate on racial grounds:

— in the terms on which accommodation is offered;
— by refusing applications;
— by the treatment of applications in relation to any other people on the register in need of such accommodation.

Disability Discrimination Act 1985

6.4. Local housing authorities must also have regard to the provisions of the Disability Discrimination Act 1985 in the allocation of housing accommodation.

7. Co-operation between Local Housing Authorities and other Agencies

Co-operation between registered social landlords and local housing authorities

7.1. **Section 170** of the 1996 Act (co-operation between registered social landlords and local housing authorities) requires a RSL, when a local housing authority requests, to co-operate to such an extent as is reasonable in offering accommodation to people with priority on the authority's housing register.

7.2. Many local housing authorities and RSLs operate mutually arranged local nomination agreements, often based on national models formulated by the local authority associations and representatives of registered social landlords. These have developed as part of local authorities' strategic and enabling roles — particularly in fulfilling their statutory duties to homeless households and to people with special housing needs — and in recognition that registered social landlords are the main providers of new social housing. In cases where a stock transfer, whole or partial, has taken place, there will need to be close liaison between all the parties involved, including the transfer landlord.

7.3. RSLs are required by the Tenant's Guarantee to make at least 50 per cent of their new lettings available to people nominated to them by a local housing authority. This requirement will continue under the new legislation and is expected to form the basis of nomination arrangements under Part VI.

Co-operation between housing, social services and health authorities

7.4. This guidance has referred several times to the importance of joint working between housing, social service and health authorities in the allocation of concil housing, and nominations to registered social landlords. Such co-operation is an important aspect of local housing authorities' work in implementing the new allocations framework.

7.5. **The Children Act 1989** and the **National Health Service and Community Act 1990** require housing authorities to work with social services. It is important, therefore, that housing authorities are fully involved in the development of community care plans and children's services plans. DoE Circular 10/92 and the forthcoming Department of Health/Department of the Environment guidance "Housing and Community Care; Establishing a Strategic Framework" provides more detail on joint working between housing, health and social services. Guidance on children's services planning was issued by the Department of Health with Circular LAC(96)10 in March 1996.

8. Offences

8.1. **Section 171** of the 1996 Act (false statements and withholding information) makes it an offence for anyone seeking assistance from a local authority under Part VI to:

— knowingly or recklessly give false information to the authority, or
— knowingly withhold information which the authority have reasonably required him/her to give in connection with the exercise of their functions under Part VI.

8.2. A person guilty of an offence under this section is liable on summary conviction to a fine not exceeding level 5 on the standard scale (£5,000).

8.3. It is for individual local authorities to determine when the provisions of this section apply and when to institute criminal proceedings. However, the circumstances in which an offence is committed could include:

— any false information given on an application form to appear on a housing register;
— any false information given in response to subsequent review letters or other updating mechanisms; or

— any false information given or submitted by applicants during the proceedings of a review.

8.4. Ground 5 in Schedule 2 to the 1985 Act (as amended by s.146 of the 1996 Act) enables a local authority to seek possession of a tenancy which they have granted as a result of a false statement by the tenant or a person acting at the tenant's instigation.

9. Preventing Homelessness: Information, Advice and Assistance

General

9.1. It is important for people to have access to good quality information and advice about homelessness: timely advice can prevent the loss of a home, and give all the parties concerned a chance to assess the most suitable course of action. The 1996 Act makes information and advice a key component of the strategy for dealing with homelessness, both for people in general who need advice and for homeless applicants specifically. In the context of homelessness prevention, local authorities are also required to take reasonable steps to secure that accommodation does not cease to be available for people with a priority need who are threatened with homelessness unintentionally.

9.2. Although the 1996 Act does not impose a specific duty on local authorities to provide general housing advice, local authorities may nevertheless wish to consider the benefits of providing a wider service: this is likely to mesh into their homelessness duties and can, in some circumstances, prevent cases from reaching the stage where the specific homelessness duties arise.

Homelessness advisory services

9.3. For the first time, local authorities have a *duty* to secure that *advice* and *information* about homelessness and the prevention of homelessness is available free of charge to anyone in their area (**s. 179**). An authority can meet this duty by: providing the service themselves; securing it from some other organisation; or securing it in partnership with another organisation. **Section 179** allows authorities to provide grants, loans or other specified forms of assistance to any person providing the service on the authority's behalf. **Section 180** (which replaces the familiar **s. 73 of the 1985 Act**) gives authorities a power to provide grants, loans or other specified forms of assistance to voluntary organisations concerned with homelessness or matters relating to homelessness.

9.4. Some authorities already secure appropriate advisory services: others may have to develop new or existing services.

Authorities may wish to liaise with any existing providers in their area to determine what changes, if any, are necessary to meet this duty and to develop appropriate strategies. They may also find it helpful to refer to the Chartered Institute of Housing's 'Good Practice Guide to Housing Advice Services' (June 1996) and (although Scottish local authorities operate under different legislation) to scottish Homes' national standards and good practice manual for housing advisory services. The Department of the Environment's publication 'Models of Practice in Housing Advice Services' provides examples of current practice.

Assessing existing advice provision

9.5. Authorities should consider what housing advice is currently being provided in their area. For example, there may be a service provided by a specialist voluntary organisation such as Shelter or the Catholic Housing Aid Society (CHAS), or a general advice service including housing advice, such as that provided by a Citizens Advice Bureau or a neighbourhood advice agency.

9.6. Authorities may find it useful to carry out an "advice audit" to assess current provision and need in their areas. DoE research suggests that such an audit should:

- ascertain the nature of the provision and the role(s) of the agency(ies);
- identify any gaps or overlaps in the provision;
- clarify the role which the local housing authority themselves wish to play and the implications for voluntary sector agencies;
- develop liaison arrangements for the strategic planning and delivery of services;
- consider funding sources; and
- consider the quality and effectiveness of services.

What service should be offered?

9.7. It is important that people in the area are aware of the service and of what it offers. Advice and information are not defined in the 1996 Act but, as a minimum, are likely to comprise:

a) *advice*:

— setting out a person's options or courses of action;
— obtaining information from another source;
— help with letters or form filling; and
— referral to another source of help or a specialist service such as a money advice service or law centre; and

b) *information*:
— providing written or verbal information and/or explanation;
— "signposting" to other available resources or services.

9.8. Some advisory services may wish to provide an advocacy service, for example representing a client in negotiation with a third party such as a private landlord, or mediating on a client's behalf. However, the provision of an advocacy service is discretionary, and is not required by the 1996 Act. If the service is provided by a voluntary sector organisation, the authority may fund it under **s. 180**.

Who provides the advisory service?

9.9. The duty requires the authority to *secure* the provision of advice and information. Whether to provide it themselves, or to secure that it is provided by another body is a matter for the authority, possibly in the light of an advice audit. Liaison with other bodies and providers can inform the authority's decision, as can other factors such as local circumstances, available resources and the effectiveness of different methods of delivery as well as the type of service they may wish to provide. If another, body is to provide the service, authorities should consider the quality assurance methods of advisory service providers. Citizens Advice Bureaux, for example, are part of a national organisation which has agreed quality assurance systems and provides resources to support them, such as information, training and specialist support. The Shelter network of Housing Advice centres is another example.

9.10. Authorities can act as strategic planners and enablers, as direct providers of housing advisory services, or in a combination of these roles. again, the Department of the Environment's 'Models of Practice in Housing Advice Services' may be helpful to authorities when considering which course to follow. Authorities might review the current funding arrangements for voluntary sector advice services in their area. Co-ordination between the various departments of authorities responsible for providing and funding advice services will help to ensure that conflicts do not arise over the purpose of any statutory funding, and also that responsibility for funding of housing advisory services is clear. In some areas it may be appropriate for an authority to fund or provide a service jointly with one or more neighbouring authorities: this may reduce costs for each participating authority and provide a better resourced service for the applicant.

What advice and information?

9.11. The precise issues to be covered by an advisory service are for each authority to determine in the light of local housing circumstances, but they must be about homelessness and the prevention of homelessness. However, information and/or advice is likely to be sought on:

— local housing opportunities, including private sector options;
— housing registers and allocations policy;
— landlords and letting agents;
— housing status, security and rights of occupation;
— harassment and illegal eviction;
— possession proceedings;
— consequences of relationship breakdown, and implications for tenancies;
— income maximisation — welfare benefits, housing benefit;
— rent levels;
— rent and mortgage arrears; and other money or debt issues which could lead to homelessness;
— local authority duties towards homeless households;
— housing conditions, grants and repairs.

Standards

9.12. Whether providing the service under s. 179 themselves or securing it from another provider, authorities should ensure that effective monitoring and evaluation procedures are in place, both to monitor the qualtity and outcome of information and advice (*e.g.* through quality audits and user surveys) and to evaluate performance against service plans. It is important to keep the effectiveness of the service under review, to ensure that it is meeting the needs of all sections of the community and is providing an approachable and accessible service. Reviews will also help to identify gaps in service, or better ways of achieving the most appropriate service.

9.13. It is important that people are not sent to and fro between departments/bodies and that they are not referred inappropriately. Liaison between the housing authority, advice providers and (where appropriate) social services, together with (where practicable) formal referral arrangements will ensure that people receive appropriate assistance as quickly as possible.

Accessibility

9.14. The homelessness advisory service should be accessible to people in the area. People need to now that the service is available to *any* person seeking information about homelessness, not only to homeless applicants, and where and to whom they should go for advice. Early and accurate advice can prevent homelessness. Authorities may wish to consider the contribution that information technology and a telephone advisory service can make, particularly in rural areas. It is important that people in the area are aware of the service and of what it offers. Authorities should consider appropriate means of promoting and publicising the service and of ensuring that information is widely disseminated, with the aim that, whenever possible, homelessness is prevented. Authorities should ensure that the information provided is accurate, up to date and accessible, *e.g.* in a range of relevant languages, and in braille and/or on tape for people with a visual impairment.

9.15. Authorities should also seek to ensure that the premises of housing advice, centres or groups providing advice and assistance are accessible to people with physical or sensory disabilities. Where this is not possible, an alternative, accessible venue for the delivery of advice and assistance should be identified, or a home visit made.

Advice and Assistance to homeless applicants

9.16. In addition to the general provision described above, authorities have a *duty* to provide *advice* and *assistance* to homeless applicants in certain circumstances specified in the 1996 Act. This duty differs from the homelessness advisory duty under **s. 179** in that it requires the authority to provide advice and **assistance** to the applicant, to enable him/her to secure accommodation.

9.17. If the authority conclude that the applicant is eligible for assistance and:

a) is homeless or is threatened with homelessness intentionally and is in priority need (**s. 190(2)(b)** and **s. 196(5)(b)**);
b) is homeless intentionally but is not in priority need (**s. 190(3)**);
c) is neither homeless intentionally nor threatened with homelessness intentionally, but is not in priority need (**s. 192** and **s. 195(5)(a)**); or
d) is not homeless intentionally, is in priority need, and the authority are satisfied that other suitable accommodation is available in their district (**s. 197(2)**),

the 1996 Act requires the authority to provide *advice* and *assistance* to the applicant. Where the advisory service is separate from the department dealing with homelessness, close liaison will be needed throughout all the stages of dealing with a homeless applicant.

9.18. In each of these cases, the authority must provide such advice and assistance as they consider is reasonably required. The duty under **s. 197** goes further, in that it also requires the authority to have regard to all the circumstances and characteristics of the applicant amd the state of the local housing market and the type of accommodation available, and give assistance that would enable him/her to secure the tenancy. Some homeless households will already have attempted to secure accommodation in the private sector before approaching the authority for assistance. Authorities should not merely require the household to take the same steps again and consider this to be a discharge of their duty. Unless there is a clear supply of vacant suitable accommodation in the area, handing out a list of accommodation agencies in the area is unlikely to be sufficient to discharge the authority's duty. Inadequate advice and assistance, or referral to unsuitable accommodation, could result in a further homelessness application to the authority and cause distress to people who may have spent protracted periods in inadequate accommodation.

9.19. Some applicants may be unable to take steps to secure accommodation for themselves, irrespective of the level of advice and assistance given. This may apply, for example, to people with a severe physical or mental illness, those with learning disabilities or people who have had a particularly traumatic experience, such as fleeing domestic violence. Others, whilst able to secure accommodation for themselves, may require high levels of assistance, such as financial assistance or help with understanding and complying with the terms of any tenancy offered to them. This will be particularly important for people whose first language is not English. It is important that authorities should take account of all the available information relating to an applicant's circumstances (**s. 197(4)**), including those that have given rise to their homelessness.

9.20. In areas where there is a plentiful supply of private rented accommodation, it will generally be easier for applicants to secure it. However, a large private rented sector will not always signify that there is a plentiful supply of accommodation available for homeless applicants. Authorities should recognise that some rents in such areas may be substantially higher than local reference rent levels or that the accommodation may largely be available as holiday lets or student accommodation. For the purposes of the duty owed under **s. 197(2)**, if rents are generally very high, authorities should consider whether the level of assistance which would be required to make accommodation available is beyond what is reasonably required, and whether such accommodation is suitable for someone on a low income.

Threatened with homelessness

9.21. The 1996 Act gives local authorities a duty in relation to those households who are eligible for assistance, threatened with homelessness unintentionally and in priority need. Under **s. 195(2)** an authority must take reasonable steps to secure that accommodation does not cease to be available for an applicant, unless they

are satisfied that other suitable accommodation is available (but see
also paragraph 20.8). Timely advice and assistance can sometimes
prevent the loss of an applicant's existing accommodation but, if
this is not possible, the authority should secure that fresh accommodation is available for the applicant if s/he would otherwise be
homeless. If the authority believe that other suitable accommodation is available in their district, they have a duty to offer such
advice and assistance as they consider is reasonably required to
enable the applicant to secure that accommodation (s. 197(2)). If
other suitable accommodation is not available, the authority must
secure that accommodation is available for the applicant for the
minimum period (two years); the advice and assistance provisions
cannot be substituted for the substantive duty in this instance.

9.22. Local authorities should normally expect family members
who are living at home to continue to be so housed, where the
accommodation is adequate. It is obviously proper for individuals
to look first to their families for accommodation before turning to
the wider community. Local authorities would naturally not
consider as a priority the housing of applicants whose family
circumstances are such that adequate accommodation is available.
They should, however, take into account the guidance (paragraphs
13.9.–13.10.) about domestic violence.

9.23. Applicants who are threatened with homelessness but are
not in priority need, or those in priority need but threatened with
homelessness intentionally, must be given appropriate advice and
assistance in their endeavours to retain existing accommodation
(s. 195(5)).

Preventing homelessness among specific groups

9.24. The following paragraphs are concerned for the most part
with guidance on the provision of advisory services under s. 179.
They set out the sort of situations in which the duty to provide
advisory services is likely to arise, and suggest specific ways in
which those situations might best be handled. As indicated above
(paragraph 9.2.), there may also be occasions where authorities will
wish to provide (or secure the provision of) advisory services on
issues which go wider than purely homelessness and the prevent of
homelessness. These are also incorporated below, the list is not
intended to be comprehensive.

Tenants of local authorities and registed social landlords

9.25. Tenants of local authorities and registered social landlords
may be threatened with homelessness as a result of eviction
because of rent arrears. Authorities may find it helpful to refer to
the Department of the Environment publication. 'Rent Arrears in
Local Authorities and Housing Associations in England', which
offers good practice guidance.

9.26. There are many measures by which authorities and registered social landlords have been able to control rent arrears. These include:

  a) ensuring that prospective tenants are fully aware of the financial commitment they are taking on, and checking that tenants are receiving any housing benefit or other relevant welfare benefits to which they are entitled. A referral to the housing advisory service for pre-tenancy advice may be helpful;

  b) monitoring the number of missed payments, to give early warning of difficulties, and enabling special arrangements for rent collection to be made;

  c) encouraging tenants who get into difficulty to approach the housing advisory service for advice;

  d) using civil proceedings to recover the debt, for example by an Attachment of Earnings Order where a person has regular employment.

Exceptionally, it is sometimes possible to get rent arrears paid by another party. (This could be done by social services authorities under **s. 17(6) of the Children Act 1989**, which empowers local authorities to give assistance in cash in meeting their duties towards children in need.)

9.27. It may be that low income tenants are not claiming Housing Benefit and other benefits to which they are entitled: action to inform people of their entitlement is one of the most important methods of preventing arrears and, ultimately, homelessness. Local housing authorities and RSLs should first seek to control the extent of any arrears (paragraph 9.25.), but if this fails and arrears start to mount, they should get in touch with the social services authority and the local Department of Social Security office to explore ways in which the debt may be paid off.

9.28. In some cases, rent arrears may be the result of an underlying problem such as drink or drug abuse or mental health problems. Housing staff may be unaware of the problem, for example if the tenant fails to respond to attempts to make contact, and the housing officer is unlikely to have all the specialist skills needed to deal with problems of this nature. It is important for the housing authority to have good liaison arrangements with social services or other agencies or organisations which support vulnerable tenants. Such arrangements can help to prevent the breakdown of tenancies, and so help both to prevent homelessness and to assist with arrears control.

Private sector tenants

9.29. Most tenants of private, non-resident landlords are protected under the Rent or Housing Acts. Where a tenant is threatened with eviction in circumstances in which an order for possession could not or would not normally be granted, the applicant may have to be referred to the housing advisory service for advice on enforcing his/her rights. Authorities should not require tenants to fight a possession action where the landlord has a certain prospect of success, such as an action for recovery of property which is let on an assured shorthold tenancy where the fixed term of the tenancy has ended. Virtually all possession orders leading to eviction originate in the county court. Liaison with the county court can therefore provide early warning. It may be possible to arrange with the court for a letter to go with the summons to the private tenant advising him/her of the assistance which is available from the housing authority and the housing advisory service which may help avert homelessness.

9.30. It is important to remember that for certain lettings which began after January 14, 1989 and where landlords and tenants share accommodation, there is no requirement for a court order and therefore homelessness in such cases could occur at any time. Homelessness advisory services must be in a position to advise people at short notice and liaise with the homelessness department where homelessness may be imminent.

Rent arrears in the private sector

9.31. Many of the suggestions above are relevant for dealing with private sector tenants who have rent arrears, particularly ensuring that there is full take-up of any benefits to which such tenants may be entitled. Authorities should be ready to act quickly where the tenant holds an assured shorthold tenancy, because landlords may seek possession for arrears where the tenant is eight weeks in arrears (where the rent is payable weekly or fortnightly), or two months or more in arrears (where the rent is payable monthly) (**amendment to Part I of Schedule 2 to the Housing Act 1988 by s. 101 of the 1996 Act**).

Owner-occupiers

9.32. Owner-occupiers may be threatened with possession by their lender, or may consider yielding possession voluntarily to the lender because of difficulty in maintaining mortgage repayments. Anyone who is falling behind with mortgage payments should be advised to contact their lender and the homelessness advisory service at an early stage, so that action can be taken to forestall possession. The Council of Mortgage Lenders has issued a statement of practice about mortgage arrears (Council of Mortgage Lenders' Statement of Practice on the Handling of Mortgage Arrears); in some instances it may be possible — with the lender's agreement — to extend the period of the loan or to reschedule it in some other way. Owner-occupiers who are entitled to Income Support may be able to get help with the interest due on their mortgages. Income Support does not, however, provide help with capital repayments. Further advice is available from local Benefits Agency offices.

People who move for work

9.33. It will be helpful to alert people who move for work reasons to the benefits to which they may be entitled if their income from work is low. People may be able to get advice from the Employment Service's Claimant Advisers, based in local offices throughout the country, about the effect on their total net income of taking a particular job.

Former members of the Armed Forces

9.34. The resettlement services of the Ministry of Defence advise service personnel to consider well before discharge where they intend to live, and should warn people against seeking to live in an area where housing is in short supply. The resettlement unit should liaise with authorities well in advance of discharge, to help prevent homelessness among ex-service personnel and their families. Authorities will wish to consider accepting on to their housing register applications from service people. The joint Department of the Environment/Welsh Office Circular, 'Housing for People Leaving the Armed Forces' (DoE 14/93, WO 59/93) (currently being reviewed) contains more advice on this subject.

9.35. The Ministry of Defence recognises that local housing authorities will often require proof that entitlement to occupy service quarters is coming to an end before they will consider an application for homelessness assistance. Authorities should not insist upon a court order for possession, and may instead accept certificates from the local service authorities. These certificates are usually issued six months before discharge. Authorities should ensure that service households approaching discharge are given timely and comprehensive advice on the housing options open to them.

Mentally ill people

9.36. There are a number of agencies who could assist the local authority in their duty to provide advice and information to mentally ill people. These agencies include day care providers, voluntary organisations concerned with Mental Illness, *e.g.* local branches of MIND or the National Schizophrenia Fellowship and the statutory providers of help, including professional providers such as the individual's key worker.

Young people

9.37 Prevention advice is particularly relevant for young people. They may not qualify as vulnerable and therefore in priority need when they apply initially, but they could become so if lack of adequate assistance causes their circumstances to deteriorate. Authorities have powers under **s. 180** to make grants or loans to voluntary organisations concerned with homelessness. The role of such bodies and of the housing advisory service in relation to young people may be germane in encouraging young people to seek advice before taking any action that might result in their becoming homeless. Organisations providing a mediation service may have a useful role to play in resolving disputes between young people and their families.

Education

9.38. Education about housing can be important in helping young people to cope with independent living, and making them aware of the risks of homelessness. Housing authorities may wish to liaise with local education authorities concerning opportunities for schools to cover housing and homelessness in their teaching programmes. In this way, young people may be able to gain a realistic appreciation of the implications of leaving home and living independently. The Youth Service, including voluntary sector agencies, may also have a role to play in providing information and other materials for use in schools and informal youth settings.

Domestic disputes

9.39. In some cases, threatened homelessness will arise because of a domestic dispute. Housing authorities should be ready to take action where household members are at risk from violence or abuse. Where young people under 18 are involved because of a breakdown in the relationship with their parents, or where there is a risk of abuse, the housing authority should alert the social services authority to the case. In other cases, depending on the severity of the dispute, the housing authority may still wish to ask the social services authority for help. In this respect housing authorities should be aware of the duties of social services and certain other specified authorities under **s. 20 and s. 27 of the Children Act 1989**. An approach to the social services authority might be directed at relieving tension within the household to enable members to continue to live together. Social Services may be able to offer counselling and support or to advise on other local services and agencies which might provide specialist help.

9.40. In assessing homelessness, authorities should also consider whether it is reasonable for a person to continue to occupy accommodation if s/he (or a person who normally resides with him/her) will thereby be subject to domestic violence, or to threats of violence (**s. 177**). This may also impact on the authority's assessment of whether a person's homelessness or threatened homelessness is intentional.

Hospital patients and prisoners

9.41. People may risk losing their home during a protracted stay in hospital or prison, if they cannot maintain their rent or mortgage payments. Where the authority has early warning of this, it can aim to ensure that appropriate arrangements are made either to retain or to terminate the tenancy. If, for example, a head of household enters hospital or prison, the authority could refer their family to the homelessness advisory service for advice on any benefits to which they may be entitled.

People affected by redevelopment

9.42. Where authorities undertake the redevelopment or improvement of residential accommodation they may have a duty, under **s. 39 of the Land Compensation Act 1973**, to ensure that people displaced are provided with suitable alternative accommodation. The duty applies whatever the household's family status, whether married or single.

Help from the Social Fund

9.43. Community Care Grants are mainly directed at particularly vulnerable people who need help to live independently in the community and have an expense which has arisen as a result of special circumstances. Interest-free Budgeting Loans are the main form of help with intermittent expenses which arise in the normal course of events but are difficult to meet from Income Support or income-based JSA. For those who are unable to get a budgeting loan, a Crisis Loan may be available to prevent serious damage or serious risk to the health or safety of themselves or to a member of their family. The Social Fund operates within a budget and consequently some applications may not attract sufficient priority to get a grant or loan. In addition, some applications may fail to meet the eligibility criteria for these payments.

9.44. Changes have been introduced recently to improve access to Community Care Grants for homeless people. In April 1995, the Secretary of State for Social Security issued revised guidance on applicants moving within the community (rather than moving from a form of institutional or residential care), advising Social Fund Officers (SFOs) to give particular consideration to vulnerable or recently homeless people if there is a danger that those people may otherwise go into care. This part of the guidance was extended further in April 1996, to encourage SFOs to consider a grant for people to move into their own, permanent accommodation as part of a planned resettlement programme.

9.45. Deposits to secure accommodation were excluded from the Social Fund because of widespread abuse of such provision under the old, single-payment system. Rent guarantee schemes are operated by many local authorities and are viewed as a more appropriate form of help than the Social Fund.

Other options

9.46. Authorities may encourage their own tenants and local owner-occupiers to take in lodgers.

PART VII OF THE HOUSING ACT 1996

10. Dealing with Homelessness Applications under Part VII of the 1996 Act

What is a homelessness application?

10.1. Under **s. 184** of the 1996 Act an authority is required to take action whenever.

— someone approaches them for help in obtaining housing; and
— the authority have reason to believe that s/he may be homeless or threatened with homelessness.

Applications need not be in writing, nor in any particular form. An application can be made by any member of a household. Authorities will need to have suitable arrangements in place to ensure that all applicants are referred speedily to the department dealing with homelessness (usually the housing department). Homeless applicants who are not already on the housing register should be given information as soon as possible about whether they qualify to go on the register.

10.2. Broadly speaking, authorities should note that applicants over 18 years of age who are owed a duty under **s. 193** or **s. 195(2)**, or have been owed a duty under **s. 192(2)** or **s. 197(2)** within the last two years (and have not subsequently been found intentionally homeless), should have the right to go on the housing register.

Applications to more than one authority

10.3. Authorities need to be alert to instances where an applicant has applied as homeless to other local authorities at the same time. Multiple applications are not unlawful. Authorities can ask the applicant at the initial interview if s/he has applied to another local housing authority and, if so, contact the other authority or authorities to agree which authority will take the responsibility for carrying out enquiries.

Who makes the enquiries?

10.4. As soon as a homeless application is received, under s. 184 of the 1996 Act authorities must make enquiries to satisfy themselves whether the applicant is eligible for assistance; and what duty, if any, is owed to them. They may also make enquiries to determine whether the applicant has a local connection with the area of another housing authority in England, Wales or Scotland. Authorities must then make a reasonable decision in the light of these enquiries. Authorities should remember that any delegation to officers, committees or others must comply with **s. 101 of the Local Government Act 1972.**

Service provision for applicants

10.5. It is important that the housing staff are trained in the requirements of the 1996 Act, the use of this Code, and the authority's own policies. Staff will need to have good interviewing and interpersonal skills and to be equipped to deal with people who are distressed, embarrassed or confused. Reception staff will have a useful role to play in recognising people who may be homeless or threatened with homelessness and directing them to the appropriate officer(s), but unless they are thoroughly trained they should not be expected to exercise any kind of informal 'first screening' of applicants and care will need to be taken that they do not treat as informal inquiries approaches which should be treated as actual applications. The assessment process requires a skilled and objective approach, in which elected members should not be involved.

10.6. The need for assistance can arise at any time, and the legislation assumes that authorities will operate on this basis. Authorities should therefore provide access at all times during normal office hours, and many already have arrangements in place for 24 hour emergency cover, *e.g.* by enabling telephone access to an appropriate duty officer. This need not be the homelessness officer. The police and other relevant services will need to have any emergency phone number.

10.7. Authorities are advised to pay considerable attention to ensuring physical and geographical access to the homelessness service. Any office dealing with homeless applicants preferably needs to be easily reached by public transport and to be accessible to people with disabilities, and/or young children. Where geographical access is difficult to achieve an authority may wish, for example, to consider offering a telephone service followed up by a home visit, if appropriate. Confidential interviewing facilities are strongly advised and authorities may wish to consider offering same-sex interviewers, if requested. It is desirable for premises to have public lavatories and telephones, a children's play area and access to refreshments. Appointments systems for those threatened with homelessness can help relieve the stress of the application process for the applicants and authorities' own officers but must not be allowed to delay urgent cases.

10.8. Details of the service including the opening hours, address, telephone numbers and the 24-hour emergency contact should be well publicised in plain language and, where appropriate, publicity should also be provided in relevant community languages. The needs of visually impaired people should also be taken into acocunt, for example by the provision of information in braille or on tape, and special provision may also need to be made for those with hearing impairments.

10.9. The authority may wish to consider giving each applicant a clear and simple explanation of their procedures for handling applications, and of the decisions which are open to the authority as well as the procedures for seeking a review of any decision if the applicant is dissatisfied. It is advisable that this be given in writing, perhaps in the form of a leaflet, as well as orally. Authorities will wish to give each applicant a realistic expectation of the housing assistance to which s/he may be entitled, in particular the two year duty and the policies for allocation of tenancies through the housing register. Applicants can be spared a lot of anxiety if at every stage in the process they are told in a sympathetic manner what is happening to their applications and the timescale involved. Applicants should be advised that they must report any change in their circumstances between the initial interview and the authority's decision, including any change of address where s/he can be contacted to be informed about the progress of the application. They should also be warned that it is an offence to make a false statement with the intent of inducing the authority to secure accommodation or other assistance for him/her (**s. 214**). This needs to be done sensitively so as not to intimidate the applicant, and at the earlist opportunity.

Target timescales for enquiries

10.10. Target setting is consistent with a performance-oriented approach, which providers are being encouraged to adopt across all local authority services. In dealing with enquiries, it is suggested that authorities aim to meet specific target dates, for examples:

— interview and carry out an initial assessment of the eligibility of the applicant on the day of application or on the first working day therefore in the case of applications made out of office hours: if the interim duty to accommodate arises, the authority will need to comply with the duty straightaway;

— complete their enquiries as quickly as possible and preferably within 30 working days, from the time they accept a duty under s. 184, except in cases where exceptional circumstances apply; and

— issue written decisions to the applicant within three working days of the completion of those enquiries.

10.11. Authorities should bear in mind that target timescales are a maximum and that they should seek to deal with applications as quickly as possible. Effective monitoring should be able to identify specific problems in dealing with applications. Authorities need to ensure that accurate measures of workloads are in place and aim to maintain a manageable caseload for each staff member taking into account the complexity of cases, the level of investigations carried out, the number of inactive cases etc. Periodic reviews are advisable to ensure that caseloads are reasonable and achievable.

Interim duty to accommodate

10.12. As soon as they receive a homelessness application an authority must assess whether the applicant needs to be offered interim accommodation pending the completion of their enquiries. **Section 188** requires that if an authority have reason to believe that an applicant may be:

— eligible for assistance;
— homeless; and
— in priority need,

they have a duty to secure that accommodation is available pending the outcome of their enquiries and a decision on any further duty they may owe.

11. Carrying out enquiries

What enquiries?

11.1. Enquiries are necessary to satisfy the authority whether the applicant's eligible for assistance; and if any duty, and if so what duty, is owed to the applicant (**s. 184(1)**). The authority may also enquire whether a local connection exists with the area of another authority in England, Wales or Scotland (**s. 184(2)**).

11.2. The obligation to make enquiries rests with the authority; it is not for the applicant to "prove" his/her case. Clearly the nature and scope of enquiries will vary in individual cases, but authorities will wish to ensure that they are always undertaken quickly, sympathetically and, as far as possible, in confidence. The authority may request another relevant body to assist in discharging the enquiry duty under **s. 213** (co-operation between relevant housing authorities and bodies); if they do the other body will be under a duty to co-operate in rendering such assistance in the discharge of the function to which the request relates as is reasonable in the circumstances.

11.3. Equiries need to be careful, but not over elaborate. A long, period of uncertainty may be stressful, and could incur extra costs for the authority if they are providing interim accommodation. It may be helpful for applicants, especially those who are under particular stress, to be accompanied during interviews by someone they know and trust. The applicant should always have the opportunity to explain his/her circumstances fully, particularly on matters which may lead to a decision against his/her interests, *e.g.* intentionally. This may be difficult for those applicants for whom English is not the first language and authorities will need to ensure access to competent interpreters for the community languages of the area. People with hearing or speech disabilities may also need an intermediary.

11.4. In cases involving violence or the threat of violence, the applicants may be in considerable distress. Wherever possible, an officer of the same sex as the applicant should conduct the interview, preferably someone trained in dealing with circumstances of this kind. If the applicant reports violence or threats of violence, the authority should not normally seek proof directly from the alleged perpetrator, since doing so may delay the assessment and may generate further violence.

11.5. Where applicants appears to have care, health or support needs, the authority should liaise with the social services and health authorities when making their enquiries.

12. Eligible for Assistance

GUIDANCE TO FOLLOW: this will supersede Guidance on the provisions of s. 9 of the Asylum and Immigration Act 1996, issued on September 12, 1996.

13. Homeless or threatened with homelessness

13.1. Under **s. 175** of the 1996 Act a person is homeless if s/he has no accommodation available in the United Kingdom or elsewhere. Accommodation is only available for a person's occupation if it is available for occupation by him/her, together with any other person(s) who normally live with him/her as a member of his/her family or can reasonably be expected to reside with him/her. A person is threatened with homelessness if it is likely that s/he will become homeless within 28 days.

Persons who live with the applicant

13.2. The phrase "as a member of his/her family" (**s. 176(a)**) will clearly cover established households where there is a close blood or marital relationship. "Any other person" (**s. 176(b)**) insofar as they do not form a family, might cover, for example:

— cohabiting couples, *e.g.* a man and a woman living together as husband and wife;
— adults with foster children; or
— housekeepers, companions or carers who live with elderly people or people with a disability.

There may be a range of other situations and it is for the authority to assess whether any other person might reasonably be expected to live with the applicant. Persons who normally live with the applicant but who are unable to do so for no other reason than that there is no accommodation in which they can live together will normally be included in the assessment. When dealing with a family which has split up, authorities will need to take a decision as a matter of fact and degree — does the other person normally live with the applicant? The terms of any court orders may be relevant here.

Does the applicant have a legal right to occupy the accommodation?

13.3. Under **s. 175(1)** someone is homeless if s/he has no accommodation which she can legally occupy:

a) by virtue of an interest in it (*e.g.* as an owner, lessee or tenant) or by virtue of a court order;
b) by virtue of an express or implied licence to occupy it (*e.g.* as a lodger, as an employee with a service occupancy, or where s/he is living with relatives); or
c) by virtue of some protection given him/her by law (*e.g.* someone retaining possession as a statutory tenant under the Rent Acts after his/her contractual rights to occupy have expired or been terminated).

13.4. Someone who has been occupying accommodation as a licensee (or is an assured shorthold tenant) and whose licence (or tenancy) has been terminated is homeless because s/he not longer has a legal right to continue to occupy. This may include, for example:

— people who have been asked to leave by friends or relatives,
— those required to leave hostels or hospitals; or
— former employees occupying premises under a service occupancy which are dependent upon contracts of employment which have ended.

13.5. Authorities should be alert to be possibly of collusion in cases where people have been asked to leave by friends or relatives. For example, the request to leave may be made at the instigation for the applicant, purely so that s/he may then claim to be homeless. In some cases a home visit may be helpful to check the applicant's circumstances and, perhaps, seek to delay the home loss until alternative accommodation is obtained through the housing register or from some other source.

13.6. Homeless applicants may include those who are no longer entitled to occupy accommodation because their landlord has defaulted on the mortgage of property of which they are tenants. The Council of Mortgage Lenders' Statement of Practice on Handling of Mortgage Arrears notes that before taking possession a lender will try to liaise with the relevant local authority departments to ensure that alternative accommodation is available where appropriate. It also notes that in such cases a number of lenders send a letter addressed to the "occupier" of a property advising him/her of pending possession proceedings in a bid to inform any possible undisclosed tenants. It also advises that lenders can consult the electoral roll in order to confirm whether there are any undisclosed tenants living in the property who need to be notified of the proceedings.

Is it reasonable for the applicant to continue to occupy the accommodation?

13.7. **Section 175(3)** provides that a person shall not be treated as having accommodation unless it is accommodation which it would be *reasonable* for him/her to continue to occupy. **Section 177(1)** provides that it is not reasonable to continue to occupy if it is probable that this will lead to domestic violence or to threats of violence which are likely to be carried out by a person associated with the applicant. **Section 177(2)** provides that authorities may have regard, in determining whether it is reasonable for a person to continue to occupy accommodation, to the general housing circumstances prevailing in relation to housing in the local authority's area. Under **s.177(3)** the secretary of State may specify circumstances in which it is, or is not, to be regarded as reasonable for a person to continue to occupy accommodation. He may also specify other matters to be taken into account or disregarded in determining whether continued occupation would be reasonable.

13.8 There is no simple test of reasonableness. It is for the local authority to make a judgment on the facts of each case. Factors that may be considered include the following:

a) **affordability:** the Secretary of State for the Environment is considering making an order under **s. 177(3)** on this point; further guidance will be issued in the light of this;

b) **physical conditions:** is the condition of the property so bad in comparison with other accommodation in the area that it would be reasonable to expect someone to continue to live there?; do the physical characteristics of the accommodation make it unsuitable for the applicant (*e.g.* a wheelchair user)?;

c) **overcrowding:** authorities may wish to refer to Part X of the Housing Act 1985 on overcrowding.

However, statutory overcrowding is not, by itself, sufficient to determine whether it is unreasonable for the applicant to continue to live there but it can be a key factor if there are other factors which suggest unreasonableness. Again, overcrowding must be considered in relation to general housing circumstances in the area;

d) **type of accommodation:** some types of accommodation, for example women's refuges, direct access hostels, and night shelters intended to provide temporary accommodation in a crisis and it should not be regarded as reasonable for someone to continue to occupy such accommodation in the longer term;

e) **violence or threats of violence from persons *not* associated with the applicant:** the authority will need to consider the seriousness of the violence, or threats of violence, the frequency of occurrence and the likelihood of reoccurence. Violence or threats of violence could include:
   — racial harassment or attacks;
   — violence against a person;
   — sexual abuse or harassment; and
   — harassment on the grounds of religious creed.
   In some instances, the authority may advise an applicant to pursue any available legal remedies. This should not be done as a matter of policy but on the merits of an individual case and will need to take account of the need to ensure the proper safety of the applicant;

f) **security of tenure:** an applicant may have no security of tenure and be required to leave his/her accommodation, or it may be clear to him/her that there is no defence against possession proceedings. In these circumstances the authority may wish to start to process the application and make arrangements (if appropriate) to secure accommodation immediately. Authorities will need to be alert to the possibility of collusion between landlords and the applicant: in such cases the assessment of intentionality will be significant.

Domestic violence

13.9. **Section 177** provides that it is not reasonable for a person to continue to occupy accommodation if it is probable that this will lead to domestic violence against him/her, against a person who normally resides with him/her as a member of his/her family, or against anyone else who might reasonably expected to reside with him/her. Domestic violence is defined as meaning violence from a person with whom s/he is associated, or threats of violence from such a person which are likely to be carried out. **Section 178** provides that a person is associated with another if:

a) they are or have been married to each other;
b) they are or have been cohabitants (*e.g.* a man and a woman living together as husband and wife);
c) they live or have lived in the same household;
d) they are relatives, *i.e.* father, mother, stepfather, stepmother, son, daughter, step-son, step-daughter, grandmother, grandfather, grandson or granddaughter, brother, sister, uncle, aunt, niece or nephew (whether of the full blood, half blood or by affinity) of that person or of that person's spouse or former spouse. A person is also included if s/he would fall into any of these categories in relation to cohabitees or former cohabitees, if they were married to each other;
e) they have agreed to marry each other whether or not that agreement has been terminated;
f) in relation to a child, each of them is a parent of the child or has, or has had, parental responsibility for the child (within the meaning of the **Children Act 1989**). A child is a person under 18 years of age (**s. 178(3)**);
g) if a child has been adopted or freed for adoption (**s. 16(1) Adoption Act 1976**), two persons are also associated if one is the natural parent or grandparent of the child and the other is the child of a person who has become the parent by virtue of an adoption order (**s. 72(1) Adoption Act 1976**) or has applied for an adoption order or someone with whom the child has been placed for adoption.

13.10. The violence or threat of violence is not confined to instances within the home but extends to violence outside the home from a person with whom the applicant or a member of his/her household is associated. The fact that violence has not yet occurred does not, on its own, suggest that it is not likely to occur. Authorities should not base their assessment of a likely threat of violence solely on whether there has been actual violence in the past. Injunctions ordering persons not to molest, or enter the home of, the applicant will not necessarily deter people and the applicant should not necessarily be asked to return to his/her home in this instance. Authorities may inform applicants of the option to take out an injunction, but should make it clear that there is no obligation to do so if s/he feels it would be ineffective.

Who else is homeless?

13.11. Under **s. 175(2)** a person is homeless if s/he has a legal entitlement to accommodation to which for some practical reason s/he is **unable to gain entry** — for example:

— those who have been evicted illegally, or
— those who accommodation is being occupied illegally by squatters.

Although legal remedies may be available to the applicant to regain possession of his/her accommodation, authorities cannot refuse to assist him/her while s/he is homeless.

13.12. A person is also homeless under **s. 175(2)** if his/her accommodation is a **movable structure, *e.g.* caravan, houseboat** etc., and there is nowhere s/he can legally place it and reside in it. This could include gypsies and travellers.

When is someone threatened with homelessness

13.13. Someone is "threatened with homelessness" if s/he is likely to become homeless within 28 days (**s. 175(4)**). Authorities may find it preferable to advise and assist people where the possibility of their becoming homeless is known to the authority more than 28 days in advance, for example where an extended period of negotiation may be required to resolve a financial problem. An early referral to the homelessness advisory service may help prevent homelessness. Authorities will wish to avoid adding the stress of uncertainty to existing stresses and will wish therefore to keep applicants up to date with the arrangements that will be made to assist. Liaison between the homelessness advisory service and homelessness officers will need to be maintained to monitor progress on any preventative action being taken and to alert the authority to the need for any other appropriate action should this not prove successful.

14. Priority need

14.1. **Section 189(1)** lists those groups of people who have a priority need for accommodation. A person is in priority need if s/he:

— has dependent children living with him/her or who might reasonably be expected to live with him/her;
— is pregnant or resides with, or might reasonably be expected to reside with, a pregnant woman;
— is vulnerable as a result of old age, mental illness or handicap or physical disability or other special reason, or is someone who resides with, or might reasonably be expected to reside with, someone who is vulnerable;
— is homeless or threatened with homelessness as a result of an emergency such as fire, flood or other disaster.

It is important that authorities do not fetter their discretion by predetermining that some groups should never be considered vulnerable. Enquiries as to whether an applicant has a priority need must always be carried out where authorities have reason to believe that an applicant may be homeless or threatened with homelessness.

Dependent children

14.2. Priority need arises when an applicant has one or more dependent children living with him/her or who might reasonably be expected to do so. The 1996 Act does not define dependent children but authorities may wish to treat as dependent all children under 16, and all children aged 16–18 who are in, or are about to begin, full-time education or training or who for other reasons are unable to support themselves and who live at home. Dependent children need not necessarily be the applicant's own children but could be, for example, related to the applicant or his/ her husband or wife, or adopted or fostered by the applicant, or related to a person cohabiting with the applicant.

14.3. Where the applicant is a separated parent, authorities may wish to check that the children do depend on him/her. A child may be dependent even though s/he does not live with the applicant at all times but divides his/her time between parents or others. Court orders are an obvious starting point, but should not be required as a general rule, and authorities need to take care that each case is fully assessed on its individual circumstances. where the applicant's children are being looked after by a local authority, *i.e.* are subject to a care order or accommodated under a voluntary agreement, and are not currently living at home, the advice of the social services department will be essential in determining the nature and degree of the children's dependency, particularly since local authorities are required to take steps to settle the children back with their family and to encourage contact between them (unless either of these things would be contrary to the child's best interests).

Pregnant women

14.4. A pregnant woman, together with anyone who lives with her or might reasonably be expected to do so, has a priority need for accommodation. This is regardless of the length of time she has been pregnant. The normal doctor's letter issued to pregnant women or a midwife's letter ought to be adequate evidence of pregnancy. If a pregnant woman suffers a miscarriage or terminates her pregnancy during the *assessment* process the authority would need to consider whether she continues to have a priority need.

Vulnerable

14.5. **Section 189(1)(c)** defines someone as being in priority need if s/he is vulnerable as a result of:

— old age;
— mental illness or handicap;
— physical disability; or
— other special reasons.

The critical test is whether the applicant is less able to fend for him/herself so that s/he will suffer injury or detriment, in circumstances where a less vulnerable person would be able to cope without harmful effects. People who live or might reasonably be expected to live with a vulnerable person are also in priority need.

14.6. **Old age:** while age alone may not necessarily be sufficient for the applicant to be deemed vulnerable the authority should consider whether it is a factor which makes the applicant less able to fend for him/herself. All applications from people aged over 60 need to be considered carefully especially where the applicant is leaving tied accommodation. However, authorities should not use 60 as a fixed age beyond which vulnerability occurs automatically: each case will need to be considered on its individual circumstances.

14.7. **Mental illness or learning or physical disability:** authorities should have regard to any medical advice or social services advice that they obtain, but the final decision on the question of vulnerability will rest with the authority. Factors which an authority may wish to consider are:

— the nature and extent of illness which may render the applicant vulnerable; and
— the relationship between the illness or disability and the individual's housing difficulties.

Information about an applicant's illness or disability should be treated in strict confidence.

14.8. Health authorities have an express duty (advice contained in Department of Health circulars HC (90)23 and LASSL (90)11) to implement a specifically tailored care programme for all patients considered for discharge from psychiatric hospitals and all new patients accepted by the specialist psychiatric services. People discharged from psychiatric hospitals and local authority hostels by those with mental health problems may be vulnerable. Effective liaison between housing, social services and health authorities will assist in such cases but authorities also need to be sensitive to direct approaches from discharged patients who are homeless. Physical disability or long-term acute illness, such as those defined by the **Disability Discrimination Act 1996,** which impinge on the applicant's housing situation and give rise to vulnerability may be readily ascertainable, but advice from health or social services staff should be sought if necessary.

14.9. **Chronically sick, including AIDS and HIV:** chronically sick people, including people with AIDS and HIV related illnesses, may be vulnerable not only because their illness has progressed to the point of physical or mental disability (when they would anyway be vulnerable and in priority need under the 1996 Act) but because the manifestations or effects of their illness, or common attitudes to it, make it very difficult for them to find stable or suitable accommodation. This may be particularly true of people with AIDS, or even people who are infected with HIV without having any overt signs or symptoms if the nature of their infection is known.

14.10. **Other special reason:** authorities should determine whether applicants are vulnerable for "other special reason". Authorities should consider the following:

Young people (16 or over): vulnerability should not automatically be judged on age alone but authorities should consider the extent to which a young person is "at risk" and therefore vulnerable. Risks could arise from:

— fear of or actual violence or sexual abuse from a person with whom s/he is associated;
— the likelihood of drug or alcohol abuse; or
— prostitution.

Some young people may be less able than others to fend for themselves for example:

— those leaving or who have been in local authority care;
— juvenile offenders (including those discharged from young offender institutions);
— those who have been physically or sexually abused;

— those with learning disabilities;
— those who have been the subject of statements of special educational need;
— those who lack family contact and support.

These examples do not constitute a complete list: authorities are advised to liaise with social services authorities when considering individual cases, for example through joint assessment or other procedures.

14.11. Research has shown that care leavers are amongst the most vulnerable groups of young people and are heavily over-represented in the young homeless population. For part or most of their childhood they have been looked after (either on the basis of a Care Order or "accommodation") by local authorities. In recognition of the vulnerability of this group and the inability, in many cases, of their families to support them, the **Children Act 1989** places duties and responsibilities on local authorities to give care leavers continuing advice and assistance until their early twenties. It is therefore important that, whenever possible, any housing needs of care leavers are addressed before they leave care, and that arrangements are made for joint assessment between social services and housing authorities.

14.12. For young people who have not been in care, authorities may wish to consider the possibility of a reconciliation between the applicant and his/her family. However, such reconciliations are likely to need careful brokering and may need the assistance of social services. In some instances, it may not be possible for young people to return home safely.

14.13. The **Children Act 1989 (s. 20(3))** places a duty on social service authorities to provide accommodation for a child in need aged 16 or over whose welfare is otherwise likely to be seriously prejudiced if they do not provide accommodation; and **s. 20(1)** places a duty to provide accommodation for children in need in certain other circumstances. The social services authority may be able to provide accommodation from their own resources, or from those provided by the voluntary or private sector. Where they are otherwise unable to provide, the social services authority may seek the help of the housing authority which is required to respond **(s. 27(2))** provided this is compatible with their own statutory duties and does not unduly prejudice the discharge of their functions. Children should not be provided with accommodation by the social services authority as a result purely of family homelessness.

14.14. The Secretaries of State are concerned to prevent children and young people being sent to and fro between authorities. Each authority has a responsibility to those who approach them under the appropriate legislation. However, in order to provide an effective safety net for homeless young people it is necessary for homeless and social services to work together. Effective collaborative working is best facilitated by corporate policies and clear department procedures between social services and housing departments. Such procedures should make it clear who takes responsibility in cases where there is any room for dispute. Agreements will be most useful if they cover not only assessment, but also planning for and delivery of provision. Such agreements should be an outcome of the joint policies envisaged by the **Children Act 1989** Guidance and Regulations and of the requirement on local authorities to produce Children's Services Plans on an inter-agency basis. Authorities should consider the possibility of joint training for social services and housing department staff.

14.15. The Housing Corporation has recently published a research report on the housing needs of young people aged 16–17 and a good practice guide for registered social landlords on housing such young people.

14.16. Where accommodation is secured for a young person consideration should be given to what ongoing support and assistance s/he may need from social services or voluntary organisations to ensure that homelessness does not recur.

14.17. **Victims of violence or abuse or sexual and/or racial harassment:** authorities should consider whether men and women without children are vulnerable as a result of having suffered violence or abuse from persons with whom they are associated, or whether they are at risk of further violence or abuse if they return to those persons. They should also consider whether those who have suffered or are under threat of harassment or violence on account of their gender, race, colour, ethnic or national origin, or religion, are vulnerable — and therefore in priority need — as a result.

Homeless as a result of an emergency

14.18. An applicant has a priority need if s/he became homeless or threatened with homelessness as a result of an emergency such as fire, flood or other disaster (**s. 189(1)(d)**). A person has a priority need by reason of an emergency, whether or not s/he has dependent children or is vulnerable for one of the reasons described above.

15. Intentional Homelessness

15.1. The nature of an authority's duties towards those who are homeless and have a priority need will depend upon whether they became homeless or threatened with homelessness intentionally. **Section 191** of the 1996 Act defines the circumstances in which an applicant is to be regarded as having become homeless intentionally. **Section 196** frames the same definitions in regard to someone threatened with homelessness. Decisions on intentionality must follow from the investigations carried out on each individual case; general policies which seek to predefine what is and what is not intentional homelessness cannot be applied. Authorities should remember that it is for them to satisfy themselves whether an applicant is homeless or threatened with homelessness intentionally. The onus is not on the applicant. Authorities are required to form a view in the light of all their enquiries about the particular case. Nevertheless, authorities must always have in mind that in housing someone who has made him/herself homeless intentionally, or for whom adequate family accommodation is available, they are likely to displace those who are in a less fortunate position.

Definitions of intentional homelessness

15.2. The 1996 Act sets out three ways in which a person can become homeless or threatened with homelessness intentionally. The first (**s. 191(1) and (2) and s. 196(1) and (2)**) has three component parts:

 a) the applicant must deliberately have done, of failed to do something, in consequence of which s/he has ceased, or the likely result will be that s/he will have to cease, occupation of accommodation which was, or is available;
 b) it must have been reasonable for the applicant to have continued to occupy accommodation; and
 c) the applicant must have been aware of all the facts before deliberately taking, or failing to take, the actions referred to in a) — an act or omission in good faith on the part of someone unaware of any relevant facts is not to be regarded as deliberate.

15.3. The second (**s. 191(2) and s. 196(3)**) has four parts:

 a) the applicant enters into an arrangement under which s/he is required to cease to occupy the accommodation;
 b) it must have been reasonable for the applicant to have continued to occupy accommodation;
 c) the purpose of the arrangement is to enable the applicant to become entitled to assistance under Part VII of the 1996 Act; and
 d) there is no other good reason why s/he is homeless or threatened with homelessness.

15.4. The third (**s. 191(4) and s. 196(4)**) provides that those applicants who are given advice and assistance to secure accommodation under **s. 197** (which sets out the authority's duty where other suitable accommodations is available) but fail to secure it when it could be reasonably expected that they would do so will be treated as having become intentionally homeless or threatened with homelessness if they make a further homelessness application.

Who is intentionally homeless?

15.5. When assessing intentionality, authorities will need to ascertain the real cause of the present homelessness; this may involve consideration of accommodation occupied prior to the most recent period of occupation of accommodation which may have been available for only a limited period of time.

15.6. The act or omission referred to in paragraph 15.2. must have been **deliberate**. An applicant should always be given an opportunity to explain an act or omission. Generally the following may not be considered deliberate:

a) where the authority has reason to believe the applicant is incapable of managing his/her affairs, for example on account of old age, or mental illness or handicap. Social services may be of help in making this assessment;

b) where an applicant has lost his/her home or was obliged to sell it because s/he got into rent or mortgage arrears because of real financial difficulties (for example because s/he became unemployed or ill or suffered greatly reduced earnings or family breakdown) and genuinely could not keep up the rent payments or loan repayments even after claiming benefits, and for whom no further financial help is available. In the case of mortgagors, authorities need to look at the applicant's ability to pay the mortgage commitment when it was taken on, given his/her financial circumstances at the time;

c) where an owner occupier, who is faced with foreclosure or possession proceedings to which there is no defence, sells before the mortgagee recovers possession through the courts or surrenders the property to the lender; or

d) where a tenant, faced with possession proceedings to which there is no defence and where the granting of a possession order is mandatory, surrenders the property to the landlord.

15.7. Acts or omissions which may be regarded as deliberate could include the following examples:

a) where someone chooses to sell his/her home in circumstances where s/he is under no risk of losing it, or has lost it because of wilful and persistent refusal to pay rent or mortgage payments;

b) where someone could be said to have neglected his/her affairs having disregarded advice from qualified persons;

c) voluntary surrender of adequate accommodation in this country or abroad which it would have been reasonable for the applicant to continue to occupy;

d) where someone is evicted because of anti-social behaviour such as nuisance to neighbours, harassment etc; or

e) where someone leaves a job with tied accommodation and the circumstances indicate that it would have been reasonable for him/her to continue in the employment.

These examples do not constitute a comprehensive list.

15.8. Authorities should note that where they house someone with physical or mental health problems it is important that a proper care and support package from the social services authority is in place to ensure that any circumstances that could lead to eviction and the possibility of an intentionality determination are dealt with at an early stage. The local authority must satisfy themselves that any actions or omissions were deliberate. The draft DoE Circular 'Part V of the Housing Act 1996 — Conduct of Tenants', issued for consultation on October 16, 1996, gives advice on the handling of vulnerable tenants when they are offered introductory tenancies. The advice is equally relevant to those tenants being offered a secure tenancy.

Acts or omissions in good faith

15.9. Acts or omissions in good faith where someone is unaware of a relevant fact must not be regarded as deliberate.

Enters into an arrangement etc.

15.10. Authorities will need to be alert to the possibility of collusion by which a person may claim that s/he is obliged to leave accommodation in order to take advantage of the homelessness legislation. Collusion is not confined to those staying with friends or relatives but can also occur between landlords and tenants. Authorities need to use their experience and knowledge to identify possible collusion but must be aware that they will need to be "satisfied" that it exists, and not merely rely on hearsay or unfounded suspicions. The 1996 Act also requires that "no other good reasons exists" for the homelessness. Examples of other good reasons would include overcrowding or an obvious breakdown in relationships between the applicant and the "host" household. In most cases, home visits will be helpful in determining whether or not collusion has taken place.

Failure to secure suitable alternative accommodation

15.11. **Section 197** provides that where there would be a duty to secure accommodation but the authority are satisfied that other suitable accommodation is available in the district, the duty owed is to provide such advice and assistance as the authority consider is reasonably required to enable the applicant to secure the other accommodation. For example the applicant may be provided with information about sources of accommodation and advised about what steps to take to secure it. If the authority consider that the advice and information is sufficient to enable the applicant to secure accommodation they will have discharged their duty to him/her. However, if the applicant subsequently returns having, for example, failed to follow the advice then s/he may be treated as having become intentionally homeless if s/he makes a further application, where the authority determine that it was reasonably to be expected that the applicant would have secure that accommodation.

Whose conduct results in intentional homelessness?

15.12. It is the applicant who must deliberately have done or failed to do something which resulted in homelessness or threatened homelessness. Nothing in the 1996 Act prevents another member of the household from making a separate application. For example an applicant may have deliberately failed to pay the rent or defaulted on the mortgage payments, which resulted in homelessness or threatened homelessness, against the wishes or without the knowledge of his/her husband or wife. If the husband or wife makes a separate application then s/he might be found to be intentionally homeless if there is evidence of acquiescence, *e.g.* was s/he a party to his/her spouse's act or omission, or of a failure to take reasonable steps to prevent the homelessness. Careful consideration will need to be given to cases involving former joint tenants or mortgagors where both are legally responsible for the rent or mortgage payments, regardless of who actually makes the payments.

When can someone re-apply?

15.13. There is no period of disqualification if someone wants to re-apply as homeless after s/he has been found intentionally homeless. The authority will need to make their usual enquiries and to consider whether the applicant's circumstances have changed.

Families

15.14. All persons found to be intentionally homeless who have dependent children should be referred to the social services authority for assessment under the **Children Act 1989**.

16. Referral to Another Local Housing Authority

16.1. If an authority are satisfied that an applicant is:

— eligible for assistance;
— homeless; and
— in priority need,

and are not satisfied that s/he became homeless intentionally, they may also consider whether the conditions are met for referral of the case to another local housing authority. One of the conditions for referral is whether the applicant has a local connection with the district of another authority.

What is a local connection?

16.2. Local connection is defined in **s. 199** of the 1996 Act as a connection which the applicant has with an area:

a) because s/he is, or was in the past, normally resident in it, and that residence was of his/her own choice;
b) because s/he is employed in it (*i.e.* the applicant actually works in the area rather than that the area is the site of his/her employer's head office);
c) because of family associations; or
d) because of any special circumstances.

In assessing whether a household has a local connection with their own area, an authority should also consider whether any person who might reasonably be expected to live with the applicant has such a connection.

Transfer of the duty to secure accommodation

16.3. **Section 198** of the 1996 Act provides that if an authority would otherwise be under a duty under **s. 193** (duty to persons with priority need who are not homeless intentionally) but believe that:

a) neither the applicant nor any person who might reasonably be expected to live with the applicant has a local connection with its area; but
b) one of them has a local connection with the area of another authority; and
c) none of them will be at risk of domestic violence in the area of that authority,

then the authority may seek to refer the applicant to the other authority. In addition, the conditions for referral are also met if the applicant was placed in accommodation in the area of the authority to which his/her application is now made in discharge of a homelessness duty arising from a previous application made to another authority within a prescribed period. That period is the aggregate of five years plus the length of time between the date the application was made to the other authority and the date when accommodation was first made available (under **s. 193(2)** or **s. 195(4)**).

16.4. In other words, where an authority accept a duty to secure accommodation for two years (under **s. 193(2)** or **s. 195(4)**) and places the household in accommodation which is out-of-area, the authority retains "responsibility" for the household in the event of a further two-year duty being owed within a period of five years of the date when accommodation was first made available under the initial duty.

16.5. The referral provisions arise **only** when an authority would be under the main duty to secure accommodation under **s. 193**; they do not apply where someone is threatened with homelessness or is homeless intentionally. It arises where there is no local connection with the authority receiving the application (apart from certain cases involving domestic violence). The authority may not seek to transfer responsibility to another authority merely because the applicant has a stronger local connection elsewhere. However this need not prevent arrangements being made with another authority for that other authority to assist them in securing accommodation under **s. 213** of the 1996 Act (co-operation between authorities). The decision to seek to transfer the duty is discretionary; a local authority can decide not to transfer the duty if they do wish. Where a person has a local connection with more than one other authority, the referring authority will wish to take account of the applicant's preference in deciding which authority to notify.

Domestic violence

16.6. An authority cannot seek to refer to another authority if by doing so any member of the applicants household would be at risk of domestic violence from a person with whom s/he is associated or is at risk of threats of violence which are likely to be carried out.

Servicemen and women

16.7. For the purposes of the 1996 Act, a serviceman will not normally have a local connection solely by virtue of serving or having served in the Forces in an area (**s. 199(2)** and **s. 199(3)**). A local connection with an authority may exist for one of the specified reasons, but if the applicant or anyone who might reasonably be expected to live with him/her has no such connection with any area, then the duty to secure accommodation will rest with the authority to which s/he applies.

Ex-prisoners

16.8. Similarly, residence in prison does not itself establish a local connection with an area. However, any period of residence in accommodation prior to imprisonment may give rise to a local connection under **s. 199(1)(a)**.

No local connecting anywhere in Great Britain

16.9. If a person accepted as eligible for assistance, unintentionally homeless and in priority need has no local connection with the area of any housing authority in Great Britain, then the duty to secure accommodation for him/her rests with the authority to which s/he applied for assistance.

Procedure for transfer

16.10. When, having carried out their enquiries, the authority have notified or intend to notify another authority that they consider that the conditions for referral are met, they must also notify the applicant accordingly. At that point, the authority cease to be subject to the interim duty to accommodate (**s. 188**) but they have a duty under **s. 220(1)** to secure that accommodation continues to be available until the referral is accepted or otherwise.

16.11. The referring authority will need to notify the other authority that they believe the conditions for referral are met (**s. 198(1)**). If the other authority accept the referral, they are under a duty to secure accommodation for the applicant while they consider whether other suitable accommodation is available in their district for the applicant (**s. 200(4)**). If they believe it is available, then the duty to provide advice and assistance under **s. 197(2)** applies, and, if not, the duty to secure accommodation (**s. 193**) applies. If it is decided that the conditions for referral are not met, the referring authority are required to follow the same steps, *i.e.* to secure accommodation while they consider whether other suitable accommodation is available in their area, and then accept a duty under either **s. 197(2)** or **s. 193(2)**, as the case may be.

16.12. In the event of a dispute between the authorities, the question of whether conditions for a referral are met should be decided by agreement between the authorities concerned, but if they cannot agree, the decision should be made in accordance with arrangements directed by order of the Secretary of State. A revised Local Authority Association Joint Local Connection Agreement is now being concluded.

16.13. The applicant must be given written notice of the outcome of the referral by the notifying authority. The notice must also inform the applicant of his/her right to request a review of the decision as to whether the conditions for referral are met and the time by which s/he must make the request.

17. Notification and review

17.1. When a housing authority have completed their enquiries under **s. 184**, they must notify the applicant in writing of their decision as to whether s/he is eligible for assistance and whether any duty is owed (and if so, which duty) under Part VII. Where the authority intend to refer the applicant to another authority, they must also notify the applicant of this.

17.2. In addition, the authority must include in the notification:

— the reasons for any decision which is against the interest of the applicant, *e.g.* the applicant is not eligible for assistance, is not homeless, is not in priority need, is homeless intentionally. They must also give reasons where they have reached a decision to refer the applicant to another authority;

— information about the applicant's right to a review and the time in which a request for a review must be made.

If an authority has lost touch with the applicant, they must keep available the written statement of their decision, and any reasons for it, for reasonable period at their office for the applicant or someone who represents the applicant to collect.

17.3. It is good practice for an authority to notify an applicant of their decisions within three working days of the decisions being made. The authority will wish to aim to ensure the notification explains clearly and fully the reasons for the decisions (where required) and what, if anything, the authority will now do to assist the applicant. It will be particularly important to ensure that the applicant fully understands the nature of any housing duty that is owed. Where possible, the decisions should not only be provided in writing but also explained in person to the applicant particularly where s/he may have difficulty understanding the consequences of the decisions.

Withdrawn applications

17.4. Authorities will need to consider procedures for dealing with applications that are withdrawn or where the applicant fails to maintain contact before a decision is made on his/her application. It is good practice for applications to be considered for closure if there has been no contact with the applicant for more than three months. Any further approach from the applicant after this time may need to be considered as a new application. If the applicant contacts the authority again before his/her application is closed the authority will need to consider any change if circumstances since the last contact with the applicant.

Reviews

17.5. Under **s. 202** of the 1996 Act an applicant has the right to request a review of any decision of the local authority:

a) on his/her eligibility for assistance (**s. 184**);

   b) on what duty (if any) is owed under;
      i) **ss. 190 and 191** (intentional homelessness);
      ii) **s. 192** (no priority need and homeless unintentionally);
      iii) **s. 193** (duty to secure accommodation for the minimum period);
      iv) **s. 195** (threatened with homelessness);
      v) **s. 196** (threatened with homelessness intentionally);
      vi) **s. 197** (other suitable accommodation);
   c) to notify another authority that the conditions for referral are met (**s. 198(1)**);
   d) on whether the conditions for referral are met (**s. 198(5)**);
   e) as to the duty owed in the case of a referral (**ss. 200(3) and (4)**);
   f) on the suitability of accommodation offered under (b) or (e) above.

17.6. There is no right to request a review of a decision on an earlier review (**s. 202(2)**) and a request for a review must be made within 21 days of the applicant being notified of an authority's decision. However, the authority may specify, in writing, a longer period (**s. 202(3)**).

17.8. The authority, or authorities, concerned must notify the applicant of a decision on the review. Reasons for the decision must also be given if it confirms an original decision against the applicant's interests or confirms a decision to transfer the applicant to another authority. At the same time they must inform the applicant of his/her right to appeal to a county court on a point of law (see **s. 204**) and of the period in which the appeal must be made (**s. 203**).

17.9. The Secretary of State will, by regulation, set out the procedures to be followed by authorities in reviewing their decisions and further guidance on this will be issued in due course.

18. Decisions and Duties

18.1. Where an authority consider that an applicant may be homeless, eligible for assistance and in priority need, they are under a duty (**s. 188**) to secure accommodation pending a decision as to what further duty under Part VII may be owed. Any further duty towards a homeless applicant is determined by the outcome of their enquiries. This chapter summarises those duties for easy reference; all of the duties are described fully in this Code.

a) Not eligible for assistance:

No duty owed (apart from securing that advice is available under **s. 179**).

b) Eligible for assistance, but not homeless or threatened with homelessness:

No duty owed (apart from securing that advice is available under **s. 179**).

c) Eligible for assistance, homeless or threatened with homelessness, but not in priority need:

Appropriate advice and assistance in any attempt by applicant to secure own accommodation (**s. 192(2)**) or to prevent loss of accommodation (**s. 195(5)**);

d) Eligible for assistance, homeless and in priority need but homeless intentionally:

Accommodation for a reasonable period to give the applicant an opportunity to find his/her own accommodation and offer appropriate advice and assistance (**s. 190(2)**).

e) Eligible for assistance, threatened with homelessness and in priority need but threatened with homelessness intentionally:

Appropriate advice and assistance to prevent loss of accommodation (**s. 195(5)**).

f) Eligible for assistance, homeless, in priority need and not homeless intentionally:

Advice and assistance to enable applicant to secure other suitable accommodation (**s. 197(2)**) available in the area. If no other suitable accommodation available, duty to secure suitable accommodation for two years (**s. 193(2)**).

g) Eligible for assistance, homeless, in priority need and not homeless intentionally but applicant being referred to another local authority:

Secure accommodation until referral agreed by other authority (**s. 200(1)**).

h) Eligible for assistance, threatened with homelessness, in priority need but not threatened with homelessness intentionally:

Advice and assistance to enable applicant to secure other suitable accommodation available in the area (**s. 197**). If no other suitable accommodation available, take reasonable steps to secure that accommodation does not cease to be available (**s. 195(2)**).

19. Protection of Property

19.1. Where the authority have become subject to a duty to:

— secure interim accommodation under **s. 188** or **s. 200;**
— secure accommodation under **s. 190(2)(a);**
— secure accommodation under **s. 193(2)** or **s. 195(4);**

they are required, whether or not they are still subject to a duty, to protect the property of the homelessness person if there is a danger of loss or damage to it (**s. 211(2)**). In other cases the authority have a power to take similar action if they wish.

19.2. Applicants may be unable to protect their property if, for example, they are ill, or are unable to afford to have it stored themselves. In order to protect applicants' property, authorities can enter the applicants' homes or their last home, and deal with the property in any way which seems reasonably necessary (**s. 212(1)**). They may store the property or arrange for it to be stored; this may be appropriate where the applicant is accommodated in furnished accommodation for a period. In some cases, where the previous home is not to be occupied immediately, it may be possible to leave the property there if it can be adequately protected.

19.3. The applicant can also request the authority to move his/her property to a particular location. If the authority consider it reasonable to do so they will discharge their duty or power by doing as s/he asks and must inform the applicant that this will be the case (**s. 212(2)**). Authorities may make a reasonable charge for storing protected property, and can reserve the right to dispose of it if the applicant loses touch with them and cannot be traced after a specified period (**s. 211(4)**).

19.4. The duty or power ceases when the authority believes there is no longer any serious risk of damage to it. This may be the case, for example, where the applicant has recovered from illness or finds accommodation where s/he can put his/her possessions or where s/he is able to afford the storage costs him/herself. However, authorities have a discretion to continue to store the property (**s. 212(3)**) if they wish.

19.5. Where the authority ceases to be under a duty or cease exercising the power to protect an applicant's property they must notify the applicant and give reasons. The notification must be delivered to the applicant or sent to his/her last known address (**s. 212(5)**).

20. Securing Accommodation

Interim duty to accommodate

20.1. A duty to secure accommodation for an applicant can arise even before an authority has carried out all its enquiries. If a housing authority have reason to believe, pending full enquiry, that an applicant may:

    a) be eligible for assistance; and
    b) be homeless; and
    c) have a priority need,

they have to secure that accommodation is available for the applicant until they make a decision **(s. 188)**. This duty arises irrespective of whether the applicant has a local connection with another authority. The interim duty ends once the authority have notified the applicant of their decision on his/her homeless application, even if the applicant requests a review of the decision. Should the decision be that no further duty is owed, the authority will wish to give the applicant reasonable notice to quit the accommodation provided under the interim duty. However the local authority can, if they wish, continue to secure that the accommodation is available pending the outcome of a review. In some instances advice or support may prevent or delay homelessness and allow the applicant to remain in his/her existing accommodation until the authority have finalised their enquiries. The help that can be offered by a housing advisory service may be appropriate.

20.2. While circumstances may on some occasions require the use of bed and breakfast accommodation to provide emergency accommodation, this will generally be as a last resort, and should not be regarded as suitable accommodation for families with children. The legislation requires that all accommodation secured must be suitable.

Accommodation for those found to be intentionally homeless

20.3. **Section 190(2)** provides that where an applicant is found to be eligible for assistance, intentionally homeless and in priority need, the authority must secure that accommodation is available for a period that will give him/her a reasonable opportunity to secure accommodation for him/herself. In most areas 28 days might be expected to provide adequate time for the applicant, but authorities will need to take account of local circumstances, including how readily other accommodation is available in the area and the particular circumstances of the applicant.

20.4. Authorities must also offer an applicant found to be eligible for assistance and intentionally homeless (whether or not in priority need) advice and such assistance as they consider appropriate to help him/her secure accommodation for him/herself **(s. 190(2)(b) and (3))**.

Other suitable accommodation

20.5. The duty under **(s. 197(2)** (duty where other suitable accommodation is available) can be seen as an intermediate stage between the advisory role of the local authority and their full housing duty. The applicant is required to take responsibility for securing his/her own accommodation with the help of the authority. The authority are not required to secure the accommodation themselves (as they would be under their full housing duty). However the authority must be satisfied that suitable accommodation is available in their district. Authorities are likely to be familiar with the state of the local market and have links, perhaps through private landlords' fora, rent guarantee or rent deposits schemes, with local landlords and agencies that may have suitable accommodation for homeless applicants.

20.6. **Section 197** requires an authority to provide advice and assistance to applicants if they are satisfied that suitable accommodation is available for him/her in their district. The duty applies in cases where the authority would otherwise be under a duty to:

— secure accommodation for persons who are eligible for assistance, in priority need and not homeless intentionally **(s. 193)**; or

— prevent accommodation ceasing to be available for persons who are eligible for assistance, threatened with homelessness unintentionally and in priority need **(s. 195(2))**;

20.7. Also, where a local authority wish to exercise their power to provide a further period of accommodation **(s. 194)** they can only do so if they are satisfied that no other suitable accommodation is available in their district **(s. 194(2)(b))**. Authorities should assess whether suitable accommodation *is* available within their area at the time the accommodation is required to meet a housing duty (as specified above) and should not delay securing accommodation in the hope that other suitable accommodation *may* be available in the future.

20.8. When an applicant is threatened with homelessness, authorities should not seek to refer the applicant to other suitable accommodation if it would be less onerous for the authority to prevent the loss of the applicant's existing accommodation.

20.9. The 1996 Act requires that the advice and assistance given is commensurate with that which the authority consider is reasonably required to help the applicant secure suitable accommodation **(s. 197(2))**. In deciding what is reasonable the authority must take accound of the personal circumstances and characteristics of the applicant and the state of the local housing market including the type of accommodation available **(s. 197(4))**. For example, an applicant may have a disability which limits the type of accommodation that may be suitable and/or available to him/her or there may be a limited range of private accommodation available to families with children. The level of help will need to reflect the level of ability, disability or vulnerability of the applicant and anyone who might reasonably be expected to reside with him/her.

20.10. The authority should seek actively to assist the applicant in his/her efforts to secure accommodation. This may include offering rent guarantees or help with deposits. Authorities should seek to assist the applicant to find suitable accommodation that is available for as long a period as possible and avoid the possibility of homelessness recurring in the future. Provision of minimal assistance — such as only providing copies of local newspaper advertisements — is not likely to be sufficient to meet the duty.

20.11. It is important that authorities apply the duty sensitively and in a manner appropriate to the specific needs of the applicant. Some applicants may have little experience of dealing with private landlords and may require extensive advice and assistance to help them obtain accommodation, while others may only need to be put in touch with landlords who can offer suitable accommodation.

20.12. **Section 197(5)** provides that accommodation cannot be regarded as available if in order to secure it the applicant would require assistance beyond that which the authority consider is reasonable. For example, where substantial assistance would be required to secure the property and the authority could more cheaply provide accommodation in their own stock, the **s. 197** duty would not apply.

20.13. The accommodation must be **suitable.** In assessing this the authority should have regard to the same factors as are applied to accommodation secured by them directly **(s. 210)**. Authorities must be satisfied that suitable accommodation can be secured by that applicant, *e.g.* the landlord is prepared to offer a tenancy to a single parent who keeps normal pets. Directing applicants to accommodation which is not suitable would not discharge the authority's responsibility.

20.14. An authority cease to be under a duty towards the applicant if, having been given the appropriate advice and assistance by the authority, s/he fails to take reasonable steps to secure suitable accommodation which the authority consider is available to him/her **(s. 197(3))**. In this case, s/he will be treated as having become intentionally homeless if s/he makes a further application **(s. 191(4)** and **s. 196(4))**. Authorities should not assume automatically, without further enquiry, that failure to secure accommodation is the result of the applicant's failure to take reasonable steps: each case will need to be considered on its merits.

When is a local authority required to secure accommodation for the minimum period?

20.15. When a local authority are satisfied that an applicant:

  a) is eligible for assistance; and
  b) is homeless or threatened with homelessness (and it is not possible to secure that the existing accommodation continues to be available); and

c) has a priority need; and
d) is not intentionally homeless; and
e) the authority are satisfied that other suitable accommodation is *not* available in their district,

they are under a duty to secure accommodation for a period of two years: this is referred to in the 1996 Act as the "minimum period".

20.16. The point at which the two-year period of duty starts depends on the circumstances of the case. If the applicant is already being accommodated under **s. 188,** the period begins when the applicant is notified of the authority's decision that a duty is owed under **s. 193(2).** If the applicant is already being accommodated under **s. 200(3),** the period begins when the applicant is notified that the conditions for referral are not met. In any other case, the period starts on the first day that accommodation is made available under the two-year duty. Authorities are required to secure "suitable accommodation": wherever possible, they should avoid unnecessarily short-term accommodation once the minimum period has started.

Accommodation during the minimum period of duty

20.17. Where a duty is owed under **s. 193(2)** or **s. 195(4),** a local housing authority are required to secure that accommodation is available for a period of two years (the minimum period), at the end of which they are under no further duty unless a fresh application is successful and a new duty occurs. Any further period is at the discretion of the authority.

20.18. When accommodation is secured for the applicant is is good practice to inform him/her at the outset of the procedure which the authority intend to follow at the end of the period and the circumstances under which the authority may continue to provide accommodation thereafter. The authority will need to explain the nature of their duty clearly and that the duty is limited to two years to ensure that the applicant is fully aware of his/her position. There is no statutory requirement for giving notice at the end of a two-year period. In many cases such notice will be served where a tenancy is to be determined. Where there is no such determination, authorities will wish to ensure that notice is given nonetheless.

20.19. When accommodation has been secured for homeless people the authority will need to maintain contact with them, *e.g.* to arrange for them to move from interim accommodation, or to check that they are making use of the accommodation provided for them. Such contact provide an opportunity to identify any support needs that emerge, and to notify social services or other agencies.

20.20. Persons owed the minimum period of duty who are over 18 years of age will have the right to appear on the housing register. In many cases applicants to whom a duty is owed will, if they are in need of long term housing, fall within the reasonable preference categories for housing allocation under **s. 167** (the allocation scheme). It is open to authorities to put the names of everyone owed the minimum period of duty on the register, regardless of whether or not they request it.

20.21. The circumstances may be such that the applicant could be allocated long term accommodation through the local housing authority's allocation scheme within substantially less than the two years. The two year period of duty does not pre-empt immediate allocation of long term housing *if* the applicant has the necessary priority under the local authority's allocation scheme. Proper liaison between relevant local authority sections needs to be in place to ensure that such priority is identified and acted upon as soon as possible. The possibility that an applicant may be allocated long term housing in the near future can be taken into account in determining the type of accommodation to be secured in any intervening period, particularly in regard to any contractual commitments that the authority may have to enter into for private sector accommodation, provided of course that the accommodation is suitable.

20.22. The authority will cease to be subject to the duty to secure accommodation for the minimum period if at any time the applicant:

a) accepts an offer of accommodation through the allocation scheme **(Part VI of the 1996 Act), (s.193(6)(c))**;

b) refuses an offer of suitable accommodation, which the authority have notified the applicant as discharging the duty under **s. 193**, having been informed by the authority of the possible consequences of refusal **(s. 193(5))**;

c) ceases to be eligible for assistance as defined in **s. 185 and s.186** of the 1996 Act;

d) becomes homeless intentionally from accommodation made available to him/her under **s. 193**;

e) otherwise voluntarily ceases to occupy as his/her only or principal home the accommodation made available under **s. 193**;

f) refuses an offer of accommodation under **Part VI** (the allocation scheme) having been informed of the possible consequences of refusal **(s. 193(7)(a))**. The authority must be satisfied **(s. 193(7)(b))** that the accommodation offered was suitable and that it was reasonable for the applicant to accept it and must notify the applicant within 21 days of refusal that their duty has ceased. In the event of the applicant having contractual or other obligations in respect of his/her existing accommodation (*e.g.* a tenancy agreement or lease), under **s. 193(8)** the authority can reasonably expect on offer to be taken up if the applicant is able to bring those obligations to an end before s/he is required to take up the offer under Part VI.

A person who ceases to be owed a duty under **s. 193(2)** can make a fresh application (**s. 193(9)**).

Further periods of accommodation

20.23. Authorities have the power to continue to secure accommodation for further periods of up to two years, although most applicants in long-term housing need are likely to have been allocated accommodation through the housing register before the end of the minimum period.

20.24. An authority can determined to continued to secure accommodation for further periods of up to two years, subject to reviewing the applicant's circumstances before offering a further period. An authority may wish to put in place arrangements to ensure that two yearly reviews are carried out systematically and that applicants are kept fully informed of their situation. It will be open to the applicant to enquire of the authority what they intend to do when the minimum period ends and, if the authority determined not to offer a further period, to consider making a fresh application.

20.25. If they are considering providing a further period of accommodation, towards the end of the minimum period, or any subsequent two year period, the authority must assess the household's likely situation at the end of that period. **Section 194** requires that they must do so by making any necessary enquiries to satisfy themselves that:

a) the person continues to have a priority need (**s. 194(2)(a)**);
b) there is no other suitable accommodation available for his/her occupation in their district (**s. 194(2)(b)**);
c) the applicant wishes the authority to continue to assist (**s. 194(2)(c)**); and
d) s/he is still an eligible person.

20.26. On completing the review the authority must notify the person of the outcome and whether they propose to continue to secure accommodation. An authority must cease to exercise the power to secure accommodation under **s. 194** if any of the events listed in **s. 193(6)** or **(7)** occur, such as the person becoming homeless intentionally from that accommodation.

20.27. An authority may give notice that they propose to cease exercising their power to continue securing accommodation, either as a result of a review or at any time and, if so, must notify the person of any action they may be taking in consequence, such as deciding to evict from accommodation provided from their own stock or withdrawing any support such as rent guarantees in the case of other accommodation. A person does not have a right of appeal against the decision but can make a fresh application to the authority. The notification should be given 28 days in advance of the date they propose to cease exercising the power, in accordance with regulations made under **s. 194(6))**.

20.28. Authorities will wish to take account of a range of factors in determining whether to exercise their power to continue to secure accommodation after the minimum period of duty. A key factor will be whether the household would be homeless again if they did not, but account may also need to be taken of the efforts the household have made themselves during the period to secure their own accommodation. Where a person is likely to be allocated housing through the allocations scheme, or may secure it from some other source in the foreseeable future, an authority may decided that a further period of accommodation is in the best interests of the authority and the household. If they are clear that there is every likelihood of a further successful application under Part VII, they may feel it best to rely on the provisions of **s. 194**.

21. Discharge of Duty to Secure Accommodation

21.1. A local housing authority may discharge their duty to secure accommodation for the minimum period in a number of ways (**s. 206**):

    a) by providing accommodation themselves;

    b) by securing that the applicant obtains accommodation from another person; or

    c) by giving such advice and assistance as will enable the applicant to secure accommodation from another person.

A single offer of suitable accommodation discharges the local authority's (although a further offer may be necessary if the accommodation secured does not continue to be available for the full minimum period). Authorities need to bear in mind the need to achieve stability and will therefore wish to seek to secure accommodation which has a reasonable prospect of continuing to be available for at least the minimum period, wherever possible.

Available accommodation

21.2. The 1996 Act requires that the accommodation must be **available.** Accommodation is available only if it can take the whole household together, that is, the applicant and any other person who normally resides with him/her as a member of his/her family and any other person who might reasonably be expected to reside with him/her, *e.g.* a full-time carer.

Suitable accommodation

21.3. The 1996 Act also requires that accommodation must be *suitable*. In assessing this the 1996 Act **(s. 210)** requires authorities to have regard to **Part IX** (slum clearance), **Part X** (overcrowding) and **Part XI** (houses in multiple occupation) of the **Housing Act 1985**. The accommodation must be suitable in relation to the applicant (and to any member of his/her family who normally resides with him/her) and authorities should therefore have regard to the relevant circumstances of the applicant. Authorities also need to take account of any medical and physical needs or social considerations relating to the applicant that might affect the suitability of accommodation as well as other factors such as the risk of racial harassment or domestic violence, access to and stability in schools, and access to other facilities.

Location of accommodation

21.4. Local authorities should make every effort to secure accommodation within their own area, except where an applicant has been subject to domestic violence or is at risk of domestic violence and may need to be accommodated at a distance to reduce the risk of contact with the perpetrator(s). Authorities will wish to avoid putting people in isolated accommodation, away from public transport, shops and other facilities and need to make efforts, wherever possible, to secure accommodation within their own boundaries and as close as possible to where applicants were previously living so that they can keep the same schools, doctors, social workers, etc. Where an applicant is in paid employment account will need to be taken of his/her need to reach his/her workplace from the accommodation secured.

21.5. **Section 208(1)** requires authorities "as fas as reasonably practicable" to secure accommodation in their district but where this is not possible they are required under **s. 208(2)** to notify the local housing authority in whose area the accommodation is situated of:

   a) the name of the applicant;
   b) the number and description of other persons who nor-mally reside with the applicant as a member of his/her family or might reasonably be expected to do so;
   c) the address of the accommodation;
   d) the date on which the accommodation was made available;
   e) which function the authority was discharging in securing the accommodation.

the notice must be given in writing 14 days of the accommodation being made available. The placed household has the right to appear on the placing authority's housing register.

21.6. The Association of London Government has recently produced guidance to its members on this subject in the form of an **Inter-Borough Agreement on out-of-area placements of home-less housholds in the private rented sector.** While this was drawn up principally for use by London Boroughs, much of its content is relevant to the situation in other areas, and other authorities may wish to take note of it.

21.7. Wherever possible, households with a need for social services support should be given priority for accommodation within the authority's own boundaries. Where households have to be accommodated elsewhere, authorities need to ensure co-operation and liaison between service departments in each area *e.g.* environmental health, housing, social services, education and health services.

21.8. Authorities should be aware of the **Education (Areas to which Pupils and Students Belong) Regulations 1989,** which generally place responsibility for the provision of and payment for the education of pupils, and further education students from families placed in accommodation outside an authorities bound-aries, on the "receiving" authority. A general principle of the Regulations is that where such a pupil or student does not have ordinary residence, then s/he will be treated as belonging to the authority in which s/he is for the time being resident. The "receiving" authority is eligible for funding support for the education of such pupils.

Accommodation provided by the authority

Use of authority's own stock

21.9. In considering whether to provide accommodation in their own stock an authority will need to balance the limited require-ments in the short term from people who are homeless and the greater requirement from other for accommodation over the longer term. Priority should be accorded to long-term allocations provid-ing secure tenancies. However, local circumstances may allow, or require, the authority to set aside part of their own housing stock to provide for the needs of people accepted as homeless. Author-ities will need to consider whether the accommodation is suitable, and although hard-to-let accommodation may be suitable for emergency housing it should not generally be used as a matter of policy. Equally the concentration of homeless people in a particu-lar area or estate needs to be avoided.

21.10. The use of local authority stock which is awaiting demolition, improvement or repair, may in some circumstances offer suitable accommodation while at the same time avoiding stock needlessly standing empty. The property used should be in a reasonable state of repair and with adequate heating. The length of time that it is available needs also to be taken into account bearing in mind the need to provide stability for the houshold during the minimum period of duty.

21.11. **Section 207** require that authorities shall not provide accommodation in their own stock for more than two years continuously or two years in any three even if, during this period, more than one application for assistance has been accepted from the applicant. There are exceptions where accommodation is provided in a hostel or in accommodation leased to the authority from the private sector. From April 1, 1997, authorities will be able to lease such property for up to 10 years without setting aside capital cover equal to the cost of the lease. Under **s. 207(4)** an authority may apply to the Secretary of State for a waiver to extend the two-year limitation for up to a year at a time where the authority would not otherwise be able reasonably to discharge their homelessness functions.

Securing accommodation from another person

21.12. Where an authority secure accommodation from another landlord, they are equally bound to ensure that the accommodation is "available" and "suitable". Authorities can make use of a wide range of accommodation including housing in the private rented sector, and can ask registered social landlords to assist them.

21.13. The following paragraphs discuss the main options available to authorities:

a) Registered Social Landlords: If asked, registered social landlords are obliged (**s. 213**) to assist a local authority in carrying out their duties under the homelessness legislation by co-operating as far as is reasonable in the circumstances. In cases where whole stock transfers have taken place, assistance to the transfer landlord may need to be sought from other RSLs in the area. Most local authorities have links with registered social landlords in their area through nomination arrangements for long-term housing or through development of a common housing register. Similar links can be developed to secure accommodation for homeless applicants, although not all registered social landlords will have property which is appropriate for use in the short term. The Housing Corporation will be issuing its regulatory requirements on access to registered social landlord homes as part of its guidance on housing management (**s. 36** of the 1996 Act), which is planned to come into force on April 1, 1997. A good practice document on lettings will be issued at the same time. Where accommodation is provided to assist a housing authority to discharge an interim duty (*i.e.* under **s. 188, s. 190, s. 200** or **s. 204(4)**), a tenancy granted cannot be an assured tenancy unless the landlord notifies the applicant that it is, or unless 12 months have elapsed since the applicant was notified of the decision which brought the interim duty to an end. Where a RSL assists a housing authority to discharge any other homelessness duty, the tenancy granted will be an assured shorthold tenancy. Such a tenancy cannot be converted to an assured tenancy unless it is allocated through the housing register under Part VI (**s. 209(3)**).

    b) Private renting: An authority will benefit from building up contacts with reputable private landlords, and might consider contracts with private landlords to provide a readily accessible service. In March 1995, the Secretary of State issued a general consent to local authorities under **s. 25 of the Local Government Act 1988,** which, *inter alia,* allows, them to incur expenditure on rent deposits and guarantees to private landlords to help homeless people secure accommodation in the private sector.

21.14. Where tenancies secured in the private rented sector are assured shorthold tenancies, authorities will, where practicable, wish to ensure that accommodation is available either for an initial term of 2 years or, if less, that there is a reasonable prospect of the tenancy continuing beyond the initial shorthold term. In the event that a tenancy for less than two years is not renewed within the minimum period of duty, the authority will be under a continuing duty to secure accommodation until the end of the minimum period unless the applicant has made him/herself intentionally homeless, or there are other reasons why the duty to secure accommodation has ceased.

21.15. In some circumstances a social services authority may consider it appropriate to underwrite a tenancy agreement for people under 18 who are in priority need, for example a young pregnant women or a young person leaving care who cannot reasonably be expected to return to his/her family home.

    c) Private sector leasing: Leasing from the private sector can provide a ready source of accommodation for use by homeless people. From April 1, 1997 local authorities will be able to take out leases for up to 10 years on property owned by private landlords without being required to provide capital cover for the cost of the lease. In addition, there will be no restriction on their taking further leases on property which has been the subject of an earlier local authority lease.

    d) Lodgings: Lodgings provided by householders who are willing to offer accommodation may be suitable for some young and/or single people. It will be useful for authorities to establish a network of such landlords, and to liaise with social services who may operate supported lodgings schemes for people with support needs.

e) Hostels: As with people in lodgings there may be others who would benefit from the supportive environment provided by hostels. Hostels can offer those at crisis point some short term support to enable them to move on to independent living. Authorities should assess in co-operation with social services authorities whether a hostel can meet the continuing needs of a homeless person or whether further arrangements will have to be made before the end of the minimum period is reached. In cases where no social or other support worker is familiar with the applicant, a community care assessment may need to be requested, particularly if permanent support appears to be needed. It should not be assumed that hostels will automatically be the most appropriate form of accommodation for vulnerable people. Pregnant women in temporary hostel accommodation face particular problems where the accommodation is designed for single, childless people and is likely to be unsuitable for young children. In assessing whether it is reasonable for a woman to continue to occupy such accommodation, the authority may wish to take account of this and co-operate with hostel staff in seeking to rehouse the applicant prior to the birth of the child.

21.16. Authorities should bear in mind that some hostels are designed to meet short term needs only and are unlikely to be appropriate in fulfilling an authority's two year duty. If hostels are used authorities may seek to move homeless people into other accommodation at a suitable time, to ensure that bed space continue to be available to others in need. Authorities may also seek to provide assistance to homeless people they have placed in hostels to help them move on to other accommodation, perhaps in co-operation with social service authorities, the homelessness advisory service and other relevant statutory and voluntary organisations.

f) Other housing authorities: Another housing authority experiencing less demand for housing may be able to offer assistance with interim accommodation. This may be particularly relevant in the case of victims of violence and/or harassment who do not wish to return to the area where the perpetrator of the violence/harassment lives, or for assisting those with special housing needs. In some areas, local arrangements already exist, but even where they do not, one authority may seek the co-operation of another.

g) Other social landlords: Under s. 23 other social landlords, *i.e.* new town corporations, housing action trusts and in Scotland, registered housing associations, development corporations or Scottish Homes, have a duty to co-operate, as far as is reasonable in the circumstances, with a local authority in carrying out their homelessness functions under the 1996 Act if asked to do so.

h) Occupiers of caravans, houseboats etc, including gypsies: Under s. 175(2) someone is homeless if his/her accommodation is a caravan, houseboat, or other movable structure and s/he has no place where s/he is entitled or permitted to put it and live in it. If a duty to secure accommodation arised for this reason the authority is not required to make equivalent accommodation available, although of course it may do so if resources permit. This is particularly relevant in the case of applicants who are gypsies and travellers, who should be considered on the same basis as any other applicant. If no pitch or berth is available, it is open to the authority to arrange for some other form of suitable accommodation.

21.17. Other forms of housing sometimes used by local authorities which may be suitable in certain circumstances are:

i) Mobile homes: Although mobile homes may sometimes provide emergency accommodation *e.g.* to discharge the interim duty, they may not be satisfactory for households with children, or for the elderly or disabled people. Authorities should be satisfied that the accommodation is suitable paying particular regard to conditions and facilities on the site. Caravans designed primarily for holiday use should not be regarded as suitable for homeless people.

j) Women's refuges: Authorities are recommended to develop close links with local women's refuges in order to have access to emergency accommodation for women who have been subjected to violence or are at risk of violence. However, securing accommodation in a refuge may not count as a discharge of their duty. Refuges should be used for the minimum time necessary before securing suitable accommodation elsewhere. Authorities should not delay securing other accommodation for an applicant placed in a women's refuge in the hope that she might return to her partner. It is also important to ensure that places in refuges continued to be available for others in need. If the refuge terminates a licence to occupy because the household no longer need to be in the refuge, the authority have a duty to secure alternative accommodation straightaway.

k) Bed and breakfast: Authorities are urged to explore all alternatives before resorting to bed and breakfast hotels or other specialised bed and breakfast establishments. If, as a last resort, authorities have to use such accommodation as a short-term measure until more suitable accommodation is available they will wish to ensure that homeless people are allowed to use their rooms during the day and have adequate access to cooking facilities especially if there are young children. Authorities should ensure that such accommodation meets the statutory requirements on standards for houses in multiple occupation. Close working links between housing and environmental health departments are therefore important.

21.18. Authorities may wish to consider co-operating with other authorities in drawing up guidance to monitor conditions and safety standards in hotels used by a number of different agencies. An Agreement has been drawn up in London by the Association of London Government (ALG). Wherever possible authorities will need to try to ensure that bed and breakfast hotels and hostels in which families are placed provide adequate access to cooking and safe place areas separate from sleeping accommodation. Where breakfasts or other meals are provided by the hotel, authorities will wish to aim to ensure that the food provided is adequate. Where the authority considers food provisions is not adequate, or residents do not wish to take meals, they may wish to negotiate bed only arrangements.

Advice and assistance that will secure that suitable accommodation is available from some other person

21.19. The duty to secure accommodation can be fulfilled by giving such advice and assistance to the applicant as will secure that accommodation is available from some other person (s. 206(1)(c)). Unlike the advice and assistance duty owed to intentionally homeless and non priority homeless applicants, it requires that suitable accommodation must be secured as a result of the advice and assistance, rather than just assisting the applicant in any efforts s/he might make to find accommodation.

21.20. An example of securing accommodation in this way is where house purchase may be a possibility for the applicant. Advice on all options for financing house purchase should be made available, expecially those financial packages which may be attractive to people on lower incomes. One option for house purchase is shared ownership and authorities should maintain up to date information on the shared ownership schemes run in their area. The Housing Corporation and Housing for Wales have published separate leaflets on housing association shared ownership schemes provided by registered social landlords.

21.22. In other cases the applicant may have identified suitable accommodation and need practical advice and assistance to enable him/her to secure it. The assistance of the homelessness advisory service can be called on where appropriate. Authorities should bear in mind that the advice and assistance must lead to the securing of suitable accommodation and that applicants may need interim accommodation until the alternative accommodation is secured.

ANNEX A

Indicators of the criteria in the reasonable preference categories

Local housing authorities may devise their own indicators of the criteria in the reasonable preference categories (a) to (f) in **s. 167(2)**. The following list is included for illustrative pruposes and to assist authorities in this task: it is by no means comprehensive or exhaustive, and local authorities may have other, local factors to consider and include as indicators of the six criteria.

(a) Insanitary, overcrowded and unsatisfactory housing conditions

Lacking bathroom or kitchen
Lacking inside WC
Lacking cold or hot water supplies, electricity, gas, or adequate heating
Lack of access to a garden for children
Overcrowding
Sharing living room kitchen, bathroom/WC
Property in disrepair
Property unfit
Poor internal or external arrangements
Underoccupation
Children in flats or maisonettes above ground floor

(b) Temporary or insecure accommodation

Tied tenancies
Tenancies of a limited term
Hostel accommodation
Refuges for households escaping domestic violence
Living in homes to be demolished or modernised
Leaving institutional care
Sharing with friends or relatives
Facing eviction or repossesion
'Roofless'

(c) and (d) Families with dependent children or who may be expecting a child

Households containing at least one dependent child who lives or might reasonably be expected to live with the applicant
Households comprising or including a pregnant woman

(e) People with a particular need for settled accommodation on medical or welfare grounds (criteria may apply to any member of the household)

A mental illness or disorder

A physical or learning disability
Chronic or progressive medical conditions (*e.g.* MS, HIV/AIDS)
Infirmity due to old age
The need to give or receive care
The need to recover from the effects of violence (including racial attacks) or threats of violence, or physical, emotional or sexual abuse
Ability to fend for self restricted for other reasons
Young people at risk
People with behavioural difficulties
Need for adapted housing and/or extra facilities, bedroom or bathroom
Need improved heating (on medical grounds)
Need sheltered housing (on medical grounds)
Need ground floor accommodation (on medical grounds)
Need to be near friends/relatives or medical facility on medical grounds

(f) People whose social or economic circumstances lead to difficulty in getting settled accommodation

Lack of an actual or potential wage earner
Head of household unemployed or in part time or law paid work
Lack of capital assets
Households requiring accommodation which is unavailable at an affordable cost in the private sector (*e.g.* families requiring large housing or people requiring specially adapted accommodation).

ANNEX B

PARTS VI AND VII GUIDANCE:
Useful References

Association of District Councils/Association of Metropolitan Authorities (1995), Fair and Seen to be Fiar: A Survey of Local Authority Housing Allocations Practice, London, ADC/AMA.

Audit Commission (1992), Developing Local Authority Housing Strategies, London, HMSO.

Binns, J. and Carman, L. (1996), Common Housing Registers: A Good Practice Guide, CIH.

CHAC (1969), Council Housing Purposes, Procedures and Priorities, London, HMSO.

Chartered Institute of Housing (1995), Housing Standards Manual, Coventry, CIH.

CIH (1996) Good Practice Guide to Housing Advice Services.

CIH (1996/97, forthcoming), Allocations and Homelessness: The New Framework.

DoE (1978), Allocation of Council Housing, London, Housing Services Advisory Group.

DoE (1992), Underoccupation in Local Authority and Housing Association Housing, London, HMSO.

DoE (1993), Housing Consequences of Relationship Breakdown.

DoE (1993), Managing Social Housing, London, HMSO.

DoE (1994), Routes into Local Authority Housing, London, HMSO.

DoE (1994), Rent Arrears in Local Authorities and Housing Associations in England.

DoE (1994), Moving On, Crossing Divides, London, HMSO.

DoE (1996), Models of Housing Advice Services, London, HMSO.

DoE (1996), Evaluation of the 1991 Homelessness Code of Guidance, London, HMSO.

DoE/Welsh Office (1995), Our Future Homes: Opportunity, Choice and Responsibility, London, HMSO.

Housing Management Advisory Panel (HMAP) for Wales (1995), Seen to be Fair: A Guide to Allocating Rented Housing, Cardiff, Welsh Office.

Irvine, M. (1996), A Guide to the Housing Act 1996, CIH, ADC, AMA.

LHU, ALA, LFHA, LBA (1994), Strategic Partners.

Mullins, D. and Niner, P. (1996), Common Housing Registers: An Evaluation and Analysis of Current Practice, London, The Housing Corporation.

Parker, J., Smith, R., and Williams, P. (1992), Access, Allocations and Nominations: The Role of Housing Associations, London, HMSO.
Scottish Homes (1995), Housing Information and Advice Services — National Standards and Good Practice Manual.

ANNEX C

Local Authority Joint Tenancies

1. This guidance is about the allocation of joint tenancies by local housing authorities.

2. The Secretary of State for the Environment considers that joint tenancies can play an important role in ensuring the effective use and equitable allocation of housing.

3. In situations where the members of a household have a long-term commitment to the home, for example a married couple or when adults share accommodation as friends or unpaid live-in carers, local authorities should normally grant a joint tenancy, In this way the ability of other adult members of the household to remain in the accommodation on the death of the tenant would not be prejudiced.

4. Local authorities will wish to be assured:

— of the likely continuance of such arrangements; and
— that there are no adverse implications from the joint tenancy for good use of authorities' housing stock, for authorities' ability to continue for housing need and in particular for their being able to discharge the priority of housing families and vulnerable people.

5. It is good practice for local authorities to ensure that applicants for housing (whether new applicants or existing sole tenants) are made aware that they can be granted joint tenancies. If an authority declines to grant a jont tenancy, it should inform the applicants in writing of its reasons for refusal.

6. Where a member of a household dies and there is another member of that household who does not have the right to succeed to the tenancy, who either:

— had been living with the tenant for the year before the tenant's death, or
— had been looking after the tenant, or
— had accepted responsibility for the tenant's dependants

the local authority should grant a tenancy to the remaining person or persons, either in the same home or in suitable alternative accommodation, where the local authority is satisfied that this is a priority when viewed in the context of the other demands on their housing stock and the housing need in their area.

7. This guidance replaces that in Department of the Environment Circular 7/96 "Local Authority Joint Tenancies", which is hereby withdrawn.

8. Any queries on the contents of this Annex may be referred to Mr S. Guyon, Homelessness and Housing Management Policy Division, Department of the Environment, Room N13/14, 2 Marsham Street, London SW1P 3EB. Telephone: 0171-276-3416.

ANNEX D

Guidance on Commencement and Transition

1. The Housing Act 1996 (Commencement No. 5 and Transitional Provisions) Order 1996 (S.I. 1996/2959 (c.88)) was made on November 25, 1996. It commences, on April 1, 1997 and January 20, 1997 respectively, those provisions of Part VI and Part VII that have not been the subject of earlier commencement orders. It also has the effect of repealing Part III of the Housing Act 1985 on January 20, and s. 22 of that Act on April 1.

Part VII (Homelessness)

2. The new homelessness provisions contained in Part VII take effect on January 20, 1997. Any application for homelessness assistance made before that date will continue to be treated as an application made under Part III of the Housing Act 1985. By virtue of s. 216(2) of the Housing Act 1996, any duty owed to an applicant for homelessness assistance (even where it is not discharged until after January 20, 1997) will be as set out in Part III of the 1985 Act, which paragraph 1 of the Schedule to the commencement order saves for that purpose.

3. It is for each authority to decide how best to discharge its duty under the 1985 Act. Prior to April 1, 1997 the options open to authorities include offering the secure tenancy of a council property, and nominating a person to an assured tenancy of a property owned by a registered social landlord. From April 1, 1997, all such allocations must take place in accordance with the provisions of Part VI of the 1996 (*i.e.* in general to people appearing on the authority's housing register who have priority under the authority's allocations scheme). In deciding what accommodation to use for discharge of duty in the period prior to April 1, authorities may wish to take account of the *Awua* judgment (*R. v. London Borough of Brent; ex p. Awua* (1995) 27 H.L.R. 453), where the House of Lords ruled that the duty to secure accommodation under s. 65(2) of the 1985 Act does not import any requirement of permanence.

4. As Part VI of the 1996 Act does not come into effect until April 1, 1997 the various references to Part VI in the homelessness provisions (*i.e.* Part VII of that Act) — for example, in subsections (6) and (7) of s. 193 — have no effect during the period from January 20, to March 31, 1997.

Part VI (Allocation of Housing)

5. The commencement order provides that Part VI comes into force on April 1, 1997. Prior to that date authorities should continue to allocate housing in accordance with s. 22 of the 1985

Act. Paragraph (d) of that section refers to persons owed a duty under s. 65 or s.68 of the 1985 Act; these provisions will have been repealed on January 20, 1997. By virtue of s. 17 of the Interpretation Act 1978 (which is concerned with cases where an enactment is repealed and re-enacted with or without modifications), the Department's view is that the reference in s. 22(d) should be read as references to the corresponding provisions in Part VII of the 1996 Act. This means that the effect of s. 22 remains broadly unchanged until it is repealed on April 1.

6. From April 1, 1997 an authority must, with limited exceptions, allocate all housing within its gift to persons appearing on its housing register who have priority under an allocations scheme set up in accordance with the "reasonable preference" categories set out in s. 167(2) of the 1996 Act. Where an authority has made someone a firm offer of accommodation before April 1, but the person does not take up the tenancy until after that date, that offer would constitute the allocation of accommodation under whatever allocation arrangements the authority had in place prior to April 1. The offer would not be affected by any delay in taking up the tenancy.

7. Schedule 1 to the 1985 Act sets out cases where the secure tenancy regime does not apply, at least initially in some cases. Paragraph 2 of Schedule 16 to the 1996 Act amends those provisions to take account of the new arrangments for allocating permanent housing contained in Part VI of that Act. Paragraph 2 of the Schedule to the commencement order provides that these amendments do not have effect on any tenancy granted before April 1, 1997.

HHM
27 November, 1996

INDEX